CLIVE WOODWARD
Winning!

CLIVE WOODWARD

Winning!

Hodder & Stoughton

Copyright © 2004 by Clive Woodward and Fletcher Potanin

First published in Great Britain in 2004
by Hodder & Stoughton
A division of Hodder Headline

10 9 8 7 6 5 4 3 2 1

A CIP catalogue record for this title is available from the British Library

ISBN 0 340 83629 6

Typeset in Sabon by
Rowland Phototypesetting Ltd,
Bury St Edmunds, Suffolk
Printed and bound in Great Britain by Mackays of Chatham Ltd, Chatham, Kent

Hodder Headline's policy is to use papers that are natural, renewable and
recyclable products and made from wood grown in sustainable forests.
The logging and manufacturing processes are expected to conform to the
environmental regulations of the country of origin.

Hodder and Stoughton Ltd
A division of Hodder Headline
338 Euston Road
London NW1 3BH

CONTENTS

DEDICATION

This dedication is a little out of the ordinary in as much as the list is rather long. There are many people who have made winning the World Cup in 2003 possible. So, with my sincerest gratitude, I would like to dedicate this book to:

First and foremost, my family: Jayne, Jess, Joe and Freddie. My love and extra special thanks for all of your love and support. I would also like to thank family and friends for caring for my family in my absence.

The England World Cup Management Team: Andy Robinson, Phil Larder, Phil Keith-Roach, Dave Reddin, Dave Alred, Simon Hardy, Tony Biscombe, Simon Kemp, Sherylle Calder, Louise Ramsay, Richard Wegrzyk, Barney Kenny, Phil Pask, Dave Tennison, Steve Lander, Richard Smith, Dave Campbell and Richard Prescott – we have been on an incredible journey together. You have been fantastic in every way.

The elite rugby players in the World Cup squad: Martin Johnson, Ben Kay, Ben Cohen, Jason Leonard, Joe Worsley, Dan Luger, Paul Grayson, Danny Grewcock, Kyran Bracken, Mike Tindall, Matt Dawson, Stuart Abbott, Lawrence Dallaglio, Martin Corry, Jonny Wilkinson, Iain Balshaw, Neil Back, Trevor Woodman, Lewis Moody, Julian White, Dorian West, Mark Regan, Andy Gomarsall, Will Greenwood, Josh Lewsey, Phil Vickery, Steve Thompson, Richard Hill, Jason Robinson, Mike Catt and Simon Shaw. Add to these those players that have also contributed to the success of the squad – you have collectively risen to the challenge set before you by each of the coaching team. You should all, rightly so, be proud of what you have achieved through your dedication and hard work. What has impressed me the most, however, was the high level of standards you adhered to under intense pressure.

All those people who have worked with us over the last seven years – in the RFU, in our corporate sponsor companies, and in the Zurich Premiership clubs around the country, thank you for getting behind us when we needed it most.

And finally, the millions of rugby supporters, club members and sports fans, simply thank you for your support.

Special Acknowledgements

I would like to thank the team at Hodder and Stoughton for their great assistance in producing this book. My publisher Roddy Bloomfield for his great patience and trust, James Hughes for his invaluable help reviewing the 80+ matches in my England career, Maggie Body for her copy editing, John Griffiths for compiling the match statistics and Bob Vickers for his page layout and design.

I wish to acknowledge and thank Fletcher Potanin from Solutions Press Business Publishing in Australia. Writing this book with his assistance has been a great pleasure. Fletcher, now living in Australia with his family, is originally from the USA. He came to this story with no preconceived notions of the tradition of England rugby or of the game in general. As such we were able to give the rise of England's success a new perspective. He is a businessman specialising in the transformation of company cultures and the development of specialised business systems.

Jayne has also spent countless hours in helping me write this book. Thank you, Betsy.

A SPECIAL NOTE

This book covers four decades; it is primarily about the two careers of my life that ran side by side until 1997. From then, it's a story about the transformation of an international team into world champions.

Highly sensitive, competitive information about the work of the England coaches is just that and not for publishing; so, too, the intimate details of players and their experiences with England. This is not a book about gossip, for which I make no apologies.

Since this book covers many years over the course of my life and an intense seven-year period with England, I have tried to record the people, places and events as best I can recollect. I apologise in advance for any inadvertent error on my part or if I have forgotten to mention anyone specifically.

I have tried to write a book that reflects where my ideas have originated and to include key events and people who have been integral to the success of the team. This in turn should explain how and why we won the World Cup in November 2003.

PHOTOGRAPHIC ACKNOWLEDGEMENTS

The author and publisher would like to thank the following for permission to reproduce photographs:

Allsport/Getty Images, Associated Press, Shaun Botterill/Getty Images, John Buckle/Getty Images, Colorsport, Mark Dadswell/Getty Images, Colin Elsey/Colorsport, L'Equipe/Fevre/Offside, Stewart Fraser/ Colorsport, John Gichigi/Getty Images, Mark Leech/Offside, Joe Mann/ Offside, Mirrorpix, Adrian Murrell/Getty Images, Popperfoto.com, Craig Prentis/Getty Images, Reading Evening Post, David Rogers/Getty Images, Sandra Teddy/Photosport/Offside, Topham/Press Association.

All other photographs are from private collections.

PRELUDE: WINNING! DOESN'T HAPPEN IN A STRAIGHT LINE

Martin Johnson has it. He drives. There's thirty-five seconds to go. This is the one . . . It's coming back for Jonny Wilkinson . . . He drops for World Cup glory . . . It's up . . . It's over! He's done it! Jonny Wilkinson is England's hero yet again. And there's no time for Australia to come back. England have just won the World Cup . . . – Ian Robertson, BBC Radio Five Live 22 Nov. 2003.

In that one moment, everything came together for England rugby. Our six-year campaign of vast change, great learning, team bonding and incredible vision by many people was completed with a fairytale ending. You couldn't have scripted it any better – Martin Johnson driving up the pitch towards the goal posts, leading the England team brilliantly in the most critical moment of his career, Matt Dawson at scrum half controlling the ball and the game as always, firing back to Jonny Wilkinson for the drop kick he'd been practising relentlessly for a decade in preparation for that one moment. Combine that with the extraordinary effort of the other twelve men on the pitch, the seven on the bench and the nine players in the squad who weren't selected to play in the World Cup final in Sydney – they worked just as hard, if not harder, during the tournament than those who were fortunate enough to be selected – combine their efforts with the eighteen management and support team on tour, and what you have is a group of thoughtful, committed individuals who have, without a doubt, changed the world of international rugby.

Until this team came together, England rugby hadn't managed to string together more than three wins in a row against any southern-hemisphere rugby team for more than a hundred years. Our victory in Sydney was the first win for England in a major sporting event since the 1966 Football World Cup. I'm told that on the Saturday morning when the final was telecast live in England, the Automobile Association reported an additional 10,000,000 cars were off the road than otherwise would have been. The celebrations since our return have been massive, more than anyone involved with the team expected. Clearly something has happened. In a nation starved of sporting success, it seems winning the Rugby World Cup has inspired a nation.

It has been a magic time for England rugby, but it wasn't always this way. Not long ago our sport was clearly behind on the world stage.

Transformation

England rugby has undergone a massive transformation. In the last decade one of the largest amateur sports the world has ever known made the transition to a professional game. Here in England, more than anywhere else, the game has been through an immense period of adjustment moving into this new era. This change has been felt at the grass roots level of the game, the club level, and right through to the organisational level of the RFU, or Rugby Football Union. Without this period of growth and adjustment at all levels of the game, it simply would not have been possible to build the infrastructure essential to achieving the victory which we have all dreamed of for so long. Consequently, winning in Sydney was the culmination of a huge effort by ultimately thousands of people who pioneered this period of change in our sport. Without it our success would not have been possible.

The whole of England rugby has travelled a long hard road in the last decade, resulting in the glory of England's victory, but nowhere has that change been more pronounced than in the elite England international set-up since 1997. The England camp of today is so vastly different to just seven years ago that it is almost beyond comparison. In 1997 the RFU selected me as the first full-time professional head coach in England's history. Little did anyone know the whirlwind of events which that appointment would set in motion, least of all me.

We practically started from scratch in building the coaching systems and processes that would eventually lead us to the 2003 World Cup. The England set-up has grown into a comprehensive professional coaching and management team, and we have travelled an incredible journey from the bottom of international rugby right to the top as World Cup champions.

Winning!

Our success has not been a continual series of victories. We have had a number of devastating setbacks; how these are handled is the mark of a great team. When you read about them, you might agree to a certain extent that it is a minor miracle England rugby has managed to produce a winning side at all. It has been against all odds, but winning does not happen in a straight line. Through trials and tribulations, great victories and stunning defeats, the elite England team of coaches, management and players has stuck together to pursue our vision of arriving at the World Cup as the world number one ranked team, the odds-on favourite to win the tournament, and the best-prepared England rugby team ever to step onto the pitch.

This is also the story of my personal journey in the pursuit of winning in sport. From the time I first felt the passion sport could bring to my life, through a series of frustrating personal obstacles, to my international playing career, success in business and beyond. In my life I have always been searching for a fleeting and elusive sensation that is best described as 'winning', but in a different way from what most people understand. Playing rugby, both at club level and at international level, I learnt that you can win and yet feel like you've played the worst game of your life. You can lose but feel like you've played the best rugby of your life. It is clear there is more to winning than just putting points on the scoreboard.

Rare, even for the best elite teams, is the combination of playing flawlessly as individuals, fluidly as a team, and winning convincingly. But when you do, it's as deeply meaningful and satisfying as any sensation in the world. This is the higher ideal which true sportspeople dream about. This is Winning! It's about thinking of performance at the highest level, being the best and most prepared, getting more from the human body and human synergy than anyone else. Our victory has been a testament to the fact that in the year of the World Cup, our organisation worked better to achieve these aims than any other in international rugby.

So my story is as much a journey to discover what winning meant to me as a challenge to find out how to win in the new modern professional rugby environment. Not surprisingly, I would discover that in any team Winning! is only possible when everyone in the organisation is working well as a team, the leaders are offering strong guidance and inspiration by example, and the team is fully supported in its endeavours by its management, sponsors and fans. But, interestingly, some of my greatest insights into winning have not come from sport.

Business and sport

It's no secret that the business world has always had a fascination with sport; but having been involved in both business and rugby in England at the highest level, my mindset was and is totally different. I felt sport should have a huge fascination with business. When I started as coach, I was determined to run the England rugby team like a business, so over the years I've canvassed hundreds of sources for new business techniques in line with all my experiences in the corporate and small-business world. In finding what would work best for England rugby, I have brought together hundreds of business concepts in a totally new way. After many years in business and coaching, I've found that the principles that apply to coaching successfully also apply to business. Consequently the story of how we built a world-class team is also an account of all the business ideas that we have brought to our sporting set-up, for it is our off-the-pitch systems and processes that have created the environment of preparation for our country's best players to be victorious in Sydney.

In business, British companies are among the most successful in the world. It has always intrigued me why British national sporting teams seem incapable of winning. In so many areas we are leaders in setting world standards. In the arts and sciences, in business and banking, in the military, even in the invention and proliferation of sports like rugby, the English have proved successful.

So why, if we can win in those areas, can't we win in the sporting arena? I think it has to do with a very strong prevailing culture of 'participation' in our sporting history. It's something I encountered to my frustration in my youth, and I continued to struggle with it right into my international rugby career. This overwhelming emphasis on playing sport for the sake of 'how you play the game' was completely at odds with the way I am. I wanted to compete. I wanted to be the best. I wanted to win. My life in sport seems to have been a fight against the prevailing culture of participation in favour of winning.

The Corinthian spirit

It appears not to be a new struggle. Sportsmen in England have been aware of it for quite a few decades. Recently I picked up a book, the cherished family heirloom of a friend of mine, titled *Theory of Modern Rugby* and written in 1930 by I.M.B. Stuart, an assistant master at Harrow School. The book's Introduction gave me considerable insight into the very reason why England has not been winning at sport on an international stage.

> We have taught the world games, we have taught the world the true spirit in which to play those games, and if we no longer hold pride of place as players of the game, it matters nothing so long as we Britishers always continue to be looked up to as the truest 'players of the game' in the world. That is our greatest heritage, and one that I trust will be regarded as our most closely guarded possession – that the prize counts for nothing in comparison with the spirit in which it is struggled for. In other words, that the 'Spirit of the game' is the prize.
>
> We wonder why it is that other countries can defeat us at most sports, and the answer is to be found, not in that they are physically more endowed than we are, but that they have the temperament to practise doggedly their weakness, and endeavour to improve before they proceed any further. The Englishman, on the other hand, refuses

to identify his weakness and practise assiduously to correct it. For this reason, the average Rugby footballer cannot place-kick. He refuses to practise, what he calls 'drudge work', except just now and then.

When I read that last part, I thought how fitting that it was the golden boot of Jonny Wilkinson that kicked us to victory. That winning drop kick was the centre point of a strategy that we'd practised over and over again; Jonny performed the assigned task that he'd practised thousands of hours to accomplish. His story is the exact opposite of the Corinthian spirit that has seemed to form the prevailing culture of English sport for centuries. In a highly competitive environment, in the elite sporting environment of international rugby, that spirit of 'participation' has had a disastrous effect over many decades of elite competitive rugby. It is only through the incredible effort of a select few individuals, motivated by a stronger competitive force, that we have managed to stem the tide and change the course of England's sporting history.

I cannot begin to explain the feelings of gratitude that I have for the coaches and the rest of the management team and the players, brilliantly headed by Martin Johnson. It has been my intention in writing this book to try and set down the actions and course of events that this group of people and I have undergone in bringing the World Cup home. This is the story of England's rise to the top of the rugby world. A story of hard work, ingenuity, intense preparation . . . and perhaps even destiny.

MY FIRST DAY ON THE JOB

I really enjoy the drive into Twickenham. Crossing the bridge over the Whitton rail line on the A316, I catch a glimpse of it over the rooftops and through the oak trees. A change comes over me. I can feel myself breathing just that little bit harder. The internationally famous cauldron materialises in front of me as I drive past Harlequins where my senior rugby career started all those years ago.

It's not a match day so the place is empty, but even in its apparent silence Twickenham hums with energy. It is a truly awesome ground – the home of England rugby. Little did I know that this home would soon become a fortress.

As a player, this place filled me with pride and brought out my best. Just walking onto the pitch in 1980 with the English Rose on my chest, I felt physically larger, stronger. Here I am, seventeen years later. I wonder will it be the same? I'm the England coach now. Will I feel the same raw anticipation and excitement?

Driving around the massive stadium to the administration building, I'm struck by the heritage of this great institution. Some 130 years of history and expectations leave a legacy. In my head I hear the chattering voices of a long line of coaches who have come before me. 'Do you think he has it?' I hear them ask. 'Is he up to the job?' 'Is he the man to lead us to victory?'

Pulling into the car park, I am about to find out.

All the numbered spaces are full, so I turn into the one marked 'visitor', gather up my phone and briefcase, and head for the entrance. It is an overcast, muggy September day. The revolving door is still moving as I approach. I wait my turn and push through to the inside.

Dark clouds looming

'... OK ... right you are, then. Bye-bye.'

A cheerful receptionist finishes her call and looks up from her computer screen.

'Hello. How can I help?' she asks with a smile.

'Hi, I'm Clive Woodward.'

'And you're here to see ...?' Another smile.

'I'm here to see Don Rutherford.'

Don is director of rugby for the Rugby Football Union.

'I wasn't informed of any visitors. Do you have an appointment?' she asks, her face turning quizzical.

'Just one minute, please,' and before I can say anything she has the phone to her ear.

I tap my pen on the cover of my diary and glance around the reception area. A pot plant in the corner looks like it hasn't seen genuine sunshine in months, and it's suffering for it.

'I have a Mr Woodward in reception for Mr Rutherford. He doesn't have an appointment.' Then, after a slight pause, 'Yes ... right ... oh, of course. OK, thanks for that.' She turns, 'I'm very sorry, Mr Woodward ...'

'Please call me Clive.'

'Of course, Mr Woodward. Mr Rutherford will be right down to see you. Would you please wait right over there? He will only be a few minutes.' She points to the chairs directly to her right, next to the plant.

It's not yet 9 a.m. and I guess this wasn't the welcome I was expecting from my new employers. Perhaps I was meant to start next Monday? How odd. Sitting on the faded lounge I notice a few rugby magazines that are months out of date. Friday's paper is draped across the chair opposite. The room is stark and bare. There are no pictures of rugby players to be seen anywhere. Nothing to indicate this is the home of English rugby save the obvious presence of the stadium over my shoulder. I had been into thousands of receptions in my business life. This one would have to rank as one of the least inspiring I'd ever seen.

Lightning strikes

After fifteen minutes, Don Rutherford comes down the stairs into reception. I'd known Don for years. Don had been at the helm of England rugby for more than two decades. He is highly respected by most in the game, including me. I am pleased to see him.

'Clive. We didn't expect you. What are you doing here?'

Maybe Don had his wires crossed as well. After all, he had been responsible for finalising my contract.

'I'm here to start work. Normally I'll be in by 7 a.m., but it's only day one, so I thought I'd give you all a bit of time. I'd like to settle into my office, you know, and get things started.'

'Oh . . . but you're the coach. We thought you'd work from home and go out to the players and the clubs. What do you need an office for?'

Clunk. The penny dropped. After seventeen years in business I thought I was a pretty sharp negotiator, only to suddenly realise I had completely forgotten to discuss the most obvious of necessities in my contract, an office and a phone.

'Don, I'm the full-time coach now. I need to work from an office at Twickenham, not at home. Could I meet my secretary and we'll sort out the office later?'

'A secretary? What for? Your place is out on the pitch with the players. Why would you need a secretary?'

Looking back, I realise Don wasn't being deliberately difficult. He was in uncharted territory. I was the first professional coach in the RFU's history. For example, the previous coach, Jack Rowell, had several businesses to run while doing the job, and so needed a hands-on director like Don just to get the job done. It was the way things had been run for decades, perhaps forever. I was now the first professional coach, and clearly I was being employed to get results with none of the excuses of the amateur era.

'I've come here to do a job, Don. Most mornings except match days I'll be here to work. To start I'll need an office, phone, a computer and a secretary . . .'

'But we don't have an office prepared for you,' Don says.

'Then I'll just start work here in reception until one is ready. I have a mobile phone and several calls to make. Let's just stop all this and get on with it.'

'OK, wait here and I'll see what I can do.'

I turn, plant myself in the chair and open my briefcase on the coffee table while Don walks back up the stairs. The receptionist, who at first pretended not to listen, is staring at me aghast.

'Looks like I'll be sharing your reception for a while! What's your name?'

'Emily,' she replies.

'Hi, Emily. Nice to meet you. Can I get you a coffee?' I say in return, starting to see the amusing side of the situation. Honestly, I was looking around to see if Jeremy Beadle or the *Candid Camera* guys were about to leap out from behind the flower pot.

Getting on with the job

I pick up the mobile and call Fran Cotton, who had been the key figure in securing my appointment.

'Fran, it's Clive. I knew this job was going to be tough, but it just got tougher and its only 9.30 a.m. on day one!'

Fran Cotton and I go back a long way. We first met playing for England in 1980. Fran was at the pinnacle of his career, a hero of his time and still one to me and many others, while I was just starting out as the youngest member of the team, enjoying every moment. In one area we definitely saw eye-to-eye right from the start. We both believed the England rugby team had the potential to be the best in the world. For the last year Fran had been working to that end as a member of the management board of the RFU, his remit largely covering the well-being of the international team.

'That's right,' I say after explaining the situation. 'We forgot to put an office in the contract.' The whole situation really was highly amusing. He, like me, saw the funny side of the problem. 'As we speak I think someone's trying to find me one. Could be ages.'

The tornado hits

That afternoon a space was cobbled together for me. It was actually just a desk in the middle of the open-plan office on the northern end of the second floor. I think they might have found someone away on holiday and thrown all their possessions into a box. It was several months and numerous internal committee meetings before I eventually got my own office. Quite simply there was no space. They were totally unprepared to have a coach in the building. A secretary was eventually allocated to me whom I shared with two other people. Fully understanding the importance of a top secretary, this was not a great start and still to this day I cannot believe I overlooked it in my negotiations. It wasn't ideal, but it would have to do.

I now realise I must have been a tornado on a quiet autumn day. I never set out to deliberately shake things up, but I already believed I knew what it would take to build the world's best rugby team and it wasn't the old way of doing things. We would not achieve the results we all dreamed of with the same old level of thinking. If our goal was not just to win in Europe, which we had done in the past, but to win on the world stage, then we had to start doing things totally differently.

Rugby union had been an amateur sport in England, managed almost entirely by volunteers, for more than a hundred years. Now, as the first professional coach, I reported directly to a council of fifty-seven members who were all amateur officials and unpaid for their efforts. They in turn ran the game through the management board which represented them and also included some full-time professional staff. While there was a director of rugby who worked closely with the chairman of the management board, the RFU effectively had no full-time executive officer responsible for running the organisation. The board had been searching for twelve months, but had been unable to decide on the right person for the job. It was nearly another year after my appointment before the position would finally be filled. Imagine a business with revenues in the tens of millions of pounds that effectively had no full-time leader.

It was a huge organisation with a volunteer mentality, but the game had turned professional and a new era was upon us. The pressures of cultural change were mounting, and I was only the beginning. Unfortunately, some lost sight of what we were trying to achieve and hung on to the old ways too tightly. I'm sure they experienced great pain during that period, perhaps believing that the values and ideals they held so dear were being trampled by commercial interests and the onset of professionalism.

I'd like to take this opportunity to apologise to all those upon whose toes I stepped in my haste to get the job done in those very early days. Thank you for your decades of faithful stewardship of this great game. I hope that in time, and with our recent success for England rugby, you will see that we have protected those values and ideals, and that they prosper in the current England set-up just as strongly, and possibly more strongly, than in the amateur era.

I owe particular gratitude to Don Rutherford, director of rugby. Don was a leading figure in English rugby and had devoted his entire life to its care. Don had taken the game to a new level, but if we were serious about our quest to be the best in the world – and that was now my main reason for getting up in the morning – it was my job to question everything to do with playing and coaching England and to try and move it to a level that no one thought possible – an elite level.

England won the World Cup six years later because we had an outstanding group of players and for the first time in our history, compared to all our opponents, we had the most intense preparation, the most exhaustive analysis, and the strongest process for nurturing a powerful team spirit both on and off the pitch. Most importantly, we had a strong, dynamic organisational culture that fully supported our new approach. Without it, our systems would have been built on a foundation of sand and wouldn't have weathered the mildest of storms. My first few years as coach of the England team were a tumultuous battle between old and new, radical versus conventional.

That confrontation of beliefs was pivotal to our success. By having to fight so hard for even the smallest of changes, we were forced to question, scrutinise and vigorously defend everything we did. Although seemingly not helpful at the time, it actually was the greatest catalyst for innovation we could have had.

Now it's easy to see how it all so innocently began. I can't believe I didn't see it coming. To understand why old and new quickly squared off so resolutely against each other, you have to hear how I came to be in the job in the first place.

2
ANSWERING THE CALL

The summer of 1997 was the quiet before the storm. Life was good, I had three great kids – Jessica 11, Joseph 9 and Freddie 2 – my lovely wife Jayne, a successful leasing business, and a six handicap in golf, a game I was starting to take very seriously with a view to getting to scratch. I had just completed a great run as a coach, guiding two rugby club sides, Henley and London Irish, to the top of their respective tables, and I now had a part-time professional coaching role which allowed me to continue running my business while working with Andy Robinson at Bath where the team was really coming together. Andy and I had also been coaching the England Under-21 side together for a couple of seasons.

And yet I still felt something was missing. That's why I'll never forget the phone call that was to change my life. I was in my office in Stubbings House, a lovely old building just outside Maidenhead.

'Clive, it's Don Rutherford,' the distinctive voice said. 'Your name has come up as a possible candidate for England coach . . .'

I listened very attentively, saying nothing but taking in the somewhat extraordinary news.

'You're an outside chance, but a few members of the management board want to take a look at you. Firstly, would you be interested?'

'Thanks for the call, Don. Of course I'm interested. It's a huge opportunity . . .'

'The board is meeting tonight. Why don't I come round afterwards so we can discuss this further and I can update you on what they are thinking? Where exactly do you live?'

I told him. We set a time and hung up.

After the call I sat there with my brain really ticking over, a million and one questions going through my head at once. *Did I want it? Could I make a difference? If I didn't do it, who would? How could I do it and run my business at the same time?* Then again, when someone offers you the chance to coach your country at your sport, how could you ever say no? My mind exploded into all the areas I could change and improve. I knew then that if Don offered me the job it would be an interesting time ahead for England rugby, to put it mildly. For as long as I could remember I'd had huge issues with the way England were playing and being coached. This was an opportunity for me to put my money where my mouth was.

Then again, what was I thinking? Of course I was only an outside choice, recalling Don's words. I'd had a relatively short, albeit successful, coaching career – as an amateur coach. Rugby had just gone professional. This was the job surely every coach wanted, and there were a dozen highly qualified, full-time professional coaches who had many more years of experience than I. They were all highly traditional, trustworthy, and safe and had strong ties with the RFU. I was completely different in my coaching style, off the wall to some. Almost everything I did seemed to ruffle feathers. I had little chance, or did I?

My obsessions

I'm passionate about four things in life: first my family, second my business, third rugby and lastly sport in general – especially football where I still vividly recall the success of England in 1966. Interesting, considering I was just ten at the time.

Family, business, rugby, sport – in that order. That's my life. Nothing outside of those four things rates a mention. Jayne says I'm totally obsessive. She is probably right but it's just me.

Obviously a high-profile position such as England coach would be demanding and would impact upon my family and my business. This wasn't a decision I could make alone. I left work early that day. I wondered what Jayne would think.

The sacrifices the family would have to make for me to do this job successfully would be huge. I was certain that the upside to me doing this job would far outweigh the downside, but I knew there would be times, especially if things were not going well on the pitch, that this philosophy would be hard to maintain.

Indeed there have been many incidents over the last few years when I or the team have come in for huge and scathing criticism, and it has helped that the family has known how to deal with it. The best example would be only a few months after taking the job. I was taking Jess to swimming lessons early one Sunday morning. She was twelve years old and had just started school at Queen Anne's in Caversham. England had played five games under my leadership and we didn't have a great record! I had Radio Five on when suddenly Will Carling came on the radio live from his home stating that the RFU had made a huge mistake and demanding that I should be sacked. I decided to leave the radio on, thinking that this was all part of it. When Carling finally finished his tirade of abuse I turned it off and was just about to have a grown-up conversation with my darling twelve-year-old. She would have to learn how to handle these sorts of comments.

That's when she blurted out, 'Dad, don't listen to a word people like him say . . . anyone with half a brain knows where he is coming from.' Jess, of course, was very loyal to her dad, but hers was an understanding way beyond her years.

There would be downsides to this job, but I believed talking everything through and explaining situations as they came up would really help Jess and Joe to have a balanced perspective on this part of their life, and we've done the same with Freddie as he has grown up. Importantly, we always try to see the amusing side of things, even in times of crisis.

I knew, driving home to Jayne that afternoon, that doing this job would mean that my family too would have to learn how to handle the good times and the bad.

Jayne understands me better than anyone. We both married other people as soon as we left university. Both marriages ended within a comparatively short space of time without either of us having children, so when the time came Jayne and I made a fresh start together. We have been together for more than twenty years. Jayne has supported me in everything I've done; without her it might not have happened. I think Jayne should write a book, actually – *How to Survive and Flourish while Living with an Obsessive Sportsman*. It would make fascinating reading. Going home that evening I knew she would completely understand what it would take to do this job.

'What are you doing home so early?' she asked.

'Just need to talk to you about something. Would you like a cup of tea?' I could tell she was worried. This was unusual behaviour for me – I never came home early!

'Don Rutherford called me this afternoon. Look, it's probably nothing, but . . .'

'What a fantastic opportunity!' she said with a smile before I could completely finish.

Like everyone else, Jayne had been following the drama of who would be the next coach. She knew I would love a chance at this job and would be really frustrated if I couldn't at least have a crack at putting my case forward. I knew I could do the job and wanted to make a real difference and yet, because I had a business career and had not moved into professional coaching at club level, I assumed they were not even thinking of me. The whole process of how the appointment was being made had caused me to be even more disillusioned with the RFU than ever before. They had been considering all sorts of coaches outside of the RFU, including non-English people, when I felt they had potentially the best candidates right here in this country

Only a few months earlier, while in Australia coaching the Under-21s, I had shared a cup of tea with Don Rutherford and he too asked me my opinion on the three leading candidates for the job. So it was clear I wasn't on his list of top choices. Whereas I was in business, it seemed that everyone else who had moved into full-time professional coaching had come from an education background. It might have been relatively easy for them to move into full-time coaching as the remuneration was usually slightly better. However, I simply could not afford to go from the business world into full-time coaching on the same terms. Furthermore, this position would be decided behind closed doors. The job was not advertised, and they weren't using any form of professional head-hunter, hence there was no formal method of applying for the job, so how could they possibly have known I was interested? To me the whole process was a shambles, and accurately reflected how totally unprepared the RFU were for the professional game. Even the process of selecting a head coach had become a cause of amusement and ridicule by many in the media.

Resolution: this time it will be different

Whilst talking to Jayne our conversation soon turned to what would happen in the unlikely event I was selected for the position. Tentatively we talked through what it would mean: early mornings, late nights, games on weekends, months away on tour each year . . . all part and parcel of high-pressure, high-stakes international rugby. I could see reality sinking in. Jayne was no stranger to my hours of work. She was used to me running my business as she worked in it with me and understood the commitment of coaching rugby at the same time – not to mention the golf – so it was really not too different from how my business life ran anyway. But this job came with a lot of extra baggage, one major issue being intense media scrutiny.

'But what are we talking about?' I said. 'It's an outside chance and will probably never come to that.'

'You must really go for it, Clive. If you don't, you'll always regret it. The important question is, if you can't do it on your terms, then is there any point in you doing it?'

It was a key point.

Up until now, I had been successful as a coach in club rugby when I had done things completely my way. When faced with an obstacle, I generally managed to sidestep it by thinking on my feet rather than confronting it head on. My approach frustrated some people, but in that regard I never really tried to work within the traditional coaching framework. I was fortunate that my business could heavily subsidise my desire to coach rugby successfully. There was nothing new in this – this was the amateur way. It was my way of putting something back into the game, just as thousands of others had done and many still do in the amateur areas of the game. Sometimes this was a simple matter like training kit and equipment for the team, other times I had used my financial resources to bring top players to my club where we otherwise had no way of attracting them. I never broke any rules, but thinking creatively had often given us the winning edge.

Personally I couldn't think of a better way to invest my money. But it meant that my business had been strained financially by my rugby passion. Not only that, I also spent a lot of working hours coaching rugby, and I was always thinking about the game on the weekend so my focus at work wasn't quite what it used to be. It's a wonder Jayne supported me at all. I did pay handsomely for the thrill of a few rugby matches. But what choice did I have? It was a bizarre turn-around, but winning in rugby had become even more important to me than further success in my business, and I would do anything in my power to achieve it, even if it meant using my own resources. Luckily I had good people around me. Ann Heaver, who joined the business shortly after I set it up in 1990, was practically running the company, while Jayne was working full-time on the administration side. The business was still prospering, so we didn't suffer too greatly, but it was a poignant lesson. In order to be successful in coaching, I would freely give of my time and of my business's resources to achieve my aims.

But where that might have been possible in amateur club rugby, coaching England at the international level was a different scenario. The game was now professional and the sums involved were huge. Matches at Twickenham could be sold out four times over from the massive public interest, and that's even with the three new stands that had just been completed which took the capacity of the stadium to 75,000. Many more millions were estimated to watch the games on TV. If I wanted to coach my way, I would have to set out what that meant very clearly from the start. In this case, at least, I was certain the RFU had the resources to do it the right way.

I wandered off into the back garden deep in thought. This situation needed serious consideration and I had a few hours before Don was due to arrive. I do my best thinking either in the golf net or on the putting green at the bottom of the garden. Armed with a flask of tea, BBC Radio 4, my clubs and a dictating machine I can think through just about any problem. The net and putting green are floodlit so I can often be found practising away deep in thought in the middle of the night. That evening, I considered all the aspects of England rugby that needed changing for success at the international level, gleaned both from my recent coaching experience and from my distant playing days.

I knew then that if I could set it up correctly, if I could manage the elite squad like a business, I would have the opportunity to lead England rugby through a period of significant change. It was a massively exciting prospect. That evening the golf net took a real hammering – I really did want this job.

Laying down my terms

Don did come to our house that night as planned. I had been thinking about various different scenarios of conversation most of the day. What was he going to say?

It really was a very polite conversation but not terribly long. Don had been authorised by the management board to offer me the full-time position of coach. This was the good news! At the same time it was very surprising news. Based on our conversation earlier in the day, I thought Don was calling in just to discuss the job. However, the board had made their decision that evening and Don had been instructed to come and see me to finalise the details.

The bad news came when we started to talk about remuneration. I really wanted to do this job; I was so excited at the prospect and the challenge that my head was buzzing. Even though my business was successful I had realised that I couldn't allow it to support me if I did this job, and I wanted to do it properly which would mean leaving others in the business to run it without me. My not being there was going to be difficult enough, let alone expecting them to continue to support me as well!

The professional era had allowed a small breakthrough for the need to balance coaching with the business. I had negotiated with Bath RFC to pay me sufficient to work with them part-time and still be able to run my business. The first time I had been able to offset my lack of time in the business with any income.

The bad news – we were way off in what I could accept in order to leave the business to coach the England side. As Don left that night I really felt crestfallen. I so wanted this opportunity but had responsibilities to my family and the people who worked for me. I thought that would be that and didn't sleep too well.

That takes care of that

Honestly, when Don walked out my door I fully expected never to hear of the matter again. I even assured Jayne that there was no possible way it would happen, and as good as promised her that our lives would not be turned upside down. The other area that had proved difficult was that I wanted the chance to do this job my way and to report to the board directly. When my phone rang next day, I was surprised to hear Fran Cotton.

Fran and I had kept in touch over the years and had enjoyed many casual talks over a pint about rugby and how it was evolving. I also knew that Fran was responsible for pushing my name forward for the coach position, along with Cliff Brittle who was chairman of the management board at the time. It was a courageous choice by both men, so I'm sure they waged a pitched battle with some of the more conservative members of the board over it, although I didn't know just how close it was at the time.

Fran suggested we met in private to discuss what it would take to get me into the job. As a matter of convenience, we agreed on the National Exhibition Centre near Birmingham, halfway between London and Manchester where he lived and worked.

Fran is a businessman. He and Steve Smith, another player from the 1980 Grand Slam side, built Cotton Traders from a two-man garage start-up to a massive £50 million sports clothing enterprise in just over a decade. He understood the practical implications of business. We talked openly about the realities of taking the job.

'Leave it with me, Clive. I'll do my best,' he assured me.

Still, despite my confidence and trust in Fran, I just did not see how the RFU could possibly come to the financial position that would enable me to do the job properly. Even with Fran's backing, we were both unsure of the outcome.

When the phone rang once again in mid-September, I was almost shocked to hear Don at the other end of the line.

'Right, Clive. You've got it. They've agreed to your terms. You're the new England coach.'

I couldn't believe it. I didn't know what to say. All I could think was, would I have the strength of conviction to carry this through, or would I bottle it? Would I bow to the traditions of English rugby?

I wanted to run this team like a business. Would it work? Would it really work in practice? And that is when reality set in. I would soon find out. We had matches against the Wallabies, the All Blacks and the Springboks at Twickenham, starting in just eight weeks – England's major competitors on the world stage.

The beginning of a journey

My journey as head coach of England rugby began shortly thereafter with my first day on the job, and a stumble start it was. Some six years later, and after many ups and downs, we would eventually achieve victory at the very top of our sport – the Rugby World Cup. However our path to glory wasn't an easy one, and it most certainly wasn't the story you might expect of a nation that had invented the game of rugby and successfully shared it with the rest of the world. Despite that, England hadn't managed to field a consistently world-beating team in more than a century. Something was obviously not right.

There's no doubt, looking back, that the one thing I'm most proud of has been creating a new culture in England rugby and a shift in the very mindset of our players and coaching staff. Where once they revered and even feared the southern-hemisphere teams, they now have absolutely no fear of any team. Where the spirit of participation once prevailed, the ideal of winning is now firmly in place. Even more than that, the success of this new culture has energised the spirit of a nation that hadn't managed to win any significant team sporting challenges for thirty-seven years.

But that of course is jumping ahead.

To understand my story as England head coach, and what has happened to create a team capable of becoming the best in the world, you should first find out why winning became such a priority for me, and how I came to bring together all the tools, resources and experiences I would need to build the elite squad into a World Championship team.

It's funny when I think about it. But for a peculiar series of events, I might never have been a rugby coach in the first place.

FRUSTRATED FOOTBALL PLAYER

3

My life, rugby and sports in general are now so intertwined that it's hard to tell where one ends or the other begins. But there's a crucial fact about my career of which most people are unaware – I really never wanted to play rugby in the first place.

I played for England and the British Lions and went on to coach the national side to World Cup glory, but underneath it all I'm just a frustrated football player.

Squadron Leader Ronald Woodward, my father, was a great dad whilst also being a serious military man. Military life is demanding on a family, and ours was no exception. We moved around a lot, so few things remained constant. When I was eleven I found myself stationed at RAF Linton-on-Ouse, just outside Easingwold, North Yorkshire. (Since our World Cup victory the officers' dining room has been renamed the Sir Clive Woodward Room. Talk about your past catching up with you!)

Like most boys, I was right into my football. It was 1967, and the England football team had only just won the World Cup the year before – football was, and still is, the country's favourite national sport. I vividly remember the incredible emotion from the very moment when England won at Wembley against West Germany. My father and I were sitting in the living room of our RAF house adjacent to the station's sports fields, over which the planes landed and took off. It had been a dramatic match, but when the final whistle blew after an action-packed extra time, the emotions coming through the little black-and-white television set were overwhelming. Even my normally staid father was beside himself with joy. I'd never seen him so happy. Running outside after the game I saw everyone out of their houses, hugging and shouting in celebration of the win.

It was my first true experience of the incredible sensation of winning. When the final whistle blew, England had won 4—2, but it was much more than that. That team achieved something that was so perfect, so powerful, that it inspired a nation. It certainly grabbed me. I was hooked. My entire sporting life since then has been a quest to understand and achieve that same ultimate level, that same incredible feeling of success, although it was some time before I realised it.

In the few years since that great victory, football had become my passion. By the age of thirteen, football totally dominated my life. I can still see the faces on the posters of the '66 legends that papered my bedroom walls. Geoff Hurst who scored the winning goal, Bobby Moore the inspirational captain, Alan Ball the red-headed dynamo and youngest member of the team who played for Everton, and especially Martin Peters who played midfield like me – these were my idols. I never missed a game on the TV, and never went anywhere without a football at my feet, much to the embarrassment of my sister, Linda, seven years my senior. I guess you could say I was nuts about football.

When I was playing football I dreamed of being in Martin Peters' boots in a thrilling World Cup final. It was said of Martin Peters that he was ten years ahead of his time. I didn't understand what that meant when I was thirteen, but I clearly understand it now. Whenever and wherever there was a match on, no matter what the age group, I was the first to arrive and the last to leave the pitch, often well after dark. The passing hours went unnoticed.

Linda always knew where to find me when mum sent her looking at tea time. I was completely dedicated to being the best, and I gave everything to it, morning, noon and night. It was the same kind of commitment I now admire so much in Jonny Wilkinson, and have read about in other great athletes such as Tiger Woods.

I was at my best when I had a football at my feet. I could do things other kids couldn't. It's hard to describe. I felt connected. It just felt . . . right. My body worked exactly the way I wanted it to, and it was magic. Absolutely magic.

This is why it was crushing when I realised a plot had been laid to take the beautiful game away from me.

Scouted . . . and scalped

I was playing above my age group in the Under-15s football team at Easingwold Grammar School. I'd been told that I was being watched by several professional clubs. Selectors from York City were known to scout our games, but word had got around that a scout from Everton, the really big Liverpool club which I loved because of Alan Ball, was coming to see me play on Saturday. In those days it was unusual for a club to look at a thirteen-year-old. There were a very few football academies emerging at the time, but they wouldn't normally be interested in anyone under sixteen years of age. It was clearly an important occasion for the school, and it was huge news for me. Were my dreams about to come true? The sidelines were unusually crowded with curious onlookers that day. But although my father usually came to every game and was a great supporter, on that day for some reason he didn't seem overly excited about my great opportunity.

Unknown to me, the headmaster of Easingwold Grammar had arranged a private meeting with my father the week before, while I was practising for the big game.

'Your son has potential, Squadron Leader Woodward. He's a smart lad. If he'd only give up his obsession with football or at least get some perspective and apply himself to the academic side of his schooling as well, he could go on to university and make something of himself.' I've imagined that conversation in my head a thousand times.

My father was a pilot trainer and a highly respected officer in the Royal Air Force. He was a really great man, too, who only wanted the best for his family. In that era, only a small handful of young adults gained places at university. It was every parent's ambition that their children would go through university and take up professional careers – as accountants, lawyers, bankers and the like. My sister had done well in her final year and earned a place at university, much to my father's delight. The headmaster's assessment of my academic ability must have been sweet words in my father's ears.

But my father was also well aware that all I wanted to do was play professional football. Even more than today, football was an adventure not a potential career for a thirteen-year-old. To my father, making good from the sport was a pipedream. His worry was that the chances of making it were very, very small. I later learned that my father had shared his concerns with his Commanding Officer over lunch in the base canteen.

'You know what you should do, Ron? As part of your officer's benefits you can send your son to a military boarding school at little cost to yourself.' Dad's CO was talking about a system designed for military personnel who were stationed abroad or constantly being posted. I lived at home. But my father had never considered boarding school before.

'I attended a top school – HMS *Conway*. I loved my years there. They're really strong on tradition, and best of all, they're rugby through and through. Certainly in my day there was no football played there at all.'

HMS *Conway* was a naval boarding school. Although an Air Force officer, my father was instructing young naval pilots in a small fixed-wing aircraft called the Chipmunk as a precursor to stepping into the Navy's rotary helicopter programme. Dad was obviously swayed by his CO's suggestion. He had made a few enquiries during the week and collared me as we walked in the door after the most important day in my young football career.

'Clive, come into the living room. We have to talk.' *Yes! The scout must have talked to him already.* But this wasn't my dad's usual way of speaking. This was the military man looking sternly back at me – a side of him I knew existed, but one I had never seen at home before. It was pretty scary, but I couldn't understand what was happening. The day had been great, really great. Our team had won in a nail-biting finish, and I had played well, the age difference making my performance stand out even more. In the midfield no one could touch me. I just had to have impressed that Everton scout.

'Clive, your headmaster talked to me this week about your marks. You're a bright boy, but you're not applying yourself to your school-work. You've got a good future ahead of you, university and a career, if only you wouldn't put all your hopes on that ruddy football.'

'But, dad, you saw me today . . .'

'Enough. Forget it,' he broke in, raising his voice. He didn't do that often. I really didn't understand what he was on about.

'You've a very high chance of getting to university, and a very slim chance of making it as a footballer. It is my job to help you make the right choices at this stage of your life. I've decided to send you away to a naval boarding school. You've got to settle down and make the most of the opportunities available to you. When the new term begins, you'll be attending HMS *Conway*. It's high on discipline, high on the academic side, high on rugby – but you need to understand there will be little football. I have spoken to the headmaster and it seems that rugby is the main game. The first thing you will do is . . .'

I didn't hear the rest of what he said. My breath faded away. My world was collapsing. Later that evening the football scout phoned our home. It was a very short conversation with my dad. I felt like my life was at an end. I felt empty, confused and isolated . . . heavy emotions for a thirteen-year-old to handle. I didn't give a monkey's about going to university, I just wanted to play football . . .

Doing what's best

Any parent would realise my father was doing what he thought best for me. As a dad, I can now understand it a little more but it was not a decision I would have made. Many would argue he was right. There is a very good chance that I wouldn't have made it at football. Let's face it, for every one David Beckham, there are 100,000 or more hopefuls who don't make it. Many of them are discarded from the academies at seventeen or eighteen with no life skills and no education to fall back on. While there are more opportunities now and academies handle this dilemma better, there are still no guarantees. There were definitely no guarantees for my father back then, but it wasn't his life. When it is *your* life, *your* opportunity, a decision by someone else may be wrong. I just do not think my dad understood. I was good. I just wanted the chance to find out how good.

I would have loved to have been a professional footballer. However, I can't second guess history too much. I went on to play rugby for my country. Along with a dedicated team of coaches and players, I helped

England win the Webb Ellis Trophy, and we stirred the national spirit. I understand my parents can feel justified in their decision but, for me, not knowing how the football would have turned out is something that will always be with me, and something that clearly has had a major affect in developing my character. Jayne says she's spent most of the last twenty years trying to redress the balance.

I came to realise that the choices we make can affect others in both good and bad ways. If it's the latter they may come to hold it against you. Whereas if you can help people to achieve something they've always wanted to do, something they couldn't have done otherwise, they'll never forget you. It's special. It became a guiding principle for me in my personal approach in managing others.

Naval school

To most, HMS *Conway* was a great school. But to this day my school days there remain the darkest days of my life. Ask any *Conway* old boy and he'll probably tell you of his many fond memories of the place. I'd say it could have been a good school, if only they had allowed me to play football. Without football, it was like a prison, my very own Alcatraz.

The school was located on the island of Anglesey in North Wales in those days, about four hours' drive from our home in Yorkshire. But it may just as well have been on the moon, it was so removed from what I knew and loved. I'll always remember the name of the local village, the longest in Wales: Llanfairpwllgwyngyll, called Llanfair (pronounced Clanfare) for short, is itself an abbreviation! The full name runs to fifty-eight letters.

'Dad, please let me come home. They don't play football here.' I pleaded with him by telephone after my first day. 'They don't even like football here. If I'm seen with a football the headmaster will go crazy and the older boys will just beat me up. All they're into is rugby.' I was vaguely familiar with rugby, having seen an international match on TV when there was nothing else on. Watching it on TV, it seemed a daft game with rules that were hard to follow.

'Sometimes you've just got to get on with it, Clive. It's character-building,' was all he would allow.

Get on with it then? Right. So I did just that. At breakfast the next morning I filled my pockets and did a runner! It took me all day, but I walked and hitchhiked my way right across the country. I was a thirteen-year-old on a mission to go back and play football.

My parents were waiting for me at the door when I arrived home. My father grabbed his coat in one hand and my arm in the other. He marched me out to the car and drove me right back the way I had come. I was seeing a side to my father I just did not know was there.

'Good job you were not Geoff Hurst's father or the bloody World Cup would be in Munich!'

Silence. Hardly a word was said the whole trip.

A few days later, I ran away again. This time, instead of driving me back, they put me on a train at York back to the nearest town to the school. Bangor, and especially that railway station, quickly became my least favourite place in the world. Still is. A week after that, I made a third break for it. Sooner or later my father would get the message: I was not going to accept this. I was coming home, and I was going to play football.

Unfortunately, it was I who got the message in the end – literally, in the form of a three-foot heavy marine rope with thick knots as hard as steel, not so fondly known as 'the teaser' by the other young cadets who were on the receiving end of it. HMS *Conway* was a tough school and discipline was handed down by the senior cadets. It was embarrassing to the school that I had run away once, let alone three times. The senior cadet captain had copped an earful from our headmaster, Mr Basil Lord, and he wasn't shy about passing it on. Corporal punishment handed out by eighteen-year-olds was no fun, but worse still this lot had never heard of Bobby Moore! I was trouble, there were consequences, and I didn't like the attention I was getting, nor did my body. As much as I had a point to prove, survival was first and foremost.

Still, I made one more attempt. My maths teacher, Mr Goode, was my last chance. He taught only one subject and so didn't live at the school like the majority of the teachers. Coincidentally, he also coached schoolboy football in nearby Bangor. We'd had a bit of a kick about one afternoon and he was amazed at what I could do with a football. He was so impressed that he even offered to pick me up and drop me off to training so that I could play with his club side.

I'll never forget the look on Mr Lord's face when I knocked on his study door that night, asking for one more chance at football. I explained how Mr Goode had offered to handle everything.

'How many times do I have to tell you, Woodward . . .' His steely expression of muted rage is etched into my mind. 'If you do not stop all this nonsense I will take the teaser to you as well.'

It was then that I realised I wasn't going to beat this. If I wanted to survive, I had to play by their rules.

Rugby, if I must

At HMS *Conway*, you could play any sport you wanted, as long as it was rugby.

They were nuts about it. They even set the school day around it. Classes ran until lunch time, and then from 1 p.m. everyone played rugby. At 4 p.m. we'd all trundle back into school for another two hours of classes. By doing it this way, we could play rugby right through the dark months of winter.

Although small for my age, I could run and I was very quick on my feet. So they did what everyone does with the little kid: they put me in at scrum-half. Sport was what I did best, so I quickly adapted and became so good at rugby that I was made captain of the Under-14s in my first season. It was no big deal. Playing rugby at least I was out of trouble with the senior cadets. Like most boarding schools at that time, if you were good at sport you survived.

I played rugby not because I loved the game, but because I had to. Soon I was better at it than anyone else in my year. Eventually in my later years at *Conway* I came to like the game but, with hindsight, it was the winning that I enjoyed most. Even then I knew that there was more to sport than just taking part. I played for one reason only, and that was to win.

It was all I had to take from a game I was forced to play against my will, but it was enough to really get me going. My approach to the game was one of a detachment that confounded my team-mates and schoolmasters. I was forever asking questions about why the game had to be played in such a ponderous way. I wasn't physically large compared with the other boys my age. I couldn't go through the opposition, so I went around them. I ran with the ball and I was fast. Of course, having a ball in my hands rather than at my feet took some getting used to, but it was a skill I honed over the next five years.

Welsh Schoolboy trials

My first taste of recognition in rugby came in my final year at HMS *Conway*, and it was a very bitter experience indeed. In their wisdom, the schoolmasters at *Conway* were not inclined to send their rugby best to the local schoolboy representative trials. If boys were sent to trials, chances were they'd miss the odd school game. Couldn't have that now, could we?

However, they made an exception with me in sixth form, the only time in five years anyone was allowed to show their rugby skills outside school – not because I was good necessarily but because the school was closing down and had largely adopted a 'who cares' attitude. If only that thought had prevailed five years before when I wanted to play football. I had done well in the North Wales trials and so in early February 1974 one of the coaches from the North Wales Schoolboys squad drove me down to Cardiff for a trial match, the annual Possibles vs the Probables – the top thirty boys in the land and I was the only representative from North Wales. I was in the Possibles.

I had grown taller and stronger in the last few years, the staple diet of chip butties had paid off. The selectors were obviously impressed. Near the end of the day the head coach called me over.

'You, Woodward, where did you really learn to run and play like that?' he asked in a thick Welsh accent.

'HMS *Conway*, sir, on Anglesey,' I replied after a moment.

'Yes, I know that. But *Conway* is a boarding school. Where are you really from, Woodward?' he returned.

'From North Yorkshire, sir. Dad's in the Air Force there.'

'Are you English then?' he asked.

'Yes, sir. Why, is that a problem?'

But with that he turned and marched straight back to the other selectors, leaving me quite perplexed as to what had just happened.

It was quietly and carefully explained to me in the car on the way home that boys from the North were rarely selected, and that no English schoolboy had ever been selected for Wales as far as he knew. This kind of not-so-subtle discrimination had been going on for years and was apparently accepted as part of the landscape.

When I finally understood I was truly shocked, in the way only a fresh-faced eighteen-year-old can be. What difference did it make where I was from? I could play rugby, I was qualified to play for the Welsh Schoolboys side because my school was in Wales, so what was the issue?

When I was first capped for England in 1980, a journalist asked about my playing history, particularly why I didn't play in the Welsh Schoolboys representative team. I lied and said I withdrew because of injury. I just couldn't tell the truth. It wasn't something that I wanted to air in public at that time – it's history now. That was my first brush with discrimination based on country of origin. I had experienced prejudice of sorts at HMS *Conway* – against football in support of rugby – and if those Welsh selectors were an example of the traditional rugby establishment, they could stick it.

I laugh now when I see players who are invited to play for a country based on the most tenuous strands of nationality through distant relatives, particularly when it's by the Welsh.

It is strange how you never forget and rarely forgive.

Enforced conformity, discipline

As the days, weeks and months passed during my five years in Wales, my dreams of football glory slowly ebbed and faded. To be truly success-ful at any sport you need to be obsessive, which with football is quite difficult when you feel your life is at risk if you're even seen with a round ball! Soon the skills which must be nurtured and honed in these formative years were lost to me forever. I eventually accepted my lot in life and altered my game to suit my new conditions. Some people take to the military school environment of discipline and structure. However I spent my five years flouting authority, resorting to humour and silly antics just to offer a little light relief. Thankfully, once I had proved myself on the pitch, I could get away with it.

At the end of 1974, the year of my A levels, the HMS *Conway* Naval School was shut down due to shrinking government funding. I can't say I was sad about it. In fact I was pleased. It was a naval school and was run like a Navy ship. Everything had to be routinely polished and cleaned, and the youngest cadets bore the brunt of the work – my form for many years, as we were the last intake of students to go through. I still have a few old photos of myself at school. I have yet to find one of me smiling!

Boarding schools have changed over the decades, but that place was definitely of the old school. Physical intimidation was part of the culture. Lying in bed at night, I remember the fear of what was to come, because something was bound to happen every night. And it wasn't like being a day boy where you could cop the abuse and go home to a sanctuary. There was no escape at *Conway*. We had to be vigilant twenty-four hours a day. It became part of every pupil's mindset. There was no hiding place.

As I progressed through HMS *Conway*, the bullying slowly ceased. I took great pleasure in personally disposing of the teaser that I came into contact with so frequently in my first few weeks. In my last year I was deputy cadet captain, but by then the culture had changed entirely. A lot of people in naval uniform loved the sort of discipline we experienced at HMS *Conway*. They just thought of it as character-building. I learned there is a fine line between character-building and institutionalised bullying. There are certain similarities in both rugby and business. As a coach or manager, you have to be very careful of the line between being tough on your team in order to strengthen them and simply running them into the ground.

I think those five years did influence my character. I learned to make the most of the situations in which I found myself. I also made a commitment to myself that in the future nobody would tell me that I could not do something ... unless there was a compelling reason for it. Struggling with the culling of my dreams, that is what moulded my psyche. The physical aspect? That was just a distraction from the real issues at hand.

If my father and mother knew of the things that went on, they would have been horrified. But having seen how I turned out, certainly my parents would argue in support of their decision. It's a valid argument, but I struggled for many years to understand, and still do. They did the best they could with the information at hand. I know they did it for all the right reasons. I'm grateful I could put this conflict with my parents behind me before my father passed away only a few years ago.

True to his word – A levels and university

To his credit, my father's belief in my academic potential was warranted.

In sending me to *Conway* he never did actually divert me from my sporting interests. I still took every opportunity to be distracted from my studies and soon played rugby with intense enthusiasm, although never with the same obsession I had for my football.

Eventually I did manage to sit for my A levels, and even passed with reasonable marks. There was every chance that I'd be accepted by the university of my choice. I decided that all this study would be put to use. I wanted to be a lawyer, and in the summer of 1974 applied to read Law at Durham University. I'm sure my parents were proud. Me, I was just happy to leave the old-school confines of the Isle of Anglesey near the little village of Llanfairpwllgwyngyll – I'll never get over that name!

Catching the train home after my final term was liberating. The first thing I did after pulling out of Bangor station for the last time was to duck into the toilet and change out of my naval uniform. I'm not sure we were even clear of the station before I was into my Levis and t-shirt, still my favourite dress today. I then grabbed my piled up uniform and threw it straight out of the window. I never wanted to see it again. It wouldn't be the last time I would throw everything out, never to bring it back into my life again. Since that day on the train I've never been back to Anglesey, not even to North Wales, not in the entire thirty-odd years since. Many old boys from HMS *Conway* still try to keep in touch. I have met Old Conways all around the world. They've even posted pictures of me on their old boys' website somewhere. However, I haven't replied to their letters and e-mails of best wishes. I don't know what to say to them. Perhaps now from reading these pages you can see why it has been difficult.

When I look back now, I smile at how far I've come in the game: the coach who took his team to become the number one rugby side in the world, the first ever northern-hemisphere World Cup champions, is a man who never really wanted to play rugby in the first place!

4
EARLY PLAYING DAYS

I kept myself busy over the summer of 1974, working at odd jobs while waiting for my final marks to arrive. My family had been posted to RAF Brize Norton in Oxfordshire, and there were a number of car factories in the Cowley area of Oxford with shift work on offer. If I was going to study Law at Durham, I could be reasonably certain of a grant to cover my university fees, but beyond that I'd have to support myself.

My marks arrived by post in early August. They weren't as good as I had hoped, but I'd still earned three reasonably good A levels. There was a very good chance that they would take me at Durham, which I had picked as one of the best universities for Law in the country. Durham required two A's and a B, which I had just missed; but they also had a reputation as a university that liked a diversity of skills, not just academic.

Shortly afterwards a letter arrived from Durham.

'Dear Mr Woodward, Thank you for your application to read Law at Durham University.' I mumbled nervously to myself. I skipped to the important bits halfway down the page. 'After much consideration, we regret to inform you . . .' And that was as far as I got. I quickly scanned the rest of the letter. The final sentence carried the punch line, 'We wish you well in finding another university, who we feel sure will be interested in your application.'

Most of the people who had been to HMS *Conway* went on to a career in the Merchant Navy. Why anyone would want to spend a life at sea was beyond me, however I was determined to go to university, and had been looking forward to studying Law. This was a major setback.

Having not been accepted by my preferred university, I had two choices. The first was a clearance scheme designed to facilitate a second round of placements. The second was to get a job and go to work. Looking through the paper, I found an advertisement for trainee positions with the NatWest Bank. 'Did you earn two A levels?' it read. 'Have you considered a promising future at the Bank? Management trainee positions in the exciting world of finance now available.' It sounded interesting enough, worth taking a punt at.

I wrote off a letter, was granted an interview and, in due course, I got the job. The really exciting thing was the positions were all in London. For years my father's postings were up in Edinburgh and all over Yorkshire and I had never been to London, which was strange because he was born and brought up in Battersea in south London, and the whole family had always supported Chelsea, and still do. I was excited to see the city now. After a summer living at home, which was very difficult after being used to the independence of school, I had to get out and on with my life. I took the job.

The world of finance

The job on offer was in the Richmond branch of the NatWest Bank, which I had to look up on a map. But I noticed one thing that interested me: it was no great distance from Twickenham, England's rugby head-quarters. In late August I was on my way to London, with a train ticket provided by the bank. This was the start of a huge adventure. What constituted my life to this point – family, school and all those little links to people and places – was all left behind me on the platform of Oxford station.

I was a bit nervous as I hopped off the train at my new home in Raynes Park, just a couple of miles south-west of the branch. My fears weren't exactly put to rest when I met the host family where the bank had got me digs in a home near the train station. They were a lovely lot, but not quite what I had in mind for living in London. Picture the scene: 7 p.m. watching TV in a cramped lounge with three boisterous kids under ten, mum, dad and me. Lying in bed that first night I thought this was not for me. *Working in a bank, sharing a kitchen and bathroom*

with two adults and three kids – even though they were kind they were
complete strangers.

My introduction to the bank had a similarly uncertain start. I arrived
for my first day at work in a tweed suit that my parents had bought
me. Boy, did I feel like some country hillbilly when I saw everyone else
in their sharp grey pinstriped suits. That I was so naïve and so badly
prepared for even the most obvious situation was another indictment
of my school. It was all part of my new life in London.

Settling in didn't take all that long though. For the first month or so
I was the lackey in the back office, doing anything and everything they
could throw at me. It was pretty tedious. There were mountains of
paperwork, and it was a bit like shelling peas, really. Everthing I did
is probably done by a machine now, but I was a fast learner. Having
a job, something productive to do, was a joy in itself, and I particularly
liked receiving my pay cheque every month, though it wasn't much.

Within a couple of months I had been promoted from the back room
to the cashiers' desk at the front. Handling the money and processing
the cheques was what most local branches of big clearing banks were
all about, and the Richmond branch of NatWest was a busy place. It
turned out I had a head for figures, which was essential, and I also
seemed to have a way with the customers. I enjoyed working on the
till best of all.

My introduction to proper club rugby

Very soon after I had arrived at my new job, I decided to investigate
the rugby situation in this part of the world. After a bit of a rocky start
I had grown to enjoy my rugby at HMS *Conway* and realised I was
good enough to have played for the Welsh Schoolboys team. I was
looking forward to perhaps playing at club level; at the least it would
be a great way to keep in shape and meet people other than those at
the bank. There were two excellent clubs nearby: Richmond near my
work, and Harlequins based a couple of miles west at the Stoop Memorial Grounds in Twickenham, near the famous stadium. I liked the
colourful Harlequins' strip, and their reputation was just as out of the
ordinary. Quins had been one of the premier rugby clubs in London

for just about forever. It was one of the original clubs that made up the Rugby Football Union over 130 years ago.

I found them in the phone book and called their number.

'Hi, is this Harlequins rugby club?'

'Yes it is. I'm the secretary. What can I do for you?'

It was obvious I had called his home. Back then running the club was a part-time job and this was probably a retired gentleman who had volunteered for the position. It was considered a privilege. That's how club rugby was run in those days.

'I'd like to join Harlequins. How do I become a member of the club?'

'We train on Tuesday and Thursday from 7 p.m. to 9 p.m. Just come on down and we'll see if we can find a place for you,' he rolled off the standard response.

I thanked him and we hung up. So one pleasant evening in early September I picked up my boots and wandered down to the Stoop Memorial Grounds.

In 1974 Harlequins was an impressive outfit. Under coach Earle Kirton's guidance, Harlequins was a serious force on the rugby scene, and they had a strong depth of players. The team was captained by England's Nick Martin and had another of England's star players, Bob Hiller, in the line-up as well.

Earle Kirton was a New Zealander who had been fly-half for the All Blacks on their tour of the British Isles a few years before. In that tour he was the quick and elusive architect of the backs in all four tests, scoring two tries against England. His international career ended in 1970, after which he came to England for a postgraduate course in dentistry. He went on to appear for Harlequins, Middlesex and the Barbarians. Kirton had a reputation as not only an accurate tactical kicker but also a fly-half who ran well, and he was noted for his skill at doubling around his outsides to create an overlap. As someone who liked to play an expansive game, Earle Kirton's rugby philosophy very much appealed to me.

Walking into the ground, I sat in a corner of the small stand to get my kit on, and then not knowing anyone, stood there like a complete lemon waiting for something to happen. After a few minutes I walked up to the first official looking person I could see to introduce myself.

'Go over there with the fourth team,' he directed, looking me up and down without much interest. The players had already been through pre-season training, so I was put in the bottom team. There actually was a fifth and sixth team, but lucky for me they didn't do any training.

Coming from the backwaters of Anglesey, I really didn't know how good I was, despite my Welsh trial. I was tall, a bit lanky and I guess hardly even looked like a rugby player – not many would have guessed that within a month I would be playing fly half in their first XV. My early success surprised me as much as anybody, and with Kirton's encouragement I began to really enjoy my rugby.

I was eighteen years old in the first team at Quins, playing with and against England internationals. At first I was in awe of their stature, but then it occurred to me – I was probably as good as most of them. But because I hadn't come through the England Schoolboys system no one had a clue who I was. It was then I started to think that maybe I could go a long way in this game – maybe I could play for England too. The thought of actually playing for my country at Twickenham began to excite me. I realised I had the chance of doing something special. I decided to go for it.

My first senior club game for the first XV was against Cardiff in early October. It was also the first time I played at Twickenham. As Quins' base was right across the road from the stadium, the club used Twickenham stadium for most of their home games through some long-standing agreement. However the old stands at Twickenham held 50,000 people, so you can imagine how vast and empty it felt playing Cardiff in front of a thousand people. It was a good crowd for us back then, but it was a strange environment. The place might just as well have been empty. Still, it was inspiring just to be there. I couldn't help but think that if I worked hard, I might have a chance of playing there for England one day. For an International the atmosphere would certainly be different.

The warmth of club rugby

One of the great things I discovered at Quins was the social aspect that the club brought to the game. No matter how fierce the match, the aggression ended as soon as the game was over. It's one of the things I loved about rugby and still do. As soon as emotions had cooled in the changing rooms, the teams always got along well over a beer. Rugby around the world has promoted a culture of trust and respect amongst its players. That's one of the reasons why I believe it's one of the greatest games around today.

In those amateur times, the more pragmatic English clubs took their rugby seriously enough, but quite a few of the Quins players were really there for a bit of social sport as they had high-pressure jobs in the City. That was one reason why Kirton's focus on a more expansive running game – which was very much *not* England's philosophy at the time – suited the club to a tee. The Quins' attitude got up the noses of some of the other clubs, especially as we won more often than not and always enjoyed ourselves in the process.

At Quins there was a feeling of camaraderie, and players tended to look after their own. Having lived away from home for so long during my years at HMS *Conway*, the club provided a very friendly reception for me. I'd soon met a couple of older players who, upon hearing of my predicament regarding accommodation, kindly offered me the use of their sofa at night.

Paddy McLoughlin was a solicitor playing in the fifth team. He loved playing rugby, although he didn't exactly scorch up the touchline with his finesse. He owned a very posh two-bedroom flat a few miles out of town in Shepperton and was sharing with 'Basher' Briggs, who worked in marketing for British Airways and played in the third team. I think that my being a regular in the first team meant they were quite pleased to be looking after me. Paddy in particular was very kind, and never charged me a penny for all the time I stayed there. It was great because I could now afford to buy a round of beers and didn't have to be embarrassed about money, or rather my lack of it! Working at the bank wasn't exactly making me rich.

After my time at Quins I lost touch with Paddy, but just a few years ago I was doing a radio interview where listeners could call in.

'Hi, Clive, is your favourite record still "You're So Vain" by Carly Simon?'

'Paddy, how the devil are you?'

It was great to hear his familiar voice once again. I used to drive him and Basher nuts blasting that song out on the stereo all the time at the flat.

I played with Harlequins for the whole of that season, camping out with Paddy and Basher. I now lived on a steady diet of cheap Chinese food and chip butties. I was the happiest I'd been in years, and rugby was making it all possible.

My first taste of public recognition

Early in the season we were playing against Coventry at the Stoop because England was playing Scotland at Twickenham later that day. Coventry was the leading club team in England in those days and so all the media came to watch, and the stands were packed with around 6,000 people. As fly-half I was playing in the pivotal position, and thanks to Kirton's preferred style of play, we did a fair amount with the ball.

In fact, I did enough to attract the notice of a sports journalist, who mentioned me in his piece the following day. The main event of course had been the International, which England had won, but the journalist wrote up that match as yet another serving-up of the boring, no-risk, forward-orientated rugby that accurately summed up the English way of playing the game.

'. . . England would do well,' he wrote, 'to look at the likes of young Clive Woodward of Harlequins to liven up the game a little.'

The journalist was by no means alone in his disappointment with England's play at the top level in those days. David Cooke usually played outside me at Quins, but he had been chosen to play against Scotland that afternoon. He hardly touched the ball at all that day. At Quins he was a great player week in, week out, but when it came to England he was hardly in the game. David explained the situation to me.

'The policy is, Woody, we only run the ball if we're 20 points up. But we never are 20 points up because we don't score any tries. And we're told to kick every time, unless we're within the opposition's 22. Only then we can move the ball around a bit. But that happens so infrequently we tend to stuff it up anyway. The old joke is, if you're in the backs for England bring your hat and gloves, because you'll wait so long just to do anything that your hands are frozen by the time you touch the ball.'

I was to find out first-hand what he meant before the end of the season.

Playing for my country

Within five months of starting with Harlequins I was selected to play for the England Under-19s representative side, the England Colts. Ironically, my first game with the Colts was against the Welsh youth team at Twickenham. I had already played against some of the Welsh players, like Terry Holmes and Gareth Davies, during my Welsh Schoolboys trial only the year before whilst at HMS *Conway*. I later played with Terry and Gareth on the 1980 British Lions tour to South Africa – the Welsh Schoolboys had quite a bit of talent the year I attended the trials there.

'How come you're playing with the England Colts?' Gareth asked in surprise, but I didn't feel like telling the story. I preferred to do my talking on the pitch and, as it happened, the England Colts dominated the game that year. Some of the Welsh selectors who had seen me play the year before were also quite surprised, especially when I scored the only try of the match.

Playing with the Colts also brought my first experience of the culture of England rugby that David Cooke had described.

'If you get the ball, kick it or give it to the forwards to take up the pitch. Kick, don't run, and only spread it wide when you're in their 22.'

It was frustrating; I was used to playing a much more open game at Quins where Earle Kirton encouraged us to use every position effectively. I think we 'hammered' the Welsh 9—6 that day.

I did feel frustrated playing this style of rugby but didn't discuss this with the coaches. The huge experience of being a new player in the England set-up was more than enough for the time being. The fact of the matter was that the culture pervading the England sides of the time had been inherited from generations of teams playing safe, no-risk rugby.

At schoolboy level as well as international level, being selected for the next game seemed to be everything. Just getting the cap, the shirt and the tracksuit seemed to be the major focus of the whole set-up, which was all very well, except that we hadn't won anything significant in rugby since 1963.

Over the years, I've encountered many different versions of inherited thinking, or tradition as some call it, in business, sport and government. The symptoms are always the same: blind faith in the 'way', nepotism to protect the institution, and a culture that heavily discourages, even punishes, any questioning of authority, and where change is an anathema.

Perhaps I should have stood up and discussed what I knew was our flawed approach with the coaches. If I had, it's possible other players would have been right behind me. On the other hand, it's more likely that I would never have played representative rugby again. You fight the battles you can win. When combating a diseased organisational culture – be it in business, sport or anywhere else – you need either strength of numbers or absolute authority to effect any real change.

When it finally came to my turn at the top, I would have both. But in 1974 I just did things their way, like everyone else, so that I'd be considered for selection the next time. It's such a shame and a regret. When I was nineteen and relatively new to rugby, I had so much to contribute about playing the game. Yet no one ever asked me for my opinion. In rugby and in business, I now try to encourage people to talk and express their views at all times, especially the newest members in the team.

In my playing career I was privileged to have played under three of the finest rugby coaches in the game: Earle Kirton at Quins, Jim Greenwood at Loughborough, and Chalkie White at Leicester. Like my football hero Martin Peters, they were all ten years ahead of their time. They came from different backgrounds and had different perspectives, but all three were coaches you could talk to and discuss things with. That was the one thing that united them. Yet none of them was ever close to being considered for a senior position within the England rugby coaching fraternity. The traditional rugby establishment were afraid of them. It was this mindset that was to continue to hold the England team back for many years to come. The culture of England rugby was set long and hard.

Rugby and banking

The little bit of notice I was now attracting from the press had another consequence. I found out that my manager at NatWest was beginning to field questions from his executives about this new trainee who was playing rugby for Harlequins and the England Colts. Rugby has long been a favourite sport for business and corporate interests because it traditionally attracts, among many other types of fan, a strong base of supporters in professional services industries. For that reason, rugby had long been the preferred sport of the banking and finance sector.

When it became clear that there was a very good chance that I could be playing for England soon, I started getting a lot of attention from senior executives. Top-level managers from several different parts of the bank would come to Richmond and take me out to lunch. For most of the conversation they'd go on about rugby, especially their own playing days! On many occasions you could find my head in my soup. Then near the end they'd typically drop in something about their part of the bank: options markets, futures exchanges, international finance. I couldn't understand what they were getting at. All I knew about the job was the till. Banking to me was about people coming down to the teller to draw out fifty quid. It was only much later that I discovered how interesting the financial world can be. Obviously these executives wanted to cajole me into their part of the bank. Only I was nineteen, loving rugby and my new-found freedom! Why would I want a serious job in banking?

In May, ten months after I had joined the bank, I resigned my trainee position. That's when the executives came in heavy with career offers, not because my performance at work merited it, but because they could see some advantage to the bank in my future rugby career. That didn't seem quite right to me at the time.

A few months before I'd had a similar experience in another quarter. It was in February, just after playing for the England Colts side, that I received an unexpected letter from Durham University. 'Dear Mr Woodward, We have recently had the pleasure of revisiting your application to read Law at Durham University. We are pleased to inform you that we now feel privileged to offer you a place to study with our distinguished faculty . . .'

That really did grate on me. Save for my rugby, I was no different a person then than when I had applied the previous year . . . and been rejected. I immediately sat down and wrote a rather direct letter telling them where they could stick their Law degree. It may seem a bit impetuous, but I had already planned my next step and even a Durham offer was not going to sidetrack me. Durham had turned me down because my marks weren't good enough. So what had changed their mind? England rugby?

Loughborough

I had basically figured out what my next step would be within two months of arriving in London. That was another reason why it was easy to turn down the offers from the bank and from Durham University. It had always been my intention to attend university. I had earned my A levels, and I wanted to get a degree. My time with NatWest in London was really more like a gap year, although I didn't exactly make that clear to them when I joined them.

Not long after I had arrived in London, I was sitting in a pub with Paddy, Basher, Cookie and a few other Quins players after a midweek practice session. Talk soon turned to rugby.

'You'd like this sort of thing, Clive,' David Cooke said as I came back to the group with a tray full of beers. 'Fifteen-man rugby with a real emphasis on using the whole pitch and everyone in the team.'

My ears pricked up. This was a story I wanted to hear. Rugby under Kirton had begun to fascinate me. I leaned in closer, straining my ears to pick up every word over the din of the pub crowd.

'It's being taken to a different level by a coach named Jim Greenwood up at Loughborough. A Scotsman. Apparently he's pretty tough. Big on fitness. He's renowned for running his players into the ground, but he's really brought a whole new range of ideas and techniques to the game.'

'Loughborough?' I knew it as a training college for PE teachers.

'That's right. Loughborough College, where you go if you want to be a teacher,' he continued. 'Next year the colleges will become part of Loughborough University and instead of a certificate in education it will now be a three-year bachelor degree in Sports Science. A couple of guys at Quins are there at the moment in their last year at the college and are so positive and enthusiastic about what Greenwood is doing. They'll be taking off soon to start their next term. They think Greenwood is the best thing since sliced bread.'

This was all music to my ears. I had to find out more.

Kirton's endorsement

My coach at Quins, Earle Kirton, seemed to like me. He would often give me the benefit of his experience after a game. His first lesson to me was: the first bit of ball you get may be your best bit of ball the whole game, so go for it! I felt I could talk to him, so casually in a conversation before training one night I asked him whether he'd heard of Greenwood.

'Jim Greenwood? The lecturer and coach at Loughborough?'

I nodded.

'Yes, of course I know him. Who in rugby coaching circles doesn't? In New Zealand he's practically a god. Same in South Africa and most other rugby nations, for that matter,' he replied. 'Why do you ask?'

'Well, I was just thinking about my future. I want to go to university and I'd heard about Jim Greenwood and Loughborough.'

Earle Kirton gave me a good hard look, almost as if to see if my interest was genuine.

'They've just created the BSc in Sports Science up there, haven't they?' he continued, gauging my response. 'A degree is a good thing, Clive. It'll take you places. And if you're going to go to university and play rugby there, that's the place to go. If I had my time over again, I'd be the first to enrol.

'Jim Greenwood is the most innovative coach around. I never could understand why your lot over here haven't given him more of an ear. He'll teach you things you never thought possible about fitness, your body and how it relates to rugby. I'd hate to lose you to him, but you couldn't be in safer hands,' he ended with a fatherly pat on the shoulder. It was time to get started at training.

'Thanks. It sounds fantastic,' I said as I wandered off deep in thought. It was kind of Earle to encourage me like that. I had no desire to be a teacher, but this sounded pretty exciting to me. Three years working exclusively on sport, coming away with a degree and being coached with someone as respected as Greenwood? Perfect.

I phoned the university and asked them to post any information they could. When I read about the curriculum – coaching, biomechanical analysis, nutrition, psychology, fitness, medical – I was even more excited. These were things I'd never heard of before in sport. Little did I know how important this was going to be in my future career as a professional coach.

I was mad on sport, and with my dark years at *Conway* behind me, it all sounded too good to be true. When I first walked into the club that September quite a few of the guys at Quins had just come back from summer holidays abroad. There I was working all day long in the bank for not very much money, and here were these guys with suntans from the south of France and Greece and goodness knows where else. They were just having a bit of fun at rugby before going back to university in the autumn. *Am I missing something here?* I thought to myself. *Or do I need to consider a different strategy!* When it came to a choice of launching into a banking career or spending a few years at university playing sport, especially rugby on a potentially full-time basis, there was no contest.

I was thinking by that stage that perhaps everything does happen for a reason and that maybe destiny does exist. Well, maybe I wasn't born to do a Law degree at Durham. My thoughts were confirmed when one executive at the bank assured me that they would welcome me back after university and that having a degree, any degree, would be all that they would require to take me back. I could have my cake and eat it too. That confirmed it. I was going to Loughborough. I was on course, and I knew it.

Filled with anticipation I wrote a letter of application. I also wrote personally to Jim Greenwood. I was granted an interview, and filled with excitement, I caught the train to Loughborough.

I first spotted Jim Greenwood while waiting in the reception of the sports hall for my interview soon after my arrival. Based on his reputation, I was expecting a giant of a man. Really that's exactly what he was, but not in physical appearance. He was in his late fifties, short grey hair and a quiet unassuming manner. I could see he was very fit, in good shape to lead any team. A coach should look the part, and this man did, in a track suit and ready to go. There he was in his job, a lecturer in Sports Science.

In the interview there was no mincing around. He was straight in your face.

'So you're Woodward, then?' he said with a nod, and I noticed his Scots burr.

'Yes, sir.'

'Jim Greenwood,' he said extending his hand.

I took it. He had a warm firm grip.

'It's nice to finally meet you, sir. I've heard a lot about you.'

'Up from the city, I hear. From Harlequins. Played with the Colts, too,' he observed, sizing me up.

'Yes, sir,' I said, fidgeting under his gaze.

'Well up here we play a different style of game, son,' he said as if completing his assessment. 'Up here we play Total Rugby, and we use the whole pitch so you need to be fit. Everyone is going to have the ball in his hands and be totally involved in the game.'

I was electrified by his words. There was no question this was the place for me. I left the interview feeling excited and nervous at the same time.

To my delight, in the closing weeks of December 1974, I was accepted to study Sports Science, starting in the autumn. It was the best Christmas present I'd ever received. Jim Greenwood had already become a hero. I couldn't wait to start working with him.

The end of my gap year

In my year in London I had enjoyed complete freedom to do things my way. I'd saved my money and bought my first car – an ancient bright yellow Mini with a white roof. It cost me all of £75, a princely sum for me then. My Mini had more miles on the clock than I had hairs on my head, which was a lot in those days. It was rough, coughed and spluttered, but it ran, even if it was on just three cylinders when it was really cold. As for most young adults, my car *was* my independence, but it didn't run on happy thoughts alone. I needed to earn money to keep it going.

I actually stayed in London in Paddy's flat until early July doing odd jobs here and there. But the rugby season had ended, and my conscience got the better of me. How could I take advantage of his hospitality if I wasn't playing for Quins any more? I didn't have anywhere else to go, so I moved back home for a short while, intent on earning money for university.

Shortly after arriving home a labourer's job came up with an industrial carpet-laying company. We laid carpet in office buildings and the like. One week we even painted a factory floor. Anything and everything, that was my boss's motto, as long as the money was good. That certainly suited me. It was a job where I was paid by the square foot, rather than by the hour. We worked hard and fast all day long, sometimes well into the night. I didn't mind. I was taking home more than five times what I'd earned at the bank! It was such a different environment. The carpet fitters were guys I could really warm to. It didn't matter who you were. All they respected was hard work. If I earned £20 in a day, the boss would give me £25. I got more than I bargained for and I sure as hell gave more than expected. It was a great feeling and a new experience for me, being paid for my results rather than for my time.

The summer passed quickly. Before I knew it, I was packing my things into my Mini and preparing for the next stage in my life. In my gap year I had learned a bit about business and the two ways I could earn money, by my time or by my results. I had been embraced by the hospitality of club rugby. I had learned to love the kind of rugby coached by Earle Kirton. I had also learned that I wanted to represent my country on the rugby pitch.

All in all had been quite a year. Indeed it was the year that shaped my life.

5
LOUGHBOROUGH

If HMS *Conway* represented the darkest period of my life, my time at Loughborough University was one of the brightest. I spent the better part of four years there, and those years were a great contrast to my school days.

That's the great thing about university. It's an environment where you can try and do all sorts of things and not have to worry too much about the risks. You can make mistakes and it doesn't have to matter that much. You learn. The real world isn't always so forgiving. University is a relatively safe environment not only to learn subjects, but also to learn about life. So, if my gap year at Richmond had been a watershed, my years at university were to prove really fulfilling, and a foundation for much of what was to come.

Loughborough is a small town about eight miles north of Leicester, and eighty miles from our home in Brize Norton, Oxfordshire. It took me about two and a half hours to drive there across the Midlands. I was full of excitement as I drew up at the main gate for the first time in the autumn of 1975. My old banger was packed full of gear and the radio was blaring, or wheezing, perhaps I should say, because it was turned right up to its limits of distortion. I was very proud of that radio – it had cost more than the car, and I'd actually installed it myself.

Cars were a rare commodity for students back then; only a handful of my colleagues at Loughborough had ascended to my esteemed four-wheeled status. But in truth I was as broke as everyone else. I had a government grant, the amount being based on my father's financial position, and I existed on my grant cheque supplemented by earnings from fitting carpets and any other job I could get hold of.

In residence

In my first year I had quite a big single room in William Morris Hall, which seemed luxury to me. There was a communal restaurant in the middle of the complex, and I felt at home there from the beginning. The place was quite empty because I had gone up a week early for pre-season rugby training. So when I went straight to the halls of residence where my room was ready and waiting, the only people back were rugby players, about thirty to thirty-five of them. I was nineteen, and some of them knew me because I had played with Quins and England Colts. Word had got round about the Harlequins fly-half who'd come to Loughborough.

Loughborough is, of course, the country's top Sports Science university today, and it was the top place then, when I arrived there for the first time, brimming with anticipation. Good people from all kinds of sports all over the UK went there because they could really train properly – it was a real centre of excellence with superb facilities. Most sports were amateur in Britain in those days, and Loughborough drew in all the really talented people from a wide range of sports.

So you had to be pretty talented both academically and at sports to get there in the first place, but to me Loughborough was also just four years of real enjoyment. And I ended with a degree, a BSc in Sports Science and Technology. Things have changed since my day, with the course now demanding A's at A level to gain entry. All I wanted to do was have four years at university, doing the things I liked doing best.

Basically, I went to Loughborough for one reason, to play my best rugby, and for one man, Jim Greenwood. If I was going to play for England, it made sense to go where the best coach was. I wanted to see how this guy would help my game. Rugby was an amateur game then of course, but Loughborough was the closest I would get to playing at professional level. I was that little bit slighter than some of the others, but pace, as in all sports, tends to be the deciding factor. As well as pace, I wanted to compete by playing differently, thinking differently. So naturally I was eager to start working with Jim Greenwood.

Living legend

Jim Greenwood had played for his home country, Scotland, and had been selected for the British Lions, so I knew he had been an outstanding player who understood the game inside and out. As it turned out, Jim and I had experienced similar frustrations in the game. He too felt there was so much more to be done on the rugby pitch, that there was so much more to the game than most people were aware of.

His whole ethos was different, and he basically taught what we would now call a standard fifteen-man rugby game compared to the then preferred style of ten-man rugby being played by the national side. In the latter, the focus is on the forwards. Keep it tight and power the ball down the pitch, basically out-muscling the opposition in the forwards, brawn not brain. England were well-known for the size and strength of their forward pack, and they habitually used this style of play. Jim Greenwood's style was almost the complete opposite in terms of central focus: use all the players on the pitch wherever possible all of the time – everyone had a role to play, even if you were on the other side of the pitch.

Jim's book, *Total Rugby*, the only rugby book I've ever read, first came out in 1978 when I was at Loughborough. It was way ahead of its time, and has since become a closely studied classic, especially in New Zealand. It's now in its fifth edition, and I enjoyed writing a foreword to it only last year.

So here was this Scotsman, a lecturer at Loughborough in the middle of England, flying in the face of conventional wisdom and re-writing all the rule books in the process. I loved it. It was exactly what I'd been searching for since I first began playing rugby at *Conway*. I played for Jim for three years, captaining the squad my last two. I respect his views on the game more than those of any other man in rugby. We're still in contact to this day, although he's well and truly retired in a little village up in Scotland now. No man has done more in our time to singlehandedly transform the modern game of rugby than Jim Greenwood.

There's no doubt Jim Greenwood was a man ahead of his time, twenty-five years ahead in terms of rugby in England. What can we be doing now that will be considered the norm in twenty-five years? For clues, it's interesting to examine the inherited thinking of conventional wisdom and look for its fundamental flaws. For a start, under him we practised weight training, analysing the opposition, and other forms of conditioning, including diet and nutrition programmes that were just way ahead. Outside Loughborough there weren't any clubs doing that kind of training, though they were starting to do it in the southern hemisphere. It so happened that Greenwood's ideas and style of play were concurrently being developed in the emerging schoolboys sides in Australia, the same group of players who would go on to demonstrate in the eighties how a well-executed running game could so thoroughly dismantle a side focused on ten-man rugby.

It's a sad fact that Jim Greenwood never coached a side at international level. As for England, in that era it was unlikely that anyone who was not English was ever going to coach the country. But I have a feeling that there was more to it: I think the conventional rugby establishment of the time were scared of the likes of Greenwood.

They simply couldn't take in the ideas of visionaries like him because his ideas would have shaken up a lot of their coaches in the way they played. It was too far from what they knew and believed in, and introducing substantially different ideas would have exposed their real lack of knowledge. To do it Greenwood's way would have required them to coach a team to take risks in front of a packed house at Twickenham – English rugby was not about innovation or risky play.

Jim continued to be ignored by the various unions in this part of the world, so he went to Japan and is responsible for the lively style of Japanese play today. His concept of Total Rugby is the antithesis of play-safe rugby. Total rugby is an open game in which every player is encouraged to show what he can do as an attacker, defender and supporting player. Jim's book has become one of the game's most important coaching manuals. Even in his seventies the man is unquestionably one of the world's most highly regarded rugby coaches. Jim Greenwood is in the National Coaching Foundation's inaugural Hall of Fame, and has also been elected as an official Legend of Scottish Rugby.

He really was the premier strategist of the game.

The core components of sport

But Loughborough wasn't just Jim Greenwood.

One of my direct contemporaries was Seb (now Lord) Coe, the legendary middle-distance runner, Olympic champion and in his day world record-holder over 1500 metres. While I was at Loughborough I had a chance to see how he trained: the psychology, the nutrition, all the things that go to making a champion. His coach was George Gandy. And just as I had gone to Loughborough to meet Greenwood, Coe would have gone there to meet Gandy.

It was great to watch Coe do something incredible, like twelve consecutive 300-metre runs, walking in between with Gandy screaming at him. I can remember sitting there thinking, *Imagine if we had a rugby team that were as powerful and as fit as that? It would be a world beater, no mistake.*

Another of my contemporaries, John Trower who threw javelin, went on to coach Steve Backley to an Olympic bronze medal. I often sat next to John, who spent half his time in the gym, and I was just fascinated to learn from him and the other people around me in different areas of sport. My unspoken thought was always, *Why is rugby so far behind?* Why were we so ridiculously amateur?

Interestingly, many of the coaches that I eventually brought into the England coaching team hail from Loughborough themselves, and so I have more to be grateful for from this institution than just my own education.

Playing rugby, Loughborough-style

I played a lot of rugby at Loughborough, and made a lot of friends. Mike Poulson was one, and he played a big part in putting me on the coaching track years later at Henley. Not that life there was entirely trouble-free – I broke my leg twice in five months during 1976 and was out for a year. The first time was in the Middlesex Sevens and then the same leg, playing football a few months later.

So Loughborough was four years of great fun for the most part – the nearest I would ever get to professional rugby – but it's a strange fact that in all that time I never played for any club. I stayed totally within the university. Some people have questioned that decision, because today a nineteen-year-old would be fast-tracked straight into a club side. But I didn't really want to play club rugby at that stage. I preferred to play with my friends on Saturday and work as closely as possible with Jim.

The England selectors were even saying to me then, 'We cannot pick you for England until you play for a proper club side.'

Sure, I would have loved to play for England whilst at university. So I adopted a pressure-with-pressure attitude and stayed firm to my views. The interesting thing was that England were doing particularly badly at the time. My four-year period at Loughborough was one of the darkest times for the country in rugby terms. I don't think they won more than seven games in all the years I was at university, from 1975 to 1979.

I could have spent all week at Loughborough doing my studies, and then on Saturday played for Leicester, which is the team I eventually joined. But the fact was that for four years I never played any club rugby, and that's why I didn't play for England until I was twenty-three. Loughborough was fantastic for me and I still have many great friends from my years there. I do like to go back from time to time. In a very kind tribute, they have just awarded me an honorary doctorate. I don't know what that means exactly, but everyone seems to be impressed.

Open to the possibilities

So at Loughborough Jim Greenwood turned out to be everything I had hoped for and more. He opened my mind to the possibilities of the game, and he planted the idea that to win against the best sides in the world you have to have a whole armoury of ways of playing. He was the first person to suggest that there are 'no rules in rugby', just like, as I later learned, there are no rules in business. He was the first person who showed me that it was all right to question traditional thinking in others who do things in certain ways because that's the way they've always been done.

It was sad in a way to leave Loughborough, the rugby was so enjoyable. However it was time to move on. First and foremost, it was time to get a real job. Four years of living off summer jobs was wearing thin. After that, I'd think about club rugby and playing for the England side, that is if the England selectors were willing to overlook my rather principled stance.

6

INTERNATIONAL RUGBY

From the moment he went down, it didn't look right.

It was a hard tackle, but it was the way he landed that made everyone wince. His leg was turned out from his side, and he hadn't been able to pull his foot free when the weight of the Ireland forward pack came crashing down. I swear I heard the crack of his leg breaking from my seat high up in the stand at Twickenham. It was like a gunshot, followed by his scream.

There he lay on the ground, the England centre Tony Bond, his face distorted in agony.

It had been a great game up to that point. Just twenty-one minutes into the second half and England were up by 9 points. Like the rest of the spectators at Twickenham, I was really enjoying watching the first match of the 1980 Five Nations competition. Then I felt a nudge on my left side which I ignored, I had my eyes on the pitch where Tony was writhing in pain. It looked bad.

Sitting next to me, Ian Peck delivered a right thump this time. 'Clive!' he shouted. 'He's not getting up. That means you're on.'

I suddenly remembered I was on the England bench, the replacement centre, and this was my moment. In those days the reserves sat high up in the West stand and so I had to be escorted by a steward down the back steps to the tunnel area. I quickly ripped off my tracksuit and started warming up next to the touchline official. Sitting in the stands watching the game like all the other spectators, I had never expected to play. Now I was frantically trying to warm my body up for the impending physical effort, trying to prepare myself.

There was slow, encouraging applause from the crowd. It took me a second to realise it was for poor Tony Bond, who was being carried towards me on a stretcher. For one brief second our eyes met. His face was ghostly pale.

For the first time in my international career, I ran onto the Twickenham pitch – nervous, excited and scared all in one adrenalin-filled moment. The remaining nineteen minutes of the game passed in a flash. The ball didn't come my way very often, but given the England tactics that was not very surprising. The only time I handled it, I was penalised for not releasing in a tackle. But we won our first match of the Five Nations: England 24—Ireland 9.

On the road to a Grand Slam

It wasn't the beginning I would have chosen for my international career, being picked off the bench. But that was how I won my first cap for England. Obviously I would have preferred it to have been as an original selection, but that was to come in the second game in the Five Nations that year against France. This time I was first choice for centre, and I was better this game, more confident. Again we won: England 17—France 13, with two neat drop goals by fly-half John Horton. That was England's first ever win at Parc des Princes, and the first in Paris for sixteen years

The next International was against Wales at Twickenham. It was a brutal game. Welsh flanker Paul Ringer of Llanelli was sent off after only fourteen minutes. As usual, most of the play was with the forwards and with just a couple of minutes of injury time remaining England were down 6—8. With a last-minute penalty, we just came out on top of a poorly-played game all around: England 9—Wales 8. It was a huge upset, as the Welsh had dominated the Five Nations for the last five years, if not the whole of the seventies. But we kicked our penalties and they missed theirs. My Leicester colleague Dusty Hare, the England full-back, had a boot as unerring in its way as Jonny Wilkinson's.

That made it three wins in a row. Just one more match and England would have its first Grand Slam since 1957.

On 15 March 1980, England faced a determined Scotland side at Murrayfield. But this day there was no stopping us. We overpowered them up front with our magnificent pack – one of the most effective

England packs ever – and scored five tries in our 30—18 victory. At last I had space to weave, step and run at my best. With a couple of breaks I set up a try on both wings, one for Mike Slemen and the other for John Carleton, who scored a hat trick that day. It was 19—3 at half-time. We were all over the Scots and, best of all, we were moving the ball around in the backs in a distinctly un-English fashion. In those days half-times were taken on the pitch with a bag of oranges. Fran Cotton was the pack leader and summed up the match so far in the best English tradition: 'Hey, guys, whatever happened to keeping the play tight!' I am still not sure to this day whether he was joking. All of the England backs were on fire – everything just clicked. There was no reason for it. It just happened.

At the final whistle the stadium erupted. England had won their first Grand Slam in more than two decades. Fran Cotton, Bill Beaumont and some of the other senior players were in tears with elation and joy. After years of bitter defeat at the international level, they had finally realised their ultimate dream. It was the greatest moment in English rugby for nearly three decades. I danced and jumped, celebrating with the rest of them, but it wasn't nearly as momentous a victory for me. We'd played pretty well in four games, and we'd won four games. I couldn't quite see what the fuss was all about. Twelve months earlier I had been playing the best rugby of my life at Loughborough yet hadn't been selected because I wasn't playing senior club rugby. Then in my first four matches in international rugby we'd played average rugby for this level and everyone was celebrating around me like our victory was heaven sent. It was all very strange really.

The end, not the beginning

What I enjoyed most about that game wasn't just the winning; it was the way we won. The England coaches always insisted on a tight game, limited to the forwards. I think because we ended up winning so much ball, we had no choice but to pass and run it around. It was totally unplanned and had nothing to do with how we were supposed to play. We had talented players in that back division, Carleton, Dodge and Slemen particularly, and in the changing room afterwards I remember thinking that to me this could be the start of something really, really special.

Unfortunately for me, the majority of players in the room saw it as the end not the beginning. Many of them were just finishing their careers, which was sad because we were a terrific team. If we had all been in our early twenties we probably would have continued our brilliant run. However most of the key players like Bill Beaumont, Fran Cotton and Roger Uttley basically stopped playing within a few months of our historic Grand Slam, and that England team were unable to keep the momentum going.

In the changing room that day I remember sitting in a corner looking at the other players getting all emotional. In one way they were all heroes because they'd been playing such a long time – for example Fran had thirty caps to his name – but in all that time they'd never won a Grand Slam, then the pinnacle of England rugby, let alone a major series against the southern-hemisphere nations. I remember thinking, *So what's the big deal? We should have won.* We were clearly the best team and had played really well.

In my first year of international rugby, in my first four matches for my country, we had won the coveted Grand Slam. The rugby supporters were going nuts. If I had known that Scotland game would be my best ever match for England, perhaps I might have appreciated it more.

Not even ten minutes of fame

Eight months earlier I had started a job with Xerox, the copier and office equipment company. When I walked into head office on Monday morning after the Grand Slam victory the congratulations, pats on the back and spirited jibes lasted for about ten minutes. Then it was right back to business. That was one of the things I liked about working for Rank Xerox in the early 1980s. The culture was all business, results-orientated and very competitive.

In May 1979, as I was nearing the end of my time at Loughborough, I had been approached by several clubs who wanted me to join them for rugby, including my old London club, Harlequins. But I needed a career, and after a year of practical teaching at Loughborough I was certain that teaching wasn't for me. I spoke to a few clubs but made it clear that I didn't want to go into education. It was clear that I wouldn't be able to play rugby in a full-time, professional environment such as Loughborough, so my focus was shifting to my business career.

There were two criteria influencing my decision in regard to club rugby. One was my work. The other was the style of rugby I'd be playing, or more importantly, who would be dictating that style. Having lived under Jim Greenwood's wing for three years, I was determined to find the best coach regardless of location. I would have liked to be back in London with Quins pursuing the offers from the bank and finance sector that, true to their words, were still on the table. Unfortunately, Earle Kirton had retired from Quins and returned to New Zealand, so it opened up the possibilities elsewhere.

Leicester was just a few miles down the road from Loughborough. We'd played them often so I knew they were a quality side, and their coach, Chalkie White, had an excellent reputation. The club network went into action and they came back to me, having arranged an introduction to a gentleman named Alan King, the regional branch manager of Xerox. In the interview Alan told me about the opportunities the company offered in terms of remuneration, training and advancement into management. Not that I was handed the job on a plate. Alan was a great supporter of the Leicester club, but there was no room at Xerox for underperformers. After exhaustive testing, I was offered a position and accepted it. I was chosen on merit, not on rugby. It was a good job with a healthy salary, a company car and an expense account. I was moving up in the world!

The Xerox competitive culture

The environment at the Leicester office of Xerox was considerably more competitive than the rugby I was playing. Xerox had mastered the art of bringing competition into the workplace. Walking into the office, any Xerox office, the first thing you'd see was the league table: the sales rankings of every sales person in the country. Your name was there and the results were posted daily. You always knew how you were performing against everyone in the room. If you had any personal pride, or wanted to maintain any shred of self-esteem, you got your sales numbers. The environment surrounding international rugby was tame by comparison, which is partly why our Grand Slam victory was diminished in my mind. Unlike in rugby, the pressure to perform here was relentless.

The daily 8 a.m. meetings stick in my memory. If we weren't meeting our targets, you'd think the world had come to an end. It was brutal. But that's why Xerox was successful. Employee turnover might have been high, but in the early eighties Xerox was at its zenith. Copier and office equipment sales were going through the roof. There was never any shortage of people willing to enter the sales environment. However it was a no-excuses environment. If you didn't make the sales calls, if you didn't get the business, there was absolutely no sympathy. It was sink or swim.

I couldn't survive simply because I played for England.

On the other hand, the training at Xerox was second to none. I learned that sales is all about listening and it's a skill you have to develop if you're to succeed. Xerox was particularly fond of employing video analysis as a daily training tool and so used to video everything, which was not an easy or inexpensive task at the time. Video analysis was becoming commonplace in professional sport, but it was still in its infancy in business. In our daily meetings the managers would video the regular sales role-play exercises right in front of the entire team. Then they'd instantly play it back. Everyone was incredibly nervous in front of the camera the first time. The pressure of knowing the whole room would be watching it was immense. I'd been used to video analysis at Loughborough, but this was different. It was up close and personal, right in your face. Even the simple act of listening was more difficult under that pressure. But that was the point. When you watch yourself on video you always see what you're doing wrong and it needed no explanation. It was a good system that gave instant feedback. Thankfully, the sales calls in real life were nowhere near as intimidating.

Top club side – Leicester

By comparison, the club rugby I was playing at the time was a lot more straightforward, and that's despite the fact that in the early 1980s Leicester was the dominant side in the national knockout competition. The year I joined the club, we won our second John Player Cup. We won a third in 1981 and reached the final once more in 1983. There was no doubt that Leicester Tigers was the best team in England at the time. It was an incredibly successful period.

The common denominator was again our coach, Chalkie White. White had joined the Tigers as a scrum-half from Camborne, but six years later, in 1965, he began to do some coaching. In those days it was unusual for a club even to have a coach. In some amateur circles it was considered unsporting, the senior players being expected to work things out for themselves. Chalkie played a huge part in making Leicester one of the most competitive sides in the country. There's no doubt he had a big influence on the club's six internationals: Dusty Hare, Paul Dodge, Nick Youngs, Les Cusworth, Peter Wheeler and myself. Les was one of the most talented fly-halves ever to turn out for the Tigers. Dusty Hare was one of England's most capped full backs, and his confident and sound kicking should have earned him more caps than he received. Paul Dodge was one of the finest and most dependable centres ever to play for Leicester, and many people thought that the centre partnership which he and I formed in the 1980s was among the world's best at that time. Peter Wheeler was an outstanding performer and captain, who in 1983 led England to a 15—9 victory over the touring All Blacks. Youngs was just Youngsy, the only prop forward ever to play scrum-half for England. I was fortunate to play with each one of them.

And it was Chalkie White who brought out the best in us. Yet he was never one to blow his own trumpet.

'There's not a lot of original thought I can take credit for,' he once said. 'I crib and steal and plagiarise. But I tell the players that if they cheat on me on the training field, they'll cheat their team-mates in the game and in all other aspects of life.'

Like Greenwood and Kirton, Chalkie White also believed that your first bit of ball might be your best bit of ball, so you'd better make the most of it – it was the one common message coming from these three great coaches. He too encouraged us to be creative with the ball and to use everyone on the pitch effectively, an approach to rugby that would have been very hard for me to give up after Loughborough.

And where other coaches in the top clubs were known to scream and yell, Chalkie always treated us with respect. At training he was clearly conscious that we'd been at work all day and made every session fun and enjoyable. I'd sometimes drive three or four hours from tough sales meetings just to get to a session. Chalkie's style was to have the groundsman there with big hot mugs of tea for everyone on arrival. He really believed in the importance of the little things, something most coaches overlooked completely. We could talk to Chalkie . . . and he'd actually listen! He might not have agreed with our views, but no one was left out of the equation if they had something to say.

His secrets to success were so simple and so blindingly obvious.

In my first season with Leicester, I came straight into the first XV team, and shortly thereafter straight onto the England bench for the 1979 autumn International. To be honest, it certainly wasn't the big momentous step everyone had been telling me it would be. By the time of my first game in the Grand Slam, I was Leicester's top try-scorer, having crossed the goal line fourteen times in the season thus far. In the final match of the Grand Slam, where we beat Scotland 30—18, I was named Man of the Match. Shortly after that Leicester won their second knockout title. I had caught the attention of the Lions selectors and was chosen for the 1980 Lions tour of South Africa. All of this in my first full year in club rugby after Loughborough.

At Leicester under Chalkie the team improved every year over the next four years. I wish I could say the same of my international rugby career. I actually think I was playing better in the years I was at Loughborough than in all the years after. At Loughborough I was playing and training more like a professional player, whereas at Leicester I definitely took an amateur approach or possibly worse, because the demands of the job at Xerox, while catapulting me forward in my business career, were actually sending me backwards in my rugby career.

I remember the day my England rugby started its decline and eventual demise.

The beginning of the end

It was 17 January at Cardiff Arms Park against Wales, the first game of the 1981 Five Nations series.

With just a few minutes remaining on the clock we were up by one point: 19—18. If we could just hang on, it would be the first time England had beaten Wales in Cardiff for eighteen years. It had been another tough, brutal battle of strength in the forward pack, which meant that in the backs once again we hadn't seen anything of the ball all game. I was anxious actually to do something.

Wheeeeet! The ref's whistle.

The ball was grounded. A Welsh scrum feed thirty metres from our line.

I got myself into position in the midfield, waiting for the scrum to pack down. My concentration was total. I ran around telling everyone, 'NO PENALTIES! . . . NO PENALTIES! KEEP YOUR SELF-CONTROL!'

'Engage!' shouted the ref, as I prepared for action.

I watched the Welsh scrum-half, Brynmor Williams, with one eye and my Welsh opposite number with the other. Williams fed the ball in to the scrum and then moved around to the back of the scrum to wait for it to emerge, poised to race off for one final attempt at the try line.

Out of the corner of my eye, I saw him bend over for the ball. He lunged towards his backs to start the attack.

I raced off with the single focus of preventing their scoring.

As if looking for me, Williams rounded the referee with his two hands held out, begging the call. The ref instantly blew his whistle and raised his hand to indicate an offside offence.

I turned around in shock to see fourteen of my team-mates all standing behind the offside line, a couple of yards away. All behind, but me. All onside, but me.

'Shit!' I screamed in complete frustration and exasperation.

I'd fallen for the oldest trick in the book. Brynmor Williams was famous for dummying to scoop up the ball and moving away as if to attack, drawing the opposition offside. It is a ruse no longer allowed under the law these days.

Wales was awarded a penalty kick thirty metres out, right in front of the posts with just seconds remaining on the clock. In that one instant I had just ended England's repeat Grand Slam hopes. We painfully endured the certainty of Welsh captain Steve Fenwick's 3-point penalty kick for victory.

Play resumed as injury time dribbled off the referee's game watch. The intense gaze of the crowd is pressing at the best of times, but in the last few minutes of the game I could feel the Welsh supporters laughing at me and the English supporters cursing me all at the same time. It was excruciating.

We were awarded a penalty forty-five metres out in the dying seconds. Dusty Hare, who had kicked us to a last-minute victory against Wales a year ago, lined up for another miracle kick. From the look on everyone's faces, you could tell it wouldn't come. We knew we'd been beaten. We were right.

At the close of play the crowds charged on around me to congratulate their home team. With one small lapse of attention I had just cost us the first game of the season.

This game is so frustrating! How could we have let a match hinge so critically on one stupid mistake? It was ludicrous. We could be so much better than this Welsh team. We should have been miles ahead with the calibre of our players, but we hadn't played as a team for nearly a year. We were so unprepared for this match. Two days of training before an international match was simply not enough.

There is no question I stuffed things up. More than that, though, I was beginning to feel that the environment of England rugby was wrong. It didn't challenge us as players. It didn't give us the preparation we needed. It didn't give us every chance. The selection system was inconsistent. The coaches insisted on a style of play from the stone age, focusing almost exclusively on forward play and leaving us backs to nearly die of boredom. We prepared for games at a level of intensity that suggested we weren't really doing everything possible, everything that needed to be done, to win.

The rugby dinner that night was painful. I just didn't want to be there.

Back to my day job

By Monday, however bad I still felt, it was time to move on. I had no choice. There was an important deal on the table and my position in the Xerox league tables was at stake. Besides, the England team wouldn't play again for another five weeks, so the rugby side could wait.

It was a difficult but necessary mindset. I was a sales manager by now, and I had put together a huge deal with Rolls-Royce, one of our best accounts. For the big deals, I liked to go with my team to the sales meetings to give them my full support. That Monday we had agreed to meet at the Little Chef just outside Derby at 8 a.m. in preparation for our appointment at the nearby Rolls-Royce engine plant. We made our way to the administration building a few minutes before 9 a.m. As we waited for the purchasing officer, the security guard who signed us in made casual conversation.

'Hey, did you see the England rugby match on the weekend?' he asked, clearly without a clue that I'd played in that game.

'As a matter of fact, I did,' Tim Buttimore, the more senior of my team, said with a sly smile. 'Great game if you are Welsh, huh?'

'Humph! What a prat that Woodward is. Any fool could have seen that dummy coming,' laughed the guard.

'Yeah, I know,' Tim quickly fired back. 'What a pillock! Can you imagine what he must feel like going to work today?'

'Yeah, what a twit. Wouldn't like to be in his shoes!'

I shook my head, laughing quietly to myself. It was pretty funny really.

The purchasing officer came through the reception door and invited us into the building. On the way past the guard, my colleague couldn't resist.

'Oh, by the way, you may not recognise this bloke. He's Clive Woodward. He's the pillock who lost us the game against Wales.'

As we disappeared through the door, the look on the poor man's face was priceless.

We had a good laugh about it with the purchasing officer, talking about rugby for another five minutes or so, and then it was right back to business.

The juxtaposition of work and rugby became quite clear in that weekend in January. My international rugby career had begun with a bang and then gradually declined over the ensuing years, whereas my work, and club rugby, went from strength to strength in the same period. We didn't win much on the international front in those lean years for England rugby, but we won at Leicester, and I was winning at work.

Woodward the maverick

At times in my international career I could be effective, but then in the very next game I would be disastrously vacant and haphazard. I so much wanted to play a more exciting game of rugby that I was desperate for the ball in order to make something happen. The other players knew me as a maverick, someone who could win a game or just as easily lose it, depending on whether or not my ploy was successful. I'm sure if you ask players like Bill Beaumont, they'd tell you that one moment they'd want to hug me and then the next minute to kick my backside. They could never be too certain what I was going to do. They weren't the only ones. Most times even I did not know what I was going to do. The good thing was, if my team-mates didn't know, then the opposition couldn't know either.

I took risks, calculated as they may have been. Sometimes they'd pay off, other times they wouldn't. At Loughborough or Leicester, that was fine. The coaches encouraged it because in that environment it won games. But in the England set-up it went entirely against the grain. Everyone's play was so safe and conservative, so predictable and boring. It was frustrating. It was like you had to change your competitive mindset when you came from your club to play for your country.

I was thought of as a maverick player, an entertainer at best. But I didn't want to dazzle. I wanted to win! Unfortunately, the England coaches, all of whom worked as volunteers on a part-time basis, couldn't provide a competitive enough environment to keep me interested. If we had played and won every game with passion, things would have been different. But it was impossible. At every training session, the coaches would sit us down and show us what the New Zealand or South African teams were doing, as if they set the standard. But by doing that, the real message they were drilling into our psyches was that we were inferior. No wonder England rarely played the southern-hemisphere teams and won. The myth of their superiority was firmly entrenched in the hearts and minds of the 'chosen ones' in the England coaching hierarchy, and they seemed only too keen to pass that myth over to the players. Then they would wonder why we continued to lose.

England rugby in the eighties

The England set-up was more about maintaining the status quo than anything else. Many of the players fell right into the routine, playing safe no-risk rugby so that they could keep their spots in the selectors' minds.

England invented the game of rugby union in the early 1830s, then exported it to the Commonwealth nations fifty years later, and here those same countries were now showing us how the game was played a century later. It just didn't make sense.

There can be no question that England's Rugby Football Union was successful in promoting and growing the game – by the mid 1980s there were over 2000 rugby clubs dotted around England alone. But by the same token, the governing body of rugby was an association of representative members and, as such, was run by committee and popular vote. By its very nature such an organisation had to be slow-moving, conservative and careful in order to survive and prosper as it had. Unfortunately, the culture required to perpetuate the survival of the amateur game was in direct conflict with the culture required to win games at an international level.

If only the cultural environment I had experienced at Xerox had been present in the set-up of the England squad, everything could have been completely different. But there was no motivation to change anything. Tickets for the international matches at Twickenham were sold out at every game, seemingly regardless of whether England won or lost. The organisation was well funded, the RFU being the only sporting body to own its home stadium outright.

There was no need to change. This was a different era for rugby union. There were no world cup to be won or global rankings.

Early retirement, sort of

I played my last game for England in the autumn of 1984. I hardly touched the ball. The rift between me and the coaches, and the style of play, was at an all time low. They didn't select me for the Five Nations later in the new year. I never formally retired, as such, but my international career was obviously over. I played out my season at Leicester, but by the summer I knew I needed a change of scenery. I had been working my butt off in the high-pressure environment at Xerox for six years, training two nights a week for weekend games with Leicester, appearing in twenty-one Test matches for England, and had toured twice with the Lions.

More and more I found myself dreaming of better times in rugby, like at Loughborough where we were fitter, faster and played an expansive game, where everything was geared around sport, where we were closer to professional standards than ever we were when I was playing for England.

ANTIPODEAN ADVENTURE

7

Brrrrrrring!

What the hell was that? Something was dragging me back to consciousness. The damn phone. I glanced at my bedside clock. 3.30 a.m. Who would be ringing at this time of night?

Brrrrrring!

I scrambled for the receiver, 'Yeah, hi . . .'

'Clive, it's Alan King here.' The voice sounded a thousand miles away. 'I'm calling from Sydney.' Twelve thousand miles away to be precise.

Alan had been my boss at Xerox's Leicester office for three years before he was promoted to the London office, but now yet another step up the ladder had taken him all the way to Sydney.

'Marvellous, Kingy. Fantastic, but what the hell are you doing calling me in the middle of the night?'

Never one to waste time on small talk, Alan came straight to the point.

'How would you like to spend some time with Xerox in sunny Australia? I've got this position that would suit you perfectly. Sales manager in Sydney.'

I'd never been to Australia. Believe it or not, in my four years as an international England had never toured there, but the Aussies had always intrigued me with their well-known passion for sport.

'Alan, it's the middle of the night. I'm half asleep. You asked so I'll tell you. I say "goodnight" and let's talk about it in the morning!'

But Alan King wouldn't take no for an answer. He persisted, I relented. By the end of the conversation I had agreed to fly down to Australia to see what he had to offer.

I was doing very well at Xerox, so the next day I got my boss's full support to take a week off for the trip. He too had been employed by Alan, and was interested to hear what Xerox was like in another continent. I'd always wanted to work overseas, and maybe get in some rugby too. The more I thought about the opportunity, the more excited I became.

Rugby, Aussie-style

The first thing Alan King did after picking me up at the airport after a gruelling twenty-four-hour flight was to drive me to meet the presidents and coaches of the two rugby clubs nearest to where he lived. First stop was the Warringah club where a young coach called Rod Macqueen was shortly to make his mark.

I have always had a tremendous respect for Rod. He is a bit older than me and came into rugby coaching some ten years before I did, but there are clear similarities in our careers as businessmen who have moved into rugby coaching. Running our own companies has exposed us to all the ups and down of business, especially the art of managing people, which is fundamental to building any high-performance team. Very few coaches in any national sport would have had that background and training. It's no coincidence that the last two World Cup-winning coaches have both had very strong business backgrounds.

After Warringah, Alan drove me nine kilometres further south to the north-eastern edge of the magnificent Sydney Harbour where the Manly club has its home grounds. The president and coach at Manly couldn't have been more welcoming, but what truly captured my imagination was the wonderful outlook of Manly beach. It was just superb. After a quick tour of the club facilities, we were invited to lunch at a nearby beachside café. My hosts insisted I take the seat facing the ocean, and I just sat there in awe. The real-life panorama was right out of the tourist brochures, only better. Having spent the last ten years in the cold blustery Midlands, Manly was truly magnificent in comparison. It was the middle of winter, the sun was shining, the beach was crowded and almost everyone had a golden tan that made my English complexion look positively pale and sickly.

Chatting about rugby, my hosts made all the right noises about a running game, and they were speaking my language. Clearly they had been well briefed by Kingy. The club had a strong support base, and a local businessman had already offered to sort out an apartment in Manly if I chose to play for them. They could not have been more helpful.

'Well, Clive, do you have any questions?'

'Yes, actually I do. Is the weather always like this?'

I think at that moment Alan King knew he had me.

The absolute worst aspect of being a sports person in England was having to get up in the dark, damp, early hours of the morning to maintain your fitness. To be honest I was staying in bed more often than not these days, which was partly why my rugby was now really suffering. This climate would be any sports person's dream.

The next few days with Alan were great. We talked about business, rugby, and the good old days in Leicester. He had a home nearby with scenic views and, with my body clock still on England time, I spent many early morning hours on his veranda soaking up the sights and sounds. At the end of my all too brief trip I left Alan at the airport terminal. I assured him I would be back.

Thinking on the plane

On the long trip home I couldn't stop thinking about my first taste of the Aussie lifestyle. Not just the climate and surroundings, but the whole strange mix. On the one hand Sydney was a vibrant city of three million people, rich in cultural diversity. On the other hand, the business market wasn't as highly evolved as in Europe.

Alan was having real trouble motivating his team to produce anything more than lacklustre results, and that didn't seem to be just a Xerox problem. For example in my particular area of expertise, financing office equipment, the market was only a fraction of its potential. The job sounded exactly like the sort of thing for me. Besides, I had been in the Leicester office of Xerox for just over six years. I was in a holding pattern. It was the right time for a change. I just don't know why it had taken me so long to figure it out.

On the rugby side, I was very eager to see how the Manly set-up worked. Alan Jones had only recently left the club to take the position as Wallabies coach. In his first and only year at Manly he won the championship, and then was selected for the top job of the Australian side. In his first tour he came to Europe and convincingly beat every northern-hemisphere team.

Like everyone, I had been impressed by the 1984 Wallabies – the Ella brothers, Campese and the rest – under Alan Jones. England's match against Australia was my last selection in the international squad. Australia had played a very dynamic game – right out of Jim Greenwood's Total Rugby text book – and had cut our line to pieces, leaving our more powerful forward pack scrambling. On one hand I was infuriated at being beaten by a style I'd been pressing the England coaches to consider for ages, on the other hand I was intrigued to see it implemented so effectively at an international level.

If that was the legacy which Alan Jones, another coach years ahead of his time, had left at Manly rugby club, then maybe there was something there still for me to discover.

Southward bound

It didn't take long to convince Jayne that we needed to go to Australia. We'd been together for quite a while by then. We had nothing to lose and everything to gain. Although she is close to her family, Jayne agreed to the adventure as long as it wasn't forever. Jayne's dog Muffin was the only real concern. Just before we left we dropped by Jayne's parents' house and asked her parents, Barry and Sylvia, to look after Muffin . . . just for the weekend! They agreed. We came back from Australia five years later. I guess it was quite a long weekend!

My Leicester colleagues were a little bit harder to convince than Jayne.

'Clive! Where have you been? We missed you at training last week,' said Graham Willars, our new coach. He had guided us to our third John Player Cup the previous season. I'd called to say that I wouldn't be around, but I didn't mention why.

'Australia, Graham! I've decided to move there to work and play for Manly!'

'What??? You can't do that! You play for Leicester!' The look of shock on Graham's face was almost amazing. Players in the first XV never left Leicester, at least not at twenty-nine when the team was so successful. Players generally stayed at their clubs for the rest of their lives.

'It's a great place and it's got nice weather, why not go?'

He looked like he wanted to throttle me.

I loved the banter with Graham. He always took the bait. It must have been frustrating for coaches back in the amateur days. He knew he couldn't do anything if I really wanted to go. Unlike at clubs these days, we weren't paid to play. I had no contract, therefore I had no ties to the club, except of course for the memory of the great times I'd had. I really liked Graham and didn't want to let him down, but I think he knew I was ready for a change.

'But what if you don't like it?'

'Well I'll just get back on the plane and see you when I get home.'

'But what about the team?' he tried again, but he was running out of steam.

'The team will get along just fine, and you know it.'

Graham just nodded his head. There was nothing he could say to that one. Sadly Graham died several years ago at a young age. At his funeral they read Graham's favourite poem and later his wife Hilary gave me a copy of the poem and said Graham would have liked me to have it. It says a lot about Graham and his thinking.

The Indispensable Man

Some day when you're feeling important,
Some day when your ego's in bloom,
Some day when you may be feeling,
You're the most important man in the room.

Some day when you feel that your going,
Would leave an unfillable hole,
Just follow this simple example,
And see how it humbles your soul.

Take a bucket and fill it with water,
Put both hands in up to the wrist,
Take them out and the hole that remains,
Is the measure of how you'll be missed.

You may splash all you like when you enter,
You may stir up the water galore,
But wait! In a minute,
It looks just the same as before.

The moral of this is quite simple:
Do just the best that you can,
Be proud of yourself, but remember,
There is no indispensable man.

Author unknown

I keep it in my wallet now, the last three lines never far from my mind.

My team-mates were no less incredulous about my new venture. I'd been with Leicester five years, and we'd fielded some great teams in that time. However they too could see that this trip was a once-in-a-lifetime opportunity. In the true spirit of the team, many team-mates and old friends called in before we left to say goodbye. To a man they all, and especially Graham, wished me well.

Turn off the waves

The first month in Australia was fantastic – Xerox had put us in the Manly Pacific Hotel for four weeks whilst we recovered from jetlag and found our feet in a new country. It became clear to both of us that Sydney was a magical place.

During that time Manly rugby club had shown us the apartment, known as a unit in Australia, that we were going to move into after our initial period at the Manly Pacific. The setting was fantastic. The unit was right on the ocean with magnificent views east over the Pacific. We were so close to the water our balcony often got wet from the ocean spray when the sea was rough.

It was an amazing piece of real estate that was highly sought after by tenants. The rugby club had kindly taken out a twelve-month lease for us through a local Manly estate agent, Bernie Berglin, who happened to be a former captain of the rugby club. We spent the next month furnishing the unit, while we were staying at the lovely Manly Pacific Hotel. But when we finally moved into the unit, one month after our arrival, we experienced our first major problem in Australia.

The unit was great, but unexpectedly there was simply too much noise from the waves crashing on the rocks right outside our bedroom window. Neither Jayne nor I could get any sleep. After four sleepless nights we were a mess. I called Bernie and asked if I could come to see him.

'Hi, Clive,' he bounded out of his chair, hand extended, as soon as I walked in his office. 'How's the unit working out?'

As two rugby nuts, Bernie and I had got on well from day one. I felt I could talk to him openly.

'It's OK, Bernie, but about the unit . . . that's why I've come to talk to you'. I shut the door as I walked into his office. He had a concerned look on his face.

'Look, Bernie, I appreciate all you've done for us, but we have to move, we have to get out of there. We just can't get any sleep because of the noise and it's driving us crazy.'

'In heaven's name, why? If it's the neighbours we can sort that out for you?'

'Well, no, uh, not exactly . . . It's the waves,' I blurted out.

I hated to say something, but I felt sure he'd fully understand.

Silence, followed by a tilt of the head and a furrowed brow.

'Say that again?'

'The waves, Bernie. We can't sleep because of the noise of the waves! They're just so loud on the rocks, right below our balcony, and they go on all night long. They never stop. We can't get any sleep.'

Silence. Pursed lips. He'd heard right.

'Hang on just a minute, Clive, I've got to write this down,' he said as he grabbed a pen and a paper from the corner of his desk.

'So let me get this straight' W.A.V.E.S. he wrote on the pad in front of him. 'You're staying in a unit right on the beach with one of the best views of the ocean in the world, and you're telling me that you want to move because the waves are keeping you awake? Is that right?'

'Ahh, well . . . yes. I guess that's right.' I was now a little less convinced this was a good idea.

The colour was rising in Bernie's face.

'Let me tell you something. I've spent all my life searching for houses where people want to know they have half the views you've got, where people can hear the soothing noise of the waves from their balconies, let alone their bedrooms, and you've come in here to tell me you *don't* want it?'

'Well, we're just not used to it.'

'I guess there aren't many waves in Leicester now, are there?' he shot back at me. 'Look, mate. You can move out if you want. Hell, I've got a dozen people who'd take that unit right now. But do me a favour, would you, before I move you out. Just give it a few more days. Just a few more days and see how you get along?'

I was starting to see his point! Maybe we were being a bit rash. I thanked him and retreated to the unit, already seeing it in a new light.

'How did you go?' enquired Jayne, as desperate for sleep as I was.

'Well, Bernie was a bit worked up about it,' I began like the hunter returning empty-handed. 'He thinks we should give it a few more days.'

For some strange reason, that night we slept like babies.

I'm just glad Bernie brought us to our senses. It was a fabulous place to live and a great introduction to the Aussie lifestyle.

Xerox – culture clash

My first day at work was another marvel. I walked three blocks east to the harbour side of the Manly peninsula, hopped on the hydrofoil ferry service right to Circular Quay in downtown Sydney, and walked another two blocks to the Xerox building. The whole trip took me around thirty-five minutes. It was the most spectacular way to commute to work I'd ever seen.

If only my work had gone as well as the journey. Turning up that first day in a tailored blue suit, pressed shirt and fine silk tie might have been the professional thing to do in England, but in the Sydney office of Xerox I stood out like a sore thumb. The standards were different – simply wearing a tie was considered a bit dressy. It certainly wasn't my intention to come in all high and mighty, but I'm afraid that's what happened. Alan had warned that it would be a bit different to what I was used to, that I shouldn't anticipate the same aggressive working environment. Still, I was ill-prepared.

I was used to offices having different styles. In England, the London office was different to the Leicester office, for example, in terms of the approach that was successful in getting the deals. The London blokes were a bit more proper and a bit slower, but they usually won the big contracts on offer in the City and so made up their numbers on the league tables. However in the Midlands, we'd sometimes have to drive for hours just to get the deals. We worked hard to get the smaller accounts, but we got more of them so we could compete on the tables. That was what it took to win in our neck of the woods.

When Alan had told me not to anticipate the same working environment, I just thought he meant a difference in terms of how people competed, just as it was between England offices. The league tables were present, but people simply weren't as interested in topping them. Quite the opposite, they seemed to have a disdain for those at the top of the list. As a consequence, my perceived superior attitude and hard competitive line went over like a lead balloon. The end of the first week saw my first direct confrontation with this strange new culture.

'G'day, Clive,' said Rob, standing in the doorway of my office on Friday afternoon. 'Just heading off now. See you on Tuesday.'

'Right, Rob. See you then.' As he turned I glanced at my watch. It was only 5.27 p.m. He was knocking off early in my books. *Wait, hang on. Did he just say Tuesday?*

'Hey, Rob. Wait a minute,' I said, walking out into the main office floor to catch up with him. 'Did you just say you wouldn't be in 'til Tuesday?' They seemed to have a lot of public holidays, but I couldn't think of anything that would make this a long weekend.

'Uh, yeah, that's right. It's my birthday Monday. So I'll see you Tuesday.'

'Yeah, right. Good one,' I replied, having a good laugh. I honestly thought he was joking.

'No,' he came back, quite seriously. 'Monday's my birthday. I don't work on my birthday. Never have. I'll be in on Tuesday.' Rob was forty-five years old, quite an experienced sales person in the team.

I don't believe it. He can't be serious? That's when things went completely off the rails.

'Bollocks!' I said rather forcefully, in front of the whole office. 'You can't take a day off because it's your birthday. What kind of attitude is that? I expect you in on Monday.' I finished with a veiled threat. I cringe now at how confrontational I was.

'You can *expect* all you like. I'll see you on Tuesday. Have a nice weekend,' Rob replied, quite composed. He then turned and walked out the door, leaving me to look pretty stupid in my fancy suit to all those who were still in the office at 5.30 p.m. on a Friday afternoon which, to be fair, was not many.

Of course he didn't come in on Monday. So I went in search of the personnel officer.

'Don't worry about it, Clive. That's just how we do things here,' it was explained to me. Well, that wasn't good enough for me. It just wasn't right. On Tuesday Rob came into the office like he said, happy as you can be, as if nothing was out of the ordinary.

'Right,' I said as I got to the first order of business in our bi-weekly meeting. That's another thing. In England we had far more sales meetings than ever in Australia. Eight a.m. every morning to plan the day, do the training and then get on with it. Broaching that subject in Australia, the look on people's faces was like someone died.

'Come off it, mate. We won't do that.' I couldn't believe my ears. I had to settle for two meetings a week, Tuesday and Thursday, at 9 a.m. This meeting hadn't started till 9.10 a.m. because everyone was strag-gling in.

'Right, there's to be a new policy,' I said looking at my watch. 'Morning meetings are to start at 9 a.m., not ten past. Not five past. At 9 a.m. I expect you to be in your seats ready to go at five minutes to. And that's another thing, No more holidays on your birthdays.'

The way I was carrying on they were probably surprised I didn't cancel Christmas, too!

'We're here to work and make the sales. How can we do that if we're not professional about it? Don't the League Tables mean anything to you? You lot are near the bottom of the list. How can you stand it?'

'Excuse me, Clive?' Rob stepped in tentatively with his hand raised. 'Does that mean if our birthday lands on a public holiday that we have to come into the office to work?'

The meeting room erupted in cynical laughter . . . at me. What can I say? I deserved it. That was the Aussie culture of the Sydney office and I didn't fit in. I could see why Alan had problems. Unfortunately, my position with the team didn't really improve from there. I learnt a hard lesson. It is important to really study the culture of a country, company, or even a sports team, before barging in. I had wrongly assumed the Xerox Leicester culture was world wide. Clearly it was not. Unfortunately, once I had created my position I couldn't see a way to change it.

Club rugby, Manly-style

By contrast, my experience with the Manly rugby club was completely the opposite. I couldn't have been made more welcome. Here was a competitive side who in the last few years had tasted real success with Alan Jones. They were willing to do whatever it took to win, and they seemed to be delighted to be gaining a player who actually said he didn't want to kick the ball away all the time.

Comparing Manly to where I'd come from at Leicester, the two clubs were quite similar. There was not that much difference in the way we trained, the tactics we employed on the pitch, or the way we won games. I soon learned that among the Australian club sides, only Randwick under Bob Dwyer was truly playing the kind of Total Rugby that had amazed the world when the Grand Slam Wallabies hit the northern hemisphere. But he had the Ella brothers and Campese on his books so his skill levels were stratospheric. As regards the other clubs, perhaps the only real difference in terms of their approach to the game was that they did try to play a good running game in the backs.

The Australian Rugby Union made a concerted effort in the seventies to promote a more expansive game in the junior development sides. It was an insightful attempt to sow the seeds of victory against the overwhelming New Zealand sides of that decade. By the time I played in Sydney, the entire competition had changed its face for the better. That crop of gifted and dynamic players, including my good friend Michael Hawker, were entering their peak years at the international level, reflected in the fact that they had so recently beaten all the Five Nations teams on their home grounds. To say the Sydney competition was fierce would be an understatement.

The rugby season in Australia starts in April and finishes in early October, which is almost the complete opposite to the timing of the season in England. So by arriving in mid-September, I was really coming in too late to play much of the season in 1985. But I did begin making my introductions around the rugby club. It was such a refreshing new beginning for me. Coming to a brand new country to meet a whole new team of players, new grounds and a new competition was exactly what I needed.

It was a magic time for me in that last few months of 1985. Sometimes I had to pinch myself and wonder at my good fortune. Just one simple phone call was all it took. It's amazing how your life can hinge on seemingly inconsequential actions. With hindsight I knew I should have done it before. My first few years in Leicester were very rewarding, with a rapidly advancing career and three outstanding years of rugby. But my stay outlasted its usefulness and I had become stuck in a rut. The dangling carrot for me, the strong force that kept me rooted, of course, was the lure of playing for England. Contemplative sunny mornings on Manly beach were a world away from my previous life in more ways than one.

Tea on the rocks

In my first week in the country I experienced perhaps the most outstanding benefit of the Aussie lifestyle – early morning training right on the beach in front of my unit! Most of the guys at the Manly rugby club lived in the suburb, and because of the shape of the peninsula forming the headlands of Sydney Harbour, it was an easy walk to the beach for practically everyone. My morning routines were wonderful. Up at 6 a.m. to meet the boys outside Manly surf club. A forty-five-minute run to North Head and back. A refreshing swim and body surf for ten minutes or so. Then back home by 7 a.m. to get ready to go to work. And all of this in warm sunny weather on long white sandy beaches with the kind of large rolling surf that you dream about. It was perfect. Over the next few years I kept up this wonderful routine religiously. I think I was the fittest I've ever been while living on Manly beach, fitter even than in my days at Loughborough.

Jayne and I would quite often walk the ten yards right back out to the beach after my training to enjoy our morning cup of tea on the rocks in that sensational setting. Being a small place, before too long we began to see and chat with friends passing by. I think they really got a laugh out of seeing us there with our cups of tea. One thing led to another and we began to bring our tea pot and a few extra tea cups for friends. Soon it became a habit, and no matter what the season you could find us out on the rocks every morning – and sometimes in the evening as well.

At the rugby club they picked up on my tea-drinking inclinations very quickly, too. I loved my tea. I'd become accustomed to it at Leicester, a big cup of tea when we arrived at the club and another round for the boys when we came off the pitch. The problem at Manly was the routine provided for ice-cold beer instead of tea. You'd come into the changing rooms and there in the middle of the floor would be this huge dustbin full of ice-cold drinks. Thinking they might be onto something I tried it, but my whole stomach cramped up in an unaccustomed violent reaction.

'Bob, I can't do this. It's just wrong,' I said to Bob Lane our coach.
'What?'
'I can't drink this cold stuff. I need tea.'
'You need tea?' he asked with eyes wide, eyebrows raised.
'Yes. I need a nice hot cup of tea after playing. It's much more refreshing.'
Well, the whole side broke into hysterics after that one.
But I wasn't going to be pushed around by this lot, so I left it at

that. However the very next session, one of the trainers waltzed up to me with his best English butler impersonation, carrying a silver tray and fancy china tea pot full of steaming hot tea.

'Your afternoon tea, sir!' he loudly announced in his best proper English accent.

Australian selection

One of the strangest situations during my stay in Australia was being selected for the Wallabies squad. Rather I should say 'being invited' to train with the Wallabies because that's as far as it went.

'Clive, hi, it's Alan Jones here,' came the voice when I picked up the phone in late February 1986.

I'd first met Alan Jones the week before at a Sydney Sevens tournament. I loved the seven-a-side game. We used to play it at Loughborough as a developmental tool to help the forwards learn how to run and pass. I went on to play with the Barbarians in the Hong Kong Sevens tournament in 1981 where, in the more open play the game affords, for the first time a British team had gone head to head with Australians, Fijians and New Zealanders and won.

Winning that year in a tight final against Australia, the first time ever for a northern hemisphere team, had been one of the highlights of my playing career. So it wasn't surprising that I was drawn to the sevens tournament in Sydney. All the top Wallaby players were on show, so it was a good chance to have a look at people's form. Between games Alan came over to say hello.

'So what are you doing in our fair country?' News must have travelled fast that I was playing for his old club, Manly.

'Oh, you know. I just thought I'd come down and show you blokes what a little real rugby is like. You know, teach you how to kick and coach rolling mauls!'

I couldn't resist the dig. It was rich, considering one year before he had brought the Wallabies to England and given us a real rugby lesson.

'It's always good to learn something new. Do you want to come and play for Australia then?' he returned, tongue in cheek.

It was an unbelievable honour to be selected to tour with the British and Irish Lions in my first full season of international rugby, 1980.

Playing against Scotland in my first international season – a Grand Slam depended on the outcome. This was to be one of my best performances in an England shirt. I wish I'd known at the time.

Offside against Wales, giving away 3 points – I still shudder at the thought. Bill Beaumont came hurrying over to give me a right bollocking.

Winning the Hong Kong 7s with the Barbarians in 1981 was one of the highlights of my playing career. Rugby 7s is the most fantastic game to play.

Playing for Leicester, 26 January 1980, with Steve Kenney and Paul Dodge. This was early days in my centre partnership with Paul. He was a great player and I think we complemented one another in our styles of play.

Six players from Leicester were selected for the England v. New Zealand game at Twickenham, 19 November 1983 – (*from left*) Dusty Hare, Nick Youngs, Peter Wheeler, Les Cusworth (on tiptoes), Paul Dodge and me. Leicester has always had a great tradition of supplying England with international players – I hope it continues.

Training at Loughborough, under Jim Greenwood's tutelage, the only time in my playing career I trained 'professionally'.

Captain of the school first XV. We had a great time as a team and there was only one more year of school to go.

That's me, aged thirteen at HMS *Conway* naval college, not looking too happy in my uniform. In the second row is high profile *Conway* old boy, the former Tory leader Iain Duncan Smith, two years my senior.

My debut game for Harlequins, October 1974, at Twickenham.

Above: Ready for my first day at Corstorphine School, Edinburgh – another player the Scots missed out on. I've a similar sort of haircut today.

Right: My sister Linda took this photo of Dad and me, aged ten, during a family holiday in Whitby.

Below: HMS *Conway*, looking more like Alcatraz. My first bed was on the third floor – third window from the right of the long block.

One of the best rugby times I've ever had, with great guys, was on the 1980 Lions tour. We managed to spend some time away from rugby, too.

My first day ever in Australia, September 1985. I stayed at the Manly Pacific Hotel – eighteen years later I was back in the same hotel with the England team to win a World Cup.

Steve Holdstock (*middle*), Wallaby Phillip Cox and I celebrate a good win in the Manly changing room after a game.

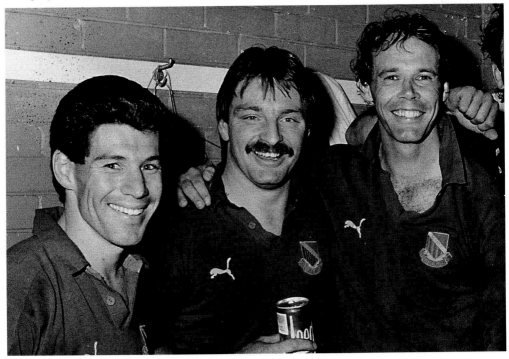

Jayne and me on Manly beach, 22 November 1985.

Our wedding day – Manly in the background and Jess as the chief bridesmaid.

We both had a good laugh. 'Wouldn't that turn some heads!'

'Well, why not?' he said suddenly with a very serious tone.

'Alan, I couldn't do that.' I also couldn't decide whether he was joking or not.

'Sure you can. What's stopping you?' Now he was getting serious.

'Well, for a start, I'm not Australian. The IRB wouldn't even let me near the pitch.'

'I haven't seen that in any rule book. Why don't you come down for a few training sessions? It'd be fun!'

Alan is a man I really admire, especially his ability to think laterally and challenge conventional thinking. He had played hardly any rugby. Alan had a background in business and politics. I found it fascinating. His success on the pitch wasn't as much about rugby skills as it was about harnessing the best resources available to get the job done. His approach was in such stark contrast to the three rugby purist coaches – Greenwood, White and Kirton – who had influenced my rugby to date. If Alan's goal was to create a winning rugby team, he didn't care how he did it. His job was to bring the right resources to bear. That was the beginning of a new era for Australian rugby.

It took Alan a full minute to convince me he was serious. He was just crazy enough to invite me down to the Wallabies training session. I was just crazy enough to agree.

A couple of weeks later I found myself walking onto the pitch.

You should have seen the looks on the faces of the Australian players.

Alan may have got a tickle out of it, but I certainly didn't. Most of the players knew me, and those that didn't quickly learned. It was like I was an enemy in the camp, which is not too far from the truth really. I just got my kit on and started mucking around with the players I knew until Alan got things started. Thankfully he acknowledged my presence by openly restating his invitation. It didn't help matters much. It felt uncomfortable and wrong. It was the most awkward training session ever.

Afterwards I couldn't get out of the place quick enough. It was interesting to see how things were managed, but honestly it was just too strange for words.

Smashing rugby

Unfortunately, my introduction to the Sydney competition wasn't as glamorous and pleasant as my welcome to the neighbourhood. Just a few weeks after my uncomfortable session with the Wallabies, in only my second game for Manly, I suffered a nasty injury.

We were playing against Warringah. I was right into it and enjoying the match when I made a standard tackle in normal play. Being at the bottom of the ruck is often a dangerous place with rugby boots flying. I'd never had a problem before, but this one time against Warringah ... WHAM! Right in the side of the face. It was like my whole head exploded. A Warringah player had really sunk the boot in with gusto. I was completely rattled and seeing stars, so I don't remember much, but you know you're in trouble when the game is stopped and everyone stares at you with horror. I must have looked a mess. The whole right side of my face was completely misshapen. At the hospital later the doctors told me my jaw was broken and my cheekbone was fully depressed.

Luckily I returned in plenty of time to play out the second half of the rugby season. We had a good team and finished strongly, with great prospects for a strong side the following year. I will admit, the competition was better overall than what I remembered in England, but primarily because nearly every team was playing a more expansive game more effectively than most of the England teams I'd played against.

However, I also recall being a little disappointed with the level of play and the strength of the coaching and management side of things. Perhaps I was expecting too much in hoping to find a Greenwood-like command of the core components of the game. At the time, I could sum it up by saying there was greater competitive spirit, and the style of play was more dynamic, in line with the current thinking of the time. But in spite of everything, Australian rugby had not turned out to be the monumental step up that I had anticipated.

The end of the rugby season did herald one life-changing event, at least. In addition to a few sleepless nights, the gently undulating waves had a different positive side effect. Jayne and I had our first child, Jess, at the Manly Cottage hospital on 5 November.

Shifting focus

I don't quite know if I could identify one specific thing that led to a shift in my focus in that first year in Australia. It could have been a result of the somewhat unenthusiastic sales culture at the office, or the warm weather and fantastic morning exercise routine, or simply the life-changing knowledge of our impending family. Whatever the cause, something in my approach to life had changed – not overnight but gradually, like the incoming tide. For the first time in many years, the office was no longer that important to me. I found myself working regular instead of murderous hours as I had at Xerox in Leicester. I'd go to work in the morning and be home for an early tea, the most pleasurable part of my working day being the ferry ride to and from the city. Unfortunately, winning wasn't a part of the culture of the Xerox office in Sydney.

I had enjoyed my club rugby experience and found being a dad just wonderful. I spent a lot of time with Jayne and Jess, just going for lots of drives and weekends away to explore the beaches and the fabulous countryside surrounding Sydney. Australians call Australia 'God's own country', and we made the most of the opportunity to take it all in. For the first time in my working life, I was more interested in enjoying life than in working. It was a really important transitional period in my life.

Hanging up the boots

In my second year with Manly, we again had a great season of enjoyable rugby. I even stepped up to captain the team on several occasions.

However, even in a leadership capacity, my rugby in Australia wasn't as fulfilling as I'd hoped it would be. The team and league were certainly very competitive, and the style of play fast and spirited. Having experienced Loughborough, where the game was semi-professional to all intents and purposes, I suppose that what I was hoping for was the competitive nature of Manly combined with a Greenwood-like command and analysis.

In the Sydney competition there was certainly a greater competitive spirit, and overall the style of play was more dynamic, but apart from those enhancements, the teams were not really that different to what I had experienced in England. It was a very high standard, at least as high as at Leicester. It just wasn't quite what I expected. The biggest difference really seemed to be the weather.

At the end of my second season with Manly I found myself, at thirty-one, one of the oldest guys on the pitch in a young man's game. It was time to move on.

Rugby had been good to me. It was sad to be closing the book on this chapter of my life. In my time as a player over the years, I had come to love the game. I had also come to love the spirit of competition, the sensation of sporting brilliance and the experience of true excellence on the pitch. I had achieved the higher ideal of winning in sport just a few times in my playing career, but that had only fuelled my quest for achieving it even more.

I often found myself daydreaming.

What if you could combine the competitive spirit I experienced at Xerox in Leicester with the core components I learned at Loughborough – fitness, nutrition, psychology, medical and analysis – along with Jim Greenwood's Total Rugby concept all co-ordinated with something akin to Alan Jones' people management skills? That combination would really be something.

Closing the lid on the copier

After a couple of years my sales team was doing reasonably well, but nothing like I wanted. I never really recovered after my rather shaky start – a poignant lesson. I came into the team as leader, a position I assumed, not one I had earned in their eyes, and I didn't have my colleagues' respect. I learned that, no matter how good you are at your job, without respect no one will really listen to you. Instead I came at them with what I *knew* was best. Only it wasn't best because it didn't work. My approach might have worked in London or another regional office in England, but I wasn't in London or another regional office, I was in Sydney, Australia. It took me a while to figure it out, but I eventually learned an important lesson about working with new teams.

It's good to set challenging goals, but if your team doesn't agree to the standards and aims that you set, in advance as you set them, then you're not really working *with* the team. You're working *at* the team. There's a big difference.

I was managing to their level of commitment while constantly trying to inspire them to higher levels. That worked with new people coming into the work environment, fresh with no preconceived ideas, but not with existing team-members, especially when I'd ruffled their feathers.

The one true high point of my Aussie Xerox career was being able to bring a couple of my old Leicester branch team over to work in the Sydney office. What's more, Steve Holdstock and Tim Buttimore both played for Manly, so we had a great time together. The team's performance in Sydney was really improved, and they were a fantastic addition to the Manly side. It's interesting to note that Tim is still heavily involved in sport himself, now managing some of the senior England players. In this game, just like in any other sphere of business, the people that you meet along the way do keep cropping up. As they say, it's a small world.

Good business

I had stopped playing rugby and had gone as far I could with my team in the Xerox environment. It was time for a new start and a new challenge. Besides I had a good reason to knuckle down with my work. As we had a new family, our little beachside apartment was quickly becoming crowded. We bought our first family home overlooking the Pacific and a few streets away from the beach. Now with a mortgage, it was time to get serious about my work again.

In Australia there existed a unique opportunity in business leasing at the time: Xerox was the only business equipment company with its own in-house finance department. Whereas other companies like NEC, Panasonic and Sharp imported their equipment from Japan and then used dealer and distributor networks to reach the business market, Xerox employed teams of direct salespeople to make things happen. Being so removed from the customer relationship, these other firms had never considered setting up finance divisions, because such details had always been in the hands of the dealers. But by the 1980s Xerox was making more money worldwide from financing office equipment than from the profit margins on the equipment itself. Other big companies like Ford and British Airways had made substantial inroads with new leasing divisions, earning a good proportion of their profits from finance businesses ancillary to their core product. Leasing was good business.

A company called Portfolio Leasing, the Australian office of US Leasing owned by Ford Motor Company, recognised that an opportunity existed to offer finance packages to these other companies. They wanted to move to fill the gap that existed in the office equipment market in Australia, so they approached me with a view to setting up and running their business finance division. I agreed. It was exactly the sort of challenge I had been waiting for.

The Managing Director of NEC, Graham Poulton, was my first call. At the time, fax machines were huge, and NEC was selling hundreds a month through its dealer network. However, these same dealers would typically sell several brands, so NEC was competing in the eyes of the consumer based on the price and features of the product.

I offered a different competitive advantage.

It was good business. Everyone got what he wanted and was happier for it.

It wasn't long before I had set up finance packages for several companies in a variety of office equipment sectors. There was no one else out there doing it. I'm just grateful that Graham could see the sense in the idea and was willing to work with me from the start. We never had a contract together. He simply listened to my idea for an hour, liked it, and said right, get out and do it. We shook hands and a great deal was done.

Exploding the myth

Though I had given up playing rugby, I still maintained a massive interest in sport in Australia. That's when I started seriously playing golf for the first time. As well as running on the beach in the mornings, you could also find me in the park down the road from our new house with a dozen balls and my pitching wedge.

My interest in sport extended beyond my back swing, however.

Australians have always been widely known for their love of sport. The English, too, are mad about sport, but I couldn't help but wonder how a country with a population one quarter the size of ours could produce competitive sports teams that consistently beat us in the very games we gave to the world. I was certain by then that the weather made it easier for athletes to train, but I still didn't have what I felt was the real answer to Australia's success in elite sports.

Throughout my entire rugby career, all the coaches in England could talk about were the three big southern-hemisphere rugby nations and what they were doing. It was as if the All Blacks, Wallabies or Springboks set the standards in the England set-up. Yet I knew that these same countries revered our coaches like Jim Greenwood. As a player I found it disappointing and sad that we weren't setting our own standards, and while living in Australia this phenomenon became a fascination. Why couldn't the European teams pull it together to convincingly beat the Antipodeans?

One day not long after I hung up my boots in Manly, I managed to set up an appointment to visit the Australian Institute of Sport. Here was a national organisation devoted entirely to developing Australia's top athletes in many different sports. Perhaps I would find some clues to this country's sporting success here.

So while in Canberra on business I called and asked for a tour. It was easy enough to do, so clearly they had nothing to hide. I ended up spending two days at the AIS walking around and observing training techniques in a variety of sports. What I found was very surprising: the competitive atmosphere was as intense and inspiring as I had imagined, yet strangely in many sports and training disciplines, the techniques were *not* as advanced as those that I had experienced at Loughborough. It was remarkable to me in that the AIS was producing superior athletes using similar (and in some cases inferior) technology. With a little probing, I finally discovered two clues as to why.

First, every athlete at the AIS was carefully selected from the best sports arenas in the country. Each was then invited to study Sports Science and performance enhancement at the Institute, mostly on fully government-funded scholarships. That was in stark contrast to

Loughborough, for example, where the prime purpose was to earn your degree. Loughborough clearly attracted outstanding athletes but you had to be bright in order to get a place and even then they only made up a small proportion of the overall student body.

However, as a result of the concentration of sporting talent at the AIS, there was a fierce spirit of competition at the elite level. The best of the best in several disciplines trained right next to each other, day after day. It was inevitable that a strong competition would evolve, and yet there was also a very healthy attitude to sharing ideas between sports. That was in stark contrast to the English sports environment, where merely a spirit of participation seemed to be the central theme and there was little cross-collaboration. I believe that was due, in a very large part, simply to the way the competitive environment was structured.

The second reason I felt the AIS was producing such excellent outcomes was that it was extremely well organised and managed. It was like a professional sporting environment in terms of everyone's commitment to their goals. Coaches were full-time professionals, and athletes were there to do a job. They all approached their training with a strong work ethic. What I was seeing at the AIS was the basic fundamentals of sport managed with a strong business ethic.

From that moment, everything became clear.

To win, you had to create the right competitive environment and engage the best specialists in each fundamental area of your sport. It all became quite straightforward. The myth of Australian sporting superiority was just that: a myth. The same must have held true of New Zealand and South Africa. Their strength lay in their competitive culture and their adequate level of preparation, not in some magic gene. It wasn't rocket science. These teams could be beaten.

The itch and the calling

I had been in Australia for over four wonderful years, during which time I had played some great club rugby and enjoyed a wonderful lifestyle. Jayne and I were married and our young family was growing – our second child, Joe, was born on 3 November 1988 – and I had realised a renewed vigour for business which was going really well.

On reflection, I was in a good position. Only I had an itch, a calling, to get back home.

Within a couple of years I had created several million pounds worth of additional business for Portfolio Leasing. They were over the moon about it. However, where the Australian business market was good, the real action was going on in London, and I knew it.

Besides, Jayne and I missed England. The first two years in Australia were like a vacation for me, a great long break from a stressful work environment and a disappointing end to an unfulfilled international rugby career. Jayne and I truly enjoyed ourselves in Australia, making the most of the lifestyle and, more importantly, of all the wonderful people – Manly really had become home – but my break was over, my batteries were charged. I was ready to get back into it. We had gone to Sydney for experience and a challenge, not because we didn't love home.

To a certain extent, I never did find what I was looking for in Australia – a winning environment both at work and in sport at the same time. Perhaps that's for the best. If I had found it I probably wouldn't have coped very well. Looking at the tempo and pace of the professional rugby player's life now, I can see that it would have been tough to manage both at the same time.

I came to realise what I really wanted was the love of sport combined with the kind of dedication that I gave to my business. What I wanted was my sport to be my business. Instead, my attention was always divided out of a necessity to earn a living. I've always been far happier when completely dedicated to just one thing, obsessive as Jayne describes it. At Loughborough it was just sport. In my leasing business in Australia, it was just business. It was a good feeling, knowing I was going home with full clarity.

I had undergone a catharsis in Australia, just like in my gap year after *Conway*. My years in Australia helped me to understand my disappointing career in international rugby. I had gone to Australia to take my sport seriously again, yet I had learned to take my work and sport lightly and my lifestyle and family seriously.

Going home

To some degree it was a huge risk to return to England. However the risk was mitigated by the fact that I was going back to work for the London branch of US Leasing. The head office liked what I'd done in Australia and they didn't want to lose me.

So, having sold our house and shipped most of our possessions by container, we trundled our young family into a cab and headed for the airport. It was the end of a great chapter in my life, and I was sad to be leaving such a wonderful place as Manly. I would never have guessed how the beautiful beachside suburb would come back into my life.

Working abroad had been a fantastic experience, something everyone should do, and it also helped me to appreciate what a great country England is, despite how many people are so quick to knock it. I think it was while living in Australia that I realised how much I enjoy being English.

I was very excited about the prospect of going home to the highly competitive leasing industry in London, and I had great plans for a prosperous future in business. I couldn't wait to get started. I couldn't have known that within a few short months those great plans would be completely tossed out of the window.

BACK HOME, A NEW LEASE... 8

It was just after 8 p.m. I was working at the headquarters of my newly created company, Sales Finance & Leasing – the converted garage of our new home in Pinkney's Green near Marlow. Starting my own business in early 1990 had been a big risk, given a young family and a new mortgage. But it was already showing great promise. I could finally close the books on a rather disappointing six months in Portfolio's London office after our return from Australia the previous year.

By the end of my first week with Portfolio Leasing in London, I knew I was in the wrong place. This company was just not right for me, so I resigned in mid-February in order to go it on my own, and set up my new leasing company on 1 April 1990.

I was up to my eyes in paperwork when the phone started ringing.

'Clive, it's Mike Poulson.'

Mike and I had played together at Loughborough, and we had great fun on and off the pitch. I was best man at his wedding shortly after university. It was good to hear from him again. We caught up on the last five years since we left for Australia, and I discovered that Mike lived in the nearby town of Henley, just twenty minutes down the road from my new home.

Henley is one of the most beautiful towns in England. On the Thames, it is of course famous for the regatta which takes place there each year at the beginning of summer, a major social occasion and one of the top rowing events in the world.

As usual with old team-mates, talk soon turned to rugby.

'So are you still playing these days?'

'No, no. Those days are over for me. I gave up a couple of years ago after my rugby in Sydney just got a little too much.'

'Yeah, I'm still kicking around. Playing down the road for the club at Henley. It's great fun. We're only small, in Southwest Division Two, but we all really enjoy our game. I'm the grandfather of the team. Captain, coach and CEO of the drinks stand all rolled into one.'

Then came an innocent remark that would eventually lead to a major shift in my life.

'Hey, why don't you come down and join us for old time's sake?'

'No, no, Mike. My playing days are definitely over.'

'Oh, come on. Just come down and talk to the guys for a few minutes? They'd really like to see you and maybe you could talk about what you learned in Australia.'

'Well ... OK, Mike. But I'm not bringing my boots! When's your next training session and I'll see if I can make it?'

'Tuesdays and Thursdays from 7 to 9 p.m., as usual. Only give me a couple of weeks so that I can spread the word and make sure everyone comes along. Why don't I give you a call when it's all organised?'

'Sounds great. Look forward to it. Thanks for calling, Mike. It's good to hear from you.'

And that was it. Another phone call that changed my life. Without Mike's simple act of friendship, I am not sure if I ever would have been tempted into coaching rugby in the first place. After this I met Mike and another old playing friend from my Leicester days, Mark Duffelin, and they persuaded me to get involved in Henley Rugby Club.

Stepping up to the crease

True to his word, Mike called a couple of weeks later to ask me to come down the following Tuesday for a bit of a talk to the players. I'll admit it felt odd stepping on the pitch in shoes and a business suit instead of boots and a jersey. As the players warmed up with passing drills, it was all I could do to stop myself from joining in. About thirty minutes into training, Mike called the boys together and introduced me to the team. I hadn't prepared anything, but I responded to their attention and interest – they wanted to learn. I don't know how training ordinarily went, but that night the team really seemed to be right into their rugby. I gave another quick talk at the end of training with a few tips about their skills and some initial thoughts on the back play that I had witnessed in training. I enjoyed it and was glad to have helped Mike out, even in such a small way.

Attracted by the warm and supportive club rugby environment, I found myself taking Jayne and the kids down to Henley for a few Saturday fixtures, but soon at Mike's invitation I was popping along to watch more training sessions. For me it was an unexpected and welcome break from my business. Two casual evenings during the week, friendly weekend matches . . . this was the bottom of Southwest Division Two after all. We were roughly a hundred teams away from the standard I used to play. It was more easygoing than I was used to, but great fun for all that. Then, at a club social barbecue after the final match of the season, Mike finally put it to me.

'You know, Clive, this team could really do with a proper coach. How would you like to give me a hand at the pre-season trainings in August? If you like it, maybe you could be our coach next year?'

I opened my mouth to say no, I wasn't interested, I was finished with rugby. But then much to my surprise something completely different came out: 'OK, that would be great!'

Mike raised his pint of lager saying, 'I expected nothing less,' and with a clink of my own glass he sealed my first multi-million pound coaching contract . . . not!

Astounded at what I'd just committed to, I rather hoped he was joking. Maybe over the next few days he would forget. He called me a week later. 'When can we meet to start planning for next season?'

Poacher turned gamekeeper

If you had asked any of my team-mates from my international days, and particularly my coaches from the time, whether they thought I would make a good coach, well, after they fell to the ground in peals of laughter you might have got a straight answer. They would probably have told you it was a bit like a poacher turned gamekeeper. As a player, I guess I was just as well-known for my odd flashes of brilliance as the occasional cock-ups. I also made it my personal responsibility to try and make all training sessions far more enjoyable than the coaches thought acceptable – smiling in training was forbidden and if a football was seen . . . well I might just have been back at HMS *Conway* and facing the teaser. I remember trying a set piece move with the England backs that involved me heading the ball to the winger. I called it a 'Jackie' after Jackie Charlton who played centre half in the 1966 World Cup and was awesome with his head. Anyway when the coach came over and asked what we were doing, I promptly showed him the new 'Jackie' move. To say he wasn't amused would be an understatement and I was promptly sent off to do rucking and contact drills with the forwards. His sense of humour finally blew a gasket when I pointed out to him that in twenty-five years' time everyone would be running this play, and what he was coaching was actually twenty-five years behind the times which, if my maths were correct, made us fifty years adrift. Needless to say my rucking and contact skills improved considerably during that period.

Coaching was probably a natural extension of my love of playing sport, combined with my training as a teacher at Loughborough. I just never really thought about it much, except to sigh at how poorly others were doing it. Any fool can criticise, and many do. Yet watching those first few games at Henley in the spring of 1990, a feeling – an instinct if you will – began taking shape within me. Here was my old friend Mike Poulson with a bunch of players, all enthusiastic about their game, laughing and having fun even in the face of defeat. In a way it was the kind of rugby I had enjoyed so much in my first year at Quins, and even though it was a lowly division, winning and losing at any club level now had consequences.

In my four years away in Australia, the rugby clubs around England had finally organised themselves into a coherent structure of divisions and leagues, whereas in my playing days fixtures were mainly set between clubs on a traditional basis or simply by mutual agreement. If you won all your matches you could probably say you were one of the best teams in the country, but even that was open to conjecture because often the best teams didn't play each other. Now however everything had changed with the official merit tables in England. If you came top of the competition tables in any division, your club would be promoted to the next higher division. And of course the converse was also true.

If you came bottom of your table you would be relegated to the lower competition, obviously a highly embarrassing outcome.

Here was a clear competition where coming top of the division tables – winning – meant that Henley could be promoted up to Southwest Division One. And who doesn't want to step up in the world in terms of standing? They wanted to win and could see the potential upside for their club. Those were still the amateur days, which meant if your club was winning you attracted more and better players. To Henley, winning would mean bigger club membership, greater financial assistance from the RFU, better games, and so bigger crowds. There was actually a lot of upside to winning, even in Southwest Division Two.

Collecting my thoughts

By the time Mike and I actually sat down to plan and plot for next season, I had convinced myself that not only would I coach, but I'd coach this team with only one aim in mind: winning the league. In as delicate a way as possible, I conveyed to Mike that I couldn't come at it halfway. It just wasn't in my nature. If he wanted me to do this thing, I had to have full rein to do it my way. Mike thought all his Christmases had come at once and was only too happy to let me do what I wanted. Being coach as well as captain is an impossible job at any level of sport, and he also had his own business to run. Mike seemed pleased to have me, and the rest was now up to me.

It was actually a great time to get involved. I had begun my leasing business only a few months before. Things were going pretty well, and I think it had a lot to do with how I planned things in the quiet time over Christmas the previous year. I like to keep things as simple as I can, so whenever I start a new project I tend to follow a rather basic three-step process. *Think, Plan, Do.* Late one Sunday night in early May I sat down to apply that process to coaching at Henley.

The first question I asked myself was, OK, *I've got to get these boys thinking correctly . . . thinking like winners. How am I going to do it?*

I wrote down a few notes on a spare piece of paper in my garage-office, things that were important to me when I was playing. In doing so, I asked myself some questions.

How can we make training fun and games enjoyable regardless of the outcome? There was no doubt that it had to be fun for everyone, otherwise it just wouldn't work. My England days had so often been heavy and tedious. They certainly didn't inspire the best in me.

What sets us apart from the other teams so that we can be different in a significant way? Who wants to be the same as everyone else? Even in Southwest Division Two, that would be pretty boring. To win we had to be better than the competition in areas that were obvious and interesting, and not necessarily always on the pitch.

How can we build on our strengths when we win and learn from our mistakes when we lose? Let's face it, this was a Southwest Division Two team that wasn't even top of their table. We were going to lose from time to time, no matter how well I did as coach. You just can't make a silk purse out of a sow's ear, at least not overnight. Success takes time, on the pitch as anywhere else. All I was hoping to do was build on that success over time, just as I had done in my leasing businesses to date.

Right, PLAN, I said to myself starting with another piece of paper. *Next thing we'll have to do is get ourselves properly organised.*

As a leader in business, I'd learned a salient lesson in the Sydney office of Xerox: you can't go anywhere if your team doesn't want to go with you. So before I did anything I needed to make sure the team were with me.

How can I get the team's full commitment to doing what it takes to win? There was no question in my mind. I was there to win. If that wasn't important for everyone on the team, it wouldn't work. Once we had that, though, I had yet another question:

How can I enlist some of the players' help in the coaching process so that everyone is actively involved? The Sydney experience had also taught me that if you don't listen to the people around you, and get them involved in the process, then you're doing it the hard way and not utilising the strength of the team. When the going gets tough, the strength of the team that pulls together will always win out over the efforts of a collection of individuals. But it wasn't just about the players in the first XV squad at Henley. There were other teams and a host of volunteers who all wanted to see us win, too.

How can we organise all the supporters at Henley to help us achieve our aim of winning? And it wasn't just the club supporters we had to think about either. If I and the players were giving up two nights a week and most of Saturday for the next year, our partners and families would have something to say about that, so we had to pay attention there as well.

OK, finally DO, I thought to myself pulling out my third piece of paper. *We have to go right back to the basic rugby skills and master them if we're to have any chance at consistently playing well.*

I'd seen this team in action. On the whole they weren't bad as such, but there was a long way to go. Consistency was our biggest issue. We missed tackles, there seemed to be several different ideas about what good scrummaging and lineout play actually were, and our passing was sometimes all right but more often sloppy and mistimed, with little or no thought or understanding of time or space. There was no question about it, I had to start everyone right back at the basics of the game of rugby so that we were all on the same wavelength. Coaching at the grass roots level, that's what these players needed. I was actually beginning to look forward to making a difference with this team.

I sat down at my computer and wrote down a summary of my thoughts so far:

WINNING AT HENLEY

THINK Correctly
- Training fun, games enjoyable
- Doing things differently
- Building success

PLAN Get Organised
- Commitment
- Help in key areas
- Support Structures

DO Coach the Basics
- Tackling
- Scrummaging
- Passing

That should just about do it. Nice and simple.

And with that I had my very first coaching plan for the first XV rugby team at the Henley rugby club. Not too surprisingly, a similar plan would form the basis of every new coaching plan I've done since.

Lights, camera . . . action!

I didn't introduce all my plan in the first day of training. Over the course of the next few weeks we put most of the building blocks in place, and really that plan wasn't fully realised until after a whole season of working on it bit by bit. In my first meeting with the squad, I kept things light and enjoyable. All we did was talk for the first hour. I asked questions, they did most of the talking and I did a lot of listening. My very first question was, 'Why are you here playing rugby?' The dialogue continued from there until I was sure that everyone in the team was with me – that they all wanted the same thing: just to do everything possible to give them a chance of becoming winners.

Only then did we talk about commitment and what it would take to achieve our aim.

'Unless we're here to win this thing, we may as well all just stay home and watch telly. We all lead busy lives. We all work outside of rugby. It is really easy to find some excuse or another for not coming to training. It's just Southwest Division Two after all, so what does it matter, right?

'Well it does matter. Winning isn't a sometime thing. It's an all-time thing.

'If we want to win, we all have to be fully committed to giving it everything we've got. For every session you miss, or for every minute you're late to training, you're letting the team down. That one missed opportunity to improve as a team could cost us the next game.

'I'll do whatever it takes to coach you through a winning season, but there is something you must all understand. If I give my total commitment to winning, it won't work unless you give your full commitment as well.

'I'll be your coach, but we all have to agree to some rules. The first is about time. I run a leasing company and I have a full schedule. I'll structure my entire diary around you guys, but in return I ask that you do the same.

'If training starts at 7 p.m., I'll be here at ten to, but I expect you to be here at 6.30 p.m. to get your kit on and be fully prepared to work. How does everyone feel about that?'

The first time at the beginning of the night when I asked the team their opinion they all just looked around dumbfounded for an uncomfortable few moments of silence. No coach had ever asked for their thoughts before.

'Sounds great!' 'OK!' came the responses.

I could tell this was going to work well. No one looked too uncertain.

It's always good to start with the things that are easy to agree on. Whenever people get together in a long-term participative team environment, keeping to time and respecting other people's time is the most important element to get right. It sets the tone for everything. Of course, being on time is a much easier habit to form when there is a great incentive. In line with making training fun and enjoyable, rather by accident I added the most successful and inspiring fitness regime that I've ever discovered in team training.

Sex sells ... even in rugby

Rather early in the season, Jayne and I were having dinner with some friends and the conversation moved to one of my favourite topics: fitness levels. It turned out that one of the lady dinner guests was also big on fitness herself and was really into aerobics. I immediately thought, *Wouldn't the guys enjoy this for something different.* The lady in question was rather attractive and in fantastic shape. She said she would be delighted to come down and take the boys through a thirty-minute aerobics session if it would help in pre-season fitness training. We agreed to meet at my house the following Tuesday evening. When the door bell rang, there was this lady dressed in full aerobics gear. I am not sure what Jayne was thinking but I certainly knew what the Henley boys would think.

For this first session, she brought her own music and, as she set everything up, I wasn't that surprised to see all the boys rushing to get their kit on and front up. She was just fantastic – it was a great aerobics session, too! By the end of it, the boys were completely exhausted while she was as bubbly as ever and had hardly broken sweat. But even in their fatigued state the men were totally attentive, riveted. I thought it was just brilliant.

Michael Poulson came up to me after training. 'If that's what it means to do things differently, then the team and I agree. We're all for it.'

Thankfully our instructor agreed to continue her sessions for the next few weeks leading up to the games. Those sessions started at 6.30 p.m. and were on top of our regular two-hour training period. Not only did everyone attend every session, but they were at least ten minutes early as well. Her aerobics certainly established a great habit of punctuality.

Livening up the rugby traditions

On the subject of having fun in training, our aerobics teacher reacquainted me with something that I'd learned while at university: the power of music in sport. Aerobics of course needs music and, because we were outdoors on the rugby pitch, her little portable CD player wasn't very loud or inspiring. We rigged up the club's PA system so that it could be used outside for the aerobics music. I decided, even when we were not doing aerobics, to keep on with the music so that things went on being fun and fast-paced. We had the PA gear set up, so why not? Music has an amazing ability to set the tone of any kind of event. I'd learned that lesson well while at Loughborough where modern pop music had been a big part of practically every physical activity we did. Yet strangely I'd never experienced music since in the England set-up or in any club rugby environment. It was fun. It was different. It was perfect. Music became a part of the way we did things.

I'll never forget the look on the boys' faces when they came back into the changing rooms after our first match. They were used to having a few pints in the changing rooms after each game. This time I had laid on four huge steaming pots of tea instead.

Ah, nothing like old traditions.

I figured that if they drank tea at Leicester then we could certainly drink tea at Henley. Besides, I didn't like beer all that much after a match and, if I was having tea, so were they. I knew I'd arrived when the tea finally came out.

I made it a habit over the cup of tea to give a quick debrief after every game. Instead of being harsh with the boys for not giving enough, or some such nonsense, I would try and focus on what they had done right, keeping it brief, and set the stage for improving for the next game.

And when we won, I would take extra time to encourage a dialogue amongst the boys so that we could openly discuss what went right and how we could reinforce those good habits and skills. It always amazed me how the players were harder on themselves than I ever would have been. Because I encouraged them to talk and speak their minds, my job was mostly to bolster and encourage their otherwise harsh self-assessment of their performance.

On the subject of beer and alcohol I took an even harder line when travelling for our away games.

'When we go away, it's really important that we conduct ourselves in the correct manner. I'm all for a good time while away – we had some great club traditions when I was younger – but I'd like you all to please be mindful of your behaviour. We don't want the team to be associated with any drunken acts of bravado.'

By this stage, the team were used to my slightly different approach, setting very high standards in almost every area of our rugby both on and, even more importantly, off the pitch. I think they understood where I was coming from. I wasn't just dictating unreasonable terms – I was appealing to higher ideals. This wasn't just about rugby. There was a lot on the line, for all of us. Winning is about more than just points on the scoreboard, or performance on the pitch. If we didn't achieve excellence in every area of our efforts as an organisation, then we weren't really winning. What a waste of time it would be if everything came together for a victory on the pitch only for a silly drunken mistake after the match to ruin everything. The whole team now had a good reason to work as a team off the pitch as well.

Setting up support

My business was now really taking off, so I couldn't just give the coaching my undivided attention. Like in my playing days, either my business or the coaching had to come second, and economics demanded it was the coaching. I decided to give some of the senior players additional responsibilities. After asking for volunteers – and I got a good show of hands because these boys were starting to see just how enjoyable rugby could be – I selected three key players, apart from the captain, and assigned them areas of responsibility in the three parts of our game upon which our early results seemed to hinge: scrums, lineouts and penalties. I gave these three players in the team a copy of Jim Greenwood's book, *Total Rugby*, and asked them to make presentations to the team on their respective areas at the next training session. From that time on, they would give reports and even a bit of coaching in their areas during our pre-training meetings.

The subject of penalties was, and still is for most teams, the greatest potential for points for or against our team. It's also one of the easiest areas to influence: all we had to do was know the rules and play to them. Unfortunately, in rugby that isn't as easy as it sounds. The rules are not as simple as in most other sports. It didn't surprise me that even though most of the guys had been playing for years, they still didn't know the detail of the rules well. This holds true today, even of most professional players: very few actually know the specific implications of the rules as set down by the International Rugby Board. They were making costly mistakes at inopportune times, and were missing obvious chances to force errors in our opposition because of their inability to understand the rules as the referees knew them. To help us in this area, I invited the traditional enemy into the very middle of our camp.

Ashley Rowden was a local referee. He still referees in the Premiership today. Ashley kindly agreed to come down to training and help us learn the rules at first hand instead of from a book. The lads were very suspicious when he first showed up. The vast majority of players are narrow-minded about refs and treat them as the enemy. They don't understand how working with referees can be so powerful. I even see this in the Premiership sides today where some of the coaches see the refs as guys with two heads and six fingers. What I don't understand is how anyone can fail to see that it is essential to work *with* an individual who has so much control over the outcome of the game. I had briefed Ashley quietly on what I wanted, so when the players made their first mistake in training, he blew loudly on his whistle, running up to the area of play and indicating a penalty to the opposition. I took my cue.

'You just lost us the game. There are thirty guys down here at training, giving it everything, sacrificing their business career, their families, their marriages and you just lost us the game because you don't know the bloody rules! Ashley, please explain what he did wrong.'

They all just looked at me as if I was completely barmy, but I think I was making my point. This was serious and I needed players who wanted to learn but also players who could think under the pressure of a game. If you are going to do things wrong in training you will have little chance when the pressure is on.

After that, Ashley came to a lot of training sessions to help coach the team. I think he was actually very pleased to give us a hand and befriend some of us in the squad. I can imagine most refs would be eager to get involved. They must sometimes feel so much like outsiders and outcasts. From that moment on, whenever Ashley blew his whistle I would emphasise that one mistimed penalty would lose us the game. Eventually, the players got the message. Controlling penalty situations won us loads of matches. The referee became one of our best coaches.

Mastering the basics

The greatest enjoyment about my new role with the team was ironically what had been my biggest disappointment while playing for England: the coaching itself. Maybe I saw it as my time to put things right. I approached this part of my role with vigour and zeal. I really had a good time teaching the boys basic rugby skills. More so than any other time since, I was utilising every coaching technique I'd either learned, devised, created or observed over the years from my mentors like Greenwood, White and Kirton. This was real grass roots rugby, and it was to prove invaluable to me in years to come, though I didn't know it at the time.

Surprisingly, even in the top levels of the game these days, there are very few coaches who are actually good at teaching basic skills. Some top coaches come into the game having had no grounding like this at the grass roots level. It makes me smile sometimes when I see big-name players turn their hand to coaching without first studying the principles of education, coaching and training in sport. A lot of coaches try to take short-cuts here, and they wonder why they quickly come unstuck.

On the other hand, a lot of good coaches are sometimes intimidated by the superstar status of some players. Would you want to teach tackling or lineout techniques to a Martin Johnson, for example? You have to, and you've got to know how to do it well. I've found that the better the player, the more he needs and wants coaching. Too many coaches want to manage, not coach, and frankly wouldn't dream of questioning their players. You need to do both. That's what I learned at Henley, and it still holds true for me today. You cannot assume even the best of your players know their basic skills.

True to form, I've never met a quality player intent on winning who didn't want to hear about ways he could improve his game. The greatest compliment I can give to players like Martin Johnson and Jonny Wilkinson would be to tell you of their thirst for knowledge. They are sponges for new ideas and real quality coaching.

In addition to a lot of detailed coaching and teaching in our sessions at Henley, I also had to break some bad habits. As a back, and having spent most of my international career watching the forwards play most of the ball, I clearly favour a running game involving all fifteen players, and so you can imagine that any policy of play that didn't support that kind of game wasn't on my list of rugby priorities. Take kicking the ball, for example. As a player with England I was completely frustrated with the official policy of kicking inside our 22-metre line every single time. In club rugby, particularly at the lower levels such as Henley, it seemed like kicking was the prime strategy. Any time the pressure was on, and sometimes even when it wasn't, the players would just go and kick the ball. Rugby matches had turned into kicking competitions, and they were boring to watch, coach and play.

Things had to change.

We weren't going to win any games by giving away possession like that.

So a month or so into the season I banned any form of kicking during play. Without kicking, you have to play the ball in your hands. When the pressure was really on, that was actually the time to keep hold of the ball, not kick it away. But a lot of the players were terrified of playing under pressure. This was real scary stuff, especially to senior players – I kept reminding them that no matter what happened during the game on Saturday, we'd all still have to go to work on Monday morning, so it wasn't really that big a deal.

That's the time when people with less skill tend to collapse under the pressure of it all. Pressure is wonderfully revealing in that way. When the pressure is on, there is just no place to hide on the pitch. I loved it. The players hated it – at first – but very quickly we became good at playing this way. If we did not become skilled at this very quickly we would be at the bottom of the table, but if we could get it right, we'd be at the top. It was compelling.

I must mention here the importance of player belief and support when you are trying to change things including a style of play or thinking. Mike Poulson and Mark Duffelin were playing. Mike at fly-half and Mark at hooker. They were fantastically supportive both on and off the pitch and I would like to think that they had as much fun as I did, playing really exciting rugby towards the end of their respective playing careers.

Victory, but not winning!

All in all, we did pretty well that first season at Henley. It was a year where we consolidated a large number of new ideas and strategies for creating a winning team. Over the course of the season we continued to make all sorts of improvements and changes to the way we did things in hundreds of different areas. By the end of the season, we were really pulling things together and the players were enjoying themselves. We won the Oxfordshire Cup at the end of the season, and finished the season by winning our last eight matches in a row, only narrowly missing out on promotion. However, the standards had been set. Everything was now in place for a serious assault with no excuses on this league.

On the bright side, because we were doing things so differently and winning, we were attracting quite a bit of attention. In the amateur game, it's not uncommon for players to move around during the season in search of a better club. Henley's player base was certainly swelling as our style of play and coaching attracted more quality players. And we even caught the eye of the local media. A couple of TV crews came down to have a look at this rather strange winning team that refused to kick the ball, had tea in the changing rooms, and played loud music during training.

I learned a lot about winning in that year. First, it was amazing to me that I could get so involved in the team that the thrill of victory was a real buzz, and the pain of defeat was so tremendous. Even Jayne was surprised at how I would mope around the house for the rest of the weekend when we lost a match. I never imagined I could become more competitive coaching Henley than I ever had been playing for club and country. I recognised that it was a potential weakness in me, how I so hated losing, and yet I was really delighted to discover that it didn't seem to matter in what division the team was playing, just as long as we were winning. I became determined that in the next season things would be different. I began to hatch a plan for building on our success that would take us to the next level, literally.

A new calibre of players

The first rule of coaching is that it really helps to have the raw material: quality players. In our first year we didn't quite have enough good players, but we'd won games through hard work – by teaching basic skills and learning to play a new game. The secret is to have both. Of course I realised rightaway that things would be different if I could just convince a few top-notch players to come and play for us. But of course, no top English player in their right mind would go down to Southwest Division Two to play for Henley, so I wracked my brain to find another way.

In the end, it was a simple matter of a bottle of wine that finally made me twig. Jayne and I were going out to dinner, and we stopped at Threshers for a bottle of wine to take with us. That's when I found the answer to my problem of quality players.

'You can't beat a good Australian really,' the shopkeeper informed me. 'Great quality, easy on the palate, and goes well with most English fare. Here, try this Penfold's red.'

Australian? After our time in Sydney I was well acquainted with the wine, but as I looked at the bottle he'd handed me something clicked in my mind. *Yes. It's a crazy idea, but why not? It just might work.* I couldn't wait to get home that night. Checking my watch I called the number I knew so well, the number that would get Bob Lane, my old coach at Manly rugby club. After a brief chat catching up on old times, I put my idea into action.

'Bob, you wouldn't happen to know a couple of gifted players who would fancy a six-month rugby holiday in London, all expenses paid, would you?'

I figured that if I once had an interest in playing rugby in Sydney, then surely two young men in Australia would welcome the opportunity of tasting the delights of Henley, London and England. It took me a few weeks to sort it out, but we managed to convince two talented young Australian players to join us at Henley for most of the rugby season. I still remembered them from my last season at Manly, now three years gone. They would do just fine. It's a good thing that the rugby calendars are on completely opposite sides of the year in the southern hemisphere. These two literally went from their game in the final of the Sydney competition one week right into our Henley team, Southwest Division Two, the next.

Suddenly at the beginning of my second season in coaching, we had two players from Australia, Rob Gallagher and Jim 'Junior' Perignon. They enjoyed the whole experience, including taking the Henley social scene by storm.

It was just brilliant.

No one really knew exactly who they were when they ran onto the pitch to warm up for their first match, apart from the fact they were Australian. However, a carefully-timed rumour of their pedigree quickly spread throughout the league. Many of the opposing teams were far from happy.

Some of them went completely nuts – 'This is just not cricket,' and 'It's not fair. Woodward's brought in two Australians,' flew the protests.

I loved it. It's fun stirring the pot a little.

I barely kept a straight face as the referee's whistle blew to signal the start of their first game, but it was very amusing.

Two players don't make a team. But with our two Aussies, we dominated the other side. In addition, all the other lads in our team lifted their game to a new level. When we added in all the quality coaching, plus a bunch of guys who were all enjoying themselves, we had the winning formula

It was excellent.

By bringing in our Aussies, we weren't breaking any rules as such. This was no different to bringing in Nottingham's Steve Holdstock and Leicester's Tim Buttimore to play for Manly, and had just as good an effect. Many more players now cross the equator in search of a contract to play the professional game – we were just a bit ahead of the times! No doubt it didn't seem fair to the other teams in our division, but this was a competition. I'm sure if the other teams could have figured out a way to attract high-calibre players to their clubs they would have done so. In more ways than one, the other teams in our division simply couldn't compete. We flew through the league in that 1991–92 season and didn't lose a game. Henley was promoted to Southwest One as champions, a feat the club had never accomplished before.

Suddenly we were a huge success and started attracting quality players in droves. By the time our Aussies left us to return to their regular seasons in Manly, we had a player base nobody had ever dreamed we would achieve. I was delighted to see, just a few years later, that one of our imports, Rob Gallagher, made the Wallaby squad.

All it took was a little creative thinking applied to a problem everyone else thought couldn't be solved.

We convincingly beat every team we came up against. We were playing our best rugby in a host of key areas, everyone associated with the organisation was really enjoying themselves, and the team were really playing well together, clicking as a team. Not only that, our supporters – all thirty-seven of them! – were going wild watching our all-out attacking style of play where our inside backs stood flat, our outside backs stood very deep and kicking was still almost banned. It was the complete opposite to the safe boring play that everyone had become accustomed to in English rugby.

Winning in coaching

For me, that season was winning at its best. To varying degrees in that magic year we achieved this grand vision of mine, this higher ideal, week after week. It was an incredible feeling, one that I never thought I would experience again after playing rugby. However, as coach I even felt I had complete control over the outcome. No longer could I criticise or complain about what was missing. It was completely up to me to create the environment I had always wanted in rugby. It was fantastic. But now of course we had been promoted up the tables and we'd lost our two superstars. We had a new division, a tougher competition and a whole new set of challenges ahead of us for the next season. I was really looking forward to it.

However, this hobby of mine, this obsession, if you will, to building a winning team had come at quite a cost in that season.

Thankfully my leasing business had gone well in its first couple of years, in spite of my starting it during one of the worst economic downturns in decades. Soon after starting the business, Jayne took over the job of managing the company's affairs and at about the same time a long-time family friend, Ann Heaver, came on board to handle the rapidly expanding workload. So by the time our two friends came from Australia, Sales Finance & Leasing had a tight team of five people in a relatively profitable enterprise. Bringing those Aussies to England and employing them while they were here was funded totally by my business. For a small growing company it clearly had a negative effect on the cash flow.

Sales Finance & Leasing was a good business and was growing quickly. To put it simply, we were winning there, too. For the first time ever, and only a few years after I'd given up on the idea, I was winning in both my work and in sport. Of course, keeping this going would prove difficult, and when something did have to give it was the business. I'm sure if I had concentrated all my energies into just my business it would have been even more successful, but winning in rugby had a firm hold. Despite my split loyalties, Jayne and Ann did a fantastic job keeping everything going, whilst I spent more time than was justifiable trying to move Henley up the tables.

More league table promotions

For the next two seasons at Henley, we continued to build on our success. Even though we didn't have our Australians, we attracted a much stronger player base now because we were winning. And we'd built our coaching systems on a strong foundation of fun, full team involvement and higher standards in our behaviour on and off the pitch. I'd much rather a unified team built on solid foundations than a collection of talented individuals with little to support them.

In the seasons between September 1991 and May 1994, Henley were unstoppable as our promotions continued. To my knowledge, no team has ever before or since dominated so completely across three divisions in as many years, ending up with promotion in 1994 to the national leagues. It's a huge credit to the players, to the coaches and support team and to the systems and processes that dozens of people helped us put in place.

By the end of my fourth season with Henley, I was beginning to wonder what we'd do next. We had won the Oxfordshire Cup in every season, and moving as far as we had into the national leagues had been a remarkable challenge, but to go right up into the top rank would be totally unrealistic, basically an impossible feat given the location, revenue base of the club, its facilities, and the players at our disposal.

My years at Henley stand among the most exciting of my coaching career. They were also my most creative in terms of doing things completely differently to what everyone expected. But, good as it had been, it was time to move on. The players, committee and members at Henley understood that. Nigel Dudding, my assistant coach, was a Henley man through and through. He took over the team and Henley has done extremely well ever since. They have never looked back, which is something I am very proud of. Being invited back every year to the president's lunch is a date I really look forward to. It was a very special time for me.

Luckily my business had still moved from strength to strength in that time. I was fortunate, too, that Jayne and Ann were willing to accommodate my love of coaching. Now I just had to figure out what I would try next.

9
THE LUCK OF THE IRISH

Quite out of the blue, Ann solved that problem for me.

Ann is Irish-Canadian. Her particular passion was the London Irish rugby club, and it was a source of great grief to her that this distinguished club had recently been relegated to the Second Division.

'How would you like to be coach at London Irish?' she asked me, more or less out of the blue.

'I can't see how that would ever happen. Ann, what's this all about?'

'I called Mike Gibson, the chairman of the committee at London Irish and told him you would consider the coaching job if he called you.'

'You did what? London Irish? Are you mad? Why on earth would you do that? I'm not even Irish.'

I knew of London Irish's predicament. When clubs get demoted, top players tend to take off in search of greener pastures. It can often lead to a downward spiral into oblivion as clubs simply go from bad to worse. London Irish was facing this grim prospect right now. Even worse, their coach, New Zealander and former All Black Hika Reid, had quit the job that very week in April 1994. The Irish can be a bit vocal, so I have heard, and he had apparently been copping plenty of abuse from the supporters and the media. In the face of so much scathing public comment, I could easily see why people walk away from these positions, which basically they're doing for little or no reward. So Ann had simply picked up the telephone and called Mike Gibson, a senior executive with Guinness and former Ireland international, and head of the playing side of the club.

Even though they were going down to the Second Division, London Irish really was a First Division team with a large stadium, a huge body of supporters, and a long and venerated history. As far as Henley was concerned, I'd come a long way with the team but it was only going to go so far. London Irish by contrast was certainly in a mess, but it would be a terrific challenge in every sense – a big club in England with a passionate support base drawn from the huge Irish community. For an Englishman to take over London Irish was a big call. The more I thought about it, the more the challenge appealed to me. When Mike Gibson's call came through, I agreed to meet him at the club and hear what he had to say.

Looking around

As Mike Gibson showed me around the large empty stadium, I could feel a pall hanging over the club. I knew the massive challenge would not just be with the players, but with the politics of the committee as well. It would be my first real exposure to such vastly differing interests amongst a huge volunteer support body. I thought as coach that I could avoid getting involved in any of it. As long as I did my job and won the matches I'd be able to stay above it all.

Mike knew of my success with Henley and asked if I could do the same with London Irish. I was clear with him. It would be a tough job. I could do it, but if the committee really wanted me they'd have to let me do the job my way, radical though it might seem at times. Even if that meant finding players who weren't Irish, I had to have full control or it wouldn't work. That day Mike and I agreed to work together with London Irish to attempt to claw our way back into the First Division.

In mid-July, just before the pre-season, I found myself once again planning for a new beginning, this time as coach of London Irish rugby club. But now I knew exactly what had to be done. In fact my written plan was remarkably similar to the one for Henley, only more detailed. Knowing what to do wasn't the problem. My biggest challenge here would be lifting the spirits of the players who had stayed with the club.

My first step was to get the team sorted, and quickly. We had just six weeks to pull ourselves into shape. Invitations to attend pre-season training had already been sent out by the club secretary. Now we were just keeping our fingers crossed that enough players would turn up for the first session.

Team meetings had customarily been held in a small bar in the downstairs of the stadium. When I walked in to find the boys, I saw twenty dishevelled young men sitting slumped in plastic chairs in a dirty dank room, heads down, eyes downcast. The little bar reeked of old beer and cigarettes. The cold light from the sparse fluorescent bulbs cast long shadows. The players were a motley crew with all different kinds of kit on, not one player in proper club gear. At least most of the senior players had turned up, but these guys were a mess.

Forgetting the introductions, the first words out of my mouth were, 'Right, we can't do this in here. Everyone grab your gear and follow me. Could you,' I pointed to an innocent-looking lad to my right, 'please pick up that flip chart and pens on your way out?'

I then promptly wheeled around and walked right back out of the door towards the pitch and the open fresh evening air.

By contrast the stadium was beautiful. There was a surreal evening twilight as all the men took a seat on the freshly cut grass. The wide open vastness of the empty stadium enhanced the dramatic change of atmosphere. This team would never meet in that depressing little bar again. Once the flip chart was set up, I felt ready to begin.

I'd like to say my opening words to the team that day were inspiring, but I don't think they were. For the most part these guys were too far gone. In their minds they had lost the season before it had even begun. In this situation words would not be enough. Only my actions would prove my intentions over the next few weeks. When people are down, I've always found it's better to tell it straight and not try and bullshit them with false promises or unknown predictions. This club was in a mess on the playing side. They knew it and I knew it.

So in my opening talk I just told it as I saw it. I acknowledged the disappointment they must be feeling, and I recognised that the future wasn't exactly bright. But I also told them quite matter-of-factly that I thought we could win this division, and that all we had to do was to play to our strengths, enjoy ourselves, and do things differently from what most people expected. Understandably, they were sceptical. Most of these players didn't remember me as a player, but I was almost young enough to be playing with them instead of coaching. Nor did they give a stuff about my success at Henley, so my credibility was more than a little shaky.

Drawing on previous experience, I asked a lot of questions, encouraged a lot of discussion, and then got them out on the pitch to focus on basic rugby skills. There was not much else I could do.

The sinking ship

At the next session one of the team's key players, an Irish international, didn't show up. He was the last of London Irish's three internationals to abandon ship. But I wasn't disappointed. All week he had been making a big deal in the media about whether he'd stay or go. I didn't care one way or another. I just wanted it settled so that I knew what I had to work with. In our team meeting at the beginning of that session conversation quickly turned to this subject and all that had been reported in the paper.

'Look,' I said. 'Let's be very clear. We need to sort this out so that we know where we stand. If he's a mate of yours, call him and tell him to go to Quins or Bath or whoever he's talking to. You may have an issue with what I am saying, but for goodness sake just tell him to get on with it because we have work to do. We can pull this thing off, and if we make it enjoyable and fun around here, players will be joining London Irish in droves just as quickly as this guy and the others left. It's happened to me before, it'll happen again. So let's get on with the business of playing rugby that we all enjoy. What do you call it? *The craic?'*

And that's exactly what we did. The players knew I was right, and I think they understood what I was saying and why I was saying it. It must have been tough for them, but it shows what tremendous dedication and trust they had for the team. With that alone a team can move mountains.

---

* **craic** noun [U] (ALSO crack) IRISH ENGLISH enjoyable time spent with other people, especially when the conversation is entertaining and amusing

Getting on with it

I really didn't try to do much in that first season with London Irish. As with Henley, the first year was really about consolidating the team and building the right foundations. Top of my list was keeping the training sessions light, fun and full of laughter. Right away I brought music into everything we did. Both at training and during the games, when players came onto the pitch or when they scored, the music blared through the loudspeaker system in the stands. It raised a few eyebrows, but it was fun and sent a clear message that things were changing.

I also introduced my preferences for a more expansive game, utilising every player on the pitch. This was a different message for the players, who had clearly never heard a coach talk like me before. They seemed to like what they heard, but the flip side of what I was saying was that everyone would have to be in great shape for that style of game to work effectively. There would be a good deal more running in the eighty minutes of the game than they were used to. But as I'd learned from my Henley experience, fitness isn't hard work at all when you're having fun.

When Mike Gibson first showed me around, I was pleasantly surprised to see that the stadium housed its own gymnasium. However when I saw what it looked like, I knew we had to find something else. With a little scouting around, I discovered St Mary's College not far down the road. It was a physical education college with a focus a little bit like Loughborough but on a smaller scale. The great thing was that it had a fantastic gym. It was there I met Angela Cumine, a conditioning and fitness expert, and asked her if she would oversee a regime of conditioning work with the players. When I introduced Angela to the team in one of our earlier sessions, it was obvious from their interest that my ploy of making fitness fun would work. The players began to get fit and to take this part of rugby seriously, and soon they were getting stronger and more powerful. Traditionally, London Irish had never been synonymous with fitness. Now Guinness and fags were replaced with nutrition and supplements.

Apart from putting enjoyment high on the priority list, getting organised, and putting the basics right, we didn't do anything hugely different that first year with London Irish. When you're consolidating a battered team, it really is the wrong time for too much radical thinking. I've always believed you have to get your foundations of team culture right and show people how you do things before you can build with new thinking and new strategies. Organisations, like people, can only handle so much change at any one point in time.

That doesn't mean my first year with London Irish wasn't exciting, though. On the contrary, this period of washing away the old and bringing in the new team culture, lifting the team spirit, is the most exciting time in the organisational development process. To most people a rising team spirit is like a long cold drink on a hot summer's day: very refreshing and tremendously rewarding.

One of my favourite players was a young guy named Rob Henderson who would go on to play for Ireland and the British Lions. Rob had a tough background. I recall asking him just before Christmas that year what he was doing for the holidays. After a bit of probing I found out he would be spending Christmas at the pub. So Rob spent that Christmas with us. It was an interesting time for him since Jayne and I had just had our third child, Freddie, and Rob found himself in a somewhat domestic scene – I think he held the baby while Jayne cooked Christmas lunch. The kids still laugh about how they put raisins in his open mouth as he snored peacefully on the sofa after lunch. He was great company. The week after Rob won his first cap for Ireland, he called in at home unannounced. He left Jayne with a Tesco bag. In it was his first Irish jersey with a note in it saying, 'Thanks, you deserve this more than I do.' It was a great moment. The highest objective for any coach or club is for your players to represent their country, no matter which country. In many ways it's why you coach and do everything possible for them, to see your players develop and do well on and off the pitch. I wrote Rob a note thanking him for his shirt and telling him that when he eventually grew up I would return it to him. I still have that green jersey at home today.

As with Henley, my first year of coaching at London Irish was one of my best ever. We didn't have the talent of our competitors, so we had to work harder than everyone else to compete. It's one of my proudest years as a coach. Our team didn't win the competition outright, but finished in the middle of the Table and had won enough games to stay in the Second Division. Towards the end we were even winning all our games confidently.

Everything was going well. We had also stopped the huge momentum of decline that had engulfed the club. My prediction was proved correct. We were having so much fun in training and playing that very soon the exodus of players stopped and the tide reversed. By the end of that 1994–95 season, London Irish had attracted a large new pool of quality players. On principle, I didn't want any of the international players who had abandoned our sinking ship back in the club, and I made sure they knew that.

I made it clear to the boys that the next year would be all about promotion back into the First Division, nothing else would matter. Only then did I start bringing in the more radical ideas that would eventually lead to our promotion, and my downfall at the club.

Irish talent

Once again when things were settling and we had created a strong team spirit and culture, I began to prepare for winning in the next season. The first rule is, you've got to have the raw material, so in one of our pre-training meetings near the end of our first season I put it to the team.

'Let's just imagine for a minute that we could pick any Irish players we wanted to play for us here at London Irish, who would you choose to be in your team?'

'Oh, come on, Clive, that would never happen,' came one unsuspecting reply.

'Fair enough, but let's just say you wanted the best player in the Irish backline, who would it be?'

'Pure speculation?' I nodded. 'That's easy. You'd pick Conor O'Shea straight off. He's young, he's brilliant ... but you'd never get him to leave Ireland.'

'OK, fair enough. It would never happen,' I assured them. 'And if you were looking for one really talented Irish forward, who would you pick?'

The players were all looking at me as if I was daft now, but still they humoured me.

'Well, all right. You'd want to go for Gabriel Fulcher. He's the shining light of the Irish team, but you'd never get him to come to London to play in the Second Division. Donal Lenihan would never allow that to happen.'

Donal Lenihan was the manager of the Irish international rugby team. At that time the Irish Rugby Union were trying to get all their players back in Ireland, and not into English clubs – a policy I would have put in place myself if the positions were reversed – so there was a bit of friction between London Irish and the Irish Rugby Union at the time.

'Yes, maybe you're right. OK then, let's get on with training . . .' and with that I turned and walked onto the pitch to start the session.

Minor miracles

Within two months, Conor O'Shea was on the pitch at London Irish for our pre-season training in the 1995–96 season. Gabriel Fulcher joined the club soon afterwards. I'd had to fly to Ireland several times to pull it off, and they did take a little convincing, but in the end both had agreed to come to London and play.

To the players and many of the club's supporters I had just performed a miracle akin to turning water into wine. Unfortunately, Irish rugby was less pleased with my resourcefulness. I heard that Donal Lenihan was furious at having his best players taken from under his nose. Of course, Gabriel and Conor were still just as eligible to play for Ireland, so I did not entirely see what all the fuss was about, especially as I saw it as key to my job in making sure they did. It was simply that they weren't playing in Ireland for Irish clubs. Part of my arrangement with the players was to give them my assurance that I would support them in playing for Ireland and all the necessary time to do this.

My move would come back to bite me many years later. Donal Lenihan was appointed manager of the 2001 Lions tour to Australia. (I still wonder why he was chosen over so many other great candidates for the job, seeing that he was an amateur official and the game had been professional for five years.) It may be that old animosity had something to do with my not being considered to coach that Lions side. I would have loved to do the job. Choosing the Kiwi Graham Henry pretty much said what Lenihan thought of me, because at the time of Graham's appointment I was coach of England and we were really going well. As a past British Lion I was disappointed at the decision to make Graham coach, and not just for myself. I felt there were other candidates from the British Isles who were also being overlooked.

Of course, getting Conor and Gabriel to London took a little more than just a smile and a good word. This was still the amateur era after all, and a big move is a big expense. This time Ann was only too pleased that Sales Finance could help, but that certainly wasn't the only attraction. Like most elite athletes, they were passionate about the challenge. All I had to do was to explain to these two intelligent young men just where London Irish was headed, and to ask them along too. To the competitive personality this was an irresistible challenge, but I had to back it up with actions. With Conor and Gabriel on board, that is exactly what I started to do.

Slip-catching

I bought a slip-catching machine, a training tool used by cricket players to improve reflexes and reaction time.

'Right, I've got something new for our training,' I said, pointing to the device on the pitch behind me.

'What's that then, a sagging park bench? You English don't build things like you used to. It's sunken in the middle!' shot out Conor O'Shea.

It's a good way to describe the look of the slip-catching machine. With its metal frame and wooden slats it does look like a piece of outdoor furniture, and it is low to the ground like an oblong concave shell, like a hammock hanging from a tree or when you cup your hands in front of you.

'No, Conor, it's a slip-catching machine. To be the best in this league, we'll have to play a fast game. Quick passing and quick reactions are critical, and not skills with which most of you are blessed! *The ball moves faster than a player can run*,' I said, quoting Jim Greenwood.

'Conor, go over there and stand about fifteen feet away from the end.'

He did so. Picking up the cricket ball at my feet I said, 'Right. Here it comes. Are you ready?'

'Yup, give her all you've got,' he said with a confident grin, arms at his side.

I wound up in a side-arm baseball-style and threw the ball with a bit of speed at the bottom of the concave bowl. The ball launched out of the other end, accelerating as it kicked right off a wooden slat and flew straight at Conor's head, missing his left ear by an inch. He never saw it coming. But he didn't move a muscle or even flinch.

The laughter from the bench died instantly. In the empty silence of the vast stadium Conor stood upright, looked over his left shoulder at the ball bouncing to a stop some fifty yards away, then turned back to face me. I had come within an inch of possibly killing him.

'See, when I say you have absolutely no reactions, I'm right.' Inwardly I made a mental note to check if my insurance policy covered me for killing a player with a cricket ball.

'Hey, that was fast! . . . Right, let's do it again!' he said with a huge grin, probably not even realising how close he had just come to visiting the local morgue.

We all had a laugh. The slip-catching machine was an instant hit. The whole team came off the bench and crowded around. Four to a side, they fell in to replace anyone who dropped a ball or let it slip past. It quickly became a very competitive and very fast game. They loved it. From that moment on, the slip-catching machine became a permanent part of our training programme.

Conor's last stand

One of the toughest skills to teach any athlete is how to think. Even my best players at London Irish were so imbued with the traditional way of playing rugby that it took all of my creative efforts to change their level of thinking. Whenever I hear people say they do something 'because that's the way it's always been done' it's an obvious sign that I'm about to challenge conventional wisdom.

'OK, guys, we're going to try something a little different this weekend,' I said one Tuesday night at training. 'I want you to switch around during the game. Conor, you're our fastest runner and you can jump the highest, so I want you to stand with the forwards during our kick-offs. You'll have a better chance of getting to the ball first and I think we can win possession right from the start.'

The players exchanged puzzled looks.

'I can't do that,' said Conor.

'What do you mean? Why not?'

'I'm a full-back. Full-backs don't stand there with the forwards at kick-off.'

'Conor, hang on. Listen to what you're saying. Can't you see? That's exactly why we must do it that way.'

He just stared at me as if I was coming from another planet.

'Just because you have a 15 on your back, you think you have to play like a full back. If I put a 2 on your back, you probably wouldn't even be able to run out on the pitch – you'd be paralysed by an identity crisis. *Am I a hooker or am I a full-back?* But think about it: what does it matter what position you play or what number you wear? It's a game with thirty men and a ball. We're here to win regardless of what we're *supposed* to be doing. You should all be playing as if there weren't *any* numbers on your back. There are no rules in rugby to say we cannot do this.'

Now they were really looking at me as if I'd lost it. But I just knew we had to do it.

That night, when I faxed the players' list through to the secretary responsible for the programme on the weekend, I just numbered the players in alphabetical order based on their surname.

The man called me next day saying I must have made a mistake, the numbers were wrong. I had to tell him three times that the numbers were right, and that it was exactly how I wanted them on the spectators' programme notes. But he bottled out, leaving the numbers the way they normally would be. When I saw the programme on game day I was furious. *Why can't they understand?*

I marched right back into the changing room.

'OK, everyone, shirts off, and line up in alphabetical order.'

I waited till they were all lined up and continued, 'Now hand your jersey to the guy next to you. I want the player this end of the line wearing No 1, and the player at that end of the line wearing No. 15, and everybody in between in sequence.'

'We can't do that! The other side won't know who to mark!'

They just didn't get it.

To their credit, they eventually did what I asked. We needed a few shirts changes due to sizing problems but we got there in the end. Then I went to the announcer's box and let him know there had been a few last-minute changes in the line-up. By the time I got back to my place on the bench, the players were just coming onto the pitch.

'Ladies and gentlemen, please welcome your very own London Irish to the pitch!' came the announcer over the loudspeakers. The music started blaring as the players made their entrance. Normally there would be a loud roar of support from the packed stadium, but this time, after a brief shout, there was just a confused murmur.

'I've been informed of a few last-minute changes in the line-up, ladies and gentlemen,' gabbled the announcer. 'There's . . . Well it looks like . . . Ladies and gentlemen, there are *fifteen* changes from your programme in the line-up today.'

There was disbelief in the stands, and on the field it wasn't much better. Everyone was so confused, but I thought it was one of the most amusing things I'd ever seen. All the same, I was doing it for a good reason. As soon as the ref blew his whistle for the kick-off, everything came together.

After only a moment's confusion, the team began to play rugby.

Real rugby. Nothing to do with numbers, titles or traditional ways of playing.

As their confidence grew, it was awesome to watch. Without their regular numbers, they were playing what they saw, not to their positions or the way rugby had traditionally told them to play. It was the best rugby we'd played all year. And in one way the men had been quite right: the opposition didn't know what to do or who to mark.

We won the game by a wide margin. From that point on the players were willing to try anything in order to improve. They'd all made a huge leap in their ability to think about the game. I only wish a small minority of the more stalwart, hard-nosed and vocal members of the club had learned the lesson as well.

All the same, everyone seemed happy enough when London Irish blitzed the Second Division and won promotion back into the First Division at the end of the 1995–96 season. It was fortunate timing for the club. Although no one in England rugby seemed to have quite caught on, the International Rugby Board had voted to make the game fully professional just six months before. Being in the First Division that first full professional year would be fantastic, and a major opportunity to recruit other Irish players who would want to come and play a higher standard of rugby week in week out than was currently available in Ireland.

I wouldn't survive as coach to see it through.

Annual General Bleating

I had coached the first XV team to win the league, and promotion back into the big time, so I expected a little bit of a hero's welcome at the Annual General Meeting. But the reception I received was quite the opposite. It turned out that my various brain waves and new ideas had been upsetting some people. Some members at London Irish proved to be a conservative bunch who fancied their traditions, and the heart pacemakers had gone into the danger zone over the rugby jerseys. I couldn't see what they were complaining about. Hadn't we won the match?

By the time of the Annual General Meeting in July, however, there were apparently several factions amongst the voting members who thought I was getting a little too big for my boots and it was time to sort me out. I had tried to remove myself from the politics of the member body. My job was coaching, and as long as the team performed, I assumed everybody would be happy. We had just pulled off a minor miracle by winning promotion back into the top division in two years. By all rights the club could have been languishing at the bottom of the Third Division if it hadn't been for our quick turnaround. As I sat in the AGM next to Ann, listening to general business, I couldn't believe my ears when a special agenda item was brought up. Instead of being rewarded for our efforts, it seems one or two people had something else in mind. Early in general business a motion was put forward for discussion of a special amendment to the club's constitution.

It took me a while to work out what they were getting at, but it became clear soon enough. One member seemed to be pushing a motion that London Irish should write into their constitution that only people of *Irish* descent could be involved in management of the club, with exceptions to be at the discretion of the committee. Not players. Just management. As far as I could tell, that meant me.

No. Surely that can't be right? I must be hearing things. Membership, even at club management level, wasn't about your nationality. It was about performance and ability. It shouldn't have mattered where any of the management team were from, just as long as they were doing the best possible job to support winning in rugby. Memories of my Welsh Schoolboy experience bubbled to the surface. As I listened to the nonsense going on around me, my emotions began to boil.

I raised my hand and waited to be recognised by the floor. Next to me, Ann had a very worried look on her face. She knew what I was thinking.

'The chair recognises Mr Woodward.'

Standing up I posed a question. 'Let me get this straight. You want to pass a motion that says anyone who isn't Irish can't be a part of the management of the club. Is that right?'

'Yes, Clive, that is the subject of the motion on the floor, but not necessarily my or any other committee member's view. Can I just point out that in a democratic club every member with the correct support is allowed to table motions such as this on any subject matter,' answered the chairman.

'Hang on. When I started this job two years ago it was on the condition that there would be none of this nonsense, that I'd have free rein to choose the players I wanted, be they Irish, English or Scandinavian for all I care. Now you're telling me you want to change all that?'

'No, no. That's not right. This ruling doesn't apply to players. Only to management,' returned the chairman, clearly on shaky ground.

'I'm English. So that means me, right?'

The roomful of 300 Irish members were starting to get excited. This looked like getting lively.

'No, of course not, Clive. The committee would have a discretionary veto to waive that rule in your case. No, no. That would never apply to you . . .'

'This is absolute nonsense. This is totally utterly wrong,' I cut in sharply.

Just then an angry old man in a faded brown suit and ancient club tie jumped up in the front row, turned around and pointed his long bony wrinkled finger right at me. 'We know what you're trying to do. You're trying to turn this into a whole team full of English players! You're trying to make this club an English club,' he shouted.

Well, Irish emotions erupted. The whole room burst into complete chaos. Everybody seemed to be screaming at once. I just stood there, holding my ground. This wasn't right, and I wouldn't have it. As the chairman tried to bring the room to order, I picked up my things and began walking towards the door. I stopped to address the chair once more.

'Look, I'm sorry. I wish you well, but I'm off. I'll have no part in a club that sanctions discrimination at any level. I thought I'd made that clear when I joined. Now I feel I've wasted two years of my life.' And with that I wheeled around and walked out of the building.

Ann was coming after me trying to calm me down and help me collect my senses, but to no avail. I wasn't going back. Apparently, the remainder of that AGM was a fierce and brutal argument between opposing factions of old and new. I was ashamed, not just for the actions of the committee, but even more for how I'd allowed the politics of the organisation to affect my position. And I was especially sad for the players. They didn't deserve this scandal in the moment of their triumph.

The newspapers the next day were rife with rumour and innuendo.

Out on my ear

After a few weeks things did calm down. With much reassurance from the committee that it was all a complete misunderstanding, and that the motion had not been voted in, I finally relented and agreed to coach the 1996–97 season. I should have listened to my instincts, though. A man should know when it's time to move on. In October of that season, my time at London Irish was over anyway. In a final twist of fate, I even chose my own successor, and this time I would never come back.

Coaching was still a hobby for me. I was passionate about it, but it was a part-time passion at that. My business wasn't getting any easier. During those two years at London Irish I devoted almost all my time to winning promotion for London Irish. Yet despite the fact that I was spending a greater proportion of my time in rugby, our leasing business was expanding. The team at Sales Finance had expanded to thirteen people. Our revenues were growing steadily and our net profit was still healthy – it was a great credit to Ann and Jayne that we kept everything going so well.

However by the end of the 1996 season I could see that both business and rugby would demand more of my time in the following season. But I knew I'd reached my limits, so even before the final that year I had begun searching for a full-time assistant coach to help out at London Irish.

During the summer I met quite a few candidates, and the stand-out option was Willie Anderson, an Irishman through and through. Better yet, I'd managed to convince the committee that there should be room in the budget for a salary for Willie as he was a professional coach and would work for London Irish on a full-time basis. That would leave me confident and assured that at least someone of real quality would be there for the players who, in the new professional era, were devoting more and more of their days to rugby training.

In October 1996, just a few weeks after the beginning of the season, Duncan Leopold, a member of the committee, met me at the changing room door on one of the evenings prior to training. He blocked the door and held his hand up to my chest.

'You can't go in there, Clive.' He was looking down as he said it, shifting from foot to foot.

'Why not? I'm the coach. I want to talk to the boys.'

'No . . . the meeting was re-arranged to start half an hour ago and you're not the coach any more. Your services are no longer required.

I mean . . . I mean, with Willie Anderson coaching full-time, we don't think it would work you doing it part-time. And we owe it to the players, you know, to give them a full-time coach.'

'Oh, I see.' It was apparent now what had happened. They'd approached Willie Anderson to take my job. The coach I'd found for them. It was amazing really. It was classic rugby politics at its best.

'Fine. Please pass on my best to all the players.' I turned and walked out of the stadium. I swear I heard a sigh of relief behind me. I suppose he feared a heated exchange. There was just no point.

The end of another eventful era

The circumstances may have been exceptional, but it sounds far more dramatic than it really was. For the most part, I had tremendous respect for everyone at London Irish as I drove out of the grounds for the last time, but I marvelled at how just a few wilful people could sway the opinions of the majority in a representative organisation. At that moment, I vowed never to leave myself exposed to the political machinations of a representative body again. For someone coming from a small business background, it just didn't make sense. That said, London Irish have a long history of success as a club and are still one of the top Premiership rugby clubs today. They must be doing something right.

It did seem a great shame to me that I left when I did. Even though we had only just been promoted back into the First Division, I knew we could have won the Premiership that year if we hadn't become lost in ludicrous distractions. With the Irish, as at Henley, it was just as I thought: get one big fish and the rest follow. As soon as we were winning with Conor O'Shea and Gabriel Fulcher on board, the top Irish players followed in droves once they could see this turnaround since my arrival two years earlier. London Irish now had no less than seven Irish internationals in its first XV team, with five more who went on to represent Ireland at an international level later. I think we would have been unstoppable in the English Premiership. Even now whenever I meet with these players, David Humphreys, Justin Bishop, Rob

Henderson, Justin Fitzpatrick, Conor O'Shea, Jeremy Davidson, Tyrone Howe, Victor Costello, Niall Woods, Malcolm O'Kelly, Gary Halpin and Kieran Dawson, it's always a great pleasure to catch up with them and shake their hands. They were a great group to coach and I still take huge delight in seeing them play for Ireland.

Within two years, all but three of those players had left the club, with Conor O'Shea as one of the remaining stalwarts. I have a huge respect for Conor. He quickly became the heart and soul of that club, epitomising all that is good and great about the Irish. His dedication and his contribution to his club over the years have been extraordinary. I was delighted to see that he was appointed chief executive of London Irish just recently. It was a horrible injury that put an end to his shining international playing career, and it was great to see that he has found a role in the club that meant so much to him. Of course, Conor did have some incentive to stay in London. He met, proposed, and is now married to Ann Heaver's beautiful daughter Alex.

The calm between storms

My two seasons with London Irish were certainly tempestuous – I'll give the Irish credit for being passionate about their interests. The exposure to club rugby in this manner was a fantastic learning ground for me, though. I reckoned that if I could survive and flourish at this club, and leave with my reputation intact, then I could do just about anything in rugby. Coaching England to win the World Cup would be a walk in the park in comparison!

They were great days and we tried to do many, many things differently. But we also would have moved mountains for each other, and you simply can't buy that kind of dedication. I realised that in smaller organisations, like Henley for example, you could do risky things and get away with them. But when you're leading bigger sides with higher profiles, those different strategies can attract a lot of adverse attention. It wasn't as if I was reckless in my intentions, I just didn't give much thought to how my actions would be perceived by other people. Winning, getting promoted, that was all I cared about. But I began to realise that you can't truly win unless all of the stakeholders in the organisation feel that they're winning right alongside you. It was an invaluable lesson.

I wasn't too upset in the end to leave London Irish, even if the circumstances did leave a bad taste, because deep down I knew it had to be done. The early years in the professional era were very difficult for all the Premiership clubs. There had been no warning and no preparation for the transition, and hence there wasn't much room in the budgets for either players or coaches. It would be years before commercial interests were balanced in these new professional environments, and indeed even today, some nine years later, many clubs have yet to pull their finances into line. Just as Duncan Leopold at London Irish had said, there was no room for me as a professional coach in London Irish as my business was too profitable for me to justify or even consider being a professional coach.

In the weeks after London Irish began playing in the Premiership with professional players, I'd resigned myself to the fact that my time as a coach was probably very limited. That was why Willie Anderson was there. I had yet again reached the level where business and rugby as a coach were no longer compatible.

No, I'd be happy to take on a part-time assistant position just to keep my toe in the water. Now I could focus on my business again. At the very least Jayne and Ann would be happy that the business no longer had to heavily subsidise my desire to be a successful rugby coach – this would certainly help our cash flow. But it was my time and attention that had been lacking. We had grown very quickly over the years, but like many organisations that experience explosive growth, our people were stretched, strained and stressed; not at all the level of enjoyment I put so much emphasis on.

Over a beer at the pub Jayne, Ann and I had lamented the good old days when there were just three of us working out of our garage in Pinkney's Green: low on creature comforts but high on good times and lots of laughs, where we celebrated every little victory. That would be my goal, to get back to enjoying my business life again.

Who knows, maybe I could even get back into my golf. It had been a great passion and a healthy release ever since I'd begun to take it seriously in Sydney after I quit rugby at Manly. Maybe I could have another go at getting my handicap down to scratch, a long-time aspiration.

And so that's exactly what I did.

But within a month the phones were ringing with clubs looking for a new coach. I was most delighted when Andy Robinson at Bath was among the first to call. We had had a great working relationship coaching the England Under-21s over the previous couple of years, and I think Andy was happy that I was only looking for an assistant position. This fitted in with his plans. He was Bath's first full-time professional coach, and was in transition from player to coach. I was at pains to make it clear that under no circumstances did I want to get involved in the politics of the club. He understood perfectly. Andy and I quickly re-formed our formidable coaching partnership, this time at Bath.

The next six months for me were a magic time once again. We tightened the ship at Sales Finance & Leasing. I employed a driver so that I could make the most of my time in the car for the two hours to Bath every Tuesday and Thursday for some great sessions with the backs, who were very special players, including the likes of Jerry Guscott and the then England captain Phil de Glanville. The whole family enjoyed the weekend matches at Bath and we quickly fell into their great club environment.

If you'd told me that within nine months I'd be appointed as England coach, I'd have said pigs might fly.

10

MY FIRST DAY WITH THE TEAM

One of the other stumbling blocks to becoming the first full-time coach of England was the need for the RFU to buy my release from the Bath RFC. Once that had been agreed I left Bath and Andy. I have the greatest respect for him and had enjoyed our relationship with the Under-21's and at Bath. I held him in such esteem that when the time was right for him and England we rejoined forces, but that was for the future.

For now here we are in September 1997 and I was due to face the press as the coach of England.

Flash, flash!

Click, click, *flash!*

I'm startled as I walk through the door.

Flash, click! *Flash, flash!*

The cameras are going off like Chinese fireworks in front of me. I'd been told what it would be like, but nothing had prepared me for the intensity of the experience – all eyes are on me. It's not just the dozens of people in the room, but the potential millions through the lens of the camera. At least on the rugby pitch there's the distraction of the game. Here it's all in my face. I am surrounded by five seasoned veterans who guide me towards the two draped folding tables at the head of the room. Six seats. I guess mine is the one behind the pile of microphones.

The five giants of the Rugby Football Union . . . and me. To my left are Roger Uttley, Cliff Brittle and Don Rutherford. On my right sit Fran Cotton and Bill Beaumont.

There's a glow on my face as I take my seat. The heat is coming from banks of lights that blind me as I lift my head to face the room. I look around, trying to see past the bright lights and television cameras.

The lenses seem so dark and bottomless, yet penetrating, like I could fall right into them.

'Whatever you do, don't squint!' I was told. 'It will make you look beady, shifty and mean. Just keep your eyes open and focus on a place just below the lights. Your eyes will adjust.'

I can make out fifty or so human shapes in front of me, sitting in two columns of what must be ten or more rows, pens at the ready. They're just shadows silhouetted by the penetrating lights.

I'm not sure quite what to do or how this kind of thing should start. It's funny the obvious things you forget to ask. *Do I start, or do they?*

The RFU media director, Richard Prescott, answers that question for me.

'Ladies and gentleman, the press conference will now begin.' I sit up straight as steely determination sets in.

'Clive . . .' 'Clive . . .'

'Clive, how do you feel . . .'

Deep breath. Here we go . . .

Probing for weakness

'How do you feel about your appointment as England coach?'

'I'm very excited, massively excited. There is a tremendous opportunity in England rugby at the moment, and we fully intend to put everything into building a winning side.'

'How do you feel about being the second choice for coach?'

'Second choice? You flatter me. I think I was more like fifth choice.'

There's almost a pause, but most of the room are starting to chuckle. My smile encourages more laughs. If the truth be known, there are probably ten people whom some of the RFU committee would have liked to have chosen ahead of me. Maybe I'm sitting here because I'm the only English coach who is actually available and is not locked up in a long-term contract elsewhere.

Technically speaking, I had never been head coach in the First Division, now called the Zurich Premiership. My last season with London Irish in the Premiership lasted one month before being cut short, and I'd only been an assistant coach at Bath for a few months.

Things were going well there, but nothing that could possibly highlight me as first choice, let alone the most proven coach in elite England rugby.

'I may not have been first choice, but I will approach it believing I will do better than anyone else the RFU may have chosen. I have no illusions. I'll be judged on results.'

'Clive,' they erupt again, once they realise I'm finished. They have to wait for me to stop talking so that they can get their sound bites. One voice at the back of the room wins out.

After a few seconds of silence my colleagues at the head table turn to look at each other, as do the journalists. I feel the expectation to continue.

'What style of play are you going for?'

There is always great debate over styles of play; ten-man, fifteen-man, expansive rugby, plan A or plan B, etc. He was fishing. I wasn't biting.

'Let's face it, this job is about winning Test matches.' I refused to declare a preference for a particular style of play. 'My view is, our style has to change to suit our opponent. We have to be good at every kind of play.'

Roger doesn't completely miss out. He's well-known to many of these journalists as he was England coach in the early nineties. He fields a couple of questions about his role as manager of the team before attention soon returns to me.

'Clive, who are your coaching influences?'

I can't see who asked it, but I think for a moment about the question. It's one of my favourites.

'I think the key is to start with a blank sheet of paper. You don't copy anyone. You may end up with similar points, but that's because you've come to the conclusion rationally. The All Blacks are the best side in the world by some distance at the moment, but we won't copy them. We have to work out the best way forward ourselves. I saw a photograph the other day of John Hart, the All Black coach, carrying a huge dice around at a training session. Why? Was it just a bluff? I bet there will be half a dozen people doing the same within a few months. That's just not the way to build a world-class team. I have strong ideas, and I can see tremendous potential. I can't wait to get started this morning.'

Dangerous thrust

'You don't have much experience at this level. How do you know your way will be the right way?'

'There's no right way to do anything. You either win, or you don't. For example, is it wrong to be a millionaire at twenty-one? You either are or you're not. It's the same with coaching. Apprenticeships are not a prerequisite. I have a lot of respect for Alan Jones, the former Australian coach. I spent a few years playing for Manly in the eighties. Jones knew stuff-all about rugby. He arrived at Manly with a business and political background. Within a year he'd won the Premiership and within two years he had won a Grand Slam over here as Australia's coach. He did it by intellect, by studying what needed to be done. He left nothing to chance. A lot of people didn't like him. I do. He had an outstanding mind.'

A room full of pens are scribbling madly, heads down, the floor completely mine.

This is going all right. Let's see if we can bump it up a notch then.

'Let me make this absolutely clear. I am the first professional coach. I'll turn to any quarter that might help us achieve our aim: the business world and even to other sports besides rugby. We'll leave no stone unturned in our search for excellence.'

More mad scribbling. A moment later . . .

'What will you do in your sessions with the team that will be different from your predecessors?'

'We have four big matches coming up in less than eight weeks. That's no time to do anything different. We're simply going to focus on thinking correctly, and the England training sessions will be dedicated to basics – lineouts, scrums and defence.'

Leadership challenge

'When will you announce a captain and can you give us an indication of who the contenders are in your mind?'

'There is no rush and I want to make sure I get this right. We have some outstanding people, especially Martin Johnson who has done great in the summer tour with the Lions. I have some criteria I use for choosing the captain and I just need a few more days in order to get this right.'

The question is hanging in the air, but I refuse to name a captain.

'It's very important that the captain is totally at one with the coach in his views and philosophy. He is the man who has to have the vision and the leadership skills to pass on what the coach is trying to do. I see no reason to saddle someone with that responsibility for scores of games. I'll be picking our team first and only then choosing the captain. He must first be worth his place in the team.'

The media director, who had been standing at the front of the room on my left the entire time, as if on guard, steps in at this point.

'Ladies and gentlemen, just two more questions, please.'

'Clive, rugby has been through a tumultuous time in the transition to professionalism. Some would say England rugby has suffered at the top level. What is the most important thing you're bringing to the table to turn that around?'

I'm passionate about this one. I've been waiting for this question.

'I think the most important thing to me is getting the right coaching and back-up team in place. People are so much more important to me than plans. It's got to be fun. I've never known a business to work if it hasn't been an enjoyable environment.

'Last question, please,' announces Richard Prescott.

'Clive, you have a rather punishing season ahead of you, including ten Tests against the big three southern-hemisphere sides. How would you judge success over the next twelve months?'

'I think I'll be happy just so as long as I don't see Cliff Brittle here in an emergency press conference having to announce that he has complete faith in me!' I give them another smile – and get a good chuckle back from Cliff.

'Thank you, ladies and gentlemen, for your attendance today,' the media director interrupts. 'We have press releases at the back for everyone. Please feel free to contact me or my colleagues in the media department for clarification on any issues.'

All of us at the head table stand up in unison. The attention is off us as a roomful of journalists move to phone their editorial teams, begin writing on their laptop computers or talk with their colleagues.

I can feel a few curious stares, sizing me up.

I'm just glad to be done with it. I think it went well, but I'll soon find out. The six of us file out the door we came in, back into a dimly lit hallway in what's known as the tennis centre at Bisham Abbey, a long-time training ground for England rugby and several other national sports teams.

No sooner does the door close than Cotton, Uttley and Beaumont spin round as Cliff Brittle and Don Rutherford engage in conversation in front of us.

'Bit intense the first time, isn't it?' says Uttley who's been there before.

'Oh, it was all right.' I say it casually, as if it hadn't been extremely intimidating.

Cotton and Beaumont exchange a knowing look.

'You did fine, Clive,' says Fran with a hand to my shoulder. Bill nods in agreement. They're old hands at this game. 'Just keep it up. If you handle the team as well as you did the media, you're off to a good start.'

'Thanks, guys. Thanks for your support. I'd better get on with it, then. I've got a roomful of players waiting. You coming, Roger?' I say, shaking hands all round, Cliff having joined us.

'Be with you in a few minutes,' Roger says.

'Good luck, Clive,' Bill says.

'Thanks, Bill, and it's time to get started.' I make my way to the nearest exit.

A good beginning

My first press conference looks better on paper than it probably was in reality. I felt pretty good about it though. I was confident, and I didn't hide, which I think the journalists there appreciated. That said, it did take them quite a while to decide finally whether my approach was genuine or pretence.

I've had much better press conferences since then, and certainly much worse. But it was a good beginning to a healthy relationship with the media that I like to think has strengthened in my tenure. I have never felt afraid or intimidated by the media, and have always been aware that they have their job to do, too. Over the years we have met regularly when not in Test-match situations, and we've all had a mutually good time. That first experience was different to what I expected though. When you see a press conference on television through the narrow view of the camera lens, the picture you get always seems so intense, so focused. Being in the room is almost completely the opposite. The apparent chaos has order and etiquette, a set of rules as to how it works. If I think about it, it's probably much the same in the way international rugby appears on television compared with what it's actually like in real life on the ground. It was good food for thought for me as I prepared to mould a new team. I was determined to be brutally honest with the media. Initially some called it naïve, but over time it worked. I never ever speak off the record, and if I know I've made an error, I own up to it and move on. You soon come to know that if you win you get a pat on the back, and if you lose, well, you got shot!

Bisham Abbey

For many years England rugby had used the facilities at Bisham Abbey for its training days with the team. I had been there as a player first with the Colts and then with the international squad as late as the mid-eighties, just fifteen years before. As I walked from the tennis centre to the main house I had a chance to observe the setting with a new set of eyes; as a coach instead of as a player.

Bisham Abbey is a government-run sports development facility near Marlow, west of London. It was the home training ground for a number of sports, from rugby to football and even hockey. Its grounds, covering some fifty acres, consist of various sports fields and facilities to accommodate the dozen or so different national sports teams training there through the year. The eastern side of the grounds held a large indoor tennis centre, behind which I had held my first press conference, and immediately to my left was a full-sized hockey pitch with artificial turf and full flood lighting. Next to that was a medical facility in a low brown brick building. To my right were full rugby and football pitches

– among the best quality pitches in England. There was, unfortunately, no gymnasium on site for weight training at that time.

We'll have to look into that.

Also on my right were the on-site accommodation facilities, a short and sprawling series of box-like two-storey buildings which could house around sixty players and coaches. The heavy, uninspiring design and the dark brown bricks made me put the date of the building at somewhere in the late sixties. By coincidence, Jayne and I and our three children had moved into the nearby village of Cookham, so thankfully I wouldn't be staying there. While the sporting grounds had always been kept in top-notch condition, even in the eighties when I last spent some time there, the rooms in the accommodation block felt tired and old. It looked like nothing had changed in the years since.

As I approached the old Abbey itself, the seventeenth-century roofline, ancient windows and mottled brickwork of the original building reminded me of its dark halls that I'd first walked when selected for the Colts in 1975. Like many old English estates, Bisham Abbey had a long heritage. To me as a player, the Abbey had felt like a natural extension of the amateur clubs of the time – a bit like a boarding school really, which was fine for a young lad not long from HMS *Conway*. However, walking up the drive as England's first full-time coach, it felt strange; slightly at odds with the professional era we were now entering. Still, it was nice to be on familiar ground as I prepared for the meeting with the players.

Laying on a bet

I stopped at my car to collect my notes, and as I closed the door I saw Austin Healey approaching with a grin. He clutched a folded newspaper in his hands. Austin was . . . well Austin; a great guy to have in your team, very passionate about playing for England, and as quick-witted as they come.

'Hi, Clive. Can I call you Clive? Did you see today's paper?'

He was holding out a copy of the paper, open at the sports pages. There had been a lot of speculation about who I would appoint as captain, and Austin was pointing to where Lawrence Dallaglio and

Martin Johnson had been listed by a bookmaker at odds of 2 to 1. Frankly I was surprised at the media interest.

'And look at me here.' Austin's name was right down the bottom of the list at 350 to 1.

'In my experience bookmakers are rarely wrong, Austin,' I said smiling. I didn't add that I had a greater chance of captaining the team that year than he did.

'No, no, you don't understand,' his grin returning. 'I can scrape together £20,000. If you can match it, well, that's £7,000,000 each! Just name me captain, and we're out of here!'

I have to admit there have been times over the last six years when I thought maybe I should have taken Austin up on his offer!

It was a great light-hearted introduction to the team. Thankfully, no matter how tough things would get over the next couple of years, there was always someone, especially Austin, to keep everything in perspective and to keep the enjoyment factor high.

Final preparation

The old musty smell of decades of cafeteria food hit me as I walked under the vaulted ceiling of what must have been the old chapel at Bisham Abbey. Most of the seventy top England players I had invited to this first meeting were sitting at long tables in the hushed quiet of what was now the dining hall. I really only knew a few to speak to. After all, I had only been coaching in the Premiership division for one season. I said a few brief hellos as I made my way to the back of the building and climbed the creaky stairs to the Elizabethan Room.

It was a long narrow room about five metres by twelve metres. The paint on the wood panelling was chipped and peeling. The patterned fabric wallpaper looked at least as old as the 150-year-old portraits on the wall. The fading, threadbare carpet covering a creaky old wooden floor had definitely seen better days. That room was certainly in keeping with the rest of the building. Bisham Abbey might have been adequate when I was young, but now it seemed the complete opposite of what I was trying to achieve. It was not at all the inspiring home of an England elite squad. Bisham Abbey has since had a refit.

At the time I'd not thought about changing the location of our training days – I had so many things on my mind to do and to arrange. It was to be some time and after a few harsh learning experiences until I realised that to be really successful I needed to manage completely and overhaul everything to do with the England team. Looking back, I should have changed it immediately. That would have been more in keeping with the new kind of thinking we would be applying to England rugby over the coming years.

The eighty chairs of odd colours, shapes and sizes seemed to pack the room to overflowing. Thankfully it wasn't a long session. In view of the large number of players who were there that day, I'd planned a quick team chat where I'd introduce myself and my thoughts to the players. After that it was home for everyone until the next scheduled training session in a couple of weeks. Our aim was to whittle the squad of players to twenty-five or twenty-six pretty quickly so that we could really focus on coaching and bringing the team together.

After checking that the room felt right, or at least as right as it was going to be, I walked into the adjoining King James Room to collect my thoughts. It was 10.45 a.m. The team meeting was scheduled to begin at 11.00 a.m.

In those few quiet moments, the distant emotion and disappointment of lost potential in my playing years bubbled to the surface. Coming back to Bisham Abbey, nearly fifteen years later, had been like stepping through time. I'd honestly forgotten what it was like coming here as a player. In the last few weeks since my appointment I'd focused so much on what I was going to *do* as coach that I forgot to think about how these players might actually be feeling right now.

Many of them had experienced relative success in the England team during the nineties. Three Grand Slam victories in the Five Nations was certainly a great accomplishment. Yet they hadn't yet realised their full potential – winning the World Cup and becoming the best team in the world.

In 1991 England had lost the final to Australia because they mistakenly changed to a completely new playing style a few days before the match, hoping to wrong-foot the Wallabies. They had dominated with their ten-man game in all the matches leading up to the last game and, by all rights, would have won if they'd stuck to their proven tactics. The World Cup is not the time to change anything so fundamental. I have no doubt that their decision still haunts those players even today. It was a hard lesson to learn.

In 1995 England was defeated by New Zealand in the semi-final of the World Cup where Jonah Lomu took the world by storm, scoring four tries against a shattered England defence. England seemed to me to be still celebrating their epic quarter-final win over Australia. After that New Zealand just took them apart.

Both were games England could have won had we been playing at our best. With my experiences at Henley and London Irish, I'd proved that with the right players and the best preparation you could win critical games. Even Lomu was later stopped when, with proper analysis, teams picked his weaknesses.

I was itching to apply my ideas to the England set-up. But I'd have to tread carefully with this team. Without their trust, we'd get nowhere. The group of players I could hear coming into the room now to take their seats included some who had just been through a tough Lions tour to South Africa. They were returning only to find wild speculation in the press about whether or not they'd even have a coach in the lead-up to what was billed as the toughest series of autumn Internationals in England's history.

I looked at my watch. Just then Roger opened the door and ducked his head in.

'Ready to go, Clive?'

'Yes. Be there in a minute.'

Checking my notes and collecting my thoughts one last time, I had a queasy nervous feeling in the pit of my stomach.

Like it or not, I had a job to do and it was time to go to work. With sweaty palms I pushed through the double set of doors into the meeting room.

Addressing the players

'Good morning, gentlemen, I'm Clive Woodward. I've spoken with many of you on the phone. It's nice to finally meet you all. You should all know Roger Uttley and John Mitchell,' I began, pointing out my two colleagues. John had been appointed as a part-time coach.

'Thanks for attending this first meeting. I am inheriting a job which I am deeply proud about, and it's a privilege to be standing here. The men you see around you are part of what we see as the squad of elite players from which we'll be drawing our international talent in the next few years. It's impossible to do anything constructive with such a large group, so I am going to pick a squad of thirty from you as a start and invite you back here for our next series of training days in two weeks' time to begin preparing for our four up-coming Internationals, starting with Australia at Twickenham on 15 November.

'If you're not chosen for the initial squad, rest assured I have no preconceived ideas on players. I will select you on your merit, your current form, and whether you're capable of playing the kind of game we'll be introducing at international level. Before we talk rugby, it's important we get off on the right foot here. So please listen carefully. Nothing you've ever done before in your international careers can prepare you for what lies ahead. From this day forth, it is vital we all start to think differently about how we play and how we train.'

Even Roger raised his eyebrow at that one.

'We're going to throw away all that we've ever done before as an international team, and we're going to rebuild it all from the ground up with a new way of thinking. We are all here to win but I now want to target the teams from the southern hemisphere. If we're ever going to be the best team in the world, and that's the only reason I'm here, we must get past these three teams, against whom we have a record of almost total failure. If you're here for any other reason, you're in the wrong room and you might want to leave now.' A few of the seasoned players cast a sideways glance at each other.

'Whatever greatness you think we might have achieved in the past means nothing, because I don't think England has ever produced a great side capable of dominating the world. We have produced very good sides, but in my opinion we have never produced a great side. Moving into the professional era, England rugby is under-achieving. We have a stronger player base, a larger support network, and a more dedicated fan base than any other international team in the world, yet we can't consistently dominate all of our European counterparts, let alone offer any menace to the real threat, the three superpower rugby teams in the southern hemisphere.

'That all stops now.

'My job is to create a world-class team. I intend to build a squad of elite players, playing an open style of rugby with a real emphasis on scoring tries. My objective is to play the fastest rugby in the world. It will demand the utmost fitness and skill levels. It won't be easy. You'll be driven harder than you've ever dreamed possible. But I can tell you this: it will be fun. If we can be successful in dominating world rugby, when we reach our goal you will consider your time with England rugby the pinnacle of your careers. Your rugby days will be the most exciting days of your lives. I still regret how in my playing days with England we never pushed the boat out – we never decided to take the world on.

'My aim is to develop a team capable of winning the World Cup in '99. To do this we have to build a squad that is capable of transforming the way we play. In order to win we'll have to take our opponents by surprise and confound them as to how they expect us to play. It will be high-risk, by definition, and we may take some time to convince critics who have got used to the subdued style that's been the hallmark of England rugby for decades.

'There is a reason the southern-hemisphere sides have dominated world rugby up 'til now. When I played for England, we'd be told at almost every coaching session what the All Blacks, or Wallabies, or Springboks were doing, and that we had to copy it. Every coaching book seemed to be written by a Kiwi. We were comfortable following others and nobody ever seemed to think we should aspire to be better than the southern-hemisphere teams.

'That all stops now, too.

'In the next year we have ten games against these sides we seem to revere. These teams can be beaten. I've lived in Australia and played with their best. They are human and their games and image have fundamental flaws. From now on, our sole aim will be not to copy them but to practise a game and a style of play that can beat them convincingly every time. We'll play, coach and manage rugby in a way that is so different to theirs that they will be copying us for a change. Until we achieve that, nothing else matters.

'And that's why we're here in this room. If we're to be the best, we first have to learn to think and plan better than everyone else. That means that from now on, when you're in the England camp, we'll spend more time thinking and planning than we will on the pitch. We won't be spending any time building fitness during these sessions. That will be done by you and us outside this environment. I fully expect you to be in the best physical condition possible, ready to play your best rugby, when you show up here. If you don't, you'll soon find yourself off the mailing list.

'The message for you all is simple. Get as fit as you can and maintain a high level of performance and you may find yourself in the England team for the greatest opportunity of your life. Any questions?

'Good. Let's get started. Grab your things and let's get down to the pitch.'

Nobody said a word as they filed out the door. Again, I could see a few of the older players exchanging looks. As if to say, *Here we go again. Just another coach who thinks he's going to change the world or something like that, won't last long!*

However, in other players like Back, Dawson, Dallaglio, Johnson, I could see I'd ignited their instincts for world success. These guys had tasted success with the Lions and if they could do the same with England – that would do fine. That would be enough for now. As long as I'd sown a seed, my actions would now have to speak louder than words – trust only comes after time and is achieved through the quality of your actions. Trust has to be earned.

We were on the right track, but would it be enough to perform well in our up-coming Internationals? Time would tell. With the first two major hurdles gone – facing the media and addressing the players – I could get on with the job of planning my coaching strategy.

It's no wonder that when I first met Don Rutherford in the reception at Rugby House I was keen to get to work. Although ideas were developing in my head for all the things I'd want to do differently, there would only be time for small changes, particularly in our thinking, for this autumn's series. With only seven weeks until our Test match against Australia and just two weeks until our next training camp at Bisham Abbey, I had so much to pull into place and so little time to prepare.

11

THINKING DIFFERENTLY ABOUT THE BUSINESS OF RUGBY

Eventually an office was found for me on the northern end of the second floor at Rugby House. It was there, the day after my first session with the team, that I began laying out the situation before me. Without really realising it, I began thinking about England rugby as I would my small business. Indeed, now England rugby *was* my business, or at least the elite international team. My small-business mindset would soon prove absolutely vital.

In commerce you learn to be very clear about managing outcomes. You have to. If you don't align your resources, deliver your product and put more money in the bank than you spend, then your business will end in misery. It's a simple equation.

For most business, including my leasing company, the biggest pressure is the time it takes to produce results. Office space, equipment and people – or overheads – all cost the same to run on a weekly basis whether you're earning the revenue or not. The trick is, then, to keep your discretionary costs low, hire the best people within your budget, and maximise your financial returns in the shortest possible time. In larger corporations where available financial resources are high, executives have more tools and better people at their disposal to plan for and manage new enterprises.

However in a small business like my leasing company, starting on a shoestring from a garage in Pinkney's Green, the owner is generally the only resource the business has to work with. Success is generally built on raw determination and the smell of a good idea. The mindset of a small-business person is literally an enthusiasm for starting from scratch with just a few resources to pull off minor miracles. It's actually quite a fun game, and hugely rewarding if you get it right. Turning my thought process to England rugby, one thing I quickly learned is that I had scarce resources with which to work.

I began to examine them.

First, time with the players.

We had a good group to select from, many of them senior and experienced campaigners, but over the course of a year I didn't have much time to work with them. We had twelve games planned from September that year to September the next, each with three full days of preparation in the week prior to the northern-hemisphere Tests. The Test-week schedule hadn't changed for years. Players would travel on Tuesday to arrive at the Petersham Hotel in Richmond, London by Tuesday night. We then had three days to train and prepare before a Saturday match.

Only there were no rugby pitches at the Petersham. It was the team hotel because of its close proximity to Twickenham, just a few miles away. Training sessions were conducted mostly at nearby pitches owned by the Bank of England, an organisation similar to the bank representative side I'd played for in my first year of club rugby working for the NatWest bank. Moving back and forth in buses and cars to the training pitch several times a day wouldn't exactly be the most efficient way to run things. The team only trained at Twickenham stadium itself for one light session the afternoon before the match. I'd have to look into that.

In addition to days during Test weeks, the RFU had negotiated with the clubs to release the players for an additional seven days during the year for training sessions at Bisham Abbey.

Doing my maths, here's what I discovered.

11 matches × 4 days of Test week	= 44 days
(3 days preparation plus 1 day for the match)	
+ 7 training days in the year	= 7 days
Total number of days with players in a year	= *51 days!*

That meant I would have roughly fifty-one days in the next calendar year – on average one day per week – in which to train, prepare and play with the best rugby players in the country against the best teams in the world. When you compare that with a business situation, most of us work fifty weeks a year, five days a week, which means that in business we have roughly 250 days in which to communicate, train, and do our work. Looking at it that way, it would take me roughly five rugby years to move as far with the rugby team as I might in one year with a business team.

On top of that, every player came from a club where there was a completely different set of plays, calls and playing styles, as well as attitudes to being an England elite player – many coaches in the Premiership were not English. New players would have huge learning curves and every player would have to discard completely what they learned in the England camp to take up their own club's coaching preferences. Put in this context we were all going to have to be unbelievably resourceful if we had any chance of being successful. The real reasons for the international team's lack of success on the world stage were becoming very clear. How could any team pull itself together to perform at a winning level under those constraints? The pressure was now really on.

As a new coach I figured I had a honeymoon period of around one year after which, if I didn't perform and win games, or at least show considerable signs that it would happen soon, there would be serious questions about my position as coach. So the pressures of time were still just as relevant in rugby as in business. Instead of cashflow considerations, however, the pressure was to win. Under those circumstances, I became quite determined to get things done quickly. With that noose hanging around my neck, and with the equivalent of half of one financial quarter to prove myself, there was considerable motivation to achieve more with less.

Second, I began to examine the coaching and support resources at my disposal.

On my immediate coaching team I had John Mitchell, plus Roger Uttley as England manager, but I must stress that these were both part-time positions. We would be going nowhere at this elite level with part-time coaches. On this issue there was great debate. In my opinion there were no 'maybes' in this job. Either you're pregnant or you're not, there is no in-between! Apart from the PA I was sharing with others, this was it; this was my management team. Things had to change and change quickly. The RFU actually employed some 130 people in various capacities around the UK, from administrative staff at Twickenham to part-time coaching and analysis teams supporting the entire rugby network. However, the flaw here was that they were employed on a part-time basis and were not accountable for success at any level. I felt we needed to focus all of our resources on the elite squad. Having coached the Under-21s for a couple of years, I was familiar with a few of the people in the system. I made a list and set it aside.

Third, I looked at the calendar for the next year.

My assessment was that there were definite windows where I could change things and implement new ideas. You can't change too much in the week before games because it becomes counter-productive for the players. Everything had to be in place before we entered a series of Internationals, the Five Nations or a summer tour. That meant there would be even less time for changing and improving how we managed events. My schedule for the next few years formed a pattern a bit like this:

November – autumn Internationals
December/January – 8 weeks preparation
February/March – Five Nations tournament (now Six Nations)
April/May – 8 weeks preparation
June – summer tour
    Already planned for '98 to Australia, '99 Australia and '00 to South Africa
July/August – 8 weeks rest over July, August
    Players into summer fitness and pre-season training
September/October – 8 weeks preparation
November – autumn internationals: in '98 against Australia and South Africa

So there were three definite windows where we could introduce change: December/January; April/May; and August/September. But then we also had to have holidays and recovery times for our management team during these windows in the schedule. *This is getting quite tight.*

Next I considered our players' capacity to perform.

Our season began in September and finished in July. That didn't leave much time for rest and recuperation for which players typically set aside the summer months. Physiologically, medical experts estimate that the battering and bruising the human body takes in the eighty minutes of a rugby match is equivalent to that experienced by people involved in a car crash at sixty miles per hour. You don't just get up in the morning and feel fine, even though modern sports medicine works hard to enhance the recovery process.

What we had to keep foremost in our minds, though, was that the top players had gruelling schedules of club fixtures on top of their international duties. If my calculations were correct, some of the players would be putting in for some forty or fifty matches in the next year, nearly twice what our southern-hemisphere competitors would have to endure. If we weren't careful, a side could disintegrate under that strain. To compete effectively at an international level, we had to manage that very carefully.

It didn't help that the RFU had no control over the requirements demanded of the players by their clubs. Our major competitors in the southern hemisphere moved quickly and decisively when the game went professional in August 1995; the respective national rugby union bodies were quick to sign contracts with all the top players so that they could control their most valuable resources. There were some at the RFU who wanted to go down this route but they failed to win this crucial battle. England had been slow to embrace professionalism and had been unprepared for the move from the amateur game. Even then, some two years after the transition, there were rumblings around that some of the RFU's committee members wanted to return to the amateur era, although there was no way that could happen.

In the meantime, the RFU had decided it did not want to enter into contracts with players and that it would leave that responsibility to the rugby clubs. The thinking was that, since the RFU distributed substantial funds out of its revenues directly to the clubs, perhaps the clubs would play along and cooperate. It was flawed thinking then and it's still flawed thinking today. Sport is about playing on a level playing field, coaching is about giving your team every chance of winning. The system England works under is just not as good as that of the southern hemisphere for the international team. I think this makes the winning of the World Cup in 2003 even more remarkable and against all logic and common sense.

The clubs, having signed contracts, would naturally do whatever it took to create the revenue to meet their subsequent financial obligations. It made perfect commercial sense that they would look after their own bottom lines before they'd think about the interests of the game at the international level. I could see now that our players, rather unfortunately, would be stuck between two interests competing for their time. It was a disaster from a coach's point of view. That was another significant limitation with which I'd have to work.

Finally, I looked at the international teams with whom we'd arranged fixtures.

I realised we might be in trouble here, too. All of the matches I could see lined up over the next few years had been organised and arranged years in advance. The RFU deserve a lot credit here. The decision by the committee finally to take the southern-hemisphere teams head on was a brave one. For years it seemed England had been ducking the hard matches and were content to increase their standing only by being the best in Europe. I wanted England to be the number one team in the world. We had to play the southern-hemisphere teams regularly in order to establish exactly where we were at any given time.

From November to November of the next year England had sixteen Test matches, ten of which were against the three most formidable rugby giants of the southern hemisphere. I had absolute faith and conviction that England could beat these teams with our best players and the right preparation, but it was without a doubt the most intimidating and gruelling series of matches in the entire history of England rugby.

It certainly wasn't for the faint-hearted.

On top of that, our competition weren't standing still. They too were embracing professionalism, and from all accounts were several steps ahead of us in getting organised. For example, Rod Macqueen was appointed Wallaby coach a few months before me and had already moved to establish a training camp at the seaside resort of Caloundia in Queensland (later changed to Coffs Harbour in northern New South Wales), where the entire team and their families would go to stay for six weeks in preparation for their winter International season. In New Zealand, where rugby is the national sport, the professional environment was even more developed. So too in South Africa, where they were still riding high on their recent win in the 1995 World Cup.

It was beginning to dawn on me why I might have been offered the top job as coach. No one else was daft enough to take it! This was the sort of challenge that would normally excite me. However, given the resources at my disposal and the calendar year ahead, it was becoming a bit daunting! I had limited control over the players in terms of time for preparation, and I had very few systems in place to bring everything together successfully; and to top it all we had a schedule that would test exactly where we were, a series of games no England team had ever attempted in the RFU's long history. To succeed in these upcoming matches, we would have to do more with less until I could bring together all the resources that I knew we'd need to reach our goal. I had to start pulling a team of coaches and players together under difficult circumstances and win in the next few games, and for that we had to think differently. Thankfully, my small-business background had prepared me for this scenario.

Raising the stakes

My first aim for the players was to make their experience of playing for their country completely the opposite of mine; something so special and unforgettable that it would represent the pinnacle of their careers, or even of their lives. In short, I wanted to redefine what it meant to the players to be a part of the England squad. In order to do that, we first needed to up the ante, to raise the stakes in terms of what our athletes were playing for.

Achieving victory in any International, a Grand Slam, or even winning the World Cup, these were obviously highly desirable outcomes. But even though we all knew this was how we would be judged, professional sports people had also to strive for more than just trophies on the wall or medals around their necks. Those ornaments were just the result of winning. I believed that winning was much, much more than that – a concept much bigger than most people could understand.

In rugby there have existed two clear and distinct levels of sporting involvement over the 130 years of the international game. For most of the amateur era the prime focus of the member clubs was participation. The Corinthian spirit of talented amateurism prevailed, and the social aspects of the game came first and foremost. At the international level there was a strong sense of competition, but it wasn't until the modern era that the spirit of competition began to take hold with league fixtures between prominent clubs. Certainly the Rugby Football Union as a whole didn't truly embrace competition until the introduction of the merit tables in the mid to late eighties. At the upper end of this competitive environment, a select group of outstanding players was picked to play for England in even more competitive international fixtures, but the game was still amateur and England teams lacked a strong and compelling desire to do whatever it took to win.

Moving beyond participating or competing, I believe there is a higher ideal of Winning!

When you're participating, your interest is to become actively involved in a sport or pastime, to enjoy being involved in the game. When you become serious about your game and securing victories, you have elevated yourself beyond participation to a level of competition. I believe it is only when you begin playing at an elite level compared to those around you, when you become obsessed with doing whatever it takes for victory, only then are you operating in the realm of winning.

It is the drive, the motivation to excel and dominate in a competitive environment. This has happened at various times in my life, notably playing club rugby at Loughborough and Leicester, and certainly at times during my business career, but *never* whilst playing international rugby.

In my years as an international I'd played in some incredible games, but had also been a part of some horrors. I'd experienced hollow victories when we had more points on the scoreboard yet had played miserably, sour victories when we were up on points but the experience behind the scenes had been horrible, and meaningless victories where the competition hadn't been strong or had not played to their potential best – at least not nearly enough to make the game interesting. Sometimes, even when we achieved a victory, we had not been winning.

That's because winning is about more than just points on the scoreboard.

Rare, even for the best elite teams, is the combination of playing flawlessly as individuals, playing fluidly as a team, and winning convincingly over formidable opponents. But when that happens, it's as deeply meaningful and satisfying as any sensation in the world. This is the peak state of which true sportspeople dream. This is what I wanted to achieve in the England set-up for our players.

Previous England teams had been aiming to compete in the knowledge that victory was defined as having more points than the opposition. In the new England set-up our goal would be different. By raising the stakes, we would settle for nothing less than the peak state of Winning! Striving for and achieving this higher ideal would be our complete focus in the years to follow. With this mindset, nothing less than playing and beating the very best teams in the world would do.

The peak state of Winning!

While I was planning for my first real session with the team, I have to admit that I didn't really have a clear definition of what winning meant to me – I just knew it was my driving passion, and if I could inspire the England internationals with a similar passion as at Henley and London Irish, we would be well on the way to victory in our up-coming clashes with the southern-hemisphere sides. Instinctively I knew that winning would only happen when we were succeeding in all areas, off the pitch as well as on it. However, having now experienced winning at an elite competitive level for many years, I have a much broader understanding of what winning actually means. For a team to be winning, many more elements have to come into play than are at first obvious.

> ### 7 ELEMENTS OF THE PEAK STATE OF WINNING!
>
> You know you're Winning! when you've achieved . . .
> 1. More points on the scoreboard.
> 2. A performance of world-class standards in the core areas of your game – all measurable.
> 3. A team that really clicks in the heat of the match – not measurable.
> 4. An experience off the pitch that is enjoyable and inspires the whole organisation.
> 5. Playing and beating teams you know can beat you.
> 6. 75,000 people on their feet going nuts – a performance your supporters wildly applaud.
> 7. Knowing you can do it on a consistent basis.

It would take some six years to discover all of these elements in England rugby, to understand what winning truly meant at this level, but looking back on the months leading up to the victorious World Cup in 2003, these seven elements were clearly at work within our set-up. The thousands of things we changed, improved and worked on over the years were clearly done with this broader context of winning in mind, and the obsession for winning would extend to all parts of our game, to our entire organisation and to our entire elite environment.

Preparing for the players

We had two sets of two training days coming up before the first autumn International against Australia – one in two weeks and the other two weeks after that. In our first meeting we'd only had a brief introduction, but next time the team really needed to see some substance in my message. Knowing what we were aiming for, and feeling as if I understood the situation in England rugby and the RFU reasonably well, I began to prepare a planning document for how I would achieve our long-term goals in England rugby. I believe England subsequently became the number one team in the world because of one critical factor at this early stage: we asked ourselves the right question before doing anything.

Other coaches before me had asked themselves, 'How can we be victorious with what we've got?' or, in other words, how could you coach and manage the players most effectively to earn victories.

To me the question was flawed; I took a different view.

Instead, I started with the end in mind – winning – and then worked out what it would take to get us there. I asked myself, 'If our goal is winning against the best teams in the world, what would our organisation need to have in place in order to succeed consistently?'

Working in my office late into the afternoon, it soon became clear to me that in my vision there were seven core components of a Winning! team. Five of them I adopted straight from my experiences at Loughborough, not just from Jim Greenwood but from all the other disciplines that were taught to us as the obvious components of any professional sporting organisation.

1. **Coaching the basic skills:** John Mitchell and I had our work cut out in this area. We needed more full-time specialists. I didn't want just a forwards coach and a backs coach, such as everyone else had. I needed coaches in all the key areas of our game: attack, defence, kicking, scrummaging, lineouts, etc. I needed to find specialists who would also all understand and enjoy my philosophy on Total Rugby.

2. **Fitness/nutrition:** We had access to fitness coach Dave Reddin on a part-time basis, but one of my first goals would be to sign him on a full-time contract to work exclusively on the elite England players. I wanted more than just running, weights and ice baths. I now wanted personal training programmes for England to become the fittest and most powerful team in world rugby.

3. **Psychology:** Dave Alred was a world-class kicking coach whom the

RFU used rarely, but he had done some work with the players. He had been working with Jonny Wilkinson since Jonny was thirteen, but this had all been paid for by Jonny's parents. Kicking is about mental preparation as well as technical expertise. We needed Dave full-time as kicking coach, but if we could also get him to work on mental and personal preparation for all players in the same way he worked with Wilkinson we would be streets ahead. But eventually we'd need even more than that. Mental preparation was a huge untapped area of the sport.

4. **Medical/Recovery:** The RFU had a strong medical contingent, but their focus was mostly on emergencies and injuries, and they were all part-time. I wanted specialists who could work preventively with all the players to reduce the chances of injury, and to improve recovery time after matches and training sessions, and also to ensure that players would not play injured because of pressure from their clubs to turn out week in week out. We had to have full-time medical staff to achieve this.

5. **Analysis/IT:** Tony Biscombe had been doing match analysis for the RFU for years, but he was covering a huge area – the whole of the RFU and all teams. He was one of the first people I would bring into the new England set-up. In addition to scrutinising our game so ruthlessly that we could measure and manage our performance, we also had to know what our opposition were doing if we were to have any chance of beating them.

To these initial five components I added two more that I had learned as a direct result of my experiences in business.

6. **Management:** We would need every little detail attended to so that all fears and expectations of our players were addressed. We would have to take away all the worries and concerns about playing for England, so that there was nothing on our players' minds but their performance in the game. We had to maximise our home-ground advantage and minimise our away-ground disadvantage.

7. **Leadership** This would be my area of responsibility in conjunction with the captain. It wouldn't be enough for the captain to be prime

spokesman and motivator, as in previous England teams. We would need to work closely together to achieve aims and maintain standards. I would need to give everyone a clear vision, direction and design for how we would achieve our aims, and we would develop a team of leaders who all could raise themselves to a level of responsibility in key areas of our game. A system involving the players just like I'd started at Henley and London Irish.

With these components in mind, I began thinking about the objectives I clearly wanted to communicate to the team in the next training day at the Abbey. I began writing a planning document that would guide the England coaching team over our first year with the England squad. After much scribbling and editing, here's the short list I came up with.

ENGLAND COACH OBJECTIVES

Mission Statement: To establish an environment of trust, elitism, excellence and fun with the England team and with everything connected with the team.

Objectives Oct 97–Oct 98

1. Establish a style of play which puts the emphasis on
   a. scoring tries (attack)
   b. speed of movement
   c. exciting to play in
   d. testing players at the ultimate level
   e. 'getting the crowd on their feet'
2. Establish selection criteria where the emphasis is
   a. form
   b. age is irrelevant
   c. fair
3. Work on five basic principles of coaching re attack
   a. Speed of ball from scrum and lineout
   b. Speed of ball from ruck and mini maul
   c. Flat ball (all phases)
   d. Buying time
   e. Going FORWARD at ALL times

4. Establish an outstanding working relationship with the England squad with the initial emphasis on the senior players, especially the captain
   a. Lawrence or Martin (undecided as yet)
   b. Jerry, Matt, Jason, Kyran, Backy, etc.
5. Establish an environment of excellence within the coaching management, medical and technical staff with the England team that would be better than any other international team.
6. Establish a rapport/working relationship with the media.
7. Establish/develop relationships with the RFU and English First-Division Rugby.
8. Look at other professional sports such as the NFL and set up *the* most professional coaching team in ANY sport.

After I had my short-term objectives clear, I began to write a document – an England Game Plan – that I could give to the players when we next met. It took me the better part of a week, but the seven-page document eventually become an 86-point strategy that would completely redefine the England playing style.

Hmmm. There's a lot there. There was too much, in fact, to communicate in just one sitting with players who had been used to doing things the same way for so long. They weren't thinking like elite rugby players yet. I had to come up with a way to get them thinking differently before any of my objectives would make sense. *But how?*

The players were all smart individuals, many holding down responsible jobs before the professional era. *That's it. Something they'll all understand.* I picked up the phone and dialled the number of my old office. Luckily Ann Heaver was still there.

'Ann, it's Clive. How many copies of that book do we still have on the shelves?'

Yes, this will get them thinking . . .

12
CHANGING OUR MINDSET

'Good morning, everyone, and welcome back to Bisham Abbey,' I said as the music died down. My favourite song at the time was a Genesis number, and I had cranked it up good and loud.

But my energetic greeting received a tired, unenthusiastic response. It was Monday. Most of the men had played club matches on Saturday and some even on Sunday. One day is simply not enough for the body or mind to recover, nor for energy levels to return – welcome to professional rugby! Besides, I still had a lot of work to do before any form of trust could be developed or expected.

'For the next hour we'll be talking and thinking about how England plays rugby. In the five weeks leading up to our autumn Internationals, we'll be doing quite a bit of talking during meetings before we even think of heading down to the pitch. You may think it unusual that rugby players should spend so much time in the meeting room. Let me try and explain why I think we need to do this at the moment. I believe there are currently five teams in the world who could win the World Cup in 1999, and we all know who they are. We all have roughly the same standard of players, the same equipment and the same physical training techniques. So what makes the difference between the winning team and the team that comes fifth? I believe the team that actually wins the World Cup will be the team that has the best mindset that encompasses new ideas and change. The difference between good teams and world champion teams is what goes on between their ears.

'So we will spend time over the next two days talking about what it will take to forge a winning side. We'll do the same in our next training days in two weeks and we'll continue into our Test week schedules. The only way we are going to function successfully as a team is if we all completely understand what we're trying to achieve and our roles in making it happen.'

Now that I had their attention, it was time for a few ground rules.

'For these meetings to work effectively there are three things we must all bring into the room. First, I'll ask you to come into these meetings with open minds. As you'll learn in the course of the morning, I believe that to be effective we have to be different, and for every three ideas we throw around the room maybe only one will turn out to be good. So please be open to new ideas and be careful about dismissing them too quickly.

A few nodding heads were the reply.

'Agreed?'

'Agreed!' said Lawrence Dallaglio, sitting forward in his chair, speaking on behalf of the team and also meaning, *Come on, cut the crap, let's just get on with this.*

With his jutting jaw and fierce expression, Lawrence was the epitome of the uncompromising and hugely-dedicated professional that would characterise the England team in the years to come. I'd selected him as captain just the week before. Martin Johnson was the more obvious choice because he had just earned huge praise as captain of the Lions side that had toured South Africa that summer. Like the true champion he is, Martin was quick to endorse Lawrence's appointment and confirmed he was right behind the England campaign and what we were trying to achieve.

'Good. Second, you've got to bring your thoughts and ideas here and be willing to share them. We absolutely must have everyone's contribution to the discussion. Whether you're the newest player in the room or the most seasoned, your thoughts are invaluable to us succeeding as a team, so please speak up. We might not always agree with each other's views, but let's all commit to making this room an open forum where everyone feels free to share their ideas.

'The third thing we must all bring to this room is the commitment that what goes on in here will be confidential. To keep an open mind and share our thoughts, we all require absolute certainty that what happens in this room stays in this room. Open minds, frank discussion and complete confidentiality are the essential foundation to everything we'll do in building a winning team.'

Author's note about confidentiality

At this point in the book, I feel it absolutely necessary to make a quick note about confidentiality. For the purposes of the story it is vital you see how everything developed because it speaks so loudly about the accomplishment the team eventually achieved by describing the difficulties they went through to achieve it. Please be aware that in the above passages, and in all those that follow, I have respected the team's confidence and will never, in any publication, show any player or member of the management in any sort of bad light.

Thinking differently

'We have to change the way we do things. Not just on the pitch, but off it as well. We have to learn to think differently about every aspect of what we do, and look at it in a way that our competitors fail to notice. However if we all come to this task with the same level of thinking that we've always had, then we'll most likely end up with the same result – England ranked sixth in the world with little or no success on the world stage, especially against southern-hemisphere teams.

'Unfortunately, inherited thinking is a curse. It's the biggest impediment to innovation in any organisation. So before we do anything, we have to change the way we think. We have to embrace a concept I call Change Thinking! That will hopefully help us to see our rugby set-up in a new light.

'There are two parts to this concept: lateral thinking or thinking differently, and vertical thinking or thinking detail. To illustrate what I mean by the first part, I'd like to tell you a story that will help you to look at the business of managing an elite international team in a new light. This story is the best example of thinking differently that I've ever come across. And if this man can do it in his profession, we can certainly do it in rugby.

'Let me start by asking a question. Does anyone here like going to the dentist . . .'

The self-confessed crazy Australian dentist

In my leasing business, I had been in the habit of attending seminars and workshops on a regular basis. A few years before I was sitting with Ann Heaver in a three-day marketing conference. The afternoon of the second day was dragging on a bit. Ann disappeared, presumably to check out the exhibitors. I wasn't going anywhere. The seminar was the most expensive I'd ever seen, costing thousands of pounds per person. I came because I simply had to see what was worth all that money. Ann soon returned with a little package under her arm. Within a few minutes she was flipping through a book. Thirty minutes later she was reading it intently.

'Ann,' I whispered, giving her a nudge. 'What are you doing?'

'It's a really good book. Shut up,' she replied, head down, eyes glued. At the next break she showed me where she had found the book with one of the other speakers outside.

I glanced at the title: *Building the Happiness Centred Business* by Dr Paddi Lund. Intriguing. I opened to the first page. It was interesting and talked about the pressures of business in a way I'd never seen before but to which I could certainly relate.

Paddi was a conventional dentist in Australia, the kind we all dread to visit. But the pressure and stress of running his business, combined with the hatred the public have for dentistry, drove him over the edge. Most people don't realise that dentists have one of the highest suicide rates of any profession in the world. Paddi didn't quite go that far, but his breakdown proved a catalyst for change. Paddi decided that he couldn't keep going unless he and his team began to enjoy their work more. So he made happiness in business his ultimate goal and began to consider what it would take to achieve it in his rather challenging profession. What followed was a period of incredible innovation in hundreds of areas.

This story was important to me because it was the best example that I had seen of thinking differently about the conventional approach to business. If only we could bring that level of thinking into how we looked at the England set-up, both on and off the pitch, then we could totally transform what it meant to play rugby at the elite international level.

Paddi thinking

'In short, because Paddi thought differently about the business of dentistry,' I concluded with the team, 'he completely redesigned his business with a new set of guiding principles, and managed to see things in a way they hadn't been considered before. He is exceptional at lateral thinking, and that's exactly what we need to do here today. I have a copy of his book here for everyone' – I picked up the box I'd collected from Ann at the office – 'and in your own time you can read the story that fits so perfectly with my approach to business and rugby. To this day, it's the only business book I've ever read twice.'

The players all looked a bit dubious. They'd never been given a business book by a coach before, let alone one by a self-confessed crazy Australian dentist.

Thinking in detail

'The second part of Change Thinking! is just as interesting, but in a different way. Before we get into it, here's a little test for you to warm us up. Would everyone please take a look at the slide on the projector screen?'

> FINISHED FILES ARE THE RE-
> SULT OF MANY YEARS OF SCIENTIF-
> IC STUDY COMBINED WITH THE
> EXPERIENCE OF MANY YEARS.

'OK, here's a question for you. How many F's – that's F for Freddie – do you see in that slide? Please keep the answer to yourself and stand up when you have it in your head.'

Within three seconds, everyone was standing . . . everyone except Will Greenwood, that is. He had his head tilted to the right at 90 degrees and was still staring intently at the screen.

'Will, what are you doing? Didn't you understand the question?'

'Yeah, I understood. I'm just trying to think like Paddi and look at it differently.'

Everyone had a good laugh, including me. That was Will. I liked him already.

'OK, would everyone now please take a seat if they saw three F's. Let me repeat that. If you saw three F's, please sit down.'

All thirty people in the Elizabethan Room, including coaches and support staff, sat down.

'Interesting . . .' I observed. 'That looks like all of us. You might be surprised to learn that there are actually six F's in that sentence.' This was a very simple test after all. It was so obvious, primary school kids would find it a breeze. Wouldn't they? In actual fact, they would probably do better than this group had.

'Take a moment to look at the slide again. Can anyone see where they are?'

After a moment, we had our answer.

'There they are,' said Jason Leonard calmly. 'In the word "of". There's two on the second line and one in the last line. Along with "finished files" and "scientific" that makes six.'

'I've only discovered this little exercise myself recently' – from an organisational consultant named Humphrey Walters: more about him later – 'and you'll be pleased to know I, too, only saw three F's. Studies have shown that in any given sample of the population, 95 per cent of people will only see three F's in that sentence. The word "of" is such a common word that our brains have learned to filter it out of our vision.

'Only the problem is, if our brains miss the word "of" because we take it for granted, what do you think we might be missing about the way we play, coach and manage rugby? What are we taking for granted in the way we play our game that might actually be the one thing that could give us an advantage on the pitch? The second part of Change Thinking! is about seeing the detail. If we expect to win on an international stage, we have to see six F's in everything we do, and I mean everything.

'So we'll spend a lot of time over the next few months examining the way we do things and we'll practise our 6-F thinking. However the good news is, there's a 95 per cent chance that the competition, the All Blacks, Springboks and Wallabies, will only see three F's. If we can learn to beat them between the ears, we can beat them on the pitch as well.

'When we last met here at the Abbey I said we'd be throwing out all that we ever knew about how to play rugby at an international level and that we'd be rebuilding it from the ground up. In short, that's exactly what we're going to do. Over the coming months we'll question everything we do and then will apply our Change Thinking! mindset to find new and better solutions.

'Any questions?'

In response I received only pensive expressions. *I think they got it.*

'Good. OK, now let's talk rugby.' I nodded to John Mitchell. Taking the cue he picked up a large pile of stapled documents and began to distribute them.

'The handouts that are coming around the room at the moment . . .'

For the next hour and a half we stepped through our plan for the England elite team on the pitch over the coming year and what it would mean to each of the players. I reproduce it here in its entirety.

England game plan

'When I analysed every successful team I have been involved with, whether it be in business or sport, it became very apparent the following three statements apply in every case without exception. They are statements I would like us to continually refer to.

'Hannibal won his wars by doing exactly the opposite to what his enemies thought and tradition had always dictated.'

I waited a few moments for that to sink in.

'Never doubt that a small group of thoughtful, committed people can change the world. Indeed it is the only thing that ever has.

'And finally, from our own estimable Sir John Harvey-Jones . . .

'To create success, EVERYONE'S noses must be pointing in the same direction.

'With that in mind, let's have a look now at how we're going to confound our opposition and change the world by pointing everyone's noses in the same direction.'

WELCOME TO THE ELITE ENGLAND SQUAD

Our Vision:
To transform England Rugby into the world leader by 1999.

Our Philosophy:
To be the best in everything we do.

Our Style of Play:
To Win.

Our Goal:
To win the World Cup in 1999.

Our Game Plan:
Scoring Tries.

However, to 'win' or 'to be the best' we must all understand and agree on 6 basic principles.

1. England's 'upper hand'

2. England's '3 key rules'

3. England's 'team commitment' to basic principles

4. England's 'leadership'

5. England's 'individual commitment' to basic principles

6. England's 'game plan'

TO BE THE BEST

1 England's 'Upper Hand'

Objective

- The most destructive defence in World Rugby
- Ability to Score off the First Phase
- Understanding the 'Hit v Time' concept
- Score Tries

Players

- Open minds
- Commitment to try anything and develop it
- Player contribution is essential
- Understanding of each move by all 15 players is essential
- A Back Row with real footballing and game reading ability – 6/7/8 should be able to play at centre

Facts

- Defences have tested systems for standard attacks
- Defences have no systems for dealing with non-standard attacks
- Non-standard attacks momentarily confuse defences as defenders are unsure of who is now their man and must decide in a split second who to cover

Key Factors To Be Exploited

- Surprise! No final positioning of attackers until last few seconds – give defenders no time to work out possible options
- Defenders lack perception of depth of each attacker
- Watching one attacker is easy, two is difficult, three is almost impossible
- Understand the importance of decoy runners to our play

Essential Requirements

- A Back Row with game-reading ability is now critical
- Player understanding that in these plays, second phase is a last resort!
- Total understanding of the geometry of each move (Starting position, Pace, Angle, Depth and Distance)
- The ability of all players to be able to 'see' the move in plan form, i.e. from above
- Wingers who can play at flanker
- A team that wants to be the best in the world

2 England's 3 Key Rules

(A) Break Tackle Lines – 'Hit'

Must get past first main line of defence. To do this we must hit contact or space very, very hard and always look to ruck, if tackled – moving ball back quickly. However, we must get over the tackle line – once past tackle line:

Avoid Contact – 'Time'

Once past tackle line must keep the ball alive whenever possible

Key Points:

- Slow down
- Stop
- Run backwards/sideways
- Deliver only 100% passes
- Change of focus of attack
- Keep the ball moving at all costs
- Stay in play
- Never kick unless you are going to score
- Call 'TIME' to tell a team-mate to slow down in order to keep the ball moving

(B) Deliver Possession

First Receiver must take the ball FLAT off ALL phases – place you take it at is dependent on what you are going to do with the ball

(C) To Play at Pace with:

SPEED of ball from LINEOUT

SPEED of ball from SCRUM

SPEED of ball from RUCK

SPEED of ball from MINI MAUL

3 Our Team Commitment to Rugby's Time-Honoured Basic Principles

The most destructive defence in WORLD RUGBY

Forwards' total commitment to 'HIT' rucks at all times

A realisation that penalties 'HURT' our team

To fight to keep the ball in play

Always make sure the ball goes out of play when kicking for touch

ATTITUDE: Toe to toe – No backwards steps against any team or any individual

4 Leadership

Captain

Responsible for ensuring all players are as one with the Coaches' Philosophy. His Key Role is at training and all team meetings and being an integral part of the Selection Process.

Tactical Decision Makers

10–9–8 in that order

Totally responsible during the game for pulling the team together to ensure we run the game and play to our strengths and to the oppositions' weakest areas. Must show leadership qualities at training and all other times.

Scrum

Front row forward to be responsible to the team for the effectiveness of this vital part of the game. Must be the leader during the game and in training and totally dedicated to England's progress in this area at ALL times. Needs to be a good communicator.

Lineout

Lock forward to be responsible to the team for the effectiveness of this vital part of the game. Must be the leader during the game and in training and totally dedicated to England's progress in this area at ALL times. Needs to be a good communicator.

Defence

    a) Backs – Inside Centre. From all set play is responsible for organising/directing our defence and being totally responsible for this part of our game functioning effectively.

    b) Forwards – Open Side Flanker. From all set play is responsible for organising/directing our defence and being totally responsible for this part of our game functioning effectively.

Summary

8 people are named above as key to putting everything in place. It must be stressed that 99% of their efforts/work takes place at:

    c) Training

    d) Meetings

    e) Phoning England colleagues

    f) Studying their appropriate areas

In the heat of the battle the whole team will be as one with the 10–9–8 taking control of our power game.

5 Players' Key Roles

The Tight 5 – ALWAYS ON THE ATTACK

- Attack at *ALL* scrums and dominate
- Be precise and accurate at *ALL* lineouts
- Clear our attacking rucks in numbers
- Have high tackle counts
- Very low penalty counts

Our total game plan starts with you

Back Row

- As for front five
- Support any ball-carrier relentlessly
- Be imaginative, creative and precise in attack
- In defence, be controlled, aggressive and totally destructive
- Very low penalty count

You are the dynamo which drives the team

Half Backs

- Handle with dexterity, accuracy and speed
- Maintain your poise in all situations
- Kick accurately, effectively and with purpose
- Be imaginative, creative and precise in attack
- In defence, reduce the attacking options of the oppositions
- Very low penalty count

You are the prime decision-makers and creators in the team

Backs
- As for Half Backs
- Have vision in attack and defence
- Be aggressive, controlled and totally destructive in defence
- Attack with poise, precision and pace
- Very low penalty count
- You are our main strike runners

6 England's Game Plan

Statistics of chances of success in international games played to the current changes in the law:

1 Slow Ball

	% Chance of scoring
1 phase slow ball	8%
2 phases slow ball	6%
3 phases slow ball	5%

If we get slow ball we must use our momentum calls to generate quick ball

2 Fast Ball

	% Chance of scoring
1 phase fast ball	17%
2 phases fast ball	45%
3 phases fast ball	60%
4 phases fast ball	75%
5 phases fast ball	85%

Scoring = Try or Penalty conceded by opponents
NB Quick ball from scrum/lineout = 1 phase fast ball

3 Tries

– 85% of international matches are now won by the team that scores the most tries – FACT

Summary

Simply based on the above stats, we must create a game that allows us to generate 4/5 phases of play that will allow us maximum opportunity of scoring tries. All our selections will be based on this simple principle.

The only other aspects that need clear consideration in addition to 1, 2 and 3 above are:
1) Weather
2) Field Position
3) Defence – Stop the opposition scoring tries
4) Scoreline

C.R. Woodward
England Head Coach

It was an exhausting morning, but an exhilarating one ... well at least for me. I'm not sure how all of the players felt. I could see the light of enthusiasm in the eyes of the younger players, but some of the more experienced players looked a little bored, as if they were covering old ground. But these ideas had been developing for decades in my brain, nurtured in Loughborough and Leicester, crystallised in Australia, tried and tested at Henley, London Irish and Bath.

Many of them were completely new to the England set-up.

IMPORTANT NOTE
In 1997 this was a top-secret document. For obvious reasons the England Team have now moved on and as such this is now an archive. This is the first time, however, that I have shared my plan with anyone outside the team there that day. Hopefully it will give you a valuable insight into our early structural planning

13
MY FIRST AUTUMN INTERNATIONALS

Sooner than I would have liked, the autumn Internationals were upon us. We were coming up against the hardest line-up of games England had ever faced: four big southern-hemisphere Internationals on our doorstep in quick succession. It seemed like only a matter of days since I had first met the team, but now we were in our final stages of preparation. It was 10 November, and already I'd been eight weeks in my new job. The first of those four Internationals, against the Wallabies at Twickenham, was just five days away.

Sitting down with Lawrence Dallaglio to thrash out the selection, there were doubts about form or fitness hanging over everyone. Some of the Lions had underperformed in the early part of the season and there were inevitably going to be some difficult calls.

The media consensus was pessimistic, but I didn't share that view. In fact, I thought it was a great opportunity. I had studied all the opposition teams carefully, and in the case of the Wallabies I knew at first hand how their team was performing because I had seen them for myself. They were coming to Twickenham having just finished a tour of Argentina, and I had flown to Buenos Aires just a week earlier to see the second of their two matches against a rugged but not especially talented Puma team. The game was not televised at home, and while I didn't go there for any other reason than to see the Wallabies first hand, my trip did send a message to my squad, to rugby followers back home and the Australians – this guy is serious, and he does his homework.

It had been Rod Macqueen's second match as Wallabies coach, and I'd watched him lose it. Argentina had shaded an experienced Wallaby team by 18—16 with scrum-half Agustin Pichot and flanker Rolando

Martin both scoring tries. So the Australians were not invincible, and I'd witnessed a superior Australian team being beaten. I knew we could beat them, particularly on our home ground.

After the game I'd bumped into Macqueen and his assistant coaches – we had all been staying in the same hotel. Though I felt a little like a spy in their camp, Macqueen rose above any awkwardness by inviting me to drinks, which was the action of a confident man. Nowadays I make a point of not mixing with opposition coaches or officials except for scheduled functions and so on, but at that time it was a little less formal as I hadn't really begun competing as a coach. My international coaching baptism was still ahead of me; it was a very nervous time.

Now that my debut was rapidly approaching, my nerves were on edge. Assembling the squad at the Petersham Hotel, the traditional venue for Twickenham games, I could feel the butterflies. Nervousness was a good sign, the start of something big. It was the old adrenalin rush, part fear, part exhilaration, the buzz of the unknown. I'd not been at this point before, but I couldn't wait to start. In fact I was fed up with talking about what might happen and was looking forward to when there would be a real performance to analyse.

Final preparations

So far it had all gone well, but there had been tense moments. When you have to tell someone that they've failed to make the team, that's when you really find out about squad spirit. But selection is all about getting on with the job. Fortune favours the bold, and I named five new caps. Of course we had a new captain too, with Dallaglio taking over from Phil de Glanville. I had been England's Under-21 coach for three seasons and was very keen to bring in some new young players that I'd been working with.

In the rooms before the game there were no last-minute tricks or surprises, it was simply a matter of giving these young professional players some space in which to prepare themselves. Earlier, I'd done the obligatory television and radio interviews, but I didn't have much to say. Nor was I saying a lot in the rooms. I knew from my playing days that this was not the time for distractions or new information; it

We honeymooned in Hawaii on the way back to England on holiday for the first time since going to Australia. Jess came too, of course.

Jess aged four months, meeting her grandparents back home for the first time.

Above: Conor O'Shea – wonderful player and charming man, my first key signing at London Irish.

Left: Henley players power through Oxford on their way to yet another promotion, February 1994. Coaching humble Henley gave me a first chance to put my ideas into practice – with highly gratifying results.

Below: I was pleased to be the new coach at London Irish but, because of the politics, coaching England later was a walk in the park in comparison.

Andy Robinson and I enjoyed happy times together at Bath.

My first press conference as the new England coach – (*left to right*) Roger Uttley, Bill Beaumont, me, Fran Cotton and John Mitchell.

André Watson, South African referee. It amazes me the number of times André and I have met in crucial games for England over the last seven years.

Lawrence Dallaglio, my first captain, seen here at Old Trafford on 22 November 1997, has never taken a backward step in anything he's ever done.

More than a bad day at the office – the lowest point of English rugby. In the first game of the Tour from Hell against Australia, we lost 76–0.

Don Rutherford, former Director of Rugby of the RFU, did an excellent job over thirty years in guiding rugby from the amateur game to professionalism.

Francis Baron, Chief Executive of the RFU since late 1998, took England into the corporate world.

England were superb against South Africa at Twickenham, 5 December 1998. Richard Hill and Neil Back took the game to them and we won the day, halting their record winning streak.

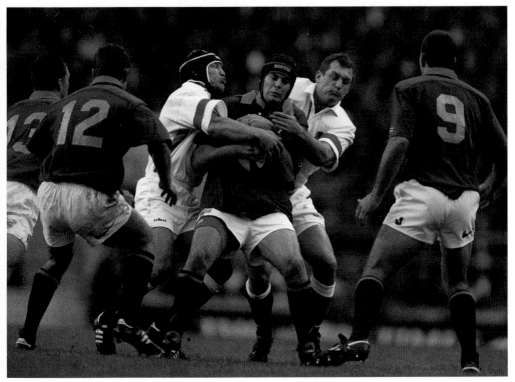

Against Wales at Wembley in 1999, we were in for the Grand Slam after a great Five Nations but, having stayed on top for eighty-two minutes, we lost by one point – crushing.

Training with the Royal Marines, pre 1999 World Cup – (*left to right*) Jason Leonard, Danny Grewcock, Richard Cockerill, David Rees.

We lost to South Africa in the quarter-final of the 1999 World Cup in Paris. The players watching de Beer drop another goal are (*left to right*) Dallaglio, Grewcock, Johnson and Vickery. Note that all of them returned from Australia victorious four years later.

The 'Winning' board was already *in situ* in the changing room before Yehuda Shinar and I ever met. Clearly, Yehuda approved of our choice of words on his first visit to Twickenham from Israel.

Humphrey Walters with Lawrence Dallaglio in the early days at the Petersham Hotel, Richmond.

was a time to keep calm and to direct the players' attention to the task in front of them. I simply asked them to go out and play like we trained, to do their own jobs and enjoy the whole experience.

Personally, I suppose I was finding the experience just as daunting as anyone, though I was trying hard not to show it. There were so many people who had invested so much in this game, and I was just one of them. Of course the rugby public was watching, but there were also my family, my business associates and countless other friends and contacts who had their own expectations and were hoping for the best for me.

The contrast between the haven of the changing rooms and the pitch could not have been greater. While I headed directly to my seat in the stands, determined to maintain a businesslike approach, the team emerged from the tunnel to an overwhelming roar from the 75,000-strong crowd. Add to that the energy and noise of the fans, the television cameras and the sheer gravity of the occasion, and you have a powerful, intoxicating mix. It could work for or against me. A brief period of silence for the national anthems, then it was time to get down to business, time for the players to go out and do their jobs.

My first International as a coach

The game itself was not what I had hoped for. The result was a 15—all draw. Some saw a draw as a moral victory, which left them not exactly ecstatic, but content. But if it was a near victory to them it was a near defeat to me.

We had started confidently and were not overawed by the occasion. By the break we were ahead 9—5. But in the second half we lost our way somewhat, and in the end we had to rely on Mike Catt's kicking to salvage the draw. A lot of people thought the result fine, but I wasn't satisfied. Far from it. Catt kicked the penalties, but the Wallabies had breached our line twice, with tries from Ben Tune and George Gregan.

Revisiting my own performance in this first game, I think I was somewhat distracted by the layout and set-up of the coaching area. In front of me was one TV, which I was not used to. Roger Uttley and John Mitchell were close at hand but the conversations were very stilted and really little to do with the game or potential tactical changes. Then there were my radio headset and microphone patching me in to the team doctors and sideline physios. It was too much – too much information and not enough clear communication. I was doing what every other international coach did, but I did not like it. It was not me and I couldn't wait to change the way we operated.

It was my head on the block and I was ultimately accountable for the team's showing, so we had to do things my way. There was no room for partnerships or committee decisions at the crucial moment. There had to be one person in charge. As coach, that person was me, and if we wanted to be successful I had to take in information and make quick and accurate decisions.

Foreshadowing

An interesting aside to this first tied match was that it was refereed by the South African André Watson, who was later to officiate in our World Cup final triumph. Watson was developing a reputation as a world-class official, and also a reputation for being in charge of close and exciting games. In another match against the Wallabies at Twickenham in November 2000 the result would just go our way courtesy of a try by Dan Luger that first had to survive the scrutiny of the video referee.

Theatre of dreams

After our draw with the Wallabies, our next opponent was the formidable New Zealand outfit, the number-one team in the world. The place was Old Trafford – what a venue – and I was delighted to be able to fulfil a childhood dream by taking a team out at the home ground of Manchester United. At thirteen I thought it just might be Everton or Chelsea (my dad's club) I would be leading out, not the England rugby team. It was just so ironic for me to be doing this, considering my earlier obsession with football. I'd always wanted to play here. Fortunately the players had little idea what was actually going through my mind.

Despite an encouraging fight-back in the second half, the All Blacks had our measure in Manchester, winning 25—8. Jonah Lomu was back for his first Test appearance after a long absence, and the press noted he was 'a constant threat for the All Blacks'. While it was true that at his best Lomu was a fantastic player, the fact was that a lot of people had a mindset problem with him after the trauma of the 1995 World Cup thrashing. Some said there was no way to stop him, but that attitude made me furious. Other countries, most notably Australia and South Africa, seemed to know how to handle him.

As a player or coach, when confronted by powerful opponents, I've never seen a benefit in buying into the 'mystique' of other teams or individual players. The All Blacks had this mystique fuelled by our media. To focus your attention on your opponent's strengths inevitably leads to revering or fearing them. You cannot spend enough time analysing your opponents, but this needs to create respect and not fear – there is a huge difference. Equally important are your own strengths, and addressing your own weaknesses where possible, and also finding areas that will set you apart from your opposition.

On the Thursday before the game I wanted to take the team on the pitch but the rain was pouring down. I thought, no way will they allow us to play on the pitch, but still I rang the groundsman, Keith Kent. To my surprise Keith said of course we could. So we trained on the pitch, which was invaluable, and, yes, we churned it up. But the moment we finished training an army of men came on and replaced all the divots, sorting it all out quickly and without fuss. That brought home to me the difference between the really professional sport of football and rugby, a fledgling professional sport.

When Sir Alex Ferguson wanted Man U to train on the pitch, that's exactly what he got. The whole thing was done with a view to winning. Whereas at Twickenham the ground committee's attitude seemed to be, 'No, no, you can't train on the pitch. We want it looking absolutely perfect.' In those days I believe there were people on the ground committee who would have been happier still if we didn't actually ever play on the pitch! We were so far away from the football people in professional terms. Today, however, I'm glad to say I think perhaps we're ahead of them. There has been a huge turnaround in a short time, and I'm pleased to say that Keith is now the head groundsman at Twickenham. He's just fantastic and the respect he has from all of us in the team is massive, all justifiably earned by the quality of his actions.

Looking back, the most exciting aspect of this week in Manchester for our team's future came with the presence of Phil Larder. I had invited Phil to join us for the week to observe and generally get a really good feel for what we were doing. The rest as they say is history. I have worked with Phil ever since and he has been truly inspirational as well as revolutionary in his work with us in defence. As a coach in his specialist domain he is unsurpassed. Not only that but a man you would want by your side when the pressure is really on. I have the upmost respect for Phil and owe him immense gratitude.

Realising it was a unique opportunity, I seized my chance to visit the Manchester United boot room and see all the players' boots. I even got to touch David Beckham's. Playing in the Theatre of Dreams literally was a dream come true. The All Blacks criticised the England players later for going back onto the pitch for what they wrongly perceived as a lap of honour. Nothing of the sort. We had never played in Manchester before and the crowd was mostly new to the game. With this in mind the players simply went to salute their spectators and thank them for coming. Taking a major International match to the north of England was a huge success, and I'm sorry it has never been repeated. We all enjoyed the experience and it would be excellent to take the game to more people that support the team in more places, more often.

Back at Twickenham a week later we could not find an opening to break away from South Africa. They were a far better side that day. It was a game they deserved to win, and we went down 29—11. I could try to make excuses, say that we lost Catt to injury at half-time and took three more injuries in the last quarter, which is all true, but the fact is they were better than us.

That said, I could see we were improving as a team, gaining in confidence.

We were getting somewhere. The elite experience was strengthening.

A moral victory

The confidence of the team was starting to show by the time the final game of the autumn Internationals came around. It was a rematch with New Zealand at Twickenham, and despite ending in another draw, 26—26, it was a terrific game.

It's interesting to consider that this was just my fourth game as coach, and it yielded the second, and so far the last draw of my entire tenure – except for the World Cup final in Sydney, of course, only we resolved that one! However, draw or not, as a team performance it was streets ahead of the Wallabies game three weeks earlier.

We played fast, exciting rugby – the ball way flying everywhere. While not yet achieving an ideal standard, there were flashes of brilliance and the style of play was approaching fifteen-man rugby. We outscored a star-studded All Black line-up three tries to two and were leading for most of the game. Sadly however, we faded badly in the last twenty minutes when we were in a position to finish off the match. Unfortunately we were nowhere near their level of fitness, either mentally or physically. We were beating them on the pitch and the scoreboard but they had been beating us in all other areas of the game At the end of the game it really started to show.

From the ecstasy shown by the England fans you would think we had just won the World Cup. To many, a draw against the All Blacks was a victory. The New Zealanders were obviously disappointed and wore very long faces, as if the world had come to an end. It was a stark contrast. To me, we hadn't won. That we stopped New Zealand from winning was indeed no victory. I knew we could have beaten that team. We would work on the aspects of our game that let us down. I can understand the New Zealanders having a laugh at the English with everyone in the stadium looking so pleased and happy with a draw, everyone except me – this would change.

One point for me to note here was the way the team improved, game on game, the longer we were together as a team. This encouraged me and made me keen to create more time for the team to be together.

A vote of confidence

The true value of fitness was something I had first really discovered at Loughborough. Our fitness coach, Dave Reddin, another Loughborough man, was beginning to get really involved. He had been part-time and I had now secured his services on a full-time basis with a very simple brief: we must be the fittest and most powerful team in world rugby. He had got together a detailed fitness programme, but that sort of thing takes years to pay real dividends. I would put Reddin above any other fitness expert in world sport – he is that good. He's the reason why England arrived at the 2003 Rugby World Cup as the fittest and most powerful team.

My overall view of those first games was: well, we hadn't won a game, but in that last match we had gained quite a bit of confidence because we had played really well. That confidence allowed us to move forward a little bit. The guys were beginning to play with self-belief; and the so-called invincibility of the southern teams was just possibly beginning to be exposed for the myth I always knew it was.

I was delighted to receive a letter from Cliff Brittle before Christmas with his full support of the work we had been doing and in the handling of the autumn Internationals.

I haven't mentioned Cliff a great deal to date but he was the one, supported by Fran Cotton, who made the decision to give me the England job. It was clearly a risky decision by Cliff but one he should be credited with. Few people in the RFU understood him, and when he lost his position as chairman of the management board, in the election a few months after my appointment, it was a major setback for the game. But only a very few people saw his real talents. He was different. He wanted change quickly, and that was the seed of his eventual downfall.

But all my attention soon went back to rugby. The real value of the autumn Internationals was to bring home to everyone, at all levels of the organisation, just how high our standards had to be in order to compete, and ultimately, to win. That message had already had a big impact on me. The other three coaches in that series – Australia's Macqueen, New Zealand's Hart and South Africa's Mallett – were all outstanding coaches. In these early stages I felt the pressure to catch up with them, and ultimately to go past them. It wasn't a comfortable feeling as they were three outstanding individuals, but it was clearly a strong motivation for me.

To make sure I stayed acutely aware of the company I was in at the international level, I hunted down pictures of these men and the other coaches from the top eight rugby nations around the world, and put them up on the wall of my office. These were professionals who would be watching my every move from now on, so they might as well have a good vantage point. Of course it also ensured I had my eye on them every day.

Sun Tzu said, *Know your enemy*. I would add, *Know his mindset and everything else you can about him as well.*

14

CHANGING OUR ORGANISATION

Don Rutherford and I hadn't exactly got off to a smashing start, what with the business about the office. While negotiating my contract I had insisted that I report directly to the management board. I wanted full and absolute control of what I saw as an emerging elite squad, a significant step up from professional management covering the whole game that Don was in charge of. In the few weeks since we'd got the office sorted out, I really hadn't had much interaction with Don. When coaches were previously only required part-time, Don and his support team had borne the brunt of the work surrounding international matches.

Don saw as his job, and that of his staff, the handling of all the management and administration requirements of the squad. As long as this aspect of the England set-up was of world-class standard, then this system would have worked well. Don's team were quite rightly operating on behalf of all the representative England teams, and they therefore did not understand, nor should they have, the different standards an elite international team required. Nor could they see how important these standards were if our goal was to be the best team in the world – not among the best, but *the* best.

When setting the terms of the position, I really didn't know what I would be changing in the England set-up, only that I'd be scrutinised for everything I did. Before late August, I wasn't even a remote possibility for the job, so it's not as if I walked in with a detailed business plan. As a result there was one thing I had no control over, and that was an operating budget covering the next twelve months. Let's face it, I'd only had a few weeks to organise my thoughts before meeting the players for the first time.

When it finally occurred to me that I'd need extra funding to do some of the things I wanted to do, I approached Don and asked him how my team's budget worked.

'Budget? We don't have an additional budget. The operating budgets for the whole organisation are set in July, so until then you just come to me with whatever you want and I'll see if I can work it in. Under no circumstance make any purchasing decisions without my signing off first.'

Don had some degree of discretion over where various items were allocated in the financial accounts. It also meant he could fit 'extraneous items' where there was room. Still, I didn't like it. I didn't have control, which was not acceptable, given it was clearly my neck on the line. Absolute statements like his always seemed to get my back up, as if I was being told all over again that I wasn't allowed to play football any more. I have a full understanding of the importance of budgets, my background is in finance. I just cannot accept 'no' if there is something that has to be done. There are some things that need to be done and need to be done now. Budget or no budget, that means we just have to find other ways to make them happen. If everyone accepted 'no' for an answer, nothing would ever get done. Don's proclamation about my lack of financial control wasn't exactly what I needed to hear.

When I went to Don for the first extraneous expenditure, it was in relation to bringing a consultant named Humphrey Walters on board.

'Sure, I know Humphrey Walters. I saw him speak with Bill Beaumont once. What are the financial implications?'

I told him.

'Oh. I see. That's a bit more than I can fit into my budget. I might have to go to the management board with this one.' They had the power to sign off non-budgeted requests from professional staff. I guess it was better than a straight out 'no'.

Another who thinks differently

I had actually first met Humphrey Walters some weeks earlier before our first international match. Bringing good people and new ideas together in business with spectacular results is incredibly satisfying, something I worked long and hard to do in my leasing business. Yet even though we were progressive for our industry, I'm sure there was more opportunity for innovation than we had the time to explore. The pressures of small business don't often leave too much time for playing around. So rather than reinvent the wheel in England rugby I was quite happy to lean on other people's expertise and creativity when we needed it. Hence I had been on the hunt for a specialist who could help us with team dynamics in the organisation between both players and coaches. It was Roger Uttley who first recommended I speak with Humphrey Walters.

'Clive, I know who you should call.'

'Who's that?'

'Humphrey Walters. He runs a training company called MaST International.'

We were chatting in Roger's office at Harrow in early October – five weeks before our first test match against Australia, just before my second meeting with the players.

'And if Humphrey can't help you, he'll know who can. I've spoken at some of his events over the years. He has worked with some very prominent companies, although I'm not sure he's ever worked in a sports environment.'

'Thanks for that, Roger. I've interviewed a few business consultants already and just haven't found what I'm looking for. England rugby will be changing over the next year and we really should involve someone with experience who can help us manage that process effectively. I also want someone who doesn't know anything about rugby and therefore has no preconceived ideas. Someone who fully understands the power of the team over a group of individuals.'

'He might be your man then, Clive. Why don't I give him a call to tell him you'll be in touch?'

Roger Uttley had been appointed manager of the England side to work in conjunction with myself as coach. It was a model that had been in place for many, many years but, taking nothing away from the excellent job Roger was doing, it was clearly outdated in the new world of professional rugby. Eventually it would cost the British Lions the Test series against Australia in 2001. It simply wasn't effective. To work around that, Roger and I had agreed that my job was everything to do with the team, both on the pitch and in the meeting room, and his responsibility was managing everything else. But there were a myriad critical details surrounding Test week and international matches. It was a huge job for someone part-time, and I learned that the smallest of oversights could have dire consequences. It would soon become clear that this was another area I'd need to manage carefully if we were serious about building a successful high-performance team.

On the way back from Harrow I looked at Humphrey's number again. It was in Maidenhead, only about ten minutes from my home. *Why don't I just call him now, and see what his reaction is then?* When Humphrey answered my call, he was surprised because he had only just hung up the phone with Roger. He was even more surprised when I said I'd be in his office in thirty minutes.

We chatted for a couple of hours that afternoon. I told him my whole story, my love of football as a youth, *Conway*, and finally my discovery of rugby. I told Humphrey of lost opportunity in my playing days, my subsequent quest in Australia, and of my eventual discovery of success in business and then in rugby as a coach. He listened intently, nodding his head at my conclusions and offering confirmation of my ideas about the future of England rugby and what it would take to build a winning team.

Our views on business were similar, and he'd been facilitating corporate change for nearly three decades. Thirty years earlier, while studying for his Masters in the late sixties, he'd actually spent several weeks with Vince Lombardi of the Green Bay Packers, regarded as the most successful coach in American football history. Humphrey had also just returned from a gruelling eleven-month yacht race around the world, the BT Global Challenge, billed as the world's toughest race because they had to travel the wrong way around the world, against trade winds and prevailing currents. Eleven yachts compete in the race. All are exactly the same design and build. They are each manned by one professional skipper and a crew of normal civilians, many of whom have never sailed before.

So with roughly the same resources and conditions, why does one yacht come first and another come last? It certainly wasn't because of a better boat or a better skipper. Humphrey showed me a business presentation based on his experiences in the race and it was this message that won him the contract to work with the team. Humphrey discovered that success could be attributed to how the team worked together under pressure, how they understood the importance of teamwork and loyalty, and how they were willing to do a hundred things just 1 per cent better. It was as if Humphrey was reading my mind. This was exactly how I saw the situation in England rugby. We had roughly the same tools as any other international team, but we had to learn to apply them differently.

Humphrey was exactly what I'd been looking for. Our thoughts were in alignment and, better still, he could look at what we were doing with a fresh and different set of eyes. As a way of introducing himself to the team, Humphrey agreed to give a brief talk about the yacht race in the lead up to the Australia match in mid-November. The talk had gone well and the team seemed to enjoy interacting with him. As a result we agreed he should facilitate a series of two-day planning work-shops, one with the management team and one with the players. The next thing I had to do was make sure the RFU would pay his bill when it came through.

Find out 'what' I wanted to do, set it all up and then find a way to make it happen. Some people consider that a bit frustrating. To me, it's just getting my priorities straight. It's the 'what' that takes most of the ingenuity. The 'how' is easy.

Bringing the management team together

'Humphrey is the right man for the job. In addition to that, I want to bring everyone who has anything to do with the elite squad or test matches into the room for this workshop so that we can all begin working together.' I handed Don a list of names on a sheet of paper.

'But there are more than twenty people on this list! We can't do that. Some of them live hours away and we'd have to pay for travel and hotels as well. Are you sure you need all of these people?'

'If we want England to win, everyone has to see the bigger picture and how they fit in. We have to get them all involved in this workshop.'

'All right, then. I'll see what I can do.'

Luckily I had already spoken at length with Fran Cotton about outside help. Fran had brought in a consultant when managing the highly successful Lions of 1997. He was supportive of my initiative and helped explain to the management board why an outside consultant and a fresh perspective were necessary. The extra finances were found.

Things were starting to happen.

Change Thinking! – organisation

'OK, Humphrey. Here's what I want to do,' I said. We were at my home in Cookham. It was a Sunday, just one week since our amazing game against the All Blacks. Everyone's confidence was riding high, and even some of the players were beginning actually to see that somewhere in the not too distant future we might go head to head against the southern-hemisphere giants on a level playing field. We could not have predicted it at the time, but it would be fully five years and another four games before we would finally beat the All Blacks at Twickenham, and even more significantly, away on their home ground in New Zealand.

'What I want is to bring everyone who has anything to do with the England squad into a room and share the vision of what we're trying to achieve, to get everyone thinking and working in the same direction. More than that, though, I want to involve them all in the process of developing the elite squad. Most of these people have had decades of coaching or managing England rugby. They are all very professional but I'm not sure they really understand the elite level we need to get to – the world-class performance standards we'll need to achieve. I think we just have to ask them the right questions and get them to do a little Change Thinking! This stuff isn't complicated. They have all the answers we need right there in their heads. We just need to get them to dream a little and to share their thoughts.'

Over the years I've canvassed hundreds of sources for new business techniques aligned to all my experiences in the large corporate world of Xerox and the small-business world of my leasing company. Now it was a case of finding what would work best for England rugby. In our very first meeting I told Humphrey about Paddi and his different approach to business. He in turn had shown me the 6F exercise. For the purposes of my session with the players, I'd then put the two together and called it Change Thinking!

'So what do you think, Humphrey?'

'I'll facilitate what I call a team effectiveness workshop, then. There are four steps. Firstly we'll identify what we're all trying to achieve, and secondly we'll establish some ground rules for how the team communicate with each other. Thirdly we'll facilitate discussions amongst the group about everyone's role descriptions, their expected outputs, as seen by others, and each individual's critical action steps in the months ahead. Lastly we'll then move into the visioning section of the workshop. Here we'll examine every aspect of the player experience in relation to their role in England rugby. You have a distinct problem. As a manager you have a workforce over which you have no control. If you want more from the players, you first have to give them good reasons why they would want to put in the extra effort.'

Humphrey was right. He confirmed my views, which I had first seen operating all those years ago at Loughborough, most notably with Seb Coe. If we wanted elite performance from our players, we first had to provide an elite environment and an elite experience. In terms of motivation, it was the difference between the carrot and the stick. If we made England rugby attractive, prestigious and exclusive enough, then the players would give everything they had within them and more. In corporate marketing terms, it was a deliberate 'pull strategy' as opposed to a 'push strategy'.

'And finally, once we've got all that together, we really should involve the players themselves in this process. Is there any chance of getting them along to the workshop?'

'Not to this one, but yes. It is something we just have to do.'

Getting clubs to agree to release players for training days was very difficult. There was a horrendous political battle raging around my ears whilst all this was going on. Unfortunately, the players were the key bargaining tool stuck in the middle.

We couldn't possibly get the players within a week, but there were some training days scheduled for mid-January. I agreed that Humphrey should hold a workshop with the team during those scheduled days –

this was far more important than the actual physical training at this stage of our development.

'Sounds good so far, Humphrey. We'll have our work cut out for the rest of the year.'

Team effectiveness workshop

The following Thursday and Friday thirteen people came together under the watchful eye of Humphrey Walters. They were:

Roger Uttley – England manager – part-time
John Mitchell – assistant coach – part-time
Phil Keith-Roach – scrummaging coach – part-time
Dave Alred – kicking coach – part-time
Phil Larder – defence coach – full-time
Pat Fox – fitness – part-time
Tony Biscombe – analysis – part-time with the team but full-time RFU
Tom Sears – media – part-time with the team but full-time RFU
Kevin Murphy – medical – part-time
Richard Wegrzyk – medical – part-time
Terry Crystal – medical – part-time
Dan Arnold – kit and equipment – full-time
And myself, Clive Woodward – head coach – full-time

See mini-CVs on page 423

Thirteen people in the room, ten of whom were in part-time positions with the team. As I looked around I couldn't help but think that if we were serious about being the best in the world, we couldn't possibly build an elite squad with part-timers, regardless of how good they were. We were clearly well behind our main rivals.

However this was the first time we'd had everyone in the same room without the time pressures of an impending Test match or a thousand things to do. By England rugby standards at that stage, it was an impressive array of people to have solely focused on the elite squad, even if it was only for two days. And everyone seemed genuinely excited to be in the room. The invitations to attend had been very specific: in this workshop we would be redesigning the elite squad of England rugby, and everyone was expected to contribute. This was the first workshop of its kind that many of them had participated in. You could tell they were looking forward to being involved, to actually having a say. The room was buzzing with energetic conversation as I stood up to open the workshop on the first morning.

'Thank you, everyone, for joining us here today. It's good to have us all together in one place. In my opening talk to the players I stressed that everything you and they ever learned about how England rugby has been run in the past is exactly that, in the past! We have no need for it here. We're going to throw away all that we've ever done as an international team, and then we're going to rebuild the England squad from the ground up with a new way of thinking.

'Imagine if you were to empty all your possessions, your entire house, onto your front lawn, then question the need for everything as you brought it back in the door. That's what we're going to do in England rugby. We have before us a unique opportunity to reinvent completely what it means to be a part of the England international rugby side, for the players, for us as a support team and even for our fans.'

I introduced Humphrey again – some had sat in on his talk to the players some weeks before – and I told the story of his life in corporate training, yachting around the world, and how his expertise would potentially be of benefit to the England set-up if we were prepared to work with him in the next two days.

He immediately took my ideas to a new level by suggesting that in reinventing England rugby we even had the unique opportunity of inspiring the nation with our sporting success. To the surprised looks on some of the group's faces he addressed the following quote by Winston Churchill: 'Never doubt that a small group of thoughtful, committed people can change the world. Indeed, it is the only thing that ever has.'

Humphrey then went on to explain that the first day of our workshop would be about our roles as a team, and the second about the player experience. Once we were warmed up, he started with critical questions about what the new ground rules in our coaching/support team would be. At Henley and London Irish, these had been the first questions I'd asked of the players, but I'd never seen it done this way in a business setting. This is the list of criteria that emerged as he guided us through a probing series of questions.

Elite Squad Management Team Ground Rules
- Be open and encourage openness in others
- No clichés or mumbo jumbo
- Have your say
- Be honest
- Ensure you spend time on self-analysis
- Have and show respect for other team-members
- Keep it in the team (confidentiality)
- Agree to disagree in a non-confrontational way
- Have loyalty for each other
- Encourage a 'no blame' culture
- No excuses
- Be up front and to the point
- No gossip
- Don't apologise for actions, get it right and be professional

It was great to see everyone start talking and the list start growing. I had seen this done in various ways, particularly at Xerox where their management training was second to none, but the difference here was the sheer enthusiasm to open up and let everyone else know exactly how they felt as individuals. This sort of openness usually took a few days, and sometimes it never happened at all. Clearly the fourteen people in the room all had the passion to work at an elite level and not just a professional level. These team-members were writing a strict code of conduct for themselves – without my having to say anything. As a manager in any other business situation, if I had tried to mandate even half of these rules there would have been a mutiny. Yet here was Humphrey asking the right questions about what they thought were the standards they would like to follow, and the most complete list I'd ever seen had emerged. It was all very powerful.

An idea was brewing in my head. *I could and would do the same thing with the players, but in a slightly different way.* I tucked that idea away for another day.

With that as just a warm-up, everyone began talking about their roles in the emerging elite squad – even people who had only minor roles were given full say. In particular we focused on specific tasks we all performed, and the outcomes of our actions and how others relied on them to do their jobs. Most people on the team never realised how much their jobs affected everyone else. It was surprising for some people to see how by missing just a few small details they could cause incredible amounts of friction elsewhere. Needless to say, this process took most of the day and by the end of the session we all had very long lists of critical action steps to improve what we did in the coming months. My list had a total of thirty-seven points, and I know it wasn't the longest list in the room.

Even though we all had lots of work to do as a result, it was still a fantastic session that everyone in the room enjoyed. The clarity it gave to what we were trying to achieve was amazing. It was exactly what the group needed and I could feel us all pulling together as a team. By the end of the evening we were exhausted but really looking forward to the next day.

Workshopping

When we came together the next morning, I again opened the session.

'As Humphrey mentioned to you yesterday, we're going to begin to dissect the entire elite player experience and then reconstruct it more in line with what we're trying to do. Before we do that though we need to talk through a concept called Change Thinking.'

Just as I'd told the players the story about the dentist, Dr Paddi Lund, I repeated the tale for the management. This time I wanted them not only to understand the concept of lateral thinking and to see that there are no rules to running a sports team, but I wanted them to free their thinking. We didn't have to do things in the same way just because they had always been done that way!

The other area of immense interest to me and one I'd first been taken with from Paddi's experience was the importance of detail, not just any kind of detail but the development of things that would and could set us apart from any other rugby team or any other sports team in the world. Paddi had called these Critical Non-Essentials, or CNe's (pronounced see nees) for short. What I wanted us to do was to develop a whole raft of these CNe's that would set us apart from the players' own club culture, to create a unique and incredibly special experience for the players in coming into the England Elite environment. The ultimate aim was to make this environment so good that once the players had experienced it they never wanted to be left out of it.

After this Humphrey and I then shared the 6F slide with them, again explaining the reasons behind the exercise.

As a result of this session with the management I was able to demonstrate my thinking. We had to assume that our main competitors would also have the same quality of players, the same resources and the same standard of coaching. If we accepted that then to be even better we had to do everything in our power to find hundreds of improvements or Critical Non-Essentials that would set us apart from our rivals. These Critical Non-Essentials would be the key factor in creating a winning mindset.

A raft of creative improvements

For the rest of the day Humphrey gently encouraged everyone in the room with probing questions about their roles and how it affected the player experience. He started at the beginning, when a player first arrived in the England camp, and finished with the time the player headed home after the match. Applied with the right level of thinking, it was an awesome process. Again, I was amazed at how many ideas the team came up with in so short a time.

By the end of another long session, we had pages and pages of notes displayed around the room. Under *'Player Experience'* we had 109 action items in the categories of Arrival Instructions, Standards of Behaviour, Dress Code, England Kit Standards, Branding/England Logo, Public Image, Twickenham, Hotel, Meeting Rooms, Player Rooms, Test Week and Departure Procedures. And each action item had initials and a date for completion next to it so that we all knew of our commitments to make things happen.

At the same time it was both an exhaustive and inspirational list of improvements. In one day the team virtually made the plan that would form the foundation of the way the entire elite England set-up would operate, although it would take us many months to implement fully – partly due to the fact that we had no budget for any of our ideas and had to think of creative ways to make them happen. It was a great day for England rugby and formed the starting point of a whirlwind of change that soon transformed the elite England set-up. Of the hundreds of ideas we floated around the room that day, the following were the most interesting to evolve in our first few months of effort:

Changing rooms: The players' changing room at Twickenham was as inspiring as a prison cell. Bare, grey breeze-block walls, a lone unpolished wooden bench underneath a row of wooden pegs. We at least wanted a coat of paint with some colour.

The ground committee with whom I discussed the problem could not understand. 'The changing room is only a few years old. What's wrong with it?' They wouldn't direct any money to the improvements, so, thinking laterally, we came up with the idea of calling the TV show *Real Rooms*, and they jumped at the chance to make over our changing room. As a surprise for the players, we kept it a secret until the Wales game of the Five Nations. When they walked in, it was a complete transformation. Fresh paint in vibrant colours, individual cubicles with hand-carved English oak name placards for each player, England imagery 'To Be the Best' everywhere, along with the England Rose and the St George Cross.

War Room/Team Room: We changed the name of our meeting room to 'War Room' and began to set it up exactly like a boardroom in any leading company – chairs and conference tables in a 'U' shape, flip charts, white boards, and a computer projector and screen. When we were in the War Room we were all business, and when our meetings finished, everyone left. There was no socialising and no messing around in the War Room. For that we had established a completely separate room we called the Team Room where players could socialise, take food, play pool, watch TV and play video games. We asked everyone to avoid socialising in hotel rooms to prevent separatism, cliques and loner behaviour.

Hotel players' rooms: We stopped twin-share accommodation immediately. Each player had his own room. They were professionals and grown men after all. Then, to make the rooms more meaningful to each of the players, we put their names on the doors, put in their rooms the most inspiring, full-action photographs we could find, and made sure they had the same rooms every visit so that they would feel comfortable and familiar with their surroundings. Next we instituted an 'open door' policy for the coaches: if the key was in the door, anyone was welcome to come in for a chat.

Team bus: During the autumn Internationals we chartered buses up to four times a day to move the team around. Many were late, some were too small, and others were completely run down. We did a deal with the coach hire company to refit one bus completely, specifically for the England team, with huge sign writing and England branding. When we arrived, everyone would know it. It was a fabulous bus and it's still the team's bus today.

This is England – welcome book: We instantly began writing a book detailing everything a player would need to know about the England set-up. We also started canvassing players for their ideas and expectations about playing for England, and together allowed them to write their own code of conduct. It would take eight months and several versions to come together in its final form, and it has been changed, enhanced and added to ever since. It's now known as our Black Book. It's a living document that constantly changes.

Players' kit: Oliver Sweeney hand-made the latest designer dress shoes for each player, and Hackett's began to work with players in re-designing all our England suits. When the England team showed up at a function, we looked like a professional organisation, and we had the stated aim of turning heads.

Driveway to Driveway

Over the coming year we would repeat many times this process of examining the player experience with the players and management team together, part of our ever-growing schedule of meetings during training days and Test weeks. Eventually I came to describe it as 'Transforming the Experience – Driveway to Driveway' to cover the entirety of the players' time devoted to the England set-up from when they left home to play for their country to when they returned, hopefully victorious.

We soon applied the same level of thinking to the family and spouses of the players, so that their experience was also considered. From my point of view, I want happy players. They do not need to be worrying about their families when they have so many other things to concern themselves with in Test match build-up. From Jayne's point of view she could see the things that needed to be done to make the overall experience for family and spouses important to the players. Jayne went into action in this area and the work she does here cannot be over-estimated. It is hugely appreciated by all players and their families, and has been fundamental to the success of the team.

As a natural extension, we expanded the process to encompass our interaction with our corporate sponsors, the members of the RFU, the media, and even our supporters – all of our partners in making England rugby the best it can be. It's a powerful process that has application in a variety of ways. It needs a lot of thought and hard work but produces amazing results when facilitated correctly.

As we wrapped up the meeting that Friday in mid-December, we all realised that we had much to think about over the holiday period and a lot of work to do in the new year. There was a buzz of energy and excitement in the room. Everyone was itching to get started. We'd created the blueprint for the type of elite professional sports experience that would support our overarching goal of winning on the rugby pitch. Now all we had to do was pull it off. With just seven weeks including the holidays before the first match of the Five Nations against France, there was simply not enough time to do it all.

15

FIVE NATIONS AND THE TOUR FROM HELL

'Clive, I've got it. I'm at Mount Nelson Hotel. Everyone calls it the Pink Palace. It's the best place in Cape Town, and they have enough rooms for all of us.'

'Great,' I said to Jayne at the other end of the phone. 'Look, it's getting serious over here. I'll jump in a cab and be right over. Would you see if you can find the general manager? I'll be there in thirty minutes.'

We were in South Africa for the last game in our gruelling seven-game, three-country tour of the southern hemisphere. I was fully supportive of the RFU wanting us to take the southern teams head on. However to do it without our top players and send out a third team was not my idea of fun.

Four months earlier, entering our first Five Nations season, I felt a strong sense of synergy growing among the coaches and support team. Our meetings and planning sessions had worked to bring everyone together. Every new idea and advance on our thinking had been implemented, adding to our growing confidence. As far-fetched as it all sounded when I first floated my various ideas for England elite rugby with the players and subsequently in our management team meeting, there was a sense, a feeling that yes, we could do this thing.

Five Nations, 1998

The first match of the 1998 Five Nations tournament got off to a poor start. We were playing France away at their new state-of-the-art stadium, the recently built Stade de France on the outskirts of Paris. It was impressive, yet despite the £270 million construction cost, the winter had really set in and the ground was like concrete. There was some doubt whether the match could be played at all. With the practice pitch frozen and unusable, we were reduced to training in the garden of the team hotel, a situation that could only be described as hopeless. Faced with that same situation now we would handle it with ease, considering it an advantage as we would believe we could handle the conditions better than the opposition. But that's the benefit of experience. Instead it was a frustration.

Before the game we felt we had a good chance, to the extent that France had just been hammered by the Springboks while we had given quite a good account of ourselves against the three southern sides. As it turned out the French won 24—17, and deservedly so. If anything, the scoreline flattered us, because their front row was very strong and for most of the game we were on the back foot as a result. So after five games we still hadn't notched up a win. In performance terms, while we were just about treading water, we certainly weren't walking on it! The French, by contrast, went on to win back-to-back Grand Slams.

The Friday before we played Wales at Twickenham I snatched an hour to drive to Heathrow to meet Jayne and the children just back from a skiing holiday we'd booked before I started the job. It had been an interesting time for the family – the pressure of heavy criticism was beginning to build, especially from one or two past players – but I still wanted the kids to go on holiday, at least with their mum. They'd had a great time. Just after we'd loaded up the car and climbed in, Radio Five Live rudely interrupted their homecoming.

'. . . So does Woodward have a future if England doesn't win tomorrow?' asked the anchor.

'No, it was a bad appointment and it's time to get rid of him!' came the reply from the ex-international.

Jayne looked across at me. The kids went quiet.

'I take it I've missed an interesting week,' she said.

Joe followed with, 'Hey, dad, it's OK by me if they sack you 'cause then you can come with us on holiday next time!'

He was nine, bless him.

Thankfully, we did do a lot better against the home sides, particularly against Wales. We won by 60—26. That was the side's first Test win under my watch, and it was by a record margin for any international championship match. Things were beginning to come together. We went on to win a Triple Crown with victories over Scotland 34—20 and Ireland 35—17.

The results from those first eight games were not brilliant, but I felt the situation overall was very heartening, proof that all our ideas across everything we were doing would be achievable. A major plus was that the players were enjoying what they were doing – a high enjoyment factor is an essential ingredient in my formula for winning – and some people were beginning to talk about our rising stock as contenders for the 1999 Rugby World Cup.

That's why it was so shocking when the ensuing five weeks slowly became England rugby's worst nightmare . . . and I was the man at the helm.

The Tour from Hell

I invited Brian Ashton to join the management team just before our departure to Australia for this tour. I have to say that the further development of the coaching structure at this point remains one of the high points of that particular summer. Brian is an exceptional coach and a joy to work with. I had known him for a long period of time and had recently been an adversary of his in his capacity as coach of Ireland in the recent Five Nations. Brian had parted ways with the Irish Rugby Union and I seized the opportunity to bring him on board. He enabled me to continue to change the approach to coaching the game in moving away from the more traditional approach of having a backs coach and a forwards coach. I wanted to break down the game into attack and defence, and concentrate on the development of basic skills for all of the players, in all areas of the game. Coming from a background of long-term success and experience at Bath, Brian was the perfect addition at this time. His special remit was in attack.

However on the playing front in the eight weeks leading up to our summer tour of the southern hemisphere, later to be known simply as the Tour from Hell, the wheels started to fall off England rugby in a very dramatic way. As the weeks passed into May and events unfolded, it became more and more apparent that the ongoing clash between the interests of the players, the clubs and the RFU was going to have a real and dramatic effect on the England team, one that visionaries like Cliff Brittle and Fran Cotton had foreseen.

The majority of England's best players were declaring themselves ineligible for selection for the summer tour due to injury and fatigue. To be fair, the physical punishment their bodies were being subjected to was immense. Some England players were walking onto the pitch that year for nearly twice as many games as any other elite players around the world. While other teams considered twenty-five games a season as the maximum their players could play while still maintaining peak physical performance, some of our best players had competed in nearly fifty games in the previous twelve months.

The players clearly did need a rest. Typically, summer was the time they could count on it, but instead England had the most gruelling seven-match series ever devised for an England team against the three southern-hemisphere sides. The competition and the schedule made even the fiercest Lions tour pale into insignificance. Something had to give. Unfortunately for me, it was the summer tour. Facing the most challenging task an England rugby coach could imagine, my top players were dropping like flies. Their bodies and fitness levels simply couldn't cope with the immense workload.

It was at that time I realised first, that we simply had to become the strongest and most powerful team in the world in order to win on the world stage; and second, that the RFU and the England team had to begin working together with the professional clubs and players as partners, otherwise the whole thing would collapse in on itself. For the present, I had a job to do, and it had disaster written all over it.

In the end, there was no way we could call the tour off, as it would signal the collapse of international rugby. We went ahead in the knowledge of what was to come. However I was determined to make the most of the situation. English rugby would have to learn its collective lesson. Still, boarding that plane to Brisbane, Australia for our first test against the Wallabies, I couldn't help but think, *This is what it must feel like to be a crash-test dummy.* Would you hop into a car, knowing it would shortly hit a brick wall at 60 mph? It was an obvious fatal conclusion, yet the sheer momentum of events meant we were all power-less to stop it. Everything had caught up with us.

We went with a third-string team. Only six players had more than ten caps to their name and fully twenty out of our thirty-seven-strong touring side were debutants – ten in the forwards and ten in the backs. Obviously the results against full-strength southern-hemisphere sides were terrible, but if you look at that squad list from that tour you'll see some of those players really came good later on. Jonny Wilkinson played in that first test in Brisbane along with Vickery, Dawson and Lewsey. All four were to play in the World Cup final five years later.

All the same, losing 76—0 at Brisbane was a terrible failure for all of us but it was a result that has helped me to keep my feet on the ground every since. The Australians reported it was the biggest massacre since Gallipoli. ARU chief executive John O'Neill said after the eleven-try slaughter, 'This is not what international rugby is about. It wasn't a contest. Those poor players, as determined and proud as they are, were not Test players.'

I could not entirely disagree with his words. Clearly, there were some Test match players, but there were not enough of them. We were letting the whole of international rugby down. Why weren't we putting our full-strength side in Internationals against teams like Australia and New Zealand? I vowed it would never happen again if I had anything to do with it.

After losing in Brisbane we went on to New Zealand, where we were defeated 64—22 at Dunedin on 20 June. Danny Grewcock was sent off. Jonny Wilkinson received an injury in the forty-third minute that put him out of the tour and, as with the Wallabies, it was England's worst ever defeat by a New Zealand side. The second Test went a little better. Matt Dawson captained brilliantly and his example enabled England to show some spirit in their best performance of the tour.

I often hear the words 'character-building' in reference to that tour. Indeed it was a major turning point for me. I had been called home in an emergency the week before the second test in Auckland. Very sadly, my father had passed away. It was not a complete shock as he had been very ill for a long time. I was away for five days to attend my dad's funeral, but if things weren't bad enough losing him, I really needed to be back with the team.

On the flight back to New Zealand, for the first time, I looked at my situation as my father would and knew what he would be asking me: was I really doing this job properly or just trying to keep everyone happy? Losing my father put many things into perspective. In many ways it was time to take the gloves off and stop pussyfooting around with the dozens of people who were playing with the politics of English rugby. It was now having such a dramatic effect on the potential performance of the team that something had to be done.

I made it back to the team in time for the last match in New Zealand. Then at the end of June the England team flew to South Africa to take on the Springboks in our final test of this dreadful tour. Yet somehow I'd never been more determined in my life to make this a success.

Back to the Pink Palace

By the time Jayne had called from the Pink Palace, I was in a frame of mind for action.

Given our incredibly demanding schedule in the previous five weeks, I could sense that the team was very close to exploding. We had arrived in South Africa on Monday after being battered and beaten in a horrible string of one-sided games in New Zealand. Then to top off a twenty-seven-hour journey, we were driven by coach to a Holiday Inn Garden Court Motel in the suburb of Newlands, near the stadium where the matches were played. When we were there in 1998 the hotel had seen better days – and it wasn't a very safe neighbourhood either.

But that wasn't the only issue. While our accommodation was barely adequate for an international team of any sort, the South African team were staying across town in the lavish five-star Sun City, one of the best hotels Cape Town had to offer. It was the custom in international rugby during Tests like these for the host nation's union to arrange the accommodation of the visiting side. When the Springboks came to London, the RFU put them up at the five-star Berkeley Hotel in central London. Something was not quite right. To me, it was unacceptable.

It was an example of everything we needed to change about the mindset of England rugby. No matter how inexperienced these England players were, it was wrong of anybody to place them in such average accommodation, especially when the other side were considerably better placed. Rugby was a professional sport and our players needed to be treated accordingly, even if that meant breaking with tradition and paying for our own hotel.

Before this, I had been so busy coaching that I never even thought of getting involved with organising hotels or travel details. Don Rutherford had organised the schedule for the tour years before, and it was Roger Uttley's job to arrange the rest of the trip. It never occurred to me to question what they put together. I just assumed everything would be fine. At the time I was informed that the Lions had stayed at the same hotel the previous year. If it had been good enough for them it must have been good enough for this England team. However, I simply couldn't agree. The standard of accommodation did not meet the criteria of my new professional expectations. Even so, I might not have worried about it this time but for what happened next.

To my horror, the South African Rugby Union had also put its Under-21 team in the same Holiday Inn with us. In international rugby union terms this was unheard of. Imagine our surprise when we got off the bus to find half the South African Under-21 side in the hotel lobby. It was an insult, and everyone knew it. Their not-so-subtle reference to the youthful status of the England team was probably accurate. However, with the painful tour we'd just been through, things were at boiling point in the team. This situation might just have been the straw that broke the donkey's back. I had to do something about it, so I'd asked Jayne to do a little scouting around to see if she could find a more appropriate venue. She had arrived to spend the last week of a very difficult tour with me. I arrived at the Pink Palace by taxi very soon after Jayne called. By late Thursday afternoon I was utterly convinced that I needed to act. The hotel and lack of decent food were creating undercurrents that weren't good – the players had hardly slept all week because the hotel was so noisy. On top of that, laundry we sent away never came back and various items over those few days disappeared and I was worried about the hotel's security. It was time to be decisive and demonstrate to the players that they were special and that they did matter to England rugby.

The Pink Palace

The Mount Nelson is one of South Africa's most famous hotels. It's a hundred-year-old landmark building situated on nine acres of park-like gardens at the base of Table Mountain, placing it right in the very heart of old Cape Town. 'Why do they call it the Pink Palace?' I asked my taxi driver. 'Because it's pink and looks like a palace,' was his response. It was easily the Ritz or Savoy of Cape Town. I knew I had come to the right place as my taxi drove through the enormous gates, past the elaborate guard houses and outrageously uniformed guards, up the majestic drive, to the palatial main building. Another uniformed gentleman opened my car door.

'Good afternoon, sir. Welcome to the Mount Nelson. Mrs Woodward is in the lounge awaiting your arrival.'

Within ten minutes of meeting the general manager the arrangements were made . . . individual rooms with big beds for everyone. Now it was just a case of how we were going to pay for it! Jayne and I sat down and got out every credit card we had and handed them over. We later rang England to make sure there was enough room on the cards to cover the costs – including accommodation, food and the meeting facilities we'd need for the rest of the weekend. We also needed to make sure that no one travelling with us was left behind at the Holiday Inn, for we had a few team members' girlfriends and one or two parents of players with us too. If the team moved, so did they. Thankfully it was winter and not their high season.

When we returned to the hotel later that night I rewrote the notes for our morning meeting and called everyone to an early emergency session at 8 a.m., an hour before normal. We then checked that the coaches ordered for our 10.30 a.m. training would be there at 9 a.m., and finally, after a long day, I went to bed knowing I'd done the right thing.

It was unusual to change the schedule – the players would know something was wrong – but this trip had thus far delivered up quite a few surprises. I was later told that all the players expected me to come into that room and announce my resignation as coach, to quit before the tour even ended, and let someone else take responsibility for the situation we had found ourselves in on this tour. As I walked into the War Room at 8 a.m. on Friday morning, the cacophony of anxious voices died instantly.

'I'll be brief. I don't want any questions, so please listen carefully. We've all been through a difficult tour in the last five weeks, and can I just say at this point that I would like to congratulate you all on the way you have handled everything. You don't deserve the way you are being treated and this hotel sums everything up. So I want you to pack your bags. We're leaving this hotel now . . .'

The whole room burst out into spontaneous applause and laughter, I have never seen a bunch of players so happy.

'Everyone pack your bags but do not check out. I will deal with that. The team bus will be outside at 9 a.m. sharp . . . I think you'll be pleased with our new surroundings.'

No sooner had I finished than the entire group deserted the meeting room. I couldn't believe it. It was like the escape from Saigon. I've never seen a team move so fast in all my life. By 11 a.m. everyone had checked into the Mount Nelson, and the change in spirits was remarkable.

The next morning after a huge sleep they all had a great breakfast, and by the time of the game they had a spring in their step. For the first time in five weeks since our devastating loss in Brisbane the players were actually looking forward to the match.

We lost that match 18—0, but the boys put in an incredible effort, especially in defence. Fortunately it poured with rain which might have saved us from another heavy defeat. The game ended up being a bit of a free-for-all, but South Africa made fewer mistakes and our kicking was poor. Matt Perry at full-back was England's best player on the day, catching every kick the South Africans sent his way. Matt, a wonderful player and superb team member, remains the most capped England full-back ever.

International incident

Unfortunately shifting hotels wasn't as popular in other circles as with the team!

My phone didn't stop ringing for two days. I suspected the move would make big news, but it wasn't the media calling. No, the unwelcome attention came from elsewhere. Apparently the officials of the South African Rugby Union were having a major sense of humour failure and were a bit put out that I so flatly and bluntly refused their hospitality. Apparently moving to the Mount Nelson was equivalent to a very high-level diplomatic slap in the face. There were rumours of South Africa cancelling their upcoming autumn match and even banning all future tours. I had several frantic calls from council members in the UK and many more from those already in South Africa.

'You can't do that!'

'Well I have and we're not going back.'

'But the RFU doesn't pay for the team hotels when England travels.'

'Fine. I'll pay for it.' Fortunately, when the furore died down, I didn't have to. It was quite a bill. 'I am in charge here and the decision has been made. If you have an issue with this then you'll have to wait until we get back to London.' This was not bravado. They were clearly in the wrong here. This was me making cold, hard decisions based on the facts, thinking correctly under pressure.

At the formal dinner after the match, the South African captain even joked about the incident in his opening address. 'We may have won the match but the English certainly stayed in the best hotel in South Africa! Can I just say well done. Even the Springboks don't stay in the best hotel in Cape Town. You've now set the standard. I hope our union pays attention – I've always wanted to stay there!'

The day after the final match we flew back to England. To say it was good to be home would be a massive understatement. We were all exhausted, mentally, physically and emotionally, but we had survived. It's a credit to all those players, none of whom stepped out of line under incredible provocation both on and off the pitch. As I walked out of the customs hall at Heathrow at 7 a.m. that morning, all I could think about was taking a long hot shower, collapsing into bed and taking a break with the family. That's why it was interesting to see Don Rutherford approaching Jayne and me as we wheeled our trolley into the arrivals hall.

Guess he's come to check that I haven't had a nervous breakdown.

'Clive, that incident about the hotel is causing major problems. Could you come to Twickenham right now so that we can sort it out. I need to write a full report to the management board.'

Even I could not quite believe what he was saying.

'Don, we have just completed the worst tour in the whole history of English rugby, including losing to Australia 76—0, and you want me to come with you to write a report about my shifting hotels? I don't want to be rude or say something I'll regret. The answer is no. I need to go home and see the kids, OK?'

And with that I made towards the exit.

What could they do? Fire me? We'd already been through hell. It didn't get any worse than this.

It was a perfect example of the clash of different cultures in the RFU. We were just finishing the most disgraceful international tour ever in terms of results. The schedule of the tour would have been fine – challenging but do-able – if you had the players in great shape with time to prepare for it. Without that it was always going to be tough if not impossible.

The RFU, the coaches, the clubs, the players ... everyone, we all failed that summer. We let our country down badly. That one moment in the crowded arrivals hall was the lowest point in more than 130 years of England rugby history ... and I was in charge.

Unfortunately, the lessons learned from this tour were never really taken on board by those responsible for running the English game. Indeed, it becomes increasingly difficult to manage many situations with the system we operate in. The break-up of the England team post RWC 2003, due to retirements, injuries, player fatigue and loss of form, would have been all far more manageable if we actually had more control over the players and worked in the same way as the southern-hemisphere teams are run. England will win if we are allowed to prepare properly and compete on a level playing field, but currently we are not and never have been since the game went professional. That is what makes winning the World Cup even more remarkable.

Cultural conflicts in the RFU

Don Rutherford and I had problems to begin with in sorting out our roles. It's not that we didn't like each other. Quite the opposite really. Don was the one who originally selected me as coach for the Under-21s in 1996. No, I realise now our approaches to rugby were so completely different. Not in our coaching ideas necessarily, but more to do with the way we thought the England elite squad should be managed and controlled.

Don had achieved an incredible amount in almost thirty years managing the game. Now I can see that was part of the problem. Before Don, the game was administered by amateurs – volunteers who were giving their time to ensure the continuation of a game they loved . . . in the Corinthian spirit, or spirit of amateur participation. Don, on the other hand, was among the first full-time professional employees in the RFU. He'd been working his entire career from within the RFU to change the organisation from a volunteer or amateur mindset to a professional one, particularly as that mindset applied to the England international teams.

The emerging business of rugby certainly required professional management. Revenues from TV coverage rights and international fixtures were blossoming. During the same time, Don personally wrote many of the coaching programmes and manuals that are still in use today at the grass roots level of rugby. In his travels representing the union, Don had visited the southern-hemisphere nations to examine successful coaching methods as well as to glean knowledge of how to manage a more competitive international team.

Don had worked consistently, quietly and carefully over the decades to bring the game into a professional era of playing, coaching and management. However, through the seventies and eighties the Corinthian spirit had been strong amongst the council members of the RFU. Don had to fight tooth and nail for every budget increase. Both his budgets and his use of funds were subject to intense scrutiny, yet for thirty years he chipped away at the problem. It takes great patience and determination to work tirelessly as he did for so long, enjoying the process no doubt, but constantly struggling to focus the volunteer mindset to the modern professional management issues involved in running a fast-growing commercial enterprise. I doubt very much that I could have done what he did. I couldn't have endured for so long his obvious fight with the volunteers who were running the game.

From my first day on the job it was apparent that my approach was going to upset the apple cart. Not necessarily all the time, but it often did, and if I'd had a little more insight this might have been avoided. That kind of understanding only comes with time and, as the coach of an international team, time was one luxury I didn't have. It's simply no good thinking, *Oh, that's a good idea. Maybe I'll try that next year* . . .

Although it wasn't as clear to me then, it's obvious now that the RFU as an organisation was in a period of transition, and the friction between the different parties was due to three distinctly different emerging interests. I must point out that everyone had the same aim – a successful and growing organisation with victories at the international level. It's just that many people had completely different views of how to achieve that aim. Not that any line of thinking was right or wrong, just different. Here's how I would picture the Rugby Football Union as it has evolved over several decades. (See diagram below.)

When the RFU was first formed in 1871, rugby was purely an ama-

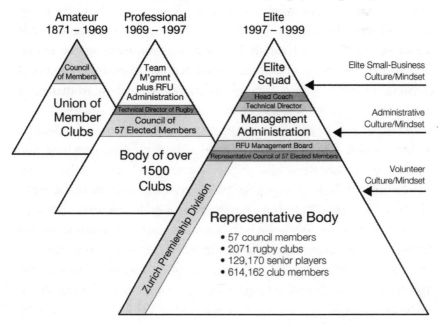

teur sport and the Corinthian spirit prevailed. In the context of winning, participation was the main aim. Over the next hundred years, the representative body of the union was managed by a volunteer committee of elected members. The union prospered, growing to hundreds of clubs and the game spread in popularity around the world. Although dominated by a voluntary culture, with decisions by committee and popular vote, it can only be said that the union has been very successful in its aims over many decades.

However, with the dawn of television and the ensuing revenue streams associated with broadcasting rights, the day-to-day operations of the union required greater management skills and resources. The union had simply become too big to be managed effectively by volunteers. Key decisions were slow and ponderous, while the commercial world demanded improved standards.

Don Rutherford's appointment in 1969 as the first full-time professional manager heralded a new age of administration and management. Over the next thirty years, Don would slowly transform the game into a network of administrative coaching support systems which were largely targeted at the grass roots of the game. However, being professionally organised and moving play to the competitive level was at odds with the Corinthian spirit that still prevailed in much of the representative council. So Don began, very carefully and very slowly, to wrest control and functional decision-making from the committee and its large number of sub-committees. This growing administrative mindset or culture simply did not mix well with the participative mindset – those inspired by voluntary participation could not understand those motivated by the spirit of competition. It wasn't as though Don or the council members had different goals. They had different views of how to achieve those goals.

Ironically, I believe that Don and I experienced a similar kind of friction, thirty years later, that he had been dealing with for all these years. My small-business mindset gave me a real advantage in running an elite team. Unfortunately, what I didn't realise at the time, was that the elite performance mindset and culture didn't exactly mix well with the administrative mindset or professional competitive culture that was there at the time.

When I look back, it's so obvious. I wonder why I didn't see it before. However, things aren't so clear when you're in the thick of it. It would take me fully five years as coach finally to understand the differences between the mindsets required successfully to manage each of these disparate yet complementary segments of the organisation. The addition of a new cultural element in late 1998, a corporate culture, was actually what helped me more than anything else to understand these groups and how they worked together. In August the management board selected Francis Baron as the first professional CEO of the union.

Indeed, even now after the World Cup we're still experiencing difficulties in balancing the interests of these groups. But we're getting better at understanding and managing them. From the coaches' point of view, and looking at how our main rivals operate, we are still skiing uphill. Why we won the World Cup in spite of the disadvantages is the key story.

16
AUTUMN INTERNATIONALS

'You've done what?' Don Rutherford was staring at me aghast.

'I said I've gone a bit over budget on our *This Is England* Black Book.'

Don had been quite adamant that I should prepare my own budgets for the England squad this financial year. That way, presumably, he felt that, once passed by the council, he wouldn't have to go back for more of my off-the-cuff expenditures. I fully understood the importance of budgets, but it was very difficult to predict, let alone work within, budgets when we had to move so fast, making the necessary improvements and innovations. We were changing things every day. I didn't know what would happen next month, let alone the next year. In spite of that, I had prepared budgets. That was in July. This was September.

'What's a Black Book? I don't remember seeing that in your budget.'

'It's under "printing, player documentation". The Black Book is the players' manual we've been putting together over the last nine months. It sets the standards for players while in the England camp; things like objectives, a code of conduct, policies and procedures, nutrition, medical and media guidelines, etc. I think it's going to play a key role in the development of the elite team.'

I was quite proud of our new work.

I told him the total figure of the final printing and pre-press bill.

'What? Clive, that's way over budget! How many of these things are you making?'

I told him.

'What?'

Don laughed for almost the first time when discussing this sort of thing.

'Well, all right. So how are we going to pay for it then?'

'I'm not sure, but it's important that we find a way.'

I think Don was starting to think on the same wavelength. But it was still incredibly frustrating. It seemed every initiative I proposed was met with the answer, 'We cannot afford to do this.'

In my opinion we couldn't afford not to do these things! In giving your team every chance of winning, no cost was too high. Nothing could be left to chance, and there must be no excuses for anyone not to succeed.

On the one hand, I had a growing team of dedicated professionals wracking their brains to come up with innovative solutions and fresh new approaches to winning with an elite rugby squad. And on the other hand, we had key decision-makers who simply didn't understand what we were trying to achieve, and why we wanted it all so quickly.

I was encouraging my team to think laterally, without limits. Yet we had to work within the restrictive management culture that pervaded the rest of the RFU, and we were moving at a much faster pace than they were even remotely used to.

It was an impossible combination of cultures, but who knows, it may be that having to struggle for every innovation forced us to be even more resourceful and creative in our thinking. If so, our Black Book would be the shining example of our hard-fought ingenuity.

The Black Book of rugby

I think our Black Book is fundamental to coaching. I'd never coach rugby or any sport without one – in fact I wouldn't even run a business without one now – and if I had to start again from scratch, it's the first thing I'd create with the new team. Since the beginning of the year we'd been working with the players at every opportunity to build this book into an everything-you-need-to-know manual about playing rugby for England. And now, after such a dismal summer tour, it was critical that we showed everyone that the Tour from Hell was behind us, and that some of us were more determined than ever to see England become the best team in the world.

What we wanted was a book that would tell the players all they needed to know in an administrative and code-of-conduct sense, so that when they arrived in the England camp they had nothing on their minds but contributing to team meetings and playing the best rugby they could produce on the pitch. More than that, I wanted our players to positively thirst for the kind of rugby we were instilling in the new elite England set-up. We'd created an elite culture. Now we needed a book that would inspire players about being a part of the England squad.

This book would be a tool that members of the squad could read in their own time, thereby bringing new players up to speed quickly and effectively. That way we wouldn't have to spend countless hours of our valuable and very limited time in the War Room going over old material.

There were roughly thirty players invited to all training days and Test week sessions. And for every series of games we played, there were roughly three new players in the set-up at any one time as a result of injury, retirement or player selection. Obviously, it's hard to function efficiently when at least 10 per cent of the room doesn't know what's going on. In our recent Tour from Hell the situation was even worse: the great majority of the players didn't know how things worked, and having to spend so much time educating everyone had caused serious problems.

A so-called Black Book would be an invaluable tool to sort that out. It was just so obvious, especially in the sporting world. I wondered why I hadn't thought of it before.

This Is England comes alive

We'd been writing solidly for the previous nine months. Our book had grown from a few loose-leaf photocopied pages into a full-colour, high-quality masterpiece. Rob Chappelhow at the Bridge Production Company in Eversholt had been working for six weeks on the design, layout and artwork . . . and it truly was a work of art. The book itself was leather-bound with the England Rose embossed on the front. Inside were the normal diary and address pages, but we'd added 96 pages to the front to make it our very own. We'd called it *This Is England* and it immediately became the cornerstone of the elite culture we'd been trying to instil in England rugby. The very first page contained an introduction from me that summarised everything we wanted the players to take to heart. But now these words were set in print, not just casually spoken out loud in a team meeting. My hope was that they would be imprinted on everyone's mind. We've changed the contents of these pages several times over the years, but this was the introduction in our very first Black Book.

The Business of Inspiration

We are in the business of inspiration. Our job is not only to inspire one another but also all those that we work with, watch us and support us. Our goal is to inspire the whole country.

Together we have achieved a tremendous amount within the last twelve months. The 26—26 game against the All Blacks and to a certain extent the win against Wales did inspire the whole country.

This document clearly shows what we have achieved together in our first twelve months and sets out what we need to aspire to in the next twelve months culminating in the World Cup.

We have worked hard on this document and all agreed its contents – now we have the platform to work from that was sadly lacking a year ago. New members to the squad will be strictly required to adhere to the contents of this document.

We are in the business of inspiration – there are no excuses anymore. Remember we work in a no 'if only' culture.

We are here to inspire our country – let's do it.

Clive Woodward
October 1998
1 year to go

'Never doubt that a small group of thoughtful, committed people can change the world. Indeed, it is the only thing that ever has.'
– Sir Winston Churchill

And on the next page . . .

How do you want to be remembered?

You are an England 'Elite' Player. You must take the full responsibility that this honour brings to you. Nothing must be left to chance and absolutely no 'if onlys' are acceptable. How does this team want to be remembered?

This text was set and printed on the highest quality paper. The colours were all in vivid England red and deep royal blue. Images of England's rose were on every page. And the inspirational sayings were set against a backdrop of the most stimulating and evocative live-action photos of the players – not old pictures from a bygone age. It was crucial to use pictures of the present players from our season thus far, some even as recent as our Tour from Hell. Opposite the 'How do you want to be remembered' page was a huge picture of the Webb Ellis Cup. This truly was an impressive book. But it didn't stop with inspirational sayings and evocative phrases. On page nine was the table of contents which read,

A Introduction

B Objectives
   ● Head Coach
   ● Players
   ● Management

C Who's Who
   ● Coaching
   ● Management
   ● Players

D Code of Conduct
   ● Players
   ● Management and Coaching

E Policies and Procedures

F Schedule up to the World Cup

G Fitness Testing

H International Week
- England Training Week
- Match Day
- Post Match Requirements

I England Support
- Medical
- Technical
- Media
- Sponsorship

J Summary

The squad had spent an inordinate amount of time through the year discussing and setting standards, ideas, goals, objectives and a philosophy of play. Now they were all set in stone and could be continually referred to, especially by new players. This Black Book of ours was a pretty impressive management tool. And because it was in a leather folder and was ring-bound, we could add and take away pages any time we liked, which we did from that time onwards about twice every year. This was a working document, and while players were in the England camp, it became their bible.

Teamship rules

Another name the team soon adopted for the Black Book was 'Teamship Rules'. This idea first came up in a discussion with Humphrey Walters. It is an incredibly simple but very powerful system that will only work when driven by the leader, i.e. me. Specifically, Teamship Rules covered the code of conduct which the players had set down and agreed that everyone should keep. They became such a dominant part of the book over the years that we soon began referring to our Black Books simply as the Teamship Rules.

I say the code of conduct was set down by the players, and that's what I mean. As a result of my observation of our own management team and our strict set of internal rules, I had put questions to the players over the previous nine months, at almost every opportunity in meetings during training days and Test weeks, about how they wanted to handle what seemed to me to be key operational activities.

Here are a few of the more widely known Teamship Rules put in place by the players and signed off by me.

Punctuality: I asked the team to discuss amongst themselves what being on time for team meetings meant to them. They came back with Lombardi Time – ten minutes early for every meeting. Nobody was ever late, and if they were the whole team would let them know that by their actions they had just cost us the World Cup.

Mobile phones: When we first came together as a team, the mobile phones were totally out of control. They were going off everywhere. After a discussion by the team they decided that mobile phones would never be seen in public, and would never be seen while players were in the England camp. They could only be used in players' rooms and in private. They also asked the team management to abide by the same rules. In the very next meeting after we agreed on the new rule a mobile phone started ringing right in the middle of my team talk.

No one moved. The phone kept ringing. Still no one moved.

'All right, whose phone is it?' I asked.

No one owned up. I started following the sound and stopped right in front of Austin Healey's chair.

'It's not mine,' he protested. 'My phone is turned off and in my room.'

He stood up. The ringing was definitely coming from the bag under his chair. He pulled it onto the table and with a very uncomfortable look picked up the ringing phone.

'Hi, Austin,' said Matt Dawson into his own phone from across the room. 'I'm just seeing if you had checked you had a phone in your bag.'

The whole room fell about. Matt had obviously planted the phone. But Austin would get his own back.

Books and press: I committed to never writing a newspaper column or a dish-the-dirt type of book spreading gossip or tittle-tattle about what happened behind England team doors, and to never, ever, betraying the team's confidence. This book for example is intended to be a management book, to set down and document the incredible hard work undertaken by both the players and the coaching team in order to win. You may be disappointed that there are no juicy bits of gossip, but I make no apologies. On their side, the players committed to ensuring that no one in the squad should be seen in a bad light in any book or column; no player, no coach, no doctor – nobody.

The Teamship Rules covered every aspect of what it meant to be a player in the England squad. We would never stop improving and adding to them. By the time we got to the World Cup in 2003, we would have 7 categories, 35 sections, and 240 individual Teamship Rules consisting of roughly 10,000 words of text. And if you think players wouldn't be interested in reading all those words, you should see how the new squad players spend a long time digesting every fact so that they won't let anyone down. It also gives them confidence about how to operate within the squad.

The Black Book is a powerful tool that has grown substantially over the years, allowing me many times in that period to reset the standards with the team's full backing. It was a key reason why we arrived at the World Cup in 2003 as such a tight-knit group in every sense of the word, and why under the greatest pressure of the World Cup the team came through in every respect.

'Now remember,' I said, as I introduced everyone in the squad to their new Black Books, 'we have all discussed and agreed these Teamship Rules over and over again during the last year. This year is all about playing. We have set these standards. Let's now agree to get on with it and stick to them.'

1998 autumn Internationals

In the autumn England played a couple of Rugby World Cup qualifiers, both staged in Huddersfield. The first, on 14 November, was against the Netherlands, and resulted in a cricket score victory of 110—0 for the home side. Neil Back collected four tries, becoming the first England forward to do so in a cap match since 1881. Paul Grayson slotted 30 points, equalling the England record for most points in a test (then held by Rob Andrew). Perhaps more importantly, this was the first time Martin Johnson played as captain for England – a role he was to assume with tremendous authority in the next five years.

But all in all this wasn't a game to remember. Frankly, it was a terrible mismatch, and I was keen that such encounters should be avoided in the future. In my view it is actually dangerous that such unequal contests should take place at all, and I would much prefer to see teams such as the Netherlands take on 'A' sides rather than expose themselves to massively fit professionals.

The next game, against Italy a week later, was a much closer match. In fact they very nearly won. In the second half their scrum-half, Alessandro Troncon, scored what looked to be a perfectly good try, only to have it disallowed by the referee. Almost to the end we were just hanging on to a one-point lead until at last Will Greenwood scored, three minutes from time.

On 28 November we took on the Wallabies, once again at Twickenham. We lost that one too, but this time there was only a one-point difference. We scored the only try in the match twelve minutes from full time. Matt Perry made a superb run from full back, and Jerry Guscott finished it in style. We missed the conversion, and soon afterwards the Wallaby captain, John Eales, kicked his fourth penalty of the match, putting the Aussies just ahead with four minutes to go. We may have won the try count but in the end we lost against a very good side.

However, even if we had beaten the Wallabies, it would have been overshadowed in people's memories by our performance at Twickenham against South Africa a week later. After a brief lack of focus at the beginning, which let through an early try for the Springboks, England fought back to put Guscott over the line. Dan Luger had taken Mike Catt's hoisted kick and unloaded to Jerry Guscott steaming up beside him. It was exactly the style of exciting rugby we wanted to play. After that, the England forwards were aggressive and forced error after error on the other side. When Dallaglio passed up the chance to kick two easy penalties in an attempt for tries, I knew the team was confident. We came in at half-time 7—7 and after the break the England forwards continued to dominate. We forced two more penalties under pressure, and England won 13—7. It was a famous English victory which ended the Springboks' amazing run of seventeen Test wins.

England had had its first southern-hemisphere victory since I had taken over, the first in a dozen matches since beating Australia in the 1995 World Cup quarter-final. It tasted sweet. I could feel the side was coming good. The Springboks, by contrast, took a long time to recover from that defeat. The expectation had been so great, the hope of achieving an all-time record in successive Tests won. But for us, that win allowed us to go into the Five Nations with a lot of confidence. We were definitely competing with the best, even if we weren't quite there yet. The Tour from Hell had been forgotten by many, but it was still at the back of my mind and has allowed me to keep my feet firmly on the floor at all times.

Laptops ... or raw meat

Just before Christmas I got the idea of giving the entire squad laptop computers.

There was clearly no budget for ideas like these. Instead I just went ahead and found another way of doing it. England rugby needed computers.

I went straight to my old friends and clients in my leasing business, Elonex Computers. As part of Sales Finance & Leasing, I'd been doing business with Michael Spiro at Elonex Computers for nearly a decade. They build and supply computers and all makes of technology to businesses. I used to arrange finance for their clients to purchase their IT hardware and even software, a burgeoning area of lending in the nineties through our leasing facility.

'Clive, happy to help if we can. What do you need?' said Michael from across the desk in his office once I'd told him why I was visiting.

'Just the normal laptops will do. I want extended battery life because they'll probably be working a lot on the road. And I want them connected to the internet and e-mail.'

'I'll see what I can do,' he said.

And that's how Elonex Computers became the official IT sponsor of the RFU. In those days no one was really worried about my making sponsorship deals with partners like Elonex. Now, however, it would go through the marketing department and a tender process, which is all fine but back then I just had to get on with it. Even when the marketing department did get involved years later to formalise their sponsorship agreements with Michael, my position and relationship with Elonex never changed – working truly in partnership is a business concept few really understand. Since day one, Elonex have been fantastic partners with us in the England team.

Now every player gets a laptop, an e-mail address and an internet dial up account from Elonex as part of their Team Induction Kit. And if for some reason a player is not selected or retires, they can choose either to give back the laptop or buy it. Most choose the latter.

When I first organised the computers, no one really knew what I was doing until the laptops showed up at Bisham Abbey. Fifty brand new laptops were crammed into the Elizabethan Room at the Abbey for our next training day. You should have seen everyone's face when they walked into the Abbey that Monday. There were boxes piled six feet high in every corner. I did give Tony Biscombe a bit of notice, seeing that he would probably be the person to whom the players would turn for technical help. However the deal I'd done with Michael would cover that, too. Part of the package was training all the players to use e-mail, plus the offer of telephone support over special help lines. Nearly 60 per cent of players didn't use a computer regularly. It only took a few months really for everyone to get the hang of things.

Some in the media were unfortunately a little harder to convince.

'What on earth do you need computers for? They're rugby players not boffins. You should be giving them more raw meat, not laptops,' came the comments.

Former Wallaby David Campese in Australia seized the opportunity once again to criticise. 'A coach who doesn't want to talk to his players?' he shouted to the world in reference to our use of e-mail. 'I wouldn't ever allow a coach to treat me that way.' Campese has always been disliked by the England players for his predictable, boring rantings against us, which I guess is fair enough. Until I read Rod Macqueen's book, however, I didn't realise how unpopular he is in Australia, too, especially with their team and coaches. Now that really does take some doing.

My detractors, and there were many, just did not understand and probably still don't. Rugby is a complex sport, and we only get eleven short weeks with our players each year, plus a handful of extra training days. In that brief time the players have to learn what is often a completely different style of game to their clubs'. We have to communicate our entire list of calls and plays; and we have to co-ordinate the schedules of some fifty high-performance individuals with hectic lifestyles and full agendas. It's simply not easy. You try reaching these guys by phone when you need to. If the diligent press can't manage it, neither could we. Computers and e-mail were the answer. E-mail will never replace the hand-shake or the face-to-face meeting, but to communicate effectively with 50-plus players it was priceless.

I will admit, we did help a few of our players to learn to use their computers at first, but it wasn't long before all our team were using these new tools like old pros. Once some of the less enthusiastic players found out what was actually on the internet it was amazing how quick the uptake was! Regular contact by E-mail has also helped the players to become a real team – they use it for good banter and keeping in touch socially.

I don't know what we would do now without the communication systems we have in place. Effective communication is at the foundation of any successful team. Without it you'll be forever mired in inefficiency. For that we owe a great thanks to Michael Spiro and Elonex Computers. They have continued to support us in the six years since.

17

THE YEAR OF THE '99 WORLD CUP

'Hi, Clive, it's Lavinia.' Lavinia was Francis Baron's secretary. 'I'm sorry to be calling so late on a Sunday night. It's important. I've got a message from Francis.'

It was 9.30 p.m. This was highly unusual.

'Go ahead. What is it?'

'Francis would like you to be seated at your desk at 7.20 a.m. tomorrow morning. Whatever you do, don't be late. He's seeing everyone in the organisation and he's only got five-minute time slots.'

'Come on, Lavinia. What's this all about?'

'I don't know, honestly, Clive. All I know is I have a list of over forty people to call with very specific instructions. Please don't be late. There is nothing else I can say to you.'

'Thanks, Lavinia. I'll be there.'

After we hung up, I began to get a little nervous. After all, I hadn't exactly set the world on fire with my win/loss record in the last year: 16 games, 6 wins, 2 draws and 8 losses – a 45 per cent success rate. But still, we'd come such a long way and we'd had such a glorious win over South Africa. Was my time as coach at an end? Francis Baron was a very hard man to read. For the previous three months since he'd started as CEO he'd kept largely to himself. He had spent the time interviewing everyone and studying the workings and the individual roles at the RFU. I had my meeting with him, and when I'd presented him with our Black Book he seemed genuinely interested in how I was operating, and seemed to nod his head when I explained my plan, but he gave absolutely nothing away. I'd not really spoken with him since. Needless to say, I didn't sleep very well that night.

I arrived early at the office as usual. The traffic before 6.30 a.m. is so much easier. Only this morning I think I would have appreciated a little extra company, perhaps a traffic jam or two, anything to delay things a bit. The office is normally quiet at that time, but on this day it was very different. A lot of people were milling around, all with a time to see Francis. It was as though word had got around and everyone knew what was coming.

At 7.20 a.m. on the dot, Francis walked into my office and shut the door.

'Clive, don't say a word. I want you to listen. I only have a few minutes, so please don't interrupt me.'

Francis then went on to explain what was about to happen.

In the few months since taking the position of CEO, he had examined the whole structure and full staff of the RFU. Today he was making his changes, all with the sanction of the management board. In a nutshell, the part-time position that Roger Uttley had filled as England team manager was no longer deemed necessary. Don Rutherford's position as director of rugby was also obsolete along with thirty-two other administrative positions. There were sweeping changes being made right across the board, but these two affected me and the England team the most.

Francis went on to thank me for what I had been trying to do and expressed his wish for me to continue. It was agreed that I would go to see Roger at Harrow and explain the position as best I could to him personally. Francis then nodded his head, extended his hand to take mine, and walked out of the door, presumably to meet the next person on his list. Our discussion had taken less than three minutes.

After my meeting with Francis, I walked out into the open-plan office. No one was speaking. No one was doing anything but wondering if they were next. As I walked through the building towards Don Rutherford's office, I saw people who'd been with the RFU for decades crying and hugging each other. By the time I got to Don's office, he was already gone. There was a security guard whom I knew well standing near his door.

'How long have you been here?' I asked.

'Since 7 a.m. Arrived with the chief executive. It was tough,' he said. 'Don just packed his things and left.'

This is going to be an interesting day! 130 people in the entire organisation and thirty-four made redundant.

I walked to my car and started the half-hour drive to Harrow School where Roger was a housemaster. On the way I put in a call to home. Jayne answered.

'Well?'

'I've still got a job, but it's been one hell of a morning here!'

I then phoned Roger to let him know I was coming. It wasn't unusual for me to drive to the school to talk about rugby and the team over a cup of tea between Roger's lessons. We'd done so many times in the past year. But driving to Roger and seeing him that morning was one of the hardest things I've ever had to do. It was difficult because nobody respected him more than I did. Roger still is one of the most outstanding individuals in the world of rugby. In the end, there was just no room in the elite squad any more for non-professional coaches. The transition between two contrasting organisational cultures was completed in one fell swoop. The management ethos of the amateur era had now been replaced with an elite performance and corporate ethic. There was no turning back. When choosing to leave my business to take on the role as coach I did not actually realise at the time what a huge decision it was. Clearly everyone had to make similar decisions about career changes if they wanted to go into professional coaching and management positions for the England team. We could not become the best in the world with part-time people, divided in their attention, regardless of how talented or respected they were.

I never did get a chance to speak with Don. I wish I had gone around to see him but would not have known what to say. I can only imagine what he must have gone through emotionally after devoting nearly thirty years of his life to the game of rugby and the RFU. However, looking at it rationally, Francis was right. The organisation did have to change. Don had created a strong professional management culture, but Francis Baron was taking the RFU into the modern corporate world, and certainly had taken on board my views on elite rugby, the need to move way beyond the levels at which it was currently working.

Change is rarely popular and one of the facts you must accept in driving it through is that you will make enemies on the way. But as long as you can look in the mirror and without reservation say you are making changes for the right reasons, no matter how difficult, then strong leaders can live with that unpopularity. Francis Baron's actions during this period, brave and forward-thinking as they were, strengthened my commitment to carry on and complete what I had set out to do.

Just fifteen short months before, five of the most influential figures in England rugby had sat by my side in that first press conference supporting my ideas. Now almost all of them had left or been removed from their positions of influence. My honeymoon period was clearly over. It was truly sink or swim time.

We had a World Cup in less than nine months. We'd done well against South Africa that autumn, thus redeeming our performance during the Tour from Hell, yet we still had so much to do. But that's the job, and I didn't have much time to dwell on it. We had the Five Nations just around the corner with a tough first game against an in-form Scotland side. We just had to get on with it. At least now there were other full-time professionals in place who were all looking to the future not the past.

1999 Five Nations

Six weeks later we were on the field again in our first match of the last of the Five Nations tournaments – from 2000, of course, it would be Six Nations, with the addition of Italy. The Scots were our first opponents, and after we ran up a 14-point lead in the first twenty minutes, the game appeared to be in our pockets. Playing a good running game, we seemed to open up holes in their midfield quite easily. But then we lost focus and let them back into the game. Scotland put up a tight and tenacious performance.

What gave us the edge was a young man of nineteen playing in his first Five Nations start for England. He was playing at centre, his name was Jonny Wilkinson, and it was his place-kicking that gave us the points we needed.

In addition to an excellent kicking game with three conversions and a penalty, none easy, Wilkinson made two try-saving tackles in the second half when we were hanging on by our fingernails to a three-point lead. Kenny Logan the Scottish kicker, by contrast, had a bad day with the boot. Scotland went down, but at 24—21 it was close.

Against the Irish at Lansdowne Road two weeks later we were warned to look out for the Irish pack, supposedly the finest in the tournament. But our guys relish a challenge, and after the game the general consensus was that, while their front three had held their own in the scrum, elsewhere we had them firmly on the back foot. I was a bit disappointed that we hadn't played a more fluent game, though our defence was impeccable (with Jonny Wilkinson again to the fore). Phil Larder's coaching in that department was really paying dividends, as the Irish discovered in the last quarter when we took everything they threw at us. The 27—15 scoreline was a reasonable indication of our improvement.

Next came the French. They arrived at Twickenham hungry for a fifth consecutive win over England, but we had other ideas. Keeping the ball in hand, Dallaglio and others too struck deep into French territory, forcing errors from a rattled defence. There was some great play with the ball in hand, with a brilliant move involving Neil Back, Matt Perry and Martin Johnson – a flanker, a full-back and a lock – which cut them to pieces. The French had to break the rules a bit to keep us out, and the ensuing high penalty count played into the hands, or rather the boot, of Wilkinson. In all he notched up seven penalties, equalling the Five Nations record for most penalty goals kicked in a match. The score was 21—3 until the game's dying moments, when, much to my annoyance, we let in French centre Franck Comba for a try in the corner. However, we had played a good open game, spreading the ball wide whenever possible, and were unlucky not to score a try: a pretty good performance all round.

Victory over Wales would bring us the Five Nations Grand Slam. The venue was Wembley, and the game was preceded by performances from the likes of Max Boyce and Tom Jones that made me wonder if I hadn't strayed into an open-air pop concert from the hippy era. The Millennium Stadium in Cardiff was being built so the WRU had moved their 'home' games to Wembley.

Wembley! First the Theatre of Dreams and now I was taking my team to Wembley! All the memories of 1966 came flooding back. In one of the rooms hangs the crossbar that Geoff Hurst hit when scoring the all important third goal – I can still see the Russian linesman signalling the score. To play this fixture at Wembley was something very special indeed. We were also playing for a trophy, a Grand Slam, so I started to picture Dallaglio taking the team up those famous steps to receive it, just like Bobby Moore did all those years ago. There we were in the actual changing room where all those celebrations must have taken place. This was a complete one off in every way – an opportunity we just had to take for a fateful win.

The organisers and promoters of the WRU had done a great job that day turning the stadium into a small outpost of Wales. Thousands of Welsh flags, painted faces, balloons, etc. adorned the grounds. It was a Sunday match and the ground was full to capacity with supporters from both sides. It seemed like half of Wales must have been there. And the Welsh rugby supporters were excited, too. New Zealander Graham Henry had arrived as their new coach, and the Welsh press were calling him the 'great redeemer'. The scene was set for an amazing game.

In the first forty minutes the Welsh had no answer to our attack, and by half time we had scored three tries and looked to be cruising to victory. Wilkinson slotted two penalties early in the second half and, although the boot of Neil Jenkins kept the Welshmen in contention, we seemed to be on course for the Five Nations Grand Slam at 31—25 ahead.

In fact we led for eighty-two minutes of the game . . . and then blew it.

Not for the first or last time, we took our collective eye off the ball. We were under a lot of pressure and didn't handle it very well. An injury time tackle on Colin Charvis by Tim Rodber was judged dangerous by referee André Watson. Whereas I thought it would go down as the tackle of the season, Watson gave a penalty – it would be another close and exciting game for his CV! Wales kicked for touch and got possession from the ensuing lineout. Our self-control cracked under pressure. Centre Scott Gibbs charged through our defence for a try. Jenkins put over the conversion, and that was it: Wales 32—England 31. Grand Slam denied.

At the final whistle I was truly shocked. I was so certain we were meant to win that game. I just stood there in the middle of the pitch at Wembley looking at the famous steps, up at the royal box, right at Peter Trunkfield, the current RFU president. He was just standing there shaking his head. The term of president is only ever one year. Peter more than anyone else I knew in rugby deserved a Grand Slam in his year. But it was not to be. To say we had blown it in the dying minutes would be a massive understatement.

That night I could not sleep at all. At 4.30 a.m. Monday morning I gave up and drove to the office. Naturally everything was locked up tight at Twickenham. The security guards were surprised to see me when I turned up in their box. They offered me a hot cup of tea and a fag, both of which I gladly accepted, although I do not smoke – in my misery it just seemed appropriate at that time.

They let me into my office at about 5.30 a.m. As I checked my e-mails I noticed one had come from a guy named Glynn Jones in Swansea approximately ten minutes after the final whistle.

'Why are the English the world's greatest lovers?' he wrote. 'Because they can stay on top for eighty-two minutes and still come second!'

The abuse from our friends in Wales had started.

Normally I would not reply, but to this one at five in the morning I just couldn't resist. I won't repeat the joke that I sent back though it's quite well known – I told the full story just once in public and subsequently got a letter from the Welsh Race Relations office.

ROYAL MARINES 18

'Who's this then?' asked Brigadier Andy Pillar OBE of the Commando Training Centre Royal Marines in Lympstone.

My jaw dropped when I saw Matt Dawson and Austin Healey getting out of their car dressed in bright floral shirts, sunnies, shorts and beach sandals.

I was sitting with Brigadier Pillar and Lieutenant Nathan Martin on the stone wall leading up to the officers' club. We were having a cup of tea while the players arrived and got themselves situated in the lounge of the modern three-storey building behind us. I'd briefed the players on how serious the Royal Marines were in terms of their kit, dress and conduct at the Marine base. It was a bit embarrassing that two of our senior players had shown up in the sort of gear you'd see people wearing on a scorching summer's day in Manly.

But then when Matt pulled a full set of golf clubs out of the boot of his car ... well, I almost fell off the wall! He swung them over his back then started walking up the steps to the entrance of the officers' club. When he got level with where we were seated I couldn't let him pass.

'Matt, what the hell do you think you are doing?'

'Damn!' he exclaimed, turning to look at Healey still in the car park. 'I just had a bet with Austin that I would actually get past the entrance before you said anything. Austin said you'd stop me here. So thanks a lot, Woody. You just cost me fifty quid.'

And with a huge smile he turned and walked back to the car. Healey was dancing around like a demented cat! Fortunately the Royal Marines beside me thought it was funny, too.

'Don't worry, Clive,' put in Lieutenant Nathan Martin, the officer who put together our training programme with the Royal Marines. 'It's good to see that kind of banter, but we have a few tricks up our sleeves, too, so we'll see who has the last laugh.'

Brigadier Andy Pillar and Lieutenant Nathan Martin were the officers who made it possible for the England rugby team to train with the Royal Marines. The idea had actually come from Humphrey Walters. He had been a good source of Change Thinking! over the previous year and a half. His ideas were a bit off-the-wall, sometimes even for me, but I'd learned to listen as there was generally something there. His thinking with the Royal Marines was that if we wanted to create an elite culture in the squad, how could we do that if the team didn't know what a true elite squad actually looked and felt like?

The Commando Training Centre is an odd collection of buildings spread over roughly thirty acres of land on the estuary just outside Lympstone. The grounds look similar to a modern university, only on closer inspection I could see this was no ordinary campus. There were several formations of uniformed men armed with fully automatic weapons marching in all directions. Very quickly I could see why Humphrey had brought me here. I observed a detailed level of training of which I'd only dreamed. Where I thought we were getting pretty good in our systems of preparation, after just a few hours with the Royal Marines, it was obvious how far we really had to go.

After my brief tour of the facility, Nathan outlined the training programme he'd devised. I could see it was exactly what the team needed. Our visit was arranged for the end of July after our southern-hemisphere tour to Australia. This would be the perfect start for our World Cup preparation.

Southern tour

In June, England had flown to Australia to play the centenary match of the Cook Cup between the two countries at Stadium Australia in Sydney. It was the opening event at their fantastic new Olympic stadium, and it was the first time Wilkinson started in the pivotal position of fly half where previously he'd been in at centre. After a good drive by the pack early on he made a neat break that split the Australian defence and put Mike Catt into space. Catt offloaded to Matt Perry and the full-back was over for a try which Wilkinson converted. But then shortly before the break there was a good bit of play from the Wallabies that ended with Ben Tune going over in the corner. And then the same guy scored again three minutes later with a move that went through five pairs of Wallaby hands.

In the second half Joe Roff grabbed another try, and David Wilson their captain was, I thought, lucky to be given another, and then for England Perry got his second not long before full-time. At the final whistle the Wallabies were up 22—15. It was a big game in the lead up to the World Cup and we'd proved we could compete, but our fitness and performance under pressure let us down in the second half again.

During our stay at Couran Cove in Australia, Dave Reddin had been working incredibly hard with players on fitness and nutrition, but clearly this is not something that could be done in such a short time span.

Commando training

We'd all had a chance to recover from our disappointing game in Australia. Now we were at the Royal Marines training ground to begin our World Cup preparation in earnest. After all the players had arrived and were waiting in the officers' mess, it was time for the four-day training programme to begin. We'd kept all the details a secret, so the players had no idea what was coming.

As Andy, Nathan and I walked into the officers' lounge, the stark contrast between the well-ordered, disciplined Royal Marines and my team was never more evident. Seemingly strewn around the room like confetti were forty-eight players in all manner of dress. I could see bits of kit from three different eras of England rugby. We clearly still had a long way to go. Some were standing, some were sitting on the floor and many were casually laid back in the huge leather lounge chairs, some with their legs hanging over the arms, others with their feet up on the coffee tables. Compared to the disciplined, uniformed Royal Marine officers coming in and out of the building, we looked like a bunch of amateurs. I knew differently, but perception is everything.

'May I have your attention, please?' I said as the conversation slowly died down. Some of the players even sat up straight, I was pleased to see. 'I'm glad you all found the place. Now that we're settled, I'd like to introduce you to Lieutenant Nathan Martin. While we're on this base you're in his hands. Over to you, Nathan. They're all yours.'

'Good evening, gentlemen,' he began. He was an imposing figure in his pressed camouflage combat dress and green beret. At 5 ft 11 in and obviously fit, he was not a large man, but had a gritty hardened look about him. He was battle tough. Not the sort of man you'd want to mess with.

'I'm Lieutenant Nathan Martin. Welcome to the Commando Training Centre Royal Marines. You might have thought you were here for a few days of casual rugby training sessions. I'm here to tell you there has been a change of plan.

'For the next four days you are mine. As of now, you're no longer England rugby players in our eyes. You'll be treated like a Royal Marine. Starting in the morning, we'll be conducting a series of military training operations designed to test your leadership capabilities, sharpen your proficiency in decision-making under pressure, and enhance your communication and teamwork skills.

'Following this briefing we'll be convening for dinner in the officers' mess over my shoulder. After that you'll be shown to your accommodation. The gymnasium in the adjacent building to the south will be open until 22.30 this evening. However I'd suggest you get an early night. Victuals will be taken in the officers' mess at 07.00. And remember, gentlemen, you're on Marine time now. Ensure you have a good night's sleep, you'll need it! That is all.'

Only I and a few others really knew the entire plan. Details had been kept very close. My instructions to Nathan had been fairly general. Put the squad in a pressurised environment where their leadership skills could be tested and expanded. I'm certain we had most of the guys fooled, and some of the guys rattled. That was the point. The Marines have a saying that even the best-laid plans go wrong. It was a central part of their training scheme. They called it Dislocated Expectations. Much like rugby, really. Over the next four days, the team would experience numerous examples of the unexpected.

I was accommodated on the ground floor in the senior officers' wing of the officers' mess. 'What's the difference between the junior and senior rooms,' I asked? 'The senior rooms have two pillows,' came the response, while the players were accommodated two to a room in the upper floors of the large building. By the next morning Nathan had relaxed a little.

'How did you all sleep?' he asked shortly after beginning our next brief.

'Terribly,' shouted one of the players. 'I didn't sleep all night. I couldn't get the thought out of my head, *You're on Marine time now.* I kept waiting for you to burst through the door with a gun.'

A few others were nodding their heads.

Nathan just laughed and continued his briefing. He informed the players that a military scenario had been created for training purposes. An enemy terrorist organisation, the 'bad guys', had established themselves in a nearby stronghold. The players were to divide into five assault teams, each with a specialist mountain-leader training instructor, and would undergo a series of training exercises in preparation for taking out this stronghold. The teams were as follows:

TEAM 1	*TEAM 2*	*TEAM 3*
Jeremy Guscott	Jason Leonard	Martin Johnson
Matthew Perry	Danny Grewcock	Richard Hill
David Rees	Richard Cockerill	Victor Ubogu
Mike Catt	Neil Back	Darren Garforth
Nick Beal	Joe Worsley	Phil Vickery
Mike Tindall	Simon Shaw	Phil Greening
Matthew Dawson	Tony Diprose	Martin Corry

TEAM 4	*TEAM 5*
Phil de Glanville	Lawrence Dallaglio
Dan Luger	Alex King
Jonny Wilkinson	Neil McCarthy
Austin Healey	Graham Rowntree
Tim Stimpson	Will Green
Barrie-Jon Mather	Trevor Woodman
Leon Lloyd	Ben Clarke

Various members of the management team were attached to each group while non-participating injured players Paul Grayson, Kyran Bracken and Will Greenwood reluctantly had to sit out the exercises.

Looking back at this list now, the most interesting point is that over 50 per cent of these men were in the World Cup-winning squad of 2003 and a staggering eleven of them played in the World Cup Final. To me this demonstrates the amount of time and commitment you need to invest in the development of leadership and the ability to perform under pressure. We were nowhere near in these key criteria by 1999 RWC.

Next Nathan explained that each team would be marked on points as to how well it performed each exercise in the next two days and that there would be a competition between teams to see which squad performed the best. There's nothing like a game to truly ignite the competitive spirit of high-performance athletes. I later learned that the teams were graded by their instructors in the areas of reaction to briefings, demonstrated understanding of briefings, team leader command and control, teamwork, and success of the mission.

After the briefing, Nathan marched us over to the stores depot where everyone was kitted out in basic military field equipment. Royal Marines are generally not big men. They are trained to be stealthy and fast, to run for days on end to reach their objective or rendezvous point. They tend to be of average size, thin, wiry and lean. So finding gear that would fit our rugby players, built for strength, was a challenge. Jason Leonard's thighs were as wide as a normal Marine's waist. It was as much fun for the Marines in the store depot as it was for us changing kit in the warm summer air.

The teams were then briefed again, under the watchful eye of their instructors now, and were put through a simulated helicopter crash scenario. Strapped into a life-size fuselage, the teams were dropped into a pool of water, turned upside down to simulate a water crash, then assessed on how quickly and calmly – while under water and upside down – they could remove their harnesses and escape as a team through a small hatch.

After passing their training, the teams were flown by Sea King helicopter to a remote disused quarry on Dartmoor. There they underwent a series of challenging physical and mental team exercises, involving rope work, problem-solving initiatives and a commando slide off a cliff face several hundred feet high into the bottom of the quarry. It wasn't for the faint-hearted.

One report was fed back to me about Team 4 during a time-limited puzzle exercise involving cords of wood. After receiving the instructions, all the team-members set to the task but one: Jonny Wilkinson. He instead stared at the puzzle for a full minute and then blurted out, 'I've got it,' whereupon a couple of the senior players in the team, after hearing his idea, shot it down and proceeded in their own way. They failed to solve the puzzle in the allotted time. However Jonny's solution had been the correct one. Needless to say they hadn't scored well on teamwork for that exercise.

At 21.00 the teams were given a compass, route card and map, along with standard issue SA80 5.56mm assault rifles common to Britain's armed forces and NATO troops. They were instructed to move on foot to Cramber Tor, from which they were airlifted at 22.00 by helicopter to Tregantle Fort where, after a final debriefing, they slept on the hard ground in their standard issue sleeping bags. The gear wasn't designed for bigger players like Martin Johnson, the fully hooded bag only coming up to his shoulders at best.

The next day the team were raised at 05.00, having had no more than four hours' sleep, which was something they were definitely not used to. After breakfast they were told that the plans had been changed and that an amphibious assault would now be the means of taking out the 'bad guys'. The teams were loaded into troop-carriers and driven to Cawsand Beach where, after a safety briefing, they boarded Rigid Raiding Craft which took them to HMS *Raleigh*. There the teams underwent various on-board fire-fighting exercises in the simulated naval frigate.

One emergency exercise in particular I found very intimidating. The teams had to descend into the hold of the ship to repair a breach in the hull below the waterline. As the players carried out the exercise, cold seawater was flooding into the compartment. The players had to complete the job by each in turn holding his breath and plunging beneath the surface. It was tough. Going down into that small, tight and confined ship's hold must have been hugely distressing for some of the men. Chatting to them later, some said it was one of the hardest things they'd ever had to do.

In a briefing after these exercises the teams were informed of another change in plans. The 'bad guys' had moved to a land-based stronghold and they would have to once again set out in Rigid Raiding Craft to Whacker Bay. Once there they split into their respective teams, each with their own directives, and proceeded to make a forward assault on Scraesdon Fort. It was incredible fun to see these grown men charge in with their fully automatic weapons, spray a magazine-load of bullets – blanks of course – at the enemy (a troop of Royal Marine recruits doing the Commando training course), and go on to take the fort in heroic style.

Finally the victorious teams climbed back into their Sea King helicopters for the ride back to the training centre, a warm meal and a comfortable bed. In a final twist of Dislocated Expectations, Nathan announced to everyone just after take-off that the helicopters would land ten miles from the base with simulated engine failure, and the teams would have to yomp (Royal Marines term for fast walk carrying heavy equipment) all the way home, 60 lb of gear on their backs, in a final test of endurance. The devastated looks on the players' faces were priceless. Even more so the look of relief as the helicopters touched down gently on the landing site at the training centre. It had been an incredible, action-packed two-day test of team-building, leadership skills, and working under pressure.

In his final debrief, Nathan brought everything together.

'Gentlemen, what you've just experienced is as near as possible a simulation of an operational mission. Your briefings changed on an hourly basis. In battle, nothing goes to plan. You might find some similarities with game plans on the rugby pitch, only in war a mistake costs you your life. Not only that, one mistake by a team-mate can cost the whole squad their lives. We have a saying here at the CTCRM when referring to fellow Marines: Would you go into battle with him? If the answer is yes, it means you'd have absolute faith in that team-member's skills and abilities, that he will think correctly under pressure, and that your life is safe in his hands.

'On the battlefield a Marine is taught to assess his situation and revaluate his mission on a constant basis. There is only one thing you can count on in a battle situation: that events never go according to plan. We call that Dislocated Expectations, and it's what we've subjected you to several times in the last forty-eight hours whilst putting you through mentally and physically challenging conditions.'

After a few more minutes of sharing the funny stories from the last two days, Nathan finished with the final points tally from the competition. It's not important which team won, but it was heart-warming to see how all the players in the other teams immediately rose to their feet to congratulate the winning team and thank the instructors with whom they had built a strong bond.

For the rest of our stay we actually did engage the team in some light training exercises. And when we returned a month later, after Test matches against the USA and Canada, we engaged the team in a heavier training programme in preparation for the World Cup as we were only a month out by that stage. The Marines have a seriously challenging high-ropes and obstacle course around which further teams of six competed on time for points. It was a fantastic experience for the players and significantly helped to bring us together as a team. It was great to train in an elite environment that was so vastly different from what these players had come to expect.

There were three huge lessons that we all took away from our experiences with the Royal Marines.

First, the Marines taught us what a true elite squad looked and felt like. They had incredible standards of dress, conduct and behaviour. We'd been telling our players for nearly two years that we were building them into an elite squad, but it was only after visiting the Marines that we truly had a vision of what that elite culture could be. Our standards lifted immeasurably as a result.

Second, Dislocated Expectations were the norm in the intense environment of Test match rugby. That phrase became a part of our vocabulary, and also a trigger to help players think on the move and under pressure.

Third, from that moment on, we had a mental image and a name for the process that begins when the players set foot on the rugby pitch for a match. We called it 'jumping out of the helicopter' – our own version of the Royal Marine saying, 'Would you go into battle with him?' – and it became a constant reminder of the faith and trust we needed to have in our fellow team-members. From that point on, whenever a new player came into the team, our version of the Royal Marines saying was applied – 'Would you jump out of a helicopter with him?' – and we wouldn't leave the War Room until we achieved universal approval.

These are powerful lessons for a team of elite performance individuals. I'm just grateful to the Royal Marines for being so open and accommodating. When we left, they presented me with their 'dagger', which is one of their emblems, and we have it displayed in the England changing room. Under it are the man of the match awards, voted by the players. Marines know better than anyone who they trust in pressure situations, and I think the same applies to players. They know who they can trust and who they really want to play with – and this was the key message we learnt at Lympstone.

19

'99 RUGBY WORLD CUP

'Judge me on the World Cup,' ran the headlines in the paper.

Only I never actually said that.

What I said was, 'All coaches will be judged rightly or wrongly on what happens in the World Cup.' I have a good relationship with the press but once 'Judge me on the World Cup' ran in the headlines of one paper there was nothing I could do to stop it.

It was a misquoted comment that would come back to haunt me.

I believed right from the start that England had every chance of winning the World Cup in 1999. Based on the assumption that I would have adequate control of the top England players, it was not an unreasonable statement to make, regardless of how it was later interpreted. The problem was that entering into our final preparation for the World Cup we still hadn't fully achieved many of our critical stated objectives. When I began my job as England coach, I identified some big problems that had threatened to hold us back – five of them to be precise. I went forward with confidence on the assumption that these problems would be solved.

Perhaps the two biggest issues – more control of the elite players in line with our main competitors, and the signing of world-class talent from rugby league – had simply failed to materialise. For me not to pursue this significant pool of talent in rugby league aggressively would have been a serious mistake. However just when I believed I had four of the very best players in league ready to switch codes, some at the RFU got cold feet and the financial and political implications overtook the obvious advantages. Of course, since then other nations, most notably Australia, have signed league players. But when I wanted to do this prior to 1999 it was seen as a risky idea and bound to upset the status quo. It left us severely disadvantaged compared to the other rugby powerhouses around the world. We were just short of one or two world-class backs, and I believe these guys would have more than filled the holes. Seeing what Jason Robinson has done not only for England but the game as a whole just makes me think of what could have happened in 1999 if I had managed to convince the RFU to back my plan.

It's interesting that when I had a meeting with Rod Macqueen in late 1997, very soon after we had each been appointed coach in our respective countries, the only time he seemed to get worried about what England was doing was when I talked about signing our top-line league players. I wonder if he was thinking about our conversation when Jason Robinson went over for a terrific try in the 2003 final. At the time of my conversation with Rod our major competitors saw our forward pack as worrying but demonstrated little concern over the quality of our back division.

Despite these setbacks, everything else the RFU provided for the final build-up to the 1999 World Cup was as good as it could be. Our week at Couran Cove in Queensland during the summer tour had been our first thorough foray into the new player fitness and nutrition programme that Dave Reddin designed. While we were in Australia, Dave had even organised a seminar at Twickenham for the players' spouses and families with a leading nutritional expert, Dr Adam Carey. Dave and Adam had been working very closely to design the new programme, and they wanted the players' direct supporters briefed on what the players needed to be eating under their new regime. The families have been a fantastic support to the players in so many ways.

Unfortunately, although these fitness and nutrition improvements were huge, four or five months is very little time to see marked differences. Dave was working at it like a Trojan but needed more time. I always believed Dave had something special about him. Knowledge is one thing, which he has in bucketloads, but gaining the respect and trust of players is everything. He drives all our players to the limit and yet you can see his popularity with them. He is a priceless asset to everyone involved in England rugby, and one we have to protect.

We were also working hard on the technical side of our game to bring our skills up to world-class standards. Our time with the Royal Marines had helped demonstrate what a well-trained elite environment looked like, and everyone was approaching their World Cup preparation with a new level of professionalism. The team improved dramatically in our first four months of genuine concentrated training time, but would it be enough against the highly professional set-ups being fine tuned by Macqueen in Australia, Hart in New Zealand and Mallett in South Africa?

Warming up

In August England played the United States at Twickenham in the first of two so-called World Cup warm-up games, which England won 106—8. You can't warm up for the World Cup with this sort of game, where the opposition is totally outclassed. When I took over the coaching job eighteen months before, there just wasn't enough time to organise games against real quality opposition. It hadn't been thought through. But the next time we played warm-up tests, in 2003, they were against proper opposition – two against France and one against Wales – with our top thirty players fully involved. That was the way it should be.

Having said that, the US match was as fine an exhibition as you could hope to watch, but that's exactly what it was, an exhibition. Unfortunately, World Cups are not exhibitions. US coach Jack Clark said after the game, 'I feel like we were hit with a lethal cocktail: one part world-class team, one part perfect form, and one part something to prove.'

The second warm-up game was a week later against Canada, and it resulted in a 36—11 victory. Considering our overwhelming domination, that wasn't very impressive. Dallaglio was outstanding, and with Richard Hill and Neil Back they made a world-class back row. I was also pleased that Will Greenwood was back and in form – he scored two tries – after injury had put him out of rugby for nearly a year. But I was disappointed by the number of opportunities England missed. To create so many opportunities was encouraging but to convert so few was quite annoying. In terms of preparation, such games were not adequately challenging and, worse, didn't give us any real indication of where we actually were as a team.

October eventually arrived, after what seemed an incredibly long month of September preparing for the big event, and it was time for the '99 World Cup. Moving into the tournament, I still genuinely believed we had a good chance of winning because everything seemed to be going our way in respect of injuries, availability and preparation. However, we didn't arrive at the World Cup as the best prepared team compared with our main rivals. Not even close. Ours was a truly 'fingers crossed' approach. No one would run a business in this way if his livelihood depended on it.

Our first pool match

The first pool match was on 2 October against Italy, which resulted in a 67—7 win for England. This was a far cry from the dour and disappointing match against the Azurri in Huddersfield the previous year, when we had been lucky to scrape a win. England played some pretty good rugby, scoring eight tries and playing a running game that everyone watching at Twickenham greatly enjoyed.

The first try set the tone when Matt Dawson went over by the corner flag after chipping down the right wing for Austin Healey, then running up in support as Healey popped it back to him. The last try, when Martin Corry took a behind-the-back pass from Dawson to score in the third minute of injury time, put the seal on a dominant performance. Wilkinson, playing with great assurance, orchestrated England's win, adding 32 points of his own to the score – setting a new England record for most points in a Test.

The All Blacks – make or break

Our next match was the make or break game against the All Blacks. I had never been more confident going into a match of such importance as I was on that day. We had our tactics covered, and I thought I had our selection right. However looking back now I realise I made a fundamental mistake in selection. I played Wilkinson at fly-half with

De Glanville and Guscott in the centre. I should have played Grayson at fly-half with Wilkinson and Guscott in the centre.

Selection is the most important part of this job. Selection wins or loses you more matches than anything else. This was a major error on my part. The pressure to play Wilkinson at fly-half instead of Grayson was immense, but this was not the right call. Jonny had played most of the season at centre, with Paul Grayson at fly-half. Playing Grayson at fly-half would have given us real leadership and experience, which Wilko was still acquiring.

World Cups are not about experimenting or developing players – World Cups are won by experienced teams with outstanding leadership. Jonny would arrive at the next World Cup as one the most talented fly-halves the game has ever seen, with a huge amount of experience in this position and leadership qualities second to none. However, 1999 was too early for him.

But it wasn't Jonny who lost the game. Nor was it the centre pairing that I chose. Rather it was my selection. In the first twenty minutes alone we missed several scoring opportunities, and we never recovered our momentum from that point. Along with the loss to Wales at Wembley earlier that year, it was the most disappointing game of my coaching career – a game I still refer back to with the players even today. Basically we bottled it. Not physically, where everyone gave their all, but mentally. Our mindset let us down badly, and under the pressure of the game we reverted to type and played a very typical English game.

We lost to New Zealand 16—30.

This defeat brought us down to earth with a sickening thud. Winning the World Cup would now be incredibly difficult. That was the key game, a game we should have won. I believe that match cost us the World Cup. Instead of England, the All Blacks were on the fast track to the knock-out stages, while we were lumbered with an extra game before the quarter-final and a trip to Paris to meet the waiting South Africans.

A disastrous situation

The following week saw the rout of Tonga 101—10 in a game which resulted in several injuries for England players. Hill was decked with a punch that would have won praise from Sonny Liston. After Ngalu Ta'ufo'ou was sent off just before half-time the game became very one-sided, with England having the advantage of an extra man to add to their technical superiority. Altogether Tonga got one red and two yellow cards in a match that no one who saw it would want to remember. Jerry Guscott came up to me in the changing rooms after the game, informing me he had torn his groin – his World Cup was over and he never played for England again. Losing one of our very few world-class backs was a massive blow.

Another Pacific side, Fiji, were our next opponents in a somewhat closer game which we eventually won 45—24. It was the play-off match for the quarter-finals, and once again we incurred multiple injuries. Wilkinson took a massive hit from the Fijian captain, Greg Smith, while Perry, Luger and Healey also picked up injuries. Jonny Wilkinson kicked seven penalties, and Dan Luger scored a great try before going off with a groin strain.

Against inferior sides we had gone through, but, at an incredible cost in injuries and energy levels. We'd won both matches, but it was a disastrous situation. We were in bits and just did not have enough quality players to cover the loss of our first-choice team. With just three days to travel and prepare, we were off to Paris to meet a well-rested and determined South African side in the quarter-final. How the organisers could so seriously hamper one of the sides in a quarter-final still beggars belief. But it was our loss to New Zealand that was the real nail in the coffin.

A horrific quarter-final

It's difficult to ask any team to play South Africa in Paris with only a day's preparation when they had been waiting for us for nine days. We travelled from London to Paris by train on the Thursday after the Fiji match, then had just Friday to prepare for our Saturday quarter-final.

It was an obscene schedule for any professional team and should never have been allowed. I would still like to know who actually devised this system. So often decisions like this have a dramatic effect on people's lives and careers, while those who make them have scant regard for what has happened.

I need hardly say that our game against South Africa was the third most disappointing match of my career as England coach. Despite the 44—21 scoreline, the Springboks only managed a couple of tries, one a rather dubious effort by scrum-half Joost van der Westhuizen. As everyone knows, it was the phenomenal drop-kicking of South African fly-half Jannie de Beer that put England away. Five drop goals in a row from de Beer in the space of thirty-one second-half minutes took South Africa to the semi-final at Twickenham and left us wondering what had happened.

South Africa were not a great side. They had a great coach but at our best, a fully fit England were a better team. This we would prove many times over the ensuing four years.

Nick Mallett, the Springbok coach, had studied England carefully and came to the conclusion that kicking would be a sound counter-attack to our more fluid game. That way they could reduce the threat of our back row, especially with Dallaglio out wide. The South Africans worked hard to ensure we got bad ball in the first phases, in the scrums and lineouts, and prevented us gaining momentum. We got in behind the South Africans on a few occasions, but turned the ball over eighteen times, a flagrant waste of precious possession. We also played right into the South Africans' hands by kicking badly. After the All Blacks game I made another error in selection. Correcting my previous mistake, I'd decided that Grayson should play fly-half again, but I should have kept Wilkinson in at centre. My mistake was not in deciding that Jonny needed more experience at fly-half, but in overlooking him for centre when he had the right experience for that position against South Africa.

When the game clock stopped and the final whistle blew, England had been soundly beaten by a much better prepared South African side. The team were devastated. I was crushed.

'Judge me on the World Cup' was what people thought I said.

Many would now try to hang me for the result.

The agony of defeat

We left Paris on Sunday morning a defeated team in every sense.

The train ride back to London was sheer agony. There I was staring out the window while right next to me the papers were calling for my head. I don't think it's overstating it to say that the weeks following the '99 World Cup were some of the hardest I've ever had to face. It quickly became obvious that the months ahead would be extremely perilous. The RFU was still a representative body governed by popular vote. There were still competing factions with different views about who should be at the helm of England rugby. If ever there was a time when my position was at risk, this was it. For the next six weeks I would be fighting for my life as England head coach.

It certainly didn't help when the French beat New Zealand in the semi-final. If they could defeat the All Blacks, why couldn't we? To make matters worse, as organised by the World Cup committee, South Africa had gleefully moved-into Petersham Hotel – *our* hotel! It only rubbed salt into the wounds.

As could be expected, the articles in the press were scathing. Keith Barwell, owner of Northampton, made harsh public statements. 'Woodward should fall on his sword and those who picked him' – meaning Fran Cotton – 'should resign, too.'

He wasn't the only one. It is amazing how some people react when others are at their lowest. Talk about putting the boot in. It was like feeding time for the sharks.

Ex-England players – who themselves had never won a World Cup, I might add – were having a field day. Non-English players were also quick to feed on the scraps. Welsh legend Ieuan Evans was reported as saying, 'Well, from a Welsh point of view, we hope he stays.' The comments bit hard, but they just served to reinforce my determination. One of my strengths – or weaknesses – is that I never forget. This lot were not going to beat me.

Of course I wasn't the only one feeling the heat. The players too were physically and mentally exhausted by the experience. To make matters worse, many of them drew further criticism because they physically couldn't perform when they went back to play club rugby in the coming weeks.

My lowest point came when I attended a club match at Leicester on one of my regular visits about three weeks later. I decided it was time to get out and face the music. When it was announced over the loudspeaker just before kick off that I was in the stands, people started booing before my name was even finished. This wasn't detached criticism from a faceless name in a paper. This was personal. Sitting in my old home ground, it cut deeply. It was a moment I have never forgotten, despite my many happy memories there as a player.

They say the darkest hour is just before the dawn. In this case, it was true.

Coming to terms

During December I spent many hours at the golf net in my back garden thinking about what had gone wrong. We had worked so hard in the year leading up to the tournament. *What had held us back?* We had the potential to be such a strong dynamic team. *How could we get to the quarter-finals and have so many injuries?* The structure of the tournament just was not right. *Why weren't we allowed to compete on a level playing field?* With the weight of the nation on our shoulders, it was hard to get a proper perspective on our failure. But slowly, with the passing of time, it started to become clear.

Some people wonder about the things that drive highly competitive people. To add fuel to my fire, I decided I had to try and thrive on all the criticism that had come my way, some fair and some not. I was angry with myself more than anything. If our group of players had been fit, fresh, and properly prepared for that South Africa match, we could have beaten that team on the day. I still fully believed we had the potential to win the tournament, but there again, if we had won, it would have been against all logic and common sense. The problem was, we had all agreed in the England set-up that there would be no 'if only' excuses. Those unexpected events that assisted in derailing the England team are part of what every team had to contend with in a high-pressure World Cup environment. Under those circumstances, winning the World Cup would have been a chance fluke, due to the vagaries of sport, not because we deserved or earned it.

We'd lost. Deep down I knew that there were reasons for this.

During this time I must have been very difficult to live with at home, even more so than normal! My family, too, were deeply affected by our 1999 World Cup defeat. Other kids were saying things at school, and the whole media onslaught was almost enough for me to question whether it was right for me to carry on. The final conviction to get stuck in came from my family: the great chats and advice from Jess, the cups of tea that Joe brought me in the golf net, the wonderful hugs from Freddie and, of course, Jayne's unwavering faith in me.

One morning after I'd rested and found the energy to move on again, I took a good hard look at myself in the mirror. 'Right,' I said to the haggard face staring back at me. 'Either quit as a loser or get back to it and make this thing work.'

No matter what I was feeling inside, it was time to get on with it. The allure of winning, particularly in the shadow of defeat, is a highly motivating force to the true competitor.

Figuring out what went wrong

Rather than spending the next six months wallowing in self-pity, we would confront our failures head-on. By confronting them, we would say what needed to be said. We would feel the pain, and we would move on.

For the first time since I'd written my initial plan for the players almost two years previously, I sat down to write a report of our '99 World Cup to the management board. It was my own 'warts and all' analysis of what went wrong, and my recommendations for fixing the problems before the next World Cup in 2003. In that report I summarised our predicament, saying we had been working in a 'fingers crossed environment'. It was so true.

When everything was working for us – if the gods of rugby were smiling on us – we won. But reliance on divine intervention did not constitute a plan. No, if we wanted to win, we had to be fully preypared for every eventuality, and that's how I spelt it out in my report.

For the previous two years I had been focusing almost exclusively on the internal structure of our team, getting our player experience, coaching procedures and behavioural standards in place. But that obviously wasn't enough. We hadn't prepared for the extraneous forces that I had regarded as outside my control, such as the never-ending problem of access to players; an impossible schedule of pool matches and travel times; and last-minute changes in the rules. As an example of the last, the IRB made a significant change in the lineout law only days before our first game. This caused us a great deal of trouble. But to be fair it was causing every other team problems too, and the team that managed the change best would clearly have an advantage, although I didn't see it that way at the time.

I laid it all out for the management board of the RFU because they were the only body with real power to change the important things. They were the ones with the clout to negotiate with the clubs, and they had influence through their representatives on the IRB to ensure sensible World Cup fixtures. Behind closed doors, I delivered my twenty-six-page report. I knew the spotlight was firmly fixed on me, but I felt I had nothing to gain by holding anything back.

For those on the board who were with me and agreed with my view of how to bring England to a winning position in world rugby, the report was a revelation. Board members had very little to do with the day-to-day running of the England team, and many of the problems the team had faced were quite new to them. It was clear to most of them that England simply had not created an overall rugby environment which was conducive to pulling a well-prepared team together with the best chance of winning.

Unfortunately for my detractors, telling the truth when they didn't want to hear it was fraught with danger. The report only added fuel to the fire in their quest to remove me from the England coaching set-up. To my absolute horror, the most controversial elements were splashed across the papers that weekend. The entire report had been leaked.

For several weeks the pressure to 'sack the coach' was intense.

I regretted ever writing that report. I learned that putting the 'truth' on paper can be very perilous. Since that time I have only ever written one more official document discussing the England team, which was after the World Cup 2003. People often say that I'm secretive and give nothing away. Well, I have a very good reason to be. I'm still just as open and up front with my thoughts. Now I'm just more careful about the timing and setting in which I share them.

My saving grace

Thankfully, the call to inform me my services were no longer required never came. I remained as England coach. The RFU had told me they wanted me to stay in the job until the end of August 2000, the end of my three-year contract. However they had not yet indicated whether or not they would renew my contract. That left the axe dangling precariously over my head. I had two options: resign and regret it for the rest of my life, or carry on, accept the criticism, and show courage.

Three people saved my coaching career.

The first was Fran Cotton. Although he had left the management board some eighteen months before, Fran had still retained his position as one of the fifty-seven council members and was shortly afterwards elected chairman of another committee in the RFU, Club England. In that time Fran hadn't been sitting on his hands, but had been campaigning tirelessly in support of the new initiatives we were implementing. When we lost so dismally to South Africa, his dedication and support didn't waver – it only escalated. His opinions held considerable sway amongst the member body of the RFU, and consequently among the fifty-seven members who ultimately controlled my fate. His appointment was a bold and courageous step for the benefit of England rugby.

The second was Francis Baron. As a CEO with vast corporate and commercial experience, he was highly respected by the management board who appointed him. Indeed he had already created a considerable turnaround in the revenues and profits of the organisation in just one year. So when Francis came in with his full support for my plans to modernise the elite performance set-up, it was a great endorsement.

The third 'person' or factor that came to my support, and therefore granted me a second chance with England rugby was, most importantly, the players themselves. I say 'importantly' because so often in the past the players were marginalised in the decision-making process at the RFU. On the face of it, everything we do revolves around the players and their performance on the pitch. Whether they perform well or poorly, win or lose, radically affects the financial position of the RFU. It can create a situation where one million people are playing at the grass roots level, and two million are attracted to the game, and it has the even wider effect of uplifting or deflating the spirits of our sports-mad population. And yet so often the players had been no more than the meat in the sandwich in the tussle between the RFU and the clubs, their opinions rarely considered.

So when in my darkest moment the players started voicing their support for me as coach, it was one of the proudest moments of my life. The two players I recall most vividly were Neil Back and Richard Hill, so seeing those two on the winner's podium in Sydney was very special for me. Most of the top players had newspaper columns, and they were speaking openly about what the new England set-up meant to them. They weighed in with their full support, and I think that tipped the balance in my favour. Even if I had been removed, with their comments I would have considered my time in the England set-up a success. The players' support was proof positive that we were finally coming together as one.

Objectively speaking

In business, it's common knowledge that 85 per cent of new enterprises fail within their first three years. It's no wonder that successful entrepreneurs are among the most competitive individuals, or that elite athletes are often highly successful in business. Coming into the England set-up as the first professional coach was much like starting from scratch with a new business. Even though we had been soundly defeated in the World Cup – my stomach still churns whenever I think of our campaign – I had to look back at our two years as a team from an objective point of view. We had come a long way in that time. We had also done the best we could under intense pressure; however, I realised we had probably pushed a little too far in changing so much in the year of the '99 World Cup. The twelve months before the World Cup should be about consolidating, not rebuilding.

If we had won in 1999 it would have been against all logic and common sense. That is not what winning at the highest level is all about. In fact it's the complete opposite. My aim is to arrive at any tournament as favourites, ranked number one in the world, and clearly the best-prepared team.

The main function of a coach is to give his players every chance of winning. But he can actually do no more than that. In 1999, due to many factors already mentioned and including my lack of experience in the job – especially in preparing for a World Cup – we were far from being the best prepared team on many fronts. To be successful you must have everyone's nose pointing in the same direction. Only then do you have a real chance of success. In this we were adrift in 1999 but not by much and most importantly the key lessons had all been learned.

In one respect, I should be thankful that we did lose so miserably in the quarter-final. Everyone in the RFU organisational body was so upset and desperate to find out what went wrong that it was a great time to demand change. The RFU, the clubs, the players, and the supporters all had serious questions about the England set-up. They wanted answers. They wanted solutions, and that's exactly what I would now give them. I was going to try and be even more focused and determined to see through with new conviction ideas that would create a World Cup-winning side, such as utilising Rugby League players. I was not going to take no for an answer even on the really big issues.

REBUILDING WITH RENEWED VIGOUR

20

On Monday 20 December 1999 I called a meeting with the players who would form the future of England rugby. It had been two months since the World Cup, and it was time to move on.

'Good morning, everyone, and welcome to Pennyhill Park.'

There were forty players in the room along with Fran Cotton, Francis Baron and Brian Baister, the current chairman of the management board and the management team. Pennyhill Park was an immaculate five-star hotel set on a 120-acre estate thirty minutes southwest of Twickenham in a secluded part of Surrey near Bagshot. It had its own nine-hole golf course and a full-size rugby pitch. It was quiet, private, and perfectly suited to the intense mental preparation that had become so much a part of our game – no more back and forth between Bisham Abbey, the Petersham and the Bank of England practice pitches. Best of all, the feel of the place was exactly what I wanted for the new elite England rugby set-up, an atmosphere of understated excellence and professionalism. We were moving on and not looking back.

'The last two months have been hard on everyone. We lost. It was a major setback and not something we deserved, but it's over. Now it's time to examine our mistakes and move on. We'll be looking for a few key lessons that we can take forward with us to make sure that we arrive at the next World Cup in a completely different position. In Australia in 2003 I want us to arrive as favourites, ranked number one in the world, with a full squad of players who are in peak physical condition and have had the best preparation of any team in the tournament. That will be our focus from now on.'

At this point I introduced Fran, Francis and Brian. I'd asked them to attend the meeting so that they could address the players themselves.

This was the first time we'd come together in the two months since our defeat, and the first game in the Six Nations was against Ireland in a little over six weeks. We didn't have the luxury of time to wallow in our misery. This meeting was about purging the pain of the past, and hearing a strong endorsement from the three top executives at the RFU would really bring the message home.

Success from setbacks

After Fran, Francis and Brian finished with their message of strong support of the team, I devoted the next three hours to presenting a detailed analysis of what I felt went wrong in our World Cup campaign, as well as what went right. This wasn't about pointing any fingers, except at myself. I ultimately made some critical mistakes and so shouldered the responsibility for our performance. This was about explaining the situation as I saw it so that the players could put things in the right perspective. It was the first time I had formalised my strategy for building successes from setbacks. I believe that all too often, in the business world particularly, managers and coaches make too much of defeat and too little of success. Normally in business, when you lose the big deal, you're hauled into the boardroom early on Monday morning for a bollocking and a huge enquiry into what went wrong. Whereas when you win the big deal, you're usually taken straight down to the pub to celebrate.

I think most managers have it all wrong.

When you win the big deal, that's when you should be straight into the boardroom on Monday morning to analyse what happened, what went right and how you can learn from your success to do it again the next time. However, when you lose the big deal or the big game, the last thing you need is to dwell on the mistakes. That's the time to head down the pub. It's a management concept I call 'Success from Setbacks and Build on Success'.

It hadn't been my style to lay into the team after a defeat, either in the changing room or at meetings, but the tidal wave of negative press in the weeks after the World Cup had achieved nearly the same effect.

The best thing I could have done would have been to throw a party – perhaps it should have been a wake – in the week after the game. However, international rugby just doesn't provide those opportunities. We left Paris the day after the match with South Africa, and the players were scattered to all parts of the country with their clubs.

When you have a setback, the most important thing the leader must do is make sure his team realise it is only a setback, that it isn't the end of the world. Our success in England rugby to date had not been a linear progression. We had experienced ups and downs, and they weren't always tied to the result on the scoreboard. To build a winning team you first have to learn how to build on your successes, when you have them, and how to minimise the damage to self-confidence and momentum when things go wrong – and things will go wrong, as the World Cup tournament had shown. In order to win you have to know how to lose. You have to know how to handle your setbacks in order to move forward.

For me, there were three critical lessons to be drawn from our World Cup defeat: logistics, my management skills, and what I call 'energy sappers'. And that is what I focused on with the players that Christmas.

As regards logistics, moving to Pennyhill Park made a huge difference in our preparation, even though it wouldn't become apparent until the next Six Nations. At last we had a proper, decent-sized War Room where we could spread out and communicate comfortably in meetings. The rugby pitch was just a three-minute walk away, and we could keep all our kit permanently set up at the house during training days and Test matches. And not having to drive anywhere on a coach during Test week, except to the match on Saturday, saved a huge amount of distraction from our play. As I explained why I thought it would be better, the players visibly brightened. But it wasn't until I explained the other two big lessons that the weight of self-doubt and criticism lifted from the broad shoulders of the elite players who had been part of our failed World Cup campaign.

Managing versus coaching

In our meeting I stressed to the team that it wasn't the principles upon which we'd based our rugby that were in question, it was our thoroughness in preparing for them. Ultimately, I had to step up and manage every aspect for the elite team. John Mitchell had been a great asset, but he was only coaching part-time, and at some stage would return to New Zealand. Phil Larder and Brian Ashton were both full-time. I wanted to bring in a full-time coach to work with me and the newly created coaching team. That would then give us far greater scope to work with the team when we had them to train with as a group and, more importantly, to go to their clubs and work with them there too. With more resources in the coaching department of the management team, it meant from that point on, in addition to being responsible for selection, plus some key coaching areas such as our attacking play, I would oversee the management of everything off the pitch. Putting forward the needs and demands of the international team wouldn't necessarily bring me any popularity, but if the coach didn't do it, who would? My immediate priority was preparation time and signing rugby league players.

In my first two years on the job I took the view that my role was coaching the team and leading the elite squad. I left many of the details surrounding England rugby to people in the RFU to handle. However, I realised now that there were too many things outside my current control that could severely affect our preparation, and hence our success. Until that World Cup 1999, it had never dawned on me how serious the consequences could be.

The pressures in this job are great. John Hart, the All Blacks coach, went through a terrible time after his team went down to the French in the semi-final. New Zealand had gone into the tournament as favourites, and that rugby-mad nation had very high expectations. When the team lost, Hart was vilified in the press, spat on in the streets of Auckland and summarily dismissed from his post. He even suffered in his business. New Zealand were winning comfortably in that match – France hadn't been playing well the whole tournament – but with eighteen minutes to go and nothing to lose, the French, from being fourteen points behind, scored two quick tries off risky plays, then two drop goals within two minutes, and finally won comfortably 42—31.

That's just how rugby goes sometimes. But for John Hart, it was like the end of the world. In eighteen minutes he went from national hero to despised villain. It was wrong, but it was also the reality of this sport. Doing this job, your whole life could change in twenty minutes. If England had lost in 2003 in the quarter-finals against Wales I have no doubt I would have suffered the same consequences, probably worse.

No one would protect me if the tide really turned, and no one else involved in the game was exposed like I was. My mindset changed after seeing what happened to John Hart. I realised that my job was to do everything possible to bring the players into every match with the best possible chance of winning. If people got in my way, I would need to be far more confrontational and sometimes brutal if the situation called for it. Being head coach of an international team sounds prestigious but, at the end of the day, the law of the jungle will prevail: only one person will survive. To ensure my success, and consequently that of the team, I had to be prepared to fight. I was used to this in the business world, but hadn't anticipated it in sport.

Insight, Royal Marine-style

It was a hard fact to accept, but I realised that for two years I had been making some fundamental errors on player selection. Certainly, I had been selecting players on their merit and the strength of their perform-ance in games, as I had promised the players I would in our first meeting at Bisham Abbey; however, a critical factor in selection had eluded me. It was thanks to our visit with the Royal Marines that I first put into words something my instincts had been telling me all along.

On the last day of our visit, I'd asked several of the senior officers for an honest assessment of the players in their drill teams. They looked at me cautiously, careful not to overstep the mark.

I waited.

'OK, if you want to hear it,' eventually began one of the senior training instructors, dropping his voice to a whisper and leaning forward in his chair in the officers' lounge. 'There are men in your squad whom we wouldn't go into battle with.' He then rattled off the names in quick succession.

The other instructors all nodded their heads. Obviously they had discussed it.

Quite frankly I was amazed. They had listed all the players who in my own mind had question marks over them. Yet all were players whose rugby skills and talent you simply could not fault.

'But why? What is it about these players? They're clearly great at the game. Why wouldn't you go to war with them?'

'It's not about their skills, Clive. It's about their attitude and their effect on the team. There are hundreds of soldiers who can run for three days, think on their feet, and handle a weapon. But some of them simply aren't suited to working in high-pressure team situations. It might be the smallest trait, like a bit of a moan when the going gets tough. Under normal circumstances that wouldn't have any effect. But in high-pressure combat situations just that one negative trait can destroy a whole team. We are trained to identify these clues because the consequences for us are so serious. It's the difference between life and death. One wrong team player can sap all the energy from the group.'

In two days these Royal Marines had confirmed what it had taken me two years to figure out. I guess that's why those guys don't jump out of helicopters with just anybody. Unfortunately, I could do nothing more than catalogue these thoughts. We were eight weeks out from the World Cup. It was not the time to do anything about it, but that conversation would linger in my mind.

To the people in the room at Pennyhill Park I admitted I'd made a mistake. I had weakened the team by hiding behind those players, even with their all too obvious experience. I admitted that, if I had my time again, I would make the hard choice and bring in the new players immediately so that they could gain the experience sooner. I would much rather have lost in the World Cup knowing we had chosen the best team. It would have been easier to live with myself in the face of defeat if I knew that at least I'd done what was right and that the team ethic had been kept intact. I've often thought since that we actually would have had a greater chance of winning. Post World Cup it was now all about making the correct decisions under pressure.

Energy sappers into energisers

For the previous month the Marines' words had been ringing in my ears.

It's not about skills. It's about attitude and the effect on the the team. One wrong team player can sap all the energy from the group.

This was exactly what happened. I sensed that it was essential to find a way to bring the lesson into the elite squad, but it was a difficult concept to grasp. I looked up a few words in the dictionary. The definition of 'sap' was perfect. That's exactly what players were doing when they complained about conditions, pressure and the workload required to become champions, or when they resisted change. International rugby is hard enough without those added distractions. What we needed was a team without any energy sappers. What we needed was a team of energisers, people for whom there was no personal price too high for winning, who were open to new ideas, who were willing to contribute to the team and keep everyone's energy levels high.

Energy Sappers	Energisers
sap *v.* bleed, deplete, devitalise, drain, erode, exhaust, undermine, weaken, wear down.	**energy** *n.* drive, efficiency, exertion, fire, force, intensity, power, spirit, stamina, strength.

When I shared these definitions and explained what they meant, the players sat in silence. Many knew what I meant and exactly which players I was referring to. No names needed to be mentioned. Even those new to the elite squad recognised truth when they saw it. Patently, there are good teams and there are bad teams. I think energy sappers are the biggest obstacle to success. Every team that ever existed has struggled with this problem at some time.

I went on to explain the point I was trying to make. 'If ever I have to talk to you about anything other than your ability to play rugby, then you are potentially sapping my and everyone else's energy. Let me make this clear. When we run out on that rugby pitch it's like the Marines jumping out of that helicopter. We cannot afford any weak links. If I think any of you are becoming energy sappers, first I'll meet with you in private and we'll discuss it openly. However, if that fails, you will not be selected in future.'

I now do everything humanly possible to switch over the energy sappers, usually just by sitting down with the Black Book and pointing out the definition. These definitions are simple ways to explain what otherwise are very complex team issues. They are not at all obvious, and it took me until after the '99 World Cup truly to understand and vocalise them. If I can't switch them over, they have to go. It's a tough call, but it's a necessary one. I believe entire organisations can be brought down by just one energy sapper who is not confronted and sorted out as soon as you are aware of a problem.

After the World Cup, the energy sappers were all sorted out. Some I managed to turn around. In every case none of them had actually realised that what they'd been doing behind the scenes could cause so many problems. I'm proud to say that England arrived at the Rugby World Cup 2003 with a thirty-strong squad of energisers, plus another twenty at home hoping to take part, led brilliantly by Martin Johnson, not an energy sapper in sight and not a single player with whom I wouldn't jump out of a helicopter.

That afternoon on the way home from Pennyhill Park, I finally felt like we'd begun to put the World Cup behind us. When we walked into the room, energy levels were low. Leaving the room, everyone was motivated and ready to work harder than they ever had before. The effect of the energisers was immediate. That was building success from setbacks.

The process of Winning!

Feeling much more positive about the team and our future, I had a better Christmas with my family than I would have thought possible. In building our new elite organisation we had largely stumbled along, guided by instinct in terms of what was right for us. Looking back now, I can see that we followed a basic series of steps in transforming England rugby (see diagram p. 265.)

First, winning was obviously our overriding goal and dominating influence, and not just on the scoreboard. To achieve it we set out to create an elite squad of coaches, players and support team focused exclusively on our aim of winning.

Second, we created an elite player experience that fully supported the players in focusing all of their attention on mental preparation before the match and world-class performance on the day.

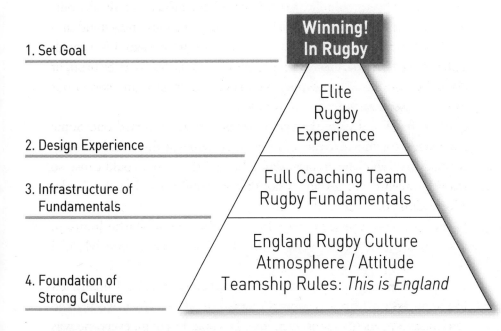

	Winning! In Rugby
1. Set Goal	Elite Rugby Experience
2. Design Experience	
3. Infrastructure of Fundamentals	Full Coaching Team Rugby Fundamentals
4. Foundation of Strong Culture	England Rugby Culture Atmosphere / Attitude Teamship Rules: *This is England*

Third, we had assembled a team of specialist coaches in each of the key areas of our game, just as I'd dreamed: Brian Ashton in attack, Phil Larder in defence, Dave Alred in kicking, Phil Keith-Roach in scrummaging, Dave Reddin in fitness and nutrition and Tony Biscombe in analysis. These were world-class professionals in every sense of the world. We'd then begun measuring key performance indicators in these areas during matches and training sessions and had placed coaches and players in charge of each area.

Fourth and finally, in support of these fundamentals our elite culture formed the foundation of everything we did, and was embodied in the attitude of everyone involved, as well as the atmosphere that pervaded our training days and Test weeks. That elite culture was further set in stone in our Black Book of Teamship Rules.

It was a good but bare framework for what we'd been trying to achieve. Obviously we had a lot of fleshing out to do before the picture would be complete. In terms of our elite culture, rugby fundamentals and player experience we could be so much better.

Our performance in the '99 World Cup tournament was a catalyst for change in each of these areas. We moved from the Petersham to Pennyhill Park so that the logistics of training days and Test weeks could run more smoothly. We'd reorganised our coaching structure, and I would have more time to manage outside influences to ensure we had the necessary training time with the players to win. With 'energisers' introduced to our Teamship Rules, we had the basis for a strong team culture within the squad.

Whereas on the surface these may seem like small and minor changes, we felt they would have major positive consequences for our rugby. Only time would tell and, as usual, time was short with just four weeks to pull everything together for our first Six Nations match against a determined Ireland side.

Six Nations – will we perform?

Actions speak louder than words, so the best answer to the criticism after the World Cup disappointment was to put in top performances in the first ever Six Nations. First up was Ireland, and in that first match at Twickenham we may have given our critics food for thought. We not only put a half century of points past the opposition, but we also did it in considerable style, running in six tries and notching up our highest ever score against Ireland. Mike Tindall and Ben Cohen were making their debuts for England, at centre and wing respectively, and the combination produced two tries for Cohen, one for Tindall, and two for Austin Healey on the other wing. The new players were outstanding. We were only two months past the World Cup and already a strong new team was forming.

Change kit – half time

There was a nagging problem that Tony Biscombe had drawn to my attention for quite a few matches. We had been developing a more sophisticated analysis and the statistics were showing a worrying trend that we kept trying to alter, but which was proving stubborn to address. We were starting games well in the first ten minutes of the match, but needed to find a way of starting the first ten minutes after half time just as well. These are critical periods in the game and we were just not getting it right immediately after the break.

I discussed the whole thing with Humphrey and he simply asked what we did at half-time. After we'd gone over the whole routine he made one of the simplest suggestions that made us question our half-time procedure. 'Why don't you change shirts at half-time? You've got to get back to the same mindset as at the start of the game!'

Humphrey was right about creating the same mindset but I scoffed at his idea of changing shirts, mostly because it had never been done for this purpose before and as a rugby player myself I was slow to see the sense in the idea.

Second-Half Thinking

The following morning after a restless night's sleep it dawned on me that Humphrey might just be right. When that half-time whistle blows, the players need to recover during the break, but the last thing every player does before leaving the pitch is to look at the scoreboard. You can't help it. Generally it's all you think about in the changing room, and often it's what the coaches talk about. I realised that might be the problem. The players were coming back onto the pitch as if they were in the middle of the game. What I really wanted to see was the players performing as if it was the first-half all over again.

It was so obvious. To fix the problem, we had to change our mindset going into the second half of the match. Not only would we change shirts, we also needed to change our whole half-time routine so that it concentrated on getting the players to focus on the rest of the match. Thinking about it, it seemed to me that when we went into the second half it should be irrelevant what the scoreboard said. If we were up, we would need to play a great game to maintain our lead. If we were down, we'd need to forget the first-half and play a great game to come back. In both situations it wouldn't matter what the scoreboard said, you would still have to win the half to win the game.

From that point on, our mindset going into the second-half would be as if the scoreboard was 0—0 and it was a brand new game. And changing shirts? Well, it had never been done before, but I was determined to try it. It would be a physical act to trigger our minds to 0—0, fresh-start, Second-Half Thinking. I went back to the team with the idea at our first meeting in the lead-up to France. After recounting the statistics of our performance against Ireland and the trend they had shown, I launched into 'my idea'.

'We've been wracking our brains for a way to solve the problem. I think we've finally got it. We're going to change our shirts at half-time . . .'

'No way, we're not doing it,' was the general consensus before I'd even fully explained Second-Half Thinking. I wouldn't swap these guys for anyone in the world, and I mean anyone, but I can promise you they are not yes-men. In fact they're the complete opposite. We all have strong opinions and fight for what we think is right, which is what makes the England camp so passionate. At times it can really kick off – it's an awesome environment to work in.

'Why not?' I questioned.

'We don't have the time . . .'

'We've never done it before . . .'

'I have my own routine in the changing room . . .'

The multitude of reasons why we should not do it came through loud and clear. They could however see that I was serious about this one.

'Right, I hear you, but I don't give a stuff! This is an idea we just have to try. We must get our mindset back to the start of the game where we are playing well. Look, if it's a total cock-up we won't do it again, but we have to try it.'

They rolled their eyes, but knew we had to give it a go. One of the team's great strengths is that we'll always try new things, no matter how strange they may sound.

I then proceeded to set out a new half-time routine and explained the reasons why I wanted to change our Second-Half Thinking.

HALF TIME ROUTINE – SECOND-HALF THINKING

0000–002 minutes
Absolute silence
Think about performance
Shirts off
Towel down
New kit
0–0 on the scoreboard

0002–0005 minutes
Coaches' assessment
Take on food and fluids

0005–0008 minutes
Captain/Coach final word
Take on food and fluids

0008–0010 minutes
Absolute silence
0–0 on the scoreboard
Visualise kick-off

As I explained it, the players started to come around. They weren't convinced, but they agreed to try it against France at the weekend.

One of the great moments comes when you know your rivals are not only watching what you are doing, but copying. A few months later we noticed that all the other teams were changing their strip at half time too. We were winning the mindset battle. For the first time in the history of English rugby, other teams were copying England.

Rolling on

We knew that the second Six Nations game against the French at their beloved Stade de France would be no cakewalk – it turned into a tough, gritty match. Our ability to play different types of rugby according to the conditions and opposition was very much in evidence this time as our forwards took on and beat the biggest pack in French history. We forced turnovers and numerous errors from them in the first half, and Wilkinson punished every penalty, nailing five of his six kicks for goal and notching up all England's points. In the process he became, at twenty, the youngest player ever to score more than 200 points in Test rugby. His tackling was exemplary too, and one fearsome hit on French wing Ntamack will remain in the memory of all who saw it, especially Emile Ntamack's.

This game was the first to feature our half-time thinking.

After the break the going got even tougher. We didn't make things easier for ourselves by landing two sin-binnings: lock Simon Shaw and wing Austin Healey. We were down to thirteen men as France threw everything at us. But we held on. Our defence was rock solid, and the French just could not get through. At the final whistle we were victorious by 15—9, and their flanker Olivier Magne spoke for them in saying, 'The English were stronger than us today . . . We've got work to do.'

When the game was finished and we were back in the dressing room, we got everyone round. It was a very proud moment. It had been a huge low for us losing in Paris the previous October, but that day in the changing room the atmosphere was fantastic. In many ways, this victory was more important to me than beating South Africa at Twickenham in 1998 – this game was the key turning point in my career. But at 15—9 it was a slim margin. Just one score by the French, one interception try, was all it would have taken to reverse the result. The difference one small event can make to your entire life is amazing. It we had lost that game I have no doubt I would not have been allowed to carry on even if I had wanted to.

For those who complained that the win over France had been try-less, the England side showed what could be done in that department in the next match at Twickenham against the Welsh. For me, this game combined the free-flowing rugby we had delivered in our victory over the Irish with the tough discipline we had shown against the French. Our hooker Phil Greening scored the first try from the left wing after thirty minutes. That score, plus Wilkinson's conversion, was the difference between the sides at the break, with penalties equalling each other out to make the score 19—12 in our favour. But after half-time we cut loose in a sensational run of play. We scored another four tries in a 46—12 victory, with a hat trick for the back row of Dallaglio, Hill and Back.

Going to Rome to play Italy in their first Six Nations was a real occasion, and I had no illusions that it would be an easy game. The Azurri had already shocked the Scots with a defeat at the Stadio Flaminio, and in the opening stages they really went for us. As I said after the game, they played some fantastic rugby early on, putting us under plenty of pressure. Italy coming into the tournament was excellent for the championship – I had never been to Rome before and it was good to be playing at a new venue.

Going into the last game against Scotland at Murrayfield, we could not but be aware that they had lost all their matches while we had won all of ours, averaging more than 40 points a game. We had already secured the Championship. Now, for a second time, we were playing for a Grand Slam.

As usual for away games, we flew to Scotland the week before the game and trained at Heriott Watt University in Edinburgh, staying at a hotel outside Edinburgh where everyone got bored out of their brains. During training there was an incident involving a set-up with a salacious newspaper photographer, two young women and a couple of the players which caused a major distraction – the police came and the arguments went on for hours. But the weather and conditions were superb and our training went well apart from that. Too well, in fact. On the day of the match the rain started to come down, and we weren't ready for it.

The Scots really came at us from the start – there were punch-ups all over the field – and some of our guys lost their self-control. That was what Scotland wanted, of course, and at the break we were only one point ahead, with a converted try by Dallaglio and a Wilkinson penalty against three penalties from the Scots. In the second-half the steady rain turned into a downpour, the pitch became a lake where it wasn't a bog, and the ball was as slippery as a Scottish eel. When Duncan Hodge slotted his fourth penalty to put the Scots in front, some of our players got rattled and lost their focus. The Scottish defence, on the other hand, was rock solid, and when Hodge used his aquaplaning skills to slide over next to the posts we were struggling. Somehow they kept us out, and when the whistle blew we had lost 13—19. We had missed the Grand Slam for the second year in succession.

Reviewing our progress

Taking the whole tournament into account, there were some positives. We had eight new players in the starting XV. Previously, with so many senior players from a different era, it was hard to change much without their approval. Now we had a new team without any preconceived ideas. We should have won that Scotland match, but that's rugby, that's elite competitive sports. We'd had a positive Six Nations only to miss the Grand Slam once again due to our preparation for the final match.

I could sense that we were close to really coming together as a team, but in terms of what we were trying to achieve in the broader definition of winning, we still had a long way to go. Thinking about it in a different way, in all Seven Elements of Winning we had improved considerably, but we hadn't yet achieved our true potential.

1. **Scoreboard:** We were putting more points on the scoreboard, but not enough to win the big games comfortably or the close games confidently.
2. **Performance:** Our game appeared good on paper, and certainly, Second-Half Thinking had helped in the last few matches, but Scotland indicated we had a long way to go in terms of our original goal of playing the game in a variety of ways. With the right preparation and the right plan on the day, we were unstoppable, but, as we saw in Scotland, games don't always go to plan. We clearly had to work on our thinking under pressure.
3. **Team:** With our Teamship Rules and team-building camps (like at

The game on the high veldt at Bloemfontein, 24 June 2000, was the start of a phenomenal fourteen-match winning streak against southern hemisphere teams, culminating with the 2003 World Cup final.

Our first win over Australia, 18 November 2000 – Dan Luger scores in injury time.

Martin Johnson lifts the Cook Cup for the first time, 18 November 2000.

Following our great win over Australia, we had the worst week – the players' strike. Martin Johnson and I face the cameras and press after a resolution had been found – we agreed to disagree.

The wonderful Jonny Wilkinson in action against Australia, doing what he does best. Another Cook Cup win, 10 November 2001.

England v. France, 2 March 2002 – Wilkinson 'sacked' by Betsen again. France outplayed England on this occasion but that didn't happen again until after the 2003 World Cup.

Some interesting substitutions were made for the Italy game in 2002, with four England captains taking the field together – (*left to right*) Dawson, Leonard, Dallaglio and Johnson.

Winning in Argentina, 22 June 2002, against all the odds gave Phil Vickery and other young England players the experience that was to prove priceless in our assault on the World Cup.

Working with the England players at Pennyhill Park, our training base. Ben Cohen is on the left, Lewis Moody to the right.

The view of the training pitch at Pennyhill Park from the video tower, taken by Tony Biscombe, our analysis expert.

These games against New Zealand (*above*), South Africa (*centre*) and Australia marked the laying down of the gauntlet in our build-up to the World Cup season. The three straight wins over the southern hemisphere teams were exactly what we needed twelve months out from the biggest competition of our lives.

A very proud day with (*left to right*) Joe, Jayne, Freddie and Jess, after receiving an OBE from the Queen, December 2002.

The England management team finally got what they deserved with a Grand Slam win over Ireland in 2003.

The 'White Orcs' peaked at the right time – Wilkinson kicking the All Blacks around in Wellington, June 2003.

England and Australia contest the scrum in Melbourne, June 2003 – Australia decided not to do this in the World Cup final.

the Royal Marines) the elite squad appeared to be coming together, especially since we'd begun energising our energy sappers; but we hadn't really clicked yet in our play. We had moments of brilliance, but they were all too brief.

4. **Enjoyable experience:** In this area we had come the farthest – management and players seemed genuinely excited to be a part of the elite squad. Pennyhill Park would help to solve some of the logistical hassle that accompanied an international match, yet we still couldn't get it right when we travelled for away games.

5. **Competition:** In this area we had come a long way, too. With the right preparation we knew we could soundly beat any of the Six Nations teams, and no longer were we stepping onto the pitch anticipating defeat against the southern-hemisphere teams. Even in our pool match against New Zealand, the 16—30 scoreline didn't reflect how close the match had been. I'm certain that if we had met the South Africans with our new squad we would have won.

6. **Supporters:** We had played some thrilling rugby and at times had got all 75,000 people at Twickenham on their feet going nuts – but never for a whole match. We could do more and our supporters deserved it.

7. **Consistency:** Perhaps our worst area. We were so often being let down in our performance under pressure and in our preparation. There seemed to be a thousand things to distract the team at any one time. We had to improve our efforts in preparation off the pitch before we would see any consistent improvements on it. This indeed would prove to be the last piece of the puzzle to fall into place.

Thankfully, we'd recovered from the World Cup. We'd turned our setbacks into some success, and we'd done it strongly in every game but Scotland. Even though we won the Six Nations tournament on points that year, we'd failed to capture a Grand Slam – was it becoming a bit of a monkey on our backs?

There were questions hanging over the team, questions for which I didn't have all the answers at that stage, but all were questions and experiences that the team were learning from and they would all play a key role in winning the ultimate prize.

21
ANSWERS IN ISRAEL

'So how are your players embracing our technology, then?' asked Michael as I sat in the Elonex offices in North London.

'Oh, they're getting along,' I replied. 'At first they weren't that interested in using their laptops. They couldn't see the point. Without exception they are all using them now. In fact we need to provide extra training, more programs and we should see if we can get them using Word. Mind you, with the size of their fingers we could do with you making the keyboards bigger somehow! Anyway, it's all good stuff.'

Michael Spiro laughed with me. It was good to catch up. Two years before I had sat in this same chair asking for computers for the team. E-mail had completely changed the way we communicated with the players and had given us a massive boost in productivity. That's the kind of improvement we'd been making in England rugby on a regular basis in the last couple of years. Sooner or later, I figured, it would all add up to winning. At least, that was my belief, having just scraped through a tumultuous time since the World Cup.

After Michael and I had sorted the business, our conversation took a different turn.

'You know, Clive, you might be interested in a little project we've been working on lately. It's with a guy named Yehuda Shinar who's doing extensive research on the characteristics of leadership and performance in high-performance individuals.

'His background is in handwriting analysis, but he's developed a computer program that assesses an individual's ability to perform under high levels of pressure and stress, given his or her mental acuity and psychological make-up. The program then trains you to increase your awareness and skill in a collection of key areas of competitive behaviour.'

That got my attention. Our experience with the Royal Marines had clearly shown that the only way you could really assess someone was to see how they reacted under pressure. We spent a lot of time on our ability to perform under pressure, especially Dave Alred, our kicking coach, who has earned a doctorate on the subject. Dave is really in a class of his own and was instrumental on so many fronts in helping us to win the World Cup. Clearly, as Jonny Wilkinson's kicking coach, it goes without saying how important he had been to the team. However, his skills and input go way beyond this. The work he does with all the players in terms of personal preparation and psychology is far ahead of anyone else in the sport. Anything that could help us lift individual performance even further was worth a look.

'I'd love to see what he's up to. When can I meet with this . . .'

'Yehuda Shinar. Well, here's the catch. He's in Israel. They've just completed the prototype of the training software. You're experienced in this area with respect to sport. We'd like to know what you think. Would you fly to see him?'

'Yes, of course I would. It's the least I can do.'

Israel is renowned for its technology and psychology. I'd never been there before, but if there was an outside chance of helping England rugby, I was willing to explore it. We like working with our sponsors in the spirit of partnership, so I was eager to help Elonex as well.

'When can you go?' he asked.

'How about this weekend?' This was Wednesday. No sense in mucking around.

The art of interrogation

I arrived at Heathrow's Terminal One with about an hour to spare. My secretary Karen had booked me on El Al, the Israeli national airline. As I approached the back of the line at the ticketing area a uniformed official asked for my passport and tickets. *Strange. Normally you don't need those till you reach the desk.* The officer made a thorough inspection then gave me a hard look.

'Over there,' he said, indicating a cordoned-off section to the left. *Maybe there's something wrong with my tickets. Has my passport expired*? He handed my documents to another rather stern-looking uniformed officer, this one a young Israeli lady, who in turn took a good look at my ticket and passport.

'What is the purpose of your trip to Israel?' She had now been joined by another young lady from El Al.

I told her, but she wasn't satisfied, and so began a series of direct questions about my trip. By the fifth or sixth question I was a bit perplexed. She asked where was I going, who was I going to see, why I was going for just two days, where did I live, how long had I lived there, why did I travel so much. Her questions were intensely scrutinising. They weren't just innocent queries either. Her tone and body language made them sharp and incriminating accusations. I wasn't expecting it. It only made matters worse that I didn't really know much about the man I was going to meet.

'Why do you want to learn about personal performance?'

'Because I'm a coach, a rugby coach, and it might help us win.'

'Who do you coach?'

'England rugby . . . you know, the national team . . .'

Not everybody is interested in rugby, and it clearly was not a big hit with these people. There was absolutely no sign of recognition in her eyes. This wasn't working.

'Wait, I've got a photograph.'

Once again I shuffled through my briefcase and pulled out an official photograph of me jumping out of my seat at Twickenham with my hands in the air as England scored a try.

'Here,' I said, handing over the photo, 'that's me.' She took one glance at the 8 × 10 picture and casually tossed it over her shoulder. I was beginning to worry. *What the hell is going on?*

Four large British police officers armed with fully automatic weapons had gathered outside the ticketing area. They too were staring at me intently. One of them lowered his head to speak into his two-way radio microphone.

The young lady's questions kept coming. She asked me to open my laptop and show them e-mails or correspondence with Yehuda. I couldn't. Then they asked me to show them documents proving who I was or what I did.

'Who is your employer?'

'The RFU . . . the England Rugby Football Union.'

'Do you have a business card?'

'Yes . . .'

On and on the interrogation went. It continued for what seemed like hours. I was moved to a different room. My bags were given the most thorough going over I've ever seen, an instrument being run over every square inch. They even tried calling Yehuda in Israel to verify that he knew me. He didn't answer his phone. I was body-searched, scanned, patted down for weapons, and even asked to give up my shoes. I'd been detained for the previous forty-five minutes.

It was very intimidating. I was not a terrorist, but that's clearly what it seemed they were thinking. There were now five British armed guards huddled around the exit watching me with interest.

The officer who had walked off with my passport and ticket fifteen minutes before was now returning. But instead of slapping the cuffs on, he smiled. 'Thank you, Mr Woodward,' he said, handing me my travel documents. 'You may proceed. Here is your boarding pass. Your plane is boarding at gate 56. Please go straight to the gate. Have a nice flight, and enjoy your stay.'

Guarded

In somewhat of a daze I took the documents, gathered my things and began walking towards the exit he was indicating. Quickly, before they changed their mind, I made for the exit. My two lady interrogators did not smile.

As I walked out of the ticketing area the five heavily armed police guards formed a very close walking cordon around me. The guard to my right made eye contact.

'I didn't know they played rugby in Tel Aviv?' he said with a broad grin.

I took a deep breath, stopped walking, and burst out laughing.

'What is going on!'

'Don't worry, Clive. We'll look after you from here,' and they escorted me all the way to the gate.

'What was that all about?' I asked along the way.

'Standard operating procedure. They deal with everyone that way. Pretty intimidating the first time, isn't it?'

'You're telling me. Those questions. The pressure was intense. God, they're good!'

'That's why the most prominent air target for terrorist activity in the world has only ever had one incident in its entire history. They have the best security screening procedures in the airline industry. They are very well trained and prepared.'

At the gate I thanked my escorts once again. On the five-hour flight I concluded it was no wonder the Israelis were well-known for their prowess in psychology. If Yehuda was half as good at analysing performance, we might be onto something.

Arriving in Tel Aviv

When I landed, Yehuda greeted me at the gate. At least somebody in Israel knew me. He was a warm and friendly man, of medium height and lean like a distance runner. He welcomed me into his home twenty-five minutes north of the airport in a beachside suburb that reminded me of Santa Monica in Los Angeles. It was a modern, clean and vibrant neighbourhood. After a cup of tea Israeli-style – no milk and with a lovely fresh sprig of mint – we began to discuss individual performance in competitive environments, a subject Yehuda embraced with great passion.

'Clive, you have great competitors in your team, strong athletes, yes?' he asked with a thick Israeli accent.

'Yes, Yehuda. They're the best rugby players in the country.'

'What do you believe is the difference between competitors and winners, then?'

'Well, it's a combination of preparation, fitness, skills and mindset . . .'

'Ah, yes, mindset. Thinking. That is the difference. Your mind controls your behaviours. Control your mind under the most intense pressure and you control the game.'

'What do you mean, exactly?'

'In my research of over 3,000 competitive individuals I compiled a database of common characteristics in psychological conditioning. I discovered significant trends – patterns of thinking. These trends I have developed and tested in training elite athletes, military squadrons and corporate executives over a period of fifteen years. The results are consistent. When their patterns of thinking were expertly developed, their personal performance increased in every circumstance. These competitors became winners.'

'OK, that makes good sense.'

'We have identified eleven high-performance behaviours,' he continued, 'that are consistent with winning behaviour. For example, one of the most powerful skills any high-performance individual can learn is how to apply pressure to his competitor . . .'

For the next thirty minutes Yehuda went on to describe his findings. I found his insights stimulating, his conclusions amazing. His winning behaviours covered areas like identifying opportunities, decisiveness, time management, momentum, self-control and one-on-one situations. It was one of the most remarkable assessments of the competitive situation I'd ever heard.

'. . . Yehuda, stop. Stop right there.'

'But I haven't finished yet.'

'No, stop. When can you come to London?'

'What do you mean?'

'When can you come to discuss this with my other coaches?'

'But you have not heard all of the programme yet.'

'I don't need to. I've heard enough. When can you come?'

I was getting excited. Nothing Yehuda was saying was a surprise to me. Indeed, it was everything I'd ever experienced and done when I was successful in a competitive environment both in sport and in business. But I'd just never heard anyone stating so simply and clearly what were obvious truths about winning. It was exactly the link I'd been searching for. I could sense that the England team hadn't reached its potential in critical areas of our performance on the pitch. This sounded like the perfect way to tie everything together into a tight, coherent strategy. I had to give it a try, no matter what. It was fascinating, really fascinating.

Learning by playing

After dinner Yehuda showed me his proudest accomplishment. Not only had he worked out the key mental skills of the true winner, he'd also invented a computer simulator along with a detailed curriculum that could train anyone to master the skills of mental competitive advantage. Working through the simulator which was much like a sophisticated computer game with instructional content, I was completely challenged and tested. After only ten minutes on the program I was exhausted – and I understood. It was a powerful tool, and I wanted it for the team, even though it was still at the experimental stage.

We kept working for a day and a half, then we decided to take a break. It's hard on the brain, this stuff. Yehuda put me in the car and began driving. When I saw signs for the airport, I grew curious.

'Where are we going?'

'We're going flying. I find it clears the mind.'

Yehuda pulled up outside a hangar in the general aviation section and we walked out onto the tarmac to his plane. It was a Tomahawk, a tiny craft with a single engine at the front, a bubble canopy, and only two seats.

'Are you going to fly this thing?'

Yehuda laughed. By the time we'd got off the ground, I'd forgotten my misgivings. Israel was beautiful by air, the Mediterranean sea to our left, Palestinian neighbours fifteen miles to our right. As we flew north up the coast over the bustling city of Tel Aviv, I noticed a few familiar landmarks.

'Hey, there's your house.'

'You have a great sense of direction, my friend.'

How crazy would all this seem to everyone at home with their conservative English sensibilities. I was in search of elite competitive technology with a man I hardly knew who was now flying me in an aircraft no larger than a baked bean can over the ravaged Middle East landscape. I could just see the headlines: 'England head coach shot down in two-seater plane over the Golan Heights.' Now that would be difficult to explain to the media.

Yehuda was right. Flying did clear the mind.

We had to get him to England as soon as possible. We were just starting the Six Nations but we had to see if these ideas could be harnessed into our elite environment.

By the time I returned home to England on Monday morning, my mind was in overdrive. In the car from the airport, after telling Jayne I was home, I called Michael Spiro at Elonex.

'Ah, Clive. Back already. How did you find our friend Yehuda Shinar then?'

'You've got some great potential there, Michael. Some of his ideas are fascinating from the point of view of building a winning team.'

'That's just what I wanted to hear. Thanks for that, Clive.'

'Look, I'd like to put the players through Yehuda's simulator game and ask for his assessment on them all. Is there some way we could work that out?'

'Happy to help. Clearly there are major advantages for us. I always did want to see England win something anyway. It's been a long time since 1966!'

Bringing the ideas into action

Over the course of the months leading up to our summer tour to South Africa, Yehuda visited our coaching team many times to share his ideas about winning behaviours. We also put several players through the computer simulators and began subtly focusing our training sessions on the information it revealed. Yehuda was a significant influence in helping us to think about our coaching in a new light. His training itself was very useful because it showed everyone that there was a level of competitive self-understanding that we hadn't fully explored. Yehuda's handling of behaviours wasn't entirely new to me, but what was enlightening was the way he had managed to quantify the importance of behaviour in areas I hadn't considered before. Topics like momentum, self-control and pressure are a part of every elite sportsperson's vocabulary, but even at Loughborough they weren't taught as clear and obvious aspects of the game which could be measured and controlled and coached.

When I first started coaching England, it was clear that there were key areas of our game in which we would have to excel before we could win matches on a consistent basis. For the previous two years Tony Biscombe and his team had been exhaustively analysing our performance in areas such as kick-offs, scrums, contact in rucks and mauls, lineouts, and penalties. In addition to measuring our behaviours in these areas, we had also been setting standards for world-class performance that would lead to winning games. Yehuda, however, showed me how a set of behaviours covering areas beyond just the key parts of our game could be clearly set down and consequently managed to achieve success.

Our coaching team quickly latched onto the idea and saw the tremendous benefit of creating a simple and clear list of our own winning behaviours that would suit our elite rugby environment. We made a list of behaviours and, where we could, we then critically began to assign our current world-class performance standards to each category. Over many years this list has evolved into our Nine High Performance Behaviours and it has now grown to include some thirty-four sub-behaviours broken down into more than 135 key performance indicators, all of which are measurable. That gives us an accurate indication of our performance on the pitch compared with our benchmarks in these areas measured on a world-class performance basis.

Our current nine High Performance behaviours, and the coaches primarily in charge of each, are:

1. Our Team Defence – Phil Larder
2. Our Team Basics – Andy Robinson
3. Our Team Contact Principles – Andy Robinson
4. Our Team Pressure – Clive Woodward
5. Our Kicking Game – Dave Alred
6. Our Team Attack – Clive Woodward
7. Our Team Self-control – Clive Woodward
8. Our Team Tactics – Clive Woodward
9. Our Team Leadership – Clive Woodward

We have now expanded this list of behaviours into posters and they form the basis of our coaching during Test weeks. By way of example, my area 'Our Team Self-Control' is now one of my favourite topics for discussion with the team. This is the only one that I can share with you, for obvious reasons. I do so in the hope that several referees might read this book and note the emphasis and importance that the England team give to this particular area!

7. Our Team Self-Control

Think Correctly Under Pressure – T-CUP

A. Critical Areas

A.1 Tackle	Understand the Law
A.2 Scrum	Position / Possession
A.3 Backfoot	Territory / Points

B. Self Control

B.1 Our Ball
  - Leg drive over the ball
  - Listen to the referee
    Demonstrate that you have heard
  - Ball presentation – speed of support
  - Through the gate – workrate

B.2 Their Ball
  - 'Dead' – Don't chase lost causes
  - Listen to the referee
    Shout out what he says
  - Leave 9 (scrum-half) alone
    It never works / risk / reward?
  - Through the gate – workrate

C. Work with the Referee

C.1 Body Language

D. Opposition

D.1 Intimidation – 'T-CUP'
D.2 Remember South Africa 53–3

Time management in a sporting context was one of the many things Yehuda Shinar had been talking to me about. He had a phrase called 'Correctly Thinking Under Pressure'. Despite being useless at Scrabble it didn't take me long to put it into the really English context of T-CUP – Thinking Correctly Under Pressure! That's what we had been missing in the last few minutes of our recent Scotland loss, as well as at the Wales defeat the year before. There is no greater critical component of success in sport, in either a team or an individual context, than the ability to perform and THINK correctly under pressure. And now we were measuring critical areas such as our self-control, which would allow us to improve our performance significantly in those parts of the game that had previously been difficult to manage.

The behaviours change infrequently, but the importance of certain behaviours does alter, depending on which team we're playing in the upcoming match. So our posters are flexible and we can single out the behaviours we want to stress for a particular match. And of course once the coaches have identified the strategy suitable for the opposition, the next step is to take that strategy and show how each individual contributes to it. So when we play Wales, for example, we know who their playmakers are, who their ball-carriers are, and so on. Tony Biscombe and his team can then produce DVD video analysis on each key player in the opposition to demonstrate their strengths: e.g. passing over a long distance with the left hand, pace, incisiveness, etc. and also any weaknesses: e.g. left shoulder tackle non-existent, pace, kicking left foot, etc. In these particular examples the DVD analysis can then be used as support material for either our attacking game or our team defence.

And to keep the players involved in the evolution of our High Performance Behaviours, we have integrated our Player Team system of leadership with the posters as well. Now, in addition to a coach, two or three senior players are responsible for leadership in each of the nine areas during each match – around ten players have leadership roles and so many of them have multiple responsibilities. For example, in the 2003 World Cup, in the area of our team defence, Neil Back and Mike Tindall were responsible for that part of the game. In the War Room before the match we go through each area and team leaders report on what is required for the upcoming match.

At the end of their reports I'd typically ask, 'Backy, are you happy?' i.e. that we're prepared in this area?

If the answer was 'yes', we'd move on. If the answer was 'no', we'd ask why and then turn to Phil Larder, who is the coach in charge of defence, and ask what he thought. England won the World Cup because we had the best defence in the tournament – this was without a doubt down to Phil Larder, but the importance and leadership qualities shown by players such as Back and Tindall cannot be overstated. Persuading Phil to come across from Rugby League was arguably one of the greatest factors in the development of the winning World Cup squad over the past six years. He is massive on coaching the individual on the real basics of defence, something that is rarely done now with elite sports stars in any sport, and his passion for being the best coach in world rugby has been contagious within the team.

As coaches we have been able to build and develop Yehuda's basic concepts and transform them into a coaching structure with clear emphasis on measurable world class performance standards in all areas under pressure – unless we can measure it we do not want to know about it.

In addition to the High Performance behaviours, the posters now include all the dozens of team calls used to cover the plays. Integrating everything in one place now means that these nine posters comprise a full and flexible summary of England rugby's approach to the game. When combined with our Black Book, it makes a simple yet formidable coaching combination. Although there is a complex level of detail contained within each of the posters, they are relatively simple and easy coaching tools to understand, which means that communicating all the information that new players coming into the squad need to know is far simpler than it ever was before.

Of course it would take more than a year to bring all these systems to bear in the form of our 'Nine High Performance Behaviours' as they're described here. However we might never have gone down this track if it hadn't been for a chance conversation with Michael Spiro, which led me to Israel to meet an accomplished graphologist who had applied his science to the winning behaviours of highly successful individuals.

2000 Summer Tour to South Africa

John Mitchell had returned to New Zealand at the end of the domestic season with an ambition to become the All Blacks coach.

In June we travelled to South Africa to play a two-Test series against the Springboks. This was Andy Robinson's first opportunity to start serious work with the players – we were absolutely delighted that he'd left Bath for his new position as my number two. The timing couldn't have been better. Andy was the last piece in the jigsaw in creating world-class coaches in all areas of the game. We obviously needed the players, but I have seen few sports teams succeed without world-class coaching and management support. Andy is the most competitive person I have ever met. Once he was on board, I believed winning the World Cup was a very real possibility. His coaching ability is significantly ahead of any other coach working in the sport, but what makes him such an important person within our team is his ability to transfer this expertise to all the players. He is a fantastic team-member and has always been there when I needed him most. Andy and I had worked together before, and it was great to be working together again. He was now working in the team on a full-time basis, something I didn't have with John Mitchell.

Beating the Springboks at home was a very rare event for England, but our 1998 victory at Twickenham had smashed any lingering myth of their invincibility. I felt sure we could win. The tour kicked off with a bit of déjà vu as we stayed in the Westcliff Hotel, the sister hotel of the Pink Palace. Again the South Africans were not happy about this but now I was in control of budgets and had realised long before that if you want your players to be the world's best you must look after them in the same way. This group deserved five-star treatment because they gave us five-star performances.

On the morning of the first test, Jonny Wilkinson woke up feeling really sick. By the time we arrived at the Loftus Versfeld stadium in Pretoria, he was violently ill. It was literally an hour to kick-off. We had to give up on him and switch to Austin Healey at No. 10. It was a big change in a critical position so close to the start of a match.

Dan Luger scored the only try in the game after a string of penalties had gone against us. In the second-half we had enough possession to win the game but, credit to the Springboks, they made it hard for us to turn that possession into points. When full-time came there were some very relieved South Africans, and some very disappointed Englishmen. We lost the first Test 18—13, although a lot of people said we were unlucky not to win. In the last few minutes Tim Stimpson was tackled by South African captain Andre Vos while touching the ball down over the line. All of us in the England camp – and plenty of the South Africans around me, too – thought that England was looking at seven points. But the South African video referee had other ideas.

It was some consolation that we played well, but the fact is that to be Number One you really need to win by a margin wide enough to rule out any question of a bad call here or there influencing the outcome of the game.

Wilko's illness was eventually traced back to some off milk in a milkshake. It's impossible to say what impact that had on the match, but had Jonny not become sick, we would not have had the forethought to bring a chef with us in future. So maybe it was destiny. The incident brought home to me that to be fully prepared we had to cover every base, even as far as controlling food intake. During the World Cup 2003 we had our own chef, a Scotsman called Dave Campbell. Do you win World Cups because of a chef? All I know is we had thirty healthy, fit and energised players for the final.

In the second Test we were determined not to let anything get in our way.

South Africa looked good in the early stages before we got our hands on the ball, but once we did things started to go our way and the Boks seldom looked close to crossing our line. Jonny Wilkinson put in an immaculate performance, scoring all England's points with eight penalties and a drop goal. He hardly put a foot wrong in the whole match. But it was a team effort, with everyone giving it 100 per cent to make a famous victory – a credit to everyone involved. England have had some great matches, but this ranked right up there with the best of them.

The Springboks were trailing by 12 points until the eightieth minute, when van der Westhuizen scored a controversial try. The video referee,

André Watson, ruled that the Boks' scrum-half had reached over and grounded the ball from a ruck on the England line, another call I found impossible to agree with, especially when he had time to watch it in slow motion. So it was another close, exciting game with Watson again at the centre of the key moment.

We won the second match at Bloemfontein 27—22. It was the first win by any northern-hemisphere national side on Tri-Nations soil since England's quarter-final win in the 1995 World Cup, and it was only the third win by England on South African soil in twenty-eight years. What nobody knew then was that this would also be the start of eleven successive England Test victories. Even better, we would not lose to a southern-hemisphere side again, home or away, right up to the 2003 World Cup. We were on the verge of a winning sequence of twelve matches, including the final against Australia.

The tide had well and truly turned. But winning doesn't happen in a straight line. The team would nearly break apart before we'd finally pull together to demonstrate our potential.

FALLING DOWN 22

On Monday 20th November 2000 I learned from the players that they were unanimous in their decision to strike. By this they meant that they did not intend to play for England on Saturday against Argentina. Twickenham was sold out, the Pumas were in town and everyone expected an England team to kick off at 3 p.m. on Saturday!

The contrast of this situation from two days earlier was remarkable.

England had just played one of their best games in my time as coach in a thrilling victory against Australia at Twickenham. The Test against Argentina was in five days, and there was another against South Africa the week after that.

A players' strike in the middle of our autumn Internationals felt wrong. Wrong for the players, wrong for the fans, wrong for the RFU, wrong for the very good of the game.

England versus Australia, Twickenham

18 November 2000 is an important date in England's rugby history, because it was on that day that our team psychologically broke Australia's back at Twickenham with a victory over the Wallabies. It also happened that this win would be the start of an unparalleled five-match winning streak against the Wallabies. A great achievement, but as I said at the time, it would have been a massive setback if we had lost that day. We certainly didn't play as well as we could have, but perhaps that made it all the better. It showed we could still get a win even when we were not at our best.

The Wallabies were ahead 19—15 and it was well into injury-time. We had a lineout on their line, our last chance, but we blew the throw-in and the whole of Twickenham groaned. But then it happened. With seconds remaining the Aussies kicked for touch. It would have been game over, but they missed the touchline. Our team just did not panic under the pressure of the situation but continued to attack, keeping hold of the ball, recycling phase after phase.

With seconds of the match left, Iain Balshaw, seeing there was no full-back or cover defence, chipped ahead into the left-hand corner behind the Wallaby line and Dan Luger outpaced the opposition to make the touchdown. But Luger's dramatic last-minute try had André Watson going to the TV replay before he could make his decision. Why he had to go to the video replay when the touch judge had clearly seen the touchdown and told him it was a try is still beyond me. Once again Watson was the referee of yet another cliffhanger.

A nail-biting interval ensued as we waited for the ref to decide, and then ... TRY! The decision appeared on the screen to an incredible wall of noise as Twickenham erupted in celebration. Wilkinson converted from the touchline with an amazing kick, and there wasn't even time to re-start the game before Watson blew his whistle for full time. We had won in dramatic fashion. England 22—Australia 19.

The Australians weren't happy at all. England were not supposed to snatch victories in the last second – it was very un-English behaviour! That was how we lifted the Cook Cup for the first time. It was a real thriller. Not the most elegant of games, but England played with tremendous self-belief. Rod Macqueen was less than amused afterwards. It was my first win against him and one I cherished. We had just beaten the world champions and hadn't even played our best.

Twenty seconds to score

That last-minute try wasn't as lucky as some might have thought and all Australians believed. We'd had good preparation before the game with an adequate number of training days in September and October, but during Test week we had been training for just such a last-minute situation as we found ourselves in against the Wallabies. We discussed and trained for two strategies designed to win the tight match: first, our drop goal routine and, second, time management.

Since we'd implemented our new half-time routine and worked on our Second-Half Thinking, England had reversed the trend by which our worst performing period came in the first ten minutes of the second-half. This post-break period was now on par with the rest of our game, which was excellent. However once we'd resolved that one, another trend emerged. It was only the week before the Wallabies match that our analysis showed that in the last five minutes of matches our performance consistently fell away. But it wasn't our fitness that was lacking. Our work rates were just as high in those closing minutes. It appeared as if we were losing our composure in close games as the clock dwindled. It was our time management and our thinking that were suffering as the end was getting near.

Video footage of the Grand Slam game in the wet conditions against Scotland proved the point with more than six minutes, or 360 seconds, to go. We played right into the Scots' hands by playing high-risk rugby with little or no chance of success when there was plenty of time to get the decisive score. We lost that game by six points, but it wasn't the only time our senses seemed to desert us in the closing minutes of the match. We had lost to Wales by one point at Wembley, but looking at the tape again there were still another five minutes of rugby after Jenkins converted the Gibbs try. Again plenty of time to score and win.

We showed the Scotland footage to the team and then went on to explain to the players that repeated video analysis showed that it only took twenty seconds to score a try. Tony Biscombe produced further footage of try after try where the duration of the series of plays that led to the score was repeatedly less than twenty seconds.

The tactic Twenty Seconds to Score was a part of our training programme all week leading up to the Wallabies as we worked diligently on our T-CUP – Thinking Correctly Under Pressure. Twenty Seconds to Score paid off on the day. The team was four points behind as we went into injury time. This game no-one panicked. Instead I saw very clear thinking; especially from Martin Johnson and Matt Dawson, two of our key leaders.

The difference, in my view, was that now we were coaching 'between the ears'. Johnson's leadership was fantastic. He understood what we were trying to do and his contribution in the team environment cannot be overstated. His enthusiasm to listen and then take on these ideas was contagious. It was one of his many great attributes. In fact, all the players were becoming sponges for new ideas, thoughts and concepts. We had a room full of energisers. We now knew we could win, so we wanted to concentrate on why we were winning in order to keep raising the bar.

With our result against the Wallabies, we had now won two games in a row against southern-hemisphere teams, with every chance of three with South Africa coming up. England had never done that before. Suddenly we had back-to-back victories and the team not only believed they could win but knew they *deserved* to win. We were starting to believe that we could really take on the world.

But just as we were finally pulling things together, that's when the wheels nearly fell off, well and truly. I'm not overstating things when I say that what followed was the second darkest day in England rugby history, and once again I was at the helm.

Grinding to a halt

From the beginning of my appointment as coach of England I had consciously decided not to get involved in any contract negotiations with the players. I felt I should leave the finances totally to the RFU. I thought my job was to coach the team, but after this episode I realised I was wrong.

Of course I had been aware that new contract negotiations were going on. They had been dragging for some time, but the differences, to me, seemed to be over small details in the grand scheme of things. That was one mistake, to underestimate the importance of these matters to the players. I didn't think I needed to be involved, but this was another example of a potential disaster coming from a completely unexpected front – Dislocated Expectations at its best.

After years of hard work transforming England rugby, and massive investment in building a side capable of winning on the world stage, it was now all at risk again because of an issue I just did not see coming. Heavy-hitting corporate executive meets ultra-competitive and deter-mined group of elite players who are united and whose noses are all pointing in the same direction in everything they're doing. It was a disaster waiting to happen.

The situation had developed into a matter of principle on both sides, which made it a very, very dangerous situation. Nobody would win here, and I couldn't see either party backing down.

I thought about all the thousands of man hours the management team had spent chasing a dream, so that the players could experience what no other England player ever had: a real chance of being the best in the world. I also thought about all the huge amount of work that the players themselves had done to come so far. To me the value of this opportunity was priceless. I couldn't bear to see this all wasted. It was time to get involved.

Emergency exit

We had very little time to sort out the whole situation and still play a Test match on Saturday, so I decided to force the issue. After speaking with all of the players and getting confirmation of their intent to strike, I asked them to leave the team hotel since they were not there to prepare for a Test match.

I also advised them that if they wanted to play for England they should be back at the Pennyhill Park by 11 o'clock on Wednesday morning ready to train, or not bother coming back. In so doing I hoped to force an outcome that would be satisfactory for all concerned and resolve the conflict. How long was this going to go on for? Someone had to act.

I can't really find words to describe how I was feeling that Tuesday. I learned a lot about myself and I learned a lot about the players. Forty-nine per cent of me admired the fact that the players were 'as one' and stuck together over this issue, but 51 per cent of me couldn't agree with the way they'd acted on their resolve.

To make matters even more complicated than a whole international team going on strike, there was the small matter of a huge black tie dinner that we all had to attend that evening. Myself, Jayne, the management, the players, wives, girlfriends, the RFU, the media, about 700 people and Uncle Tom Cobbleigh and all! For the purpose of the night it was a great success, and I was delighted to see that, after my reminding the players of the dinner earlier in the day, all of them had attended as they had promised.

My emotions had been on a roller-coaster over the last twenty-four hours and I was relieved that during that Tuesday night senior players had met with the RFU and come to a settlement.

The players were all back at the team hotel by the appointed time on the Wednesday.

I wish I could say that I let it rest there and just got on with the job at hand for Saturday but too much had happened in too short a space of time. We had come so far and yet the fact that everything could so easily be jeopardised in such a way absolutely floored me. Of course I realised this was not a personal matter between me and the players, but at the time I was incredibly angry. That Wednesday night in a team meeting, fuelled by my emotions and clouded by fatigue, I made the worst ever display of myself with the team. I completely lost it. I'm passionate about this job of mine, it had become a way of life. If you want to do it well you have to feel it, you have to care. The events of this particular week had struck deeply. I lost my temper. It was awful. It was the one time I can truly say I was disappointed with how I handled things.

Time to think

Walking out of that meeting, I couldn't believe how I had handled the situation. At the end of the day the players had all come back, so why on earth did I react that way? In hindsight they were supporting me in my position and had all returned on time. Martin had handled every-thing very well again so what was the big deal?

It was a confusing time. I had to clear my head.

I walked straight to my car and began driving home. My emotions had boiled over, but it wasn't just this isolated incident. It was the whole of the previous three years. I admit to being obsessive about coaching England at rugby, but my outburst had nothing to do with the players really. Maybe some distance and perspective and a good talk with Jayne would help.

I was halfway home in my car deep in thought when the phone rang.

'Hi, Clive, it's Nathan,' Nathan Martin said in his easy, understanding way.

'Hi, Nathan.' He must have heard about the meeting.

A pause. The road noise would be coming through.

'Clive, where are you?'

'I'm in the car on the way home for the night. I need some space.'

'Stop the car.' His tone changed.

'What?'

'Pull over right now. Stop the car.'

I did as he asked.

'Clive, you can't go home. I think it's important you are here tonight. I'll call Jayne and get her to meet us at the hotel.'

He was right. What the hell was I doing?

I turned the car around and was back at the hotel within twenty minutes of leaving. Thankfully, I don't think anyone but Nathan knew I had gone.

Nathan was a coup for England rugby. The team had visited the Commando Training Centre Royal Marines once again during the summer just gone. Nathan organised another brilliant visit for us, this time focused more on fitness and team work. It was during that visit that I first asked Nathan about his military career. Although completely dedicated to the Royal Marines, Nathan was ready to leave the service for personal reasons. I'd kept that in mind and when he finally did resign, I immediately offered him a position with the England team. Nathan became the team's first official full-time manager. I figured if he could run a crack unit in the Royal Marines managing millions of pounds worth of military resources, then he could handle the logistics of a rugby team standing on his head. He was a brilliant addition to the squad, and I was even more grateful to have him around in this trying time.

Later that night Jayne did come over to the hotel. I was angry and disappointed with myself that I had 'lost it' in such a way. But by the end of the evening I knew what I had to do the next day. I had to get the week back on track and we had somehow to win a Test match on Saturday.

The morning's press conference was a good place to start.

Pulling back from the abyss

During Test weeks the England team hold a press conference on Thursday mornings. That morning I made sure all the players were in the room to hear what I had to say. There were some very uncertain faces amongst them after my previous night's tirade. I didn't sit down in front of the cameras until I could see all the players present.

The room was packed. The strike had attracted attention, and this was the media's first chance to hear my views. Outside England rugby, everyone was loving the sensationalism of this story.

Martin Johnson was sitting next to me at the head of the room.

'Good morning. Thanks for coming today. Before we take any questions I'd just like to say a few words. In the last few days, England rugby has had a major setback . . .'

For the next five minutes I openly described the events of the week so that there would be no confusion about what happened. I acknowledged that I could see both sides and that I was glad the dispute had been settled promptly. I didn't discuss my pointed approach with the players and didn't talk about my less-than-admirable behaviour. This wasn't the time to create further sensational stories. This was about moving on.

'I'd like to make this clear. I take full responsibility for what's happened here. I really should have seen this coming. The players were left exposed and felt they had no alternatives. My job is now to make sure this never happens again. We have to look at things in perspective. We've just beaten the Wallabies for the first time at Twickenham. It was a thrilling game of rugby. We have a tough match against the Pumas this weekend and the Springboks after that. We will be ready to play Saturday and look forward to the game. Again I would like to say that I take full responsibility for what has happened. We'll learn from it and will be stronger as a team because of it.'

After I finished my opening comments, the questions came thick and fast at Martin and me, probing for the slightest sign of division. There was none.

Johno made that clear. 'There are no issues between us over this.

What's done is done. It's over. We totally respect each other's views. On this one, we'll just have to agree to disagree.'

That was a clever way to put it. I looked sideways at Martin, admiring the way he was handling this. His composure under pressure was brilliant. Afterwards, Johno and I had a private word in the hall. We shook hands and have never looked back.

Back in gear

As hurt as I had been over the whole incident I was still immensely proud of how the players conducted themselves. They were a hundred per cent committed, and they had done everything as one team. It's a testament to how strong this team was under the greatest pressure. It would take time to recover fully, but we continued to meet as a team in the War Room and to enjoy doing what we did. Sometimes these situations happen. You have to get over them and move on.

The Management Team had held firm, stood by me in perhaps my darkest hour. Andy Robinson must have been wondering if England rugby was usually like this in Test week; this was his first autumn series. I am so glad that he was there. As I say it's at times like these that you learn a lot about yourself and those around you in more ways than one. Who knows, these are not the kind of experiences that anyone would like to have but until you have them, how can you learn to deal with them? There have been many times over the past seven years when we have been operating under enormous pressure and perhaps my own experiences during this time helped me.

No one wanted this strike, but it turned out to be a watershed moment for me, for the players and for England rugby. There are times when the coach and players can't be as one. In this instance we agreed to disagree, but we would have to work out in advance what would happen when it occurred in future. It was a further confirmation that my job must entail preventing anything that could possibly stop us from moving forward. We couldn't afford to ignore any issues that could influence the team, even if there was only half a chance that our efforts would help avoid the problem.

From my point of view as head coach though, there are many critical areas that it is almost impossible to have any control over – responsibility for, yes, control over the outcome, no, due to the simple fact that the players do not work for me.

Argentina, South Africa

Our match against Argentina on 25 November took place in the context of that crisis, and was coloured by it. The weather was foul, but still it was a full house. Argentina were a strong side, but we won 19—0, with Ben Cohen grabbing the only try from a grubber kick by Jonny Wilkinson. All in all, it wasn't a game to remember. Afterwards in the dressing room I got the guys together.

'Let's agree right now. What happened this week will never happen again.'

Everyone nodded.

It had been a tough, tough week, yet we could all feel that we were in the middle of doing something incredibly special – exploding the myth of southern-hemisphere superiority. This we would need to do before we could ever win a World Cup.

The next match against South Africa was a hard game, with no prisoners taken on either side. Our front five were excellent, and the captaincy of Martin Johnson was proving really strong. Overall it was a good performance, not pretty, but a big victory for us by 25—17 (and that flattered the Springboks a bit). We could have played better; however, we were winning and that is what counts. Victory over South Africa made it three wins in a row over Tri-Nations opposition. Once is an accident, but three times is a trend. It was evident, even to the doubters, that England had finally arrived as a world force.

Six Nations, 2001

The first four games of the 2001 Six Nations saw England play some of their finest rugby ever. They were all high-scoring matches, with players like Johnson, Dallaglio and Wilkinson playing out of their skins. Twenty-seven tries, an average of nearly seven per game, tell the story of a golden period of fifteen-man, free-flowing rugby that had the crowd standing on their seats – a spontaneous tribute to performances that were both spectacular and clinical. In the fourth match, against France, Jonny Wilkinson became England's all-time highest points scorer at the ripe old age of twenty-two. In addition, that quartet of matches saw the arrival of Jason Robinson from rugby league. He came off the bench in all four games and in his short time on the pitch gave people a good look at what he could do.

Graham Henry, the Kiwi coach of Wales, said that our performance against his team, a 44—15 England victory at the Cardiff Millennium Stadium, was the best he had seen by a European side. Iain Balshaw was picked for his first start at full-back in this big match, surprising the press – he was outstanding. We scored six tries, five of them in the first-half, with Will Greenwood notching up a hat trick and Matt Dawson getting two, including a superb break from halfway that left full-back Stephen Jones on his backside. Graham Henry's admission that England were now 'truly among the elite of world rugby' was no more than the truth.

Two weeks later we were at Twickenham with Italy in our sights. England were very much the favourites and, sure enough, we ended the victors by 80—23, with a try count that went into double digits. But it had taken us a long time to get going, with the Azurri pushing us all the way in the first-half. That win marked a new record for the highest score and biggest winning points margin in the international championship.

Two weeks later we entertained the Scots at Twickenham, and the memory of the previous year's defeat in the game at Murrayfield still rankled. This time we made no mistake, winning a 43—3 victory in another impressive fifteen-man display – England's biggest ever win over Scotland. Scotland held on for the first half hour, but they found it hard to counter the attacking edge that Balshaw in particular brought to our game. He got a couple of tries, as did Dallaglio, who played a blinder. At the end Robinson showed what he could do with a sprint through the tired Scots defence, feeding Greenwood for a simple try under the posts. Scotland played well, but I have never seen our team play better. Andy Nicol, the Scottish captain said afterwards, 'We were out on our feet with twenty minutes to go when I heard this huge roar from the ground . . . England were now bringing on Jason Robinson!'

It was a magical time for the team. Some of the new players who had just come in were playing as well as anyone in world rugby. Iain Balshaw was something very special. I said after the match that the mix of styles this team produced was what separated us from the team which had flopped in the 1999 World Cup. It was the ambition and variety that I liked.

Next came the French and, although they hadn't had a very distinguished tournament so far, we weren't counting on them rolling over. In fact they took the game to us early on, and we went in to the break 16—13 down. At half-time in the dressing room Martin Johnson pointed out that we were trying to play too wide against a quick defence, trying to force the little pass where we should hold onto the ball if in doubt. In the second-half, the power of our pack and the pace of our backs was overwhelming. Richard Hill, Balshaw, hooker Greening, Catt, and substitute Matt Perry all went through to put points on the scoreboard. It was a sweet feeling and an amazing turnaround to put six tries past the French – I remembered taking some real hammerings from them as a player. In the end we won 48—19.

It had been a grand day for English rugby, and we were looking forward to the Ireland match with huge anticipation. But unfortunately we would have to wait. That was the year of the foot-and-mouth scourge in farms on the British mainland, and the game was postponed until the autumn. In the meantime, the Lions were touring again, this time to Australia, and England's tremendous form in the Six Nations would ensure many of our players earned the great honour of a place in the Lions side.

2001 summer tour to North America

It was no surprise that Lions coach Graham Henry would be taking eighteen of our first-choice players with him to Australia in June. So for the tour of Canada and the USA, which had been arranged by the RFU for early June, we relied on a younger brigade, with five players making their senior debuts. Kyran Bracken stepped forward to assume the captaincy while Martin Johnson was away leading the Lions.

Although we went with a depleted squad, we put the time to good use in developing one area of our game in which we saw huge potential for improvement: lineouts. We had brought on board a new coach, Simon Hardy, after the Six Nations season for just this reason. We anticipated an easy run in Canada, so it was a great opportunity to experiment with a few of Simon's new ideas. Lineouts, like scrummages, are the bedrock of international rugby. It was Simon's job to take our lineout performance to a new world-class level. Simon also highlighted the crucial importance of the hooker's role at the lineout, above all his ability to throw accurately. We had room for improvement in this area, so we took five hookers on the tour, including Steve Thompson, who had only recently moved to that position.

A month later, I was commentating on the British Lions tour in Australia for Sky Television, and I saw the Lions lose the last test due to a lineout throw that went right where the Wallabies were expecting it. Justin Harrison stole that lineout and Australia survived. Two and a half years later in the World Cup final in Sydney, England wouldn't make the same mistake. Simon Hardy's introduction to the team was well timed.

We won all our Test matches in that tour of North America by a wide margin, but the key benefit of the trip was that we unearthed four players new to our set-up who would have a major impact on the team: Steve Thompson, Ben Kay and Lewis Moody in the forwards, and Josh Lewsey in the backs. They all made major impressions during this trip. And in Thompson we found a new hooker, but would two years be enough to bring him to world-class standard in a position he'd never played before? With our up-coming autumn Internationals, we'd soon find out.

Ireland match, October 2001

But first we had a little catching up to do. During the Six Nations in the spring, Ireland had cancelled our fixture and ruled out any England matches in Dublin until the horrendous foot-and-mouth epidemic had been sorted. Ireland decreed that they would only play England and the other affected nations once they had been declared disease-free for at least one month. We had played some brilliant rugby in our first four matches of the Six Nations, all won by a convincing margin, so the delay was disappointing, given the team's terrific form. Eventually a date was set for mid-October, but we were horribly unprepared. Our entire schedule of preparation – training days, fitness days, hotel bookings, everything – had been geared around the autumn Internationals in the middle of November. There was no way we could negotiate any additional players' release from their clubs in that time. And Ireland would be playing Scotland and Wales on successive Saturdays before playing us, which gave them a huge advantage. We were in a corner. It would prove a great challenge.

We were playing for yet another Grand Slam, come October, our third decider in as many years. Even though our preparation was negligible, everyone thought we would win easily. Perhaps if we'd played one warm-up fixture we would have identified and sorted out some of our problems.

What most people didn't build into the equation, including me, were the after-effects of the Lions tour. With no recent first-hand experience of the players to go on, I picked the team based on pre-Lions form – in my view the best England team ever. But the Lions tour had not only exhausted the team, it had also clearly led to a major crisis of form for some gifted players. When I selected the team on their form in April, I reckoned that not much could change between then and October. It was a big mistake. I totally underestimated what the Lions tour had taken out of them, and got the selection badly wrong.

I do not think it would be exaggerating to say that it took England two years to recover fully from the Lions tour of 2001 – a few players are still trying to come back from it. For the eighteen England rugby players who were selected it was a great honour, but unfortunately the Lions tour of Australia was not only unsuccessful in terms of results, but also everyone – meaning the players, coaches and all the medical team involved in the tour – came back exhausted. It was a disaster from the English point of view, and if it happens again it will be the beginning of the end for the Lions, something none of us wants to see happen. The saddest quote I have seen in rugby for a long time was Ben Cohen's in a newspaper on his return: 'I always thought playing for the Lions would be special. There is no way I am ever going on another trip with them again.'

I was still unaware of the problem as we crossed the Irish Sea a week before the match. Once again we prepared for an away game in an unfamiliar environment – it would be the last time. There were five changes from the team that demolished France in April. Matt Dawson was captain – Martin Johnson and Lawrence Dallaglio were injured – and Jason Robinson made his first England start in a Test match.

On the day Ireland showed more desire, more heart and more composure than we did. I still can't believe how many errors we made. The lineout was a disaster in the first-half and we never recovered. In that match England never settled, but that isn't to take anything away from Ireland. They played a very strong game, beating us 20—14.

It was massively disappointing, especially for the players. Collecting the Six Nations trophy seemed very much like the consolation prize. No team deserved to be Grand Slam champions more than England that year. The four tournament matches before the Lions tour were the best I have ever seen the team play in all the time I have been in charge – the rugby was something special, but a combination of factors was to deny us the result we all wanted.

In one way, that Ireland game was an example of the fine line between success and failure. England were red-hot favourites to win against Ireland and hadn't lost for ages – not since our defeat in South Africa in June of 2000, which made eleven victories on the run. The team were gathering momentum and then, once again, due to influences for which I wasn't prepared, we suffered a crushing defeat. England were going well, sometimes very well, but not in a straight line, and the huge highs and lows were like a roller-coaster. We would fight our way back, but the difference for England by the time of the Ireland match was that our setbacks were infrequent enough to make huge news. It was as if the ceiling had fallen in. We got piled by everyone.

The lessons over the loss to Ireland were many, and building success from this major setback would be the final springboard to the glory everyone involved deserved.

23
DISCOVERY – ONE TEAM

By the time we began planning our up-coming season, it's fair to say that we had experienced our first true taste of consistent success. Despite the setback in Dublin and the after-effects of the Lions tour, we had played and won three games in a row against the southern-hemisphere teams. We had also played an amazing series of matches before the Lions tour which had shown our true potential. There had been real momentum in the team and everyone could feel it. We were close to Winning!, but we weren't there yet. It was time to redouble our efforts and raise the bar in everything we did.

As part of that process the management team, too, needed to take another step forward. We had come a long way in four years, and the extensive innovations to our mindset, organisation, coaching and playing meant there had been a lot of changes. Whereas we had started out with a clear vision, I think that everyone's view of what we were doing had become a bit cloudy from the furious activity. You start out with great visions and plans, but once you get into the details, it's easy to lose sight of the bigger picture. To help plan the next phase of our quest for improvement we asked Humphrey Walters to come back for another two-day management team workshop. What I wanted for everyone was clarity on our organisational development thus far, as well as a renewed vision of what we were trying to achieve. This would be the planning session that would take us up to the World Cup. These were the participants in our workshop that year:

Elite England Management Team
- Andy Robinson – forwards, lineout, scrum
- Brian Ashton – attack
- Phil Larder – defence
- Dave Reddin – fitness
- Dave Alred – kicking, mental preparation
- Tony Biscombe – performance analysis, technical support
- Phil Keith-Roach – scrums
- Simon Hardy – throwing and lineout
- Simon Kemp – team doctor
- Louise Ramsay – team manager
- Karen Burnett – admin support to management
- Adrian Firth – media
- Steve Lander – referee
- Nathan Martin – performance division
- Clive Woodward – head coach

See mini-CVs on page 425.

In our coaching and management areas we had certainly come a long way. I finally felt that we had a solid team of specialists, close to what I had dreamed of in my first weeks on the job. There were now eleven full-time people dedicated to developing the elite squad, and another four people making significant contributions who worked full-time for the RFU, like Nathan Martin, who has since moved into the performance division to help create a new nationwide elite player development programme. Almost all the above would be at the World Cup. We would arrive in Australia with the most experienced team of players but, equally important, we would also arrive with the most experienced management and coaching team.

Louise Ramsay, our newest addition to the team, had taken over from Nathan Martin in the manager's role. Louise was an ex-pupil of Queen Anne's School in Caversham where Jess goes to school, and that certainly helped in her interview. Her previous role had been as team manager for the England swimming team, and she had co-ordinated the entire Olympic swimming team's trip to Sydney in 2000. Louise was a specialist in sports management and logistics, and would prove to be the only female team manager in the 2003 World Cup. It was good to have her on board, and particularly satisfying eventually to see her on the winner's rostrum in Sydney.

Inspirational climate survey

Before the workshop, Humphrey had first asked everyone to complete a long and detailed questionnaire entitled *Inspirational Climate Survey*. Its purpose was to measure how we were working as a management team in three key areas, which were then broken down into some sixty sub-categories. The overall categories were 1) *leadership*: perceptions of how leaders were performing their roles; 2) *partnership*: how people perceived they were working together as a team; and 3) *followership*: how effective people were at working with their leaders. As a result of the survey, Humphrey was able to give us feedback about our organisational performance in such areas as inspirational environment, building confidence, leadership support and teamworking. According to Humphrey, compared with similiar benchmarks in leading companies, we were scoring around 75 per cent overall. It was good to have an objective measure, but we obviously still had a lot of room for improvement.

The rest of the first day we discussed and refined everyone's job outputs, critical actions for the coming season and mutual expectations. On the second day we again brainstormed for new ideas, and the quantity of ideas for improving things that this generated around the room was quite remarkable. We eventually agreed on forty key improvements which would take nearly two years to implement. In medical and fitness we would explore, along with many other ideas, the possibilities of visual training, hypoxic training, a summer holiday rehabilitation programme, and even aromatherapy in the changing room. In the scrum area we committed to examining wrestling and judo techniques, and other fields of investigation, included design of our jerseys, breathing techniques and research into the best studs for traction. In the lineout area we came up with ten ideas alone which would transform that part of our game, and in a host of other fields we drew up a detailed list of critical concepts to explore.

The missing link

My whole philosophy in managing the team, right from the start, was that we should be as one in everything we did, so that's where I started. Sometime shortly after the Ireland match, I wrote the words 'One Team' at the top of a piece of paper and, using the three categories from Humphrey as my model, wrote down as I saw them the three ingredients of One Team in the England set-up.

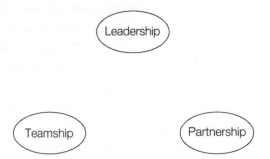

Instead of 'Followership', I put 'Teamship'. This reflected the earlier idea of creating basic teamship rules to act as a framework for our operations. This was a good model that would help us all better to understand the complex dynamics of England rugby. Over the next two years we significantly developed our understanding of these three components of One Team.

Leadership

I was under no illusion that Australia won the 1999 World Cup because of the outstanding leadership not only of the coach, Rod Macqueen, but also of the captain, John Eales, and other senior players within their squad. The importance of this cannot be overstated. Winning requires outstanding leadership, especially when under pressure.

Leadership is largely well understood – the Harvard Business School will tell you there are over 2,500 books written each year on the subject. It comes from a variety of sources and in a number of forms. We focused on Leadership across the whole of the England set-up – from myself as head coach, to our specialist coaches, to the captain, and to

our senior players in their responsibility for high-performance behaviours. Our aim is to be as one in the following areas.

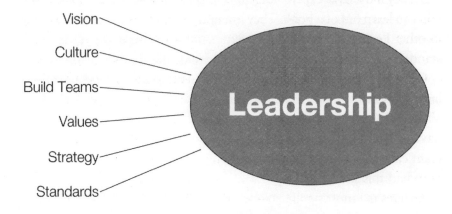

For England to be successful, the leadership from both management
and players had to be unquestionable. I've never seen any team of
people succeed without an effective influence at the helm. Thankfully,
we had a team of leaders from which to choose. My aim from the
beginning was not just to have one leader in a team of followers, but
to have an exceptional leader in a team of great leaders. Because every
key player had a leadership role of some kind in the squad, we were
never short of qualified players to fill the role when Martin Johnson
wasn't with us. At such times I had five criteria for choosing my captains.

1 Leaders had to be the best players in the team in their position.
Selection could not be an issue regarding their playing performance –
if their standards didn't exceed everyone else's then their position of
authority would be open to scrutiny.

2 They must have mastered T-CUP – Thinking Correctly Under
Pressure. When the going gets tough and the pressure is on, that's when
the team needs their leader the most.

3 Their colleagues must respect them highly – their personal standards
off the pitch and the way in which they interact with their team-mates
must be of the highest standard.

4 They must be as one with me, the coach. When we're not together
with the team, they must be relaying exactly the same message as myself.
There could be absolutely no conflicts other than behind closed doors

– we didn't want yes men, but they had to work as one with the team and in public.

5 They must have experience for the job – Leadership is not something you can learn out of a book. They must have proved themselves effective in other Leadership roles in the team, or at a level below international standards.

Over recent years, the captaincies of Martin Johnson, Lawrence Dallaglio, Jason Leonard, Matt Dawson, Kryan Bracken, Neil Back, Phil Vickery, Jonny Wilkinson and Dorian West have been outstanding, and have put us in a very strong position both on and off the field. No team can be successful without outstanding leadership. Thankfully we now had this in abundance.

Perhaps the most significant example of Leadership in relation to the England One Team set-up may be seen when things go wrong – and clearly in the course of our development they have gone wrong in major ways on several occasions. There are two ways we can look at our setbacks. Often, according to a book called *Good to Great* (which I first came across a couple of years ago) people look in the mirror and congratulate the person looking back when things are going right. But when things go wrong they prefer to look through the window and try to find someone else to blame.

However, *Good to Great* suggests there is a different view, which we in the England camp share, and that is: when things are going right, that's the time to look through the window and praise those around you. But when things go wrong, then it's time to look in the mirror, shoulder the responsibility and not blame others. When England experience setbacks, all the people in the organisation now hold themselves accountable. However, the pressure of outside criticism, particularly from the media, can be intense. This is another factor that I bear in mind when considering a player for captaincy.

Teamship

Teamship is something nobody writes about, but it's just as important as leadership, if not more so. Teamship can be described as the ability to work together in a team, or as the collective standard of behaviour understood by everyone in the team environment. It doesn't cover our performance standards in the core technical skills of rugby – our Nine High Performance Behaviours – but deals with our skills in interacting as a group.

Most leaders dictate performance standards and assume that everyone instinctively understands how they are expected to work and behave in the team environment. However, I've seen many examples of good sporting teams – as well as business organisations and even political parties – which have failed because of a lack of understanding of how to work effectively as a team. So this is an area we don't leave to chance. We have involved the whole group in the process of clearly establishing our team performance standards. My job as the leader is to identify the areas of our organisation that are critical to our success, but then it is vital that the people responsible for acting in these areas should establish their own standards. Once I'm happy that these minimum standards will allow us to achieve our aims, I sign them off. So Teamship allows a leader to lead in a totally different way – by allowing a team to set their own standards: our rules, our standards, put in place by the team, signed off by the leader.

In the England set-up, these standards are written down in the Black Book of Teamship Rules, and other contributions over the years have been added by the people responsible in each of the seven core components of the England set-up as described below.

So our Teamship covers all areas of how we operate as a group, and what is expected of each of us as individuals within the group. These rules are never formalised until they have been discussed with and agreed by those responsible for each area – to date, there's never been an issue that has not been agreed. Our players physically sign off on the Rules stating that they commit to following them, and everyone in the team is of the mindset that we have to understand and support each other's Teamship Rules.

We also encourage everyone continually to review these rules. If at any stage someone wants to change any of them, this can be done, so long as everybody is in agreement. This process is essential for the continued development of our One Team culture.

One huge essential advantage of this Living Document is the speed

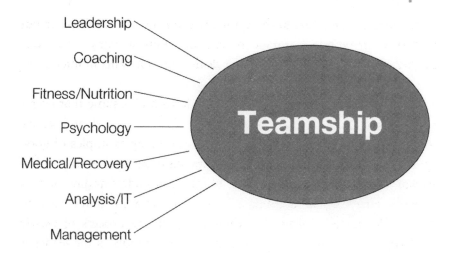

Leadership
Coaching
Fitness/Nutrition
Psychology
Medical/Recovery
Analysis/IT
Management

Teamship

at which it enables a new player to the squad to settle in. I know it is hugely exciting to be selected to join the England squad for the first time but it can also be very daunting. Knowing how the team operates and what is expected of them as a player gives the new guys great confidence. We need to bring in new players and develop the team. It could be disruptive, but using this system limits that disruption to a bare minimum.

Partnership

Working in Partnership is the third area essential for the creation of One Team. The work we have undertaken with our key sponsors, such as Nike, O_2, and Zurich, demonstrates how partnerships can increase performance to everyone's advantage. But Partnership also covers a whole range of other areas – Premiership clubs, their staff, all departments at the RFU, the media and press, our supporters and fans, and even our own spouses and families.

The message we try to get across to everyone in the set-up, particularly the players, is that if we're to receive all the support and encouragement we need to do our job properly – which is winning on the rugby pitch – we also have to give something back to the people who make it happen. When working in true Partnership with anybody, the first question that we always ask is, 'How can I/we help you?' If on the

RFU Sponsors
Zurich, O$_2$, Elonex,
Nike, Hacketts,
Oliver Sweeney

RFU and Clubs

Supporters/Fans

Management and
Players' Spouses
and Family

Partnership

other hand we take the opposite approach by asking, 'What can you do for me?' then we will quickly alienate our partners. This is a philosophy we strive to implement in every project that we undertake in England rugby.

However, Partnership has to date been the weakest of the three areas as a result of the club versus country debate. Partnership with clubs is all about working together with all our opposite numbers, directors of rugby, coaches, medical and admin personnel. It's also about ensuring that the owners and all the club management fully understand what we are trying to achieve, thereby enabling us to move forward in a genuine, progressive partnership between club and country.

From our point of view, we stress that everyone in the England set-up must clearly understand what the clubs are all about, and offer unconditional support wherever possible. This is sometimes not easy, there is a degree of conflict, but everyone can see that we absolutely have to continue working on these relationships to ensure that the Partnership component of One Team is firmly integrated with the other two.

History of One Team.

In 1997, the concepts of Leadership, Teamship and Partnership were all at a fraction of their potential. We worked very hard over the first two years to build our Leadership and Teamship, but energy sappers from all areas undermined much of what we were trying to do. By the time of the

1999 World Cup, we had only just started to get it right. Our Partnership was still way out of alignment, but the three elements of One Team. were a lot closer together than when we started. This was a fingers crossed approach to the World Cup, and if we had won it would have been against common sense and logic. We arrived at the tournament with a world ranking of sixth, and basically that's where we ended up.

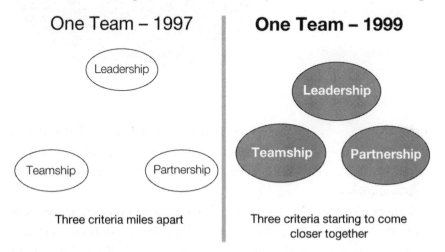

One Team – 1997

Leadership

Teamship

Partnership

Three criteria miles apart

One Team – 1999

Leadership

Teamship

Partnership

Three criteria starting to come closer together

When the One Team concept was formalised in late 2001, we had been working with our new squad for nearly two years. Our Teamship and Leadership areas were coming together. The only area truly lacking was our focus on Partnership, particularly between the elite squad, the RFU and the Premiership clubs. If only we could come to an agreement between the Premiership clubs and the RFU over access to the players and full co-operation on the training/fitness front, we would have the final pieces in place. After tireless negotiations over many months by the RFU and the club representatives, this issue was, for the eighteen months leading up to the World Cup in Sydney, finally settled. The RFU and the Premiership Clubs agreed to create the EPS or Elite Player Scheme. As well as identifying the elite players who were to come under this scheme it gave us twenty training days for the preparation of the Autumn Internationals in 2002 and the Six Nations in 2003. We would also have the players full time for us to manage from the end of May 2003 until the final whistle of the World Cup.

Quite simply, as a result of this we arrived at the World Cup as the best-prepared team. This was to be the first time in my whole career with the England Team that I really felt I could do my job.

Since the World Cup win, we have not had any training days or time with the players. The new agreement is due to start again in the autumn of 2004 with sixteen training days a year. But even these have to be agreed by all parties and will largely take place on non-productive days for training such as Mondays following tough weekend matches.

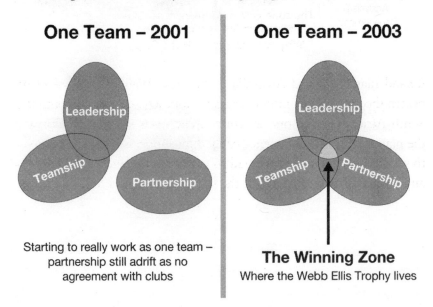

One Team – 2001

Leadership

Teamship

Partnership

Starting to really work as one team – partnership still adrift as no agreement with clubs

One Team – 2003

Leadership

Teamship

Partnership

The Winning Zone
Where the Webb Ellis Trophy lives

When all three elements came together, I knew it would create a no-excuses environment for our players, the only remaining contingencies being the vagaries of sport. If we wanted to take home the Webb Ellis Trophy from the 2003 World Cup in Sydney, we would have to work more closely in Partnership with all our sponsors, supporters and partners, as well as keep our Leadership and Teamship tight.

Back into action

Before the recent Ireland game, we hadn't lost a match in over twelve months. I viewed that defeat and the impact of the Lions as setbacks from which I was confident we would bounce back. However, as usual we didn't have much time to get it together. Three weeks after the

One Team – 2003

The zone where Winning! is possible
When One Team comes together

Why we won the World Cup?

Ireland match we had Australia – the same Wallabies who had just beaten the Lions a few months earlier – followed by Romania and then South Africa. Getting our selection right, given what I now knew of the players after the experience of the Lions tour, would go a long way to setting us straight, but we had to get our confidence back if we had any chance of winning against the southern-hemisphere sides.

24

ON THE VERGE

'The Man in the Arena'

'It is not the critic who counts, not the man who points out how the strong man stumbles, or where the doer of deeds could have done them better. The credit belongs to the man who is actually in the arena, whose face is marred by dust and sweat and blood. He who strives valiantly; who errs and comes short again and again; because there is not effort without error and shortcomings; but who does actually strive to do the deed; who knows the great enthusiasm, the great devotion, who spends himself in a worthy cause, who at the best knows in the end the triumph of high achievement and who at the worst, if he fails, at least he fails while daring greatly. So that his place shall never be with those cold and timid souls who know neither victory nor defeat.'

The whole video took around three minutes to play through. The players in the room, bitterly disappointed after our defeat by Ireland, seemed to get the message. The speech itself was an excerpt from a famous address given by Theodore Roosevelt to the Paris Convention in 1910. It's now known simply as the 'Man in the Arena', and it's one of my favourites. I explained to the team how it summed up our position perfectly. I then went on to describe how I love being in the arena. Doing it. Daring greatly. Making mistakes. Taking risks. To me, it was far better to be in there doing something than to be one of the people looking on.

Dublin was massively disappointing. It was a setback. But now we had to get back into the arena. We had Australia at Twickenham in just four days. We could listen to the harsh cries of the critics and the media, or we could learn from our setback and meet the Wallabies on Saturday playing to our full potential. It was up to us.

We regularly use video presentations such as the one about the 'Man in the Arena' to help bring the players into the right frame of mind for our more difficult matches. Tony Biscombe and his gifted IT team can do some amazing things with video. Rob Gibby in particular is a genius with the visual media. You do not win Test matches because of a great video, but it is just another good example of a critical non-essential. They had worked hard on this presentation. It had exactly the right effect.

We needed to remind everyone of how good they were, how they should not overreact to a big loss but get back on track as quickly as possible. There were issues that as head coach I had to take responsibility for, which was fine as long as I had enough control to have been responsible for the issues in the first place. England had not been together as a team since April, when we had been playing some of our most exhilarating rugby. Since then most of the squad and coaches had been on the 2001 Lions tour. I wanted training days and a pre-Ireland warm-up game. Ireland had another left-over fixture to play before our game against Scotland, and we needed one too. I went to the Ireland–Scotland game in Edinburgh, where Ireland were poor – it was their first match after the Lions tour too. The difference in their team by the following week was what I would expect after the preparation of playing. But out of necessity England met for the Test match going in cold without any time with the players. And this was a match to win the Grand Slam. Obviously, it wasn't our administrators' fault that we had had a foot-and-mouth epidemic, but just to reschedule the match without also allowing us the preparation necessary to win it was a massive mistake.

The Wallabies

We put that Ireland disappointment behind us as a good team should, and really got down to business for the autumn internationals in November. We were back to having training days and were able to have four before the autumn series. Our preparation for the Wallabies match at Twickenham was intense.

I made a lot of changes after the Ireland match – seven personnel and three positional. Unfortunately, Martin Johnson and Dallaglio were still injured and therefore not available for selection. This was an important match for England. Leadership in the team was critical. For the match against Australia, I named Neil Back as captain. It was fascinating watching him at work that week captaining in his own unique way. He is right up there as the ultimate competitor. He captained wonderfully well in one of the pivotal matches in England's recent history.

The move which raised the most eyebrows was putting Jason Robinson at full back. Having a former rugby league player as the last line of defence attracted a lot of criticism. What would Robinson know about the union kicking game? But Jason saw to it that the doubters would eat their words: his game gave the Australians all sorts of problems in defence. This guy was different, something very special, and the way he took the Wallabies' first high ball with an amazing leap could not have been bettered.

Australia played their full-strength side, but the commitment from everyone in the England team was fantastic. At the break it was 15—0 to us. Australia came back hard in the second half, but I really liked the way we didn't panic, particularly in the final minutes – a key trait now consistent in the team. We held on for a fantastic victory at 21—15, and for the first time ever in my time as England coach we hadn't used a single replacement!

Romania

A week after the Wallabies, Romania came to Twickenham. Some people claimed this was a game that should never have happened, it was such a mismatch. Of course, the RFU were trying to do something positive, to bring Romanian rugby back on course after years of problems, but there must have been better ways than submit them to a pulverising. That said, the match provided me with a welcome proof of the ruthlessness and mental strength of the England team. Most teams would have fallen off at sixty or seventy points, but in the second half we kept on coming and notched up England's highest score and biggest winning margin ever for a test match at 134—0. It was also the first time twenty tries had been scored in a Twickenham inter-national, and Charlie Hodgson, making his England debut, racked up an England record of forty-four points. This match was Jason Leonard's ninety-third England cap, overtaking All Black Sean Fitzpatrick's world record for most appearances by a forward for his country. We were fielding more or less a second team, and the fact that we could rack up a score like this without quite a few of our front-line players spoke well of the growing depth of players in the England squad.

The Springboks

A week later we played South Africa at Twickenham. In the opening minutes of the match Robinson took a dangerous and illegal tackle from the South African captain, Bobby Skinstad, and that set the tone for the first half, which was pretty physical. The Springboks were com-peting well up front and at the lineouts, but Jonny was putting away the penalties – in all he knocked over seven out of nine attempts. All the same, we were only 9—6 in front at the break. Wilkinson put two more over soon after the re-start, and then Catt's quick-thinking drop kick set clear water between the two sides. Robinson meanwhile was giving the Boks all kinds of trouble with some pinball runs, bouncing off one defender after another, and the back line was playing with real confidence. Dan Luger's beauty of an intercept try at the end sealed it. A combination of rock solid defence and clinical counter-attacking gave us victory by a record margin of 29—9.

That was a great day to be in the stands at Twickenham. It was our third straight win over South Africa and our fifth successive win against a Tri-Nations side – the first European nation ever to do so. At the end of the game I turned and jogged up the steps in the stadium to Jayne and the kids. It was a month till the holidays but I said, 'It's going to be a Merry Christmas!' There had been a lot of pressure since the Ireland game, and they probably breathed a sigh of relief to know I'd be happier over Christmas!

I was delighted that we had shaken off the Dublin nightmare and bounced back so well with such good wins against the Tri-Nations sides.

Another chance at the Grand Slam

We still weren't back to our pre-Lions strength by the 2002 Six Nations tournament in February, but those who saw England in action will always remember a series of thrilling matches, the first of which was against Scotland at Murrayfield. This time we didn't go up a week early – this approach hadn't helped at all either in Scotland in 2000 or in Ireland the previous year. This was the first away game for which we changed our preparation and didn't travel early. A lot of thought had gone into making Pennyhill Park an ideal environment for the players, so instead we flew up the day before the match after an excellent week of preparation. It paid off with two early tries from Jason Robinson.

Jason's first came after only eight minutes, with a burst down the left wing after some fine three-quarter play. Five minutes later he was over again, racing into the left corner after Wilkinson put Greenwood through with a pop pass. Greenwood offloaded to Tindall, and Tindall fed left to Robinson whose neat try was converted by Wilkinson from the left touchline, making the score 12—0. Ten minutes after the break Mike Tindall got on the scoresheet with an excellent chip and chase, and in injury time Ben Cohen broke through for his twelfth international try. That was one match where we didn't need Wilko's penalties – his first didn't come until the sixty-fifth minute. We ended up winning the match by 29—3, but our victory over the Scots at Murrayfield was businesslike rather than spectacular.

Watching the match, it looked like the old-style baggy jersey was hampering players like Jason Robinson. He was held by the shirt once or twice when he could have slipped through to score. After the game I wrote to Nike about it. Apparently my e-mail went all around the company. In the spirit of Partnership, they decided to design the most revolutionary kit in preparation for the World Cup. It would take nearly eighteen months and a lot of research and testing by Nike, but we were very pleased with the result. All the players liked the new kit because it made them that bit more elusive in the tackle. If you look at two pictures, one of Robinson being held back in the Scotland 2002 game, the other of him cutting through the Welsh in the World Cup quarter-final match, you can see the difference. It was another example of the hundreds of critical non-essentials that contributed to our World Cup campaign.

It had been our idea to make the tight-fitting shirts but Nike were also the kit suppliers for France and South Africa for the RWC 2003. They felt compelled to give the newly designed shirts to those teams as well. Fortunately they didn't have a Jason Robinson playing for either of them.

Our Scotland victory might have been clinical, but in our next game against the Irish at Twickenham there were moments of pure magic. For fifty minutes, from early in the first half to early in the second, England played the kind of rugby people dream about. It was the best period of England play since I had taken over in 1997. Jonny Wilkinson was absolutely outstanding, combining superb kicking, brilliant decision-making and a super-sharp running game. Ben Kay was a tower of strength at lock, scoring a great try after the break when he took an inside ball from Wilkinson and charged through tackles by David Humphreys and Peter Stringer to stretch his arm over the line – 'the long arm of the law' commentator Steve Smith called it, referring to Ben's father, a high court judge.

The finest moment came in the twenty-fourth minute when England, instead of clearing the lines out of their 22, ran the ball in a passage of play which went the length of the field through seven pairs of hands to finish with a simple run-in by Cohen. That score will be relished for years to come. I was criticised in the press for calling off Martin Johnson, Hill and Healey some way into the second half. There were complaints that the zing had been taken out of the match, in spite of the final score, which stood at 45—11. This was England's fourteenth successive test victory at Twickenham – a new ground record, overtaking the run set between 1913 and 1924.

France and a bright idea

Sometimes I come up with some really good ideas. Other times my initiatives come back to haunt me. Travelling to Paris in March 2002 was one of my worst ever 'bright ideas' as a rugby coach.

I got the idea driving to Paris; the tunnel under the Channel was so easy, hassle-free and fast. There was no waiting at airports and bus transfers, I even thought that it would be more relaxing for the team to enjoy the coach journey.

On the Wednesday before the match two coaches left Pennyhill Park at 4 p.m. with everyone on board. I assumed we would be arriving at the hotel by dinner time, but the first snag was a huge traffic jam on the M25 ring road around London. Then the train was delayed, so we sat waiting for hours to get through the tunnel. By the time the coaches pulled into our hotel in Paris a little after midnight – more than eight hours after we set off – you could say we weren't at our best. This was definitely not one of my shining moments. The players had a rest day scheduled for Thursday, but they wouldn't let me forget the coach ride. We will definitely fly in future.

In the match the French came out on fire. Their young No. 8 Imanol Harinordoquy was outstanding in the early stages. First he set up a try for Gerald Merceron under the posts, and then crashed over in the corner himself just a few minutes later. Merceron converted them both to make it 14—0 while the game was still in the first quarter. To make matters worse, soon afterwards Merceron slotted a penalty to make it 17—0. But just before the break, Jason Robinson took the ball at stand-off, stepped inside Merceron, eluded three cover tacklers, and was over the line for a try which Wilkinson converted. That raised England hopes, but in the second half the French held firm, even though Will Greenwood got through a few times. We dug deep, our heads never went down, and Cohen's injury-time try made the final score 20—15. By then Wilkinson had gone off after taking one hit too many from their relentless flanker Serge Betsen, and Grayson couldn't put over the conversion.

So we lost to the French at Paris, and were well beaten in the process. For some reason, the Six Nations is the only tournament in the world where to lose one game is regarded as a complete failure, especially if you are England. Well, it was tough, a setback to say the least, but we learned a few critical lessons. That was the one game when the French managed to obliterate Jonny Wilkinson. We learned how to handle that, and by the following year we had fixed it.

How severely had our logistics and poor planning for the coach journey affected our preparation and mental state? Did it cost us the match? I don't know, but most of the players mentioned it in our Monday meeting as a huge distraction from the game. As a result, we would pay even closer attention afterwards to the details of our accommodation and travel arrangements. But defeat in the Six Nations, though disappointing, was by no means the end of the world for us. We had to look at the bigger picture. My mindset was to get ahead of the three southern-hemisphere countries. That was the only way we would win the World Cup.

France, by contrast, became fixated by their success. Their celebrations after the game were amazing – you would have thought they had won the World Cup itself. They sat on that victory for two years. It seemingly became their blueprint for how to beat England. It took them a long time, perhaps too long, to change their game plan.

That was the last match in which Brian Ashton was involved with the team as an England coach. Brian had done an outstanding job since 1998, and nobody deserves more credit than him for opening up the players' and coaches' minds as to how the game could be played. However, for personal reasons he had to step down. I could have brought someone else in, but I didn't replace Brian because I believed that a new person with new ideas would disrupt the team at that time. All the same, we had to build on Brian's work, so Andy and I picked up his workload. We tightened our coaching team, and we did not lose another meaningful game right up to the World Cup.

Back on track

Against Wales two weeks later we ran up our biggest winning margin ever for a test against that country, racking up 50 points to their 10, and scoring five tries. Neil Back captained in the absence of Martin Johnson, who had incurred the wrath of the authorities for disciplinary reasons in a club game, while both Phil Vickery and Jason Robinson were on the injured list. It was another chance to show England's strength in depth. At the break we were leading 13—0 after Greenwood had benefited from a neat chip by Wilkinson, but it was in the second half that we really started motoring, with a good try by Wilkinson, and then another two for Dan Luger within three minutes of each other. Tim Stimpson, coming on as a replacement for Tindall, got the fifth and final try, Wilkinson putting over the conversion as he had done all the others. All in all, the Welsh didn't see much of the ball, thanks to a dominant performance by the pack, and the backs added their signatures to a pretty impressive display. Never mind the French setback; this was a team that was headed in the right direction.

Finishing with Italy

On a sunny afternoon in April at Rome's Stadio Flaminio we took on Italy for the last match of our Six Nations tournament. We eventually won 45—9, but it wasn't the most exciting of starts – France's victory over Ireland the day before meant we had lost the chance to win the championship on points. The main talking point before the match was about the people we'd left on the England bench, including Martin Johnson, Matt Dawson, Jason Leonard and Lawrence Dallaglio. But by now England had real strength in depth and there was more than enough talent to beat Italy without them. For many people the high point of the game was when Johnson, Dallaglio, Dawson and Leonard – 252 caps' worth of talent – came onto the field together, earning massive applause from the fans. It didn't take them long to make their mark: a break from Johnson down the centre set up a ruck for Dawson to spin the ball to Dallaglio who dotted the ball down from an unopposed run-in. Dawson added the conversion, with Wilkinson temporarily injured, and he also played a part in the next try ten minutes later. Taking a tap penalty ten metres from the Italian line, he hit a deft chip over the Italian backline for Greenwood to race onto the ball and score a well-rehearsed set-piece try, Greenwood's second. Another replacement, Austin Healey, also grabbed a try, going over in the right corner in injury time. Meanwhile, Will Greenwood's two tries brought his tally for the season to five, which made him the Championship's leading try-scorer for the second season running.

People lamented the loss of a Grand Slam for the fourth year in succession, but my driving aim was to ensure that England arrived at the World Cup as favourites to win, the highest ranked and best prepared team. We were heading in the right direction, winning by far the majority of the matches played. More importantly, with the right preparation we were beating the southern-hemisphere sides when we came up against them. Despite our setbacks, we had to continue building our success.

Summer tour to Argentina

In June an England team travelled to Argentina for a single Test against the Pumas in Buenos Aires which was played on 22 June.

That touring squad wasn't our first team, and we had a lot of critics who said it was mad to go with a number of comparatively inexperienced players – we were fielding five new caps – but in fact the experience was very valuable for everyone. Phil Vickery captained the team, displaying fine leadership qualities in a notoriously hostile environment.

What was particularly gratifying was the way the guys came back from a half-time deficit of 3—12 in that test. Charlie Hodgson's early penalty had been met with some good pressure from Argentina, with Felipe Contepomi giving their backs some fluency at centre. We gave away too many penalties in our own half, which meant that their stand-off, Gonzalo Quesada, had slotted four by the break.

The problems were sorted out in the changing room, and after the break we turned the pressure round onto them, with the likes of flanker Alex Sanderson, Moody, Vickery and Kay leading the charge. We kept hold of the ball this time, and four minutes into the half Kay was over the line after a good run by scrum half Andy Gomarsall. Hodgson put over the conversion, and then matched Quesada's penalty with one of his own to keep England within touching distance. Our second try came when Phil Christophers tore the Pumas' defence to shreds, and with Hodgson's conversion England now led 20—15. Hodgson's penalty in the third quarter meant that Argentina would have to score twice to win, and although Quesada managed one more penalty, Tim Stimpson finished off the game with a long-distance beauty not long before the end. A second-string England side had beaten the Pumas 26—18, and we didn't need to call on any players on the bench – only the second time that has happened in my career as a coach.

The Pumas are recognised as the world's best scrummaging team. But the England scrum that day was awesome. Our expert scrummaging coach, Phil Keith-Roach, is renowned as a world authority in this critical area of the game. It is his hard work that has made our scrum generally feared, with some wonderful players such as Jason Leonard, Graham Rowntree, Phil Vickery, David Flatman, Steve Thompson, Julian White, Trevor Woodman and, now, young Matt Stevens. PKR is the most wonderful team member, and touring the world with this highly respected man has always been a huge privilege, such is his support.

In many ways it was one of our best results. Argentina was certainly no pushover: just the week before they had beaten the French side that had scooped the Six Nations. That England win demonstrated our strength in depth as nothing else could and, in addition, allowed our main players to have a rest, which they had desperately needed after the Lions tour the year before. A lot of the younger players came through very strongly, which was excellent for the long term. We now had a good chance of arriving at the World Cup with thirty outstanding players.

Improving our vision

'Clive, you're never going to believe who we met in South Africa at the post-match function,' said Andy Robinson, walking into my office. He and Dave Alred had just returned from a scouting trip to watch the All Blacks play South Africa in Durban.

'We met a vision specialist. She's called Sherylle Calder, and I think she might be what we're looking for.'

Sherylle was something called an eye coach. A world-class hockey player, she was doing research for her PhD in vision technology whilst captaining her native South Africa. For some time now our coaching team had been discussing the potential advantage of really understanding the power of the eye. Led by Dave Alred, we were interested in how this might help us train the players to think better under pressure. After all, our sight is the most important sense we have in sport. Sherylle believed that the eye, like any other muscle, could be trained, exercised and measured in its performance. Today she helps high-performance athletes to improve their sports vision.

'She's been working with the All Blacks,' said Andy. 'She is very keen to meet you.'

In the course of my travels I come across dozens of specialists and analysts every year, but I tend to be attracted to the people who are a bit different, so I picked up the phone and called her. Within three hours, Sherylle Calder was booked on the next plane to London.

Sherylle had done some work with the Australian cricket team as well as the New Zealand rugby team, but to my great delight they hadn't grasped the importance of her work. It was our gain. In the early autumn we invited her into the England set-up to apply her vision principles to the way we trained for matches.

Sherylle was also the first to point out that in rugby the biggest opportunities in defence, and consequently the biggest opportunities in attack, come from the players simply seeing the space on the rugby pitch correctly. Sherylle discovered the problem was players simply weren't looking up to take in all information about the pitch. The tendency for most players was only to look up when they had the ball in their hands. At times other than that, they usually watched the ball. But a player needs information about the pitch in his head *before* the ball reaches his hands. Jonny Wilkinson was a prime example. He was so keen to play rugby, so mad to be in the game, that he would often rush into a tackle where he shouldn't have been or wasn't needed. You had to admire his enthusiasm, but it was creating unnecessary holes in our defence.

Sherylle suggested the players needed to form a habit of continually looking around the pitch throughout a game. To help retrain the players in this direction, during training we hung large banners off the goal posts emblazoned with 'CTC', and we hung similar signs at each corner of the pitch. CTC stood for 'Crossbar, Touchline, Communicate', and it became our new vision performance standard. At every phase of play each player was required to look at the crossbar, then look at each touchline on the side of the pitch. That would give them the information on their placement on the field, which was critical for playing the game effectively. In addition, they were then required to communicate that information to their team-mates.

For months in training all you could hear during the game was a chorus of 'CTC, CTC, CTC'. But it worked. It was an amazing break-through in our 2002 autumn internationals to watch the video footage where Jonny Wilkinson runs to the maul, stops mid-stride, takes a good look around, implementing CTC, and then gets himself back into position. The whole team began working that way. Scanning, scanning, scanning. It was another great example of one little thing, one critical non-essential, that helped us in our quest to win the World Cup.

COMING OF AGE 25

In the next year, the team went from strength to strength. It was the most successful year ever recorded in the history of England rugby. In that period, between our autumn international against the All Blacks and the World Cup final against Australia, we played twenty games with 95 per cent success, losing just one game, by one point, with our second team in a pre-World Cup friendly.

This was Winning! It was an amazing feeling. Without a doubt it would prove to be one of the most enjoyable years of my professional life.

If only I had known what was coming, perhaps I wouldn't have been so nervous going into the autumn internationals against New Zealand, Australia and South Africa. I had every reason to be positive. Our preparation in the lead-up to that series was phenomenal. One Team was coming together and I'd never been more confident in the England coaching and management set-up.

It was a wonder, then, that I just couldn't sleep at night. It was a worry, too.

Sleepless in Cookham

In the lead-up to the 2002–03 season I was hardly sleeping a wink. Usually I'm sound asleep within a few minutes of lying down, so I knew something was wrong. Yet this was the time when I needed my wits about me more than any other. I was beginning to be concerned that my fatigue was getting to me.

'Simon, I'm having a problem,' I said to Simon Kemp in a quiet moment between training sessions at Pennyhill Park. Simon is the

England team's medical officer. There seems to be nothing he can't fix, and if there is something he doesn't know about sports medicine then it's not worth knowing.

'I'm having trouble sleeping at night. It's been going on for a few weeks now. I'm worried it's beginning to affect my performance.'

Simon pulled out his prescription pad and began scribbling on the front.

'This is the phone number of a friend of mine you should go and see. Her name is Britt Tajet-Foxell. She is the top performance psychologist at the Royal Ballet. I think she can help. Give me twenty-four hours to speak to her first and then give her a call.'

With a name like that I had to go and see her. I wondered what a psychologist would do at the Royal Ballet. It sounded really interesting. As I later found out, Britt also works in the High Performance Centre of the Norwegian Olympic team and is responsible for some hundred elite athletes going to Athens this year. Thankfully, Britt was in town and offered to see me on Thursday, the team's day off before the Test match.

As I explained my situation Britt listened, nodded carefully in places, and asked insightful questions. Just talking with her helped me feel so much better, but she also suggested eight steps I could take to correct the situation. Britt and I only chatted for an hour, but in that time my whole perception of England rugby changed. She helped me to see all the good things we'd been doing in the elite set-up, and she urged me to ignore completely the harsh criticism in the press. She had a good point: my detractors would always be there, no matter what I did. I appreciated Britt's care and concern, but what really won me over was when she suggested I should play more golf, at least twice a week like I used to – my game had fallen away as my coaching intensity had risen over the past few years.

Since that meeting, we've kept in regular contact and Britt has become a good source for insight into the team. I followed her recommendations from our first chat and within a few weeks my sleep was right back to normal. Then again, perhaps it helped playing three pivotal matches – and winning.

New Zealand

Those three matches in autumn 2002 were the real test to see if we were fully prepared, in every detail, for the twelve-month period which would end with the World Cup final. The first game was against the All Blacks, coached by my old colleague John Mitchell. After leaving us in 2000 he returned to his native New Zealand and coached the Chiefs in the 2001 Super 12. Later that year he was appointed All Blacks coach. There were some major players left out of the New Zealand touring squad for that match, which was interesting, but it was a great game, full of pulsating passages of play which had all of Twickenham on the edge of their seats.

The game began at a terrific pace, with New Zealand making errors that Jonny punished with a couple of great penalties. The All Blacks bounced back from that, setting up an overlap from a quickly taken lineout which allowed Jonah Lomu to go over in the corner for a converted try. Then our forwards stepped up a gear, giving our backs good ball that looked like being turned into points first by Cohen, then Greenwood, then Tindall, before Wilkinson put over a neat drop goal. Soon afterwards, thanks to an interception by their centre Tana Umaga, Doug Howlett on the wing showed his speed to outdistance Jason Robinson, dotting down between the posts for a try. Wilkinson notched up another penalty in reply before Lewis Moody crashed over the line in injury time. Going into the break England was 17—14 up.

Soon after the restart Wilkinson added a further seven points when he dummied to drop kick but instead chipped over the flat All Black backline, gathering the ball himself to score brilliantly between the posts. A few minutes later Cohen grabbed onto a fumbled ball and sprinted fifty metres to score a try which Wilkinson converted. That score made it 31—14 to us with just twenty minutes to go. England were leading by 17 points, but we let them back into the game. Lomu smashed through Tindall for his second try, and then their replacement scrum half Danny Lee burrowed over from close range with ten minutes left. Andrew Mehrtens converted both, and the last minutes were edgy. With two minutes on the clock New Zealand full back Ben Blair tore away down the left wing, and looked to have a clean run-in to the line, when Cohen turned up from nowhere and bundled him into the corner flag with a try-saving tackle. In injury time Ben Kay stole a New Zealand lineout that could have spelt trouble, but then the final whistle blew and the match was ours: England 31—New Zealand 28.

ProZone

I decided to hold a press conference after the All Black game with two objectives in mind. First, we were concerned over dummy-running tactics that were being used to confuse the defence in that game, and I wanted to bring it to the attention of the IRB. I had the perfect tool to demonstrate this illegal method of blocking, *ProZone*. The use of ProZone for this purpose would achieve my second objective – I wanted to show the opposition the sophisticated level of our analysis.

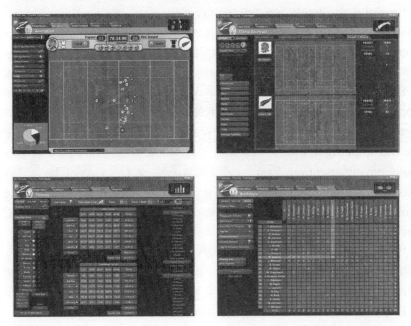

ProZone was one of the most advanced sporting analysis programs in the world. I knew that no other team could possibly source this kind of software within the year to the World Cup, and I was hoping that Eddie Jones and the Wallabies would hear about this press conference – we were playing them at Twickenham at the end of the week.

ProZone is a tool we'd been working on specifically with the designers for more than a year. It had taken a lot of hard work – and a significant investment by the RFU – to get it set up properly, but in my mind it was well worth it. We had to install twenty specialised cameras around Twickenham stadium for it to work. The great thing is, however, we get exactly the same level of information on our competitors as on ourselves. It really helps to plan for matches, and we can now send a game of data right to the players' O_2 xda phones for their own personal preparation.

When you look at the game through ProZone, it completely changes how you think about rugby. A lot of people say these days that with more teams perfecting an expansive game there isn't any space to run on the pitch anymore. All I say is, look at Figure 1 and tell me if you see as much space there as I do.

ProZone also has a function to calculate work rates on a continual basis for each and every player. That means the computer knows when you're walking! We publish competition tables in the War Room to see who's working the hardest on the pitch.

Soon after we first showed ProZone to the players and told them about the work-rate function, we were on the pitch having just completed our warm-up drills. I called everyone in to have a chat before we did some light session work. As I began talking everyone came in close, paying attention. Everyone, that is, except Will Greenwood. Will was about fifteen feet behind the group, running five paces, turning around, running five more back the other way turning around again, back and forth in quick step.

'Will,' I shouted after a moment, 'what the hell are you doing?'

'I'm just practising Shuttle runs for when the ref stops the game. With ProZone watching, I'll have to get my stats up any way I can!'

Everyone enjoyed the moment.

Australia

Unlike the All Blacks, Australia made no secret about coming at us with a full-strength side.

Australia showed a whole lot more commitment and unity in the pack than they did in the laboured 18—9 defeat they had suffered against Ireland the previous week, but we deserved to take the lead after ten minutes.

Richard Hill, a truly world-class player, caught the ball in the lineout and it was spread wide to James Simpson-Daniel, who drew three Australian defenders with a great run and scissors that let Cohen in at the corner. Matt Burke put over two penalties to bring them within a point, but we were recycling the ball pretty well in the loose, and Jonny kept easing us further ahead with penalties, giving us a 16—6 lead just before the break. I thought their lock Dan Vickerman was lucky not to get sin-binned for taking out Matt Dawson after the scrum half's brilliant fifty-metre break, but there was no questioning the try that their fly half Elton Flatley scored in the seventh minute of extra time before half time. It happened because Wilkinson slipped and lost his footing as the ball came out of the ruck, and Flatley made a very good break and cruised in under the posts. So with the conversion that made it only 16—13 at half time.

Just three minutes after the restart the Wallabies' wing, former rugby leaguer Wendell Sailor, got past Cohen to score in the corner after a good move, sparked by their flanker George Smith, had got through our defence. Almost immediately afterwards, the ball squirted out of a ruck and Flatley got his hands on it and pinned back his ears for the line, showing a great turn of pace. He hared practically the length of the field for an amazing try and no-one could catch him, not even Jason Robinson. Burke converted that one, and very soon afterwards slotted a penalty to make it 16—28 to them, turning our half-time lead into a 12-point lead for the Wallabies within about ten minutes playing time. It was horrendous.

But with twenty-five minutes left on the clock we dug deep and showed we had incredible inner reserves. Wilkinson kept putting over the penalties until we were within a converted try of them. Then Simpson-Daniel ran the ball crosswise on the Wallaby 22, dummied, and popped it up to Cohen coming in on a diagonal inward run. Cohen broke the Australian defensive line and over he went for a thrilling try with less than five minutes to go. One point down, the pressure was on Jonny Wilkinson, but he kicked the conversion and put us ahead by one point at 32—31. After a few tense minutes, where Martin Johnson's display of leadership was absolutely outstanding, the game was over and England had held on.

So we lifted the 2002 Cook Cup again, and it was three wins in a row over the Wallabies in what was one of our best games ever at Twickenham. For the team and our supporters it was marvellous, yet still my lingering self-doubt persisted.

Golf at Augusta

It's at this point that I would like to share with you one of the most wonderful personal incentives a keen golfer could ever be given to win a World Cup.

I was enjoying what was, by now, a fairly rare game of golf with a dear friend Sir Ronnie Hampel. We were about halfway round and he asked me how everything was going. We talked over a few in's and out's about the rugby and our build up to the World Cup and he finished by saying, 'Clive if you win the World Cup I'll take you to play at Augusta.'

Having thought about this for a couple of moments I asked Ronnie how he was going to do this. No-one could get to play Augusta, the most hallowed golf course in the world! Ronnie could, of course, because it turned out he was a member! I accepted his offer and thought, *If only.*

One of the first e-mails I got after the World Cup Final was from Ronnie, it read, 'When do you want to go?'

I played five rounds of the Augusta National, from the back tees, with Ronnie and Lawrence Farmer, my golf coach, in May 2004. Heaven!

South Africa

On 23 November we played the third weekend on the trot of matches against Tri-Nations teams against South Africa. By this stage we knew we would be playing South Africa in a pool stage of the World Cup next year.

We won the game 53—3, and that was the biggest margin of defeat ever suffered by South Africa in any international match. What's more, it wrapped up a unique treble for England – defeating all three Tri-Nations on successive weekends.

The key moment in the match came in the twenty-third minute when Jannes Labuschagne was sent off for following through late with a swinging arm in a tackle on Jonny Wilkinson. The Springboks lost a whole lot of discipline and self-control after that. It was a tribute to our guys' patience that they kept their composure in spite of plenty of provocation. That game was a disgrace actually. But the leadership, the self-control, the discipline of our guys that day was amazing.

When the team met again in December, I showed them all a video from every camera on the ground, which I'd sent to the IRB with a note asking what were they going to do about it. I made the video available to everyone, including the people in South Africa, and said next time we couldn't allow this to happen because someone could get seriously hurt.

Players had been shocked, but they were learning to use the experience to their advantage, and not react after the game. Self-control was the key. At the press conference I said, 'Look, you guys watched the game, you make the comment.'

As the match started we began putting points on the board early on: Wilkinson slotted a penalty after their centre Robbie Fleck had taken a swing at Ben Cohen right in front of the ref. Then Dawson's break from the base of the scrum was taken on by Dallaglio and Phil Christophers to Cohen, who ran a great angle to go over the line.

Not long after that, Labuschagne did his number on Wilkinson and was in my view a hundred per cent rightly red-carded. But what it did in terms of the match was badly to unbalance their forward capability, after which they seemed to collectively and individually lose it. They couldn't compete so they went abusive, tried to intimidate and so on.

That didn't stop Will Greenwood from going over for a try not long afterwards, thanks to an inside pass from Wilkinson. At the break we were ahead 18—3 after another penalty from each side. And that penalty by André Pretorius was South Africa's last score. Two minutes after the break it was Greenwood on the scoreboard again, dummying his way to the line from the Boks' 22. Jonny Wilkinson sent the long pass that made it for Will, but he had to go off soon after, leaving

Dawson to kick a great touchline conversion. At the end of the third quarter Phil Christophers squirmed through but received the clothesline treatment from full back Werner Greeff as he was shaping to score; the ref awarded a penalty try.

Then Neil Back scored from a rolling maul, and this time it was Andy Gomarsall who put over the touchline conversion. Our guys could do no wrong, and they were showing such self-control, it was awesome. After Back's score the rest of the back row got in on the act. Hill scored first, grabbing a cross-field kick by Healey to the right corner. Again, the try was converted from the touchline, this time by Tim Stimpson. Then, in injury-time, Dallaglio was on the end for a pushover try to take the score over the half century.

That score answered a lot of questions.

So we ended 2002 having scored 868 points and conceded just 286. We were the world's number one team according to the Zurich rankings and had stretched our unbeaten run at Twickenham to eighteen matches. We were also the first European side to defeat New Zealand, Australia and South Africa on consecutive weekends. The fact that we hadn't lost to any of the southern giants since 2000 was testimony that rugby history had been turned on its head. We totally respected the southern hemisphere teams, but guys like Martin Johnson, Lawrence Dallaglio, Neil Back, Phil Vickery, and all the others, they simply didn't have any fear of them.

World Number 1

On December 18, 2002, without much fanfare, with no special brand of announcement, for the very first time in England's long rugby history, the Elite Squad achieved the first of our three major long-term goals. England moved to number one in the Zurich World Rugby Rankings.

No one in the England camp, the RFU, nor even the media made much of a fuss over the news, but I'm sure it was deeply satisfying for all involved. The southern hemisphere pundits ranted and raved for weeks about how it was impossible for England to be number one. It was as hard for them to accept as it had been for so many in the England camp when we first started.

2003 Six Nations

For four years the Six Nations Grand Slam had slipped from our grasp. In 1999 we had lost in injury time at Wembley by one point to Wales. In 2000 the new operation at Pennyhill was up and running, and we played brilliantly all the way through until the last match. But then we went to Scotland for the week before that final match – and once again blew the Slam. In 2001, the year of the foot-and-mouth epidemic, we again went to Ireland a week ahead of the game and with no preparation, and the Irish were waiting for us. In 2002 we lost to France in Paris. We had been winning Triple Crowns and the Championship, itself, but what of the Grand Slam? Would 2003 be the year when the long-awaited prize of the Grand Slam was finally achieved? And would the final match for the Grand Slam be a showdown with Ireland at Lansdowne Road?

The Six Nations tournament put heaps of pressure on the England team to prepare for the World Cup. When I got the players together, I told them that if we were serious about the World Cup we would have to win the Grand Slam this year. We had just beaten the southern hemisphere teams, and now we had a good chance to win the World Cup. Everyone in the Six Nations was more or less on the same level of fitness and so on. I consciously put as much pressure on the players as I could, which is different from the way most coaches set about it. But I told them, 'Unless we do this we won't win the World Cup,' and built up the pressure massively in team meetings. I kept telling them, 'If you're serious about the World Cup you have to win these games.' I believe the team played better under pressure, because that's what we would meet in the World Cup.

I wanted Ireland to beat France so that we could have a massive pressure game for the Slam. An Ireland away game – that would be the Grand Slam showdown for both teams. The bonus was that Ireland were also playing for the Slam – and they were at home. History shows that we played our best game of the Six Nations in Dublin that year, and that win set up the whole year for us.

France

The first match of the Six Nations was against France at Twickenham on 15 February. We went into that game well prepared with six training days; all the clubs were behind us, the preparation time and training days were all lined up properly. In the end we didn't play especially well against les Bleus that day, but all the same we won 25—17.

Unfortunately, it was under a sad and dark cloud. The squad and I found out about Nick Duncombe's death on the Friday night. Nick had put up a lively performance at scrum half in the Scotland match the year before. At the time he earned his first cap, Nick had only played about four first-class matches, but everyone could see his talent. Thinking back to my early days as a player, I have always loved to be able to bring in young talent. If you're good enough, you're old enough. I was extremely excited about the talent this young man possessed. It was a terrible and shocking tragedy when he died, only twenty-one years old. We were all devastated, but the most affected were his own team-mates from Harlequins. If Nick had not been injured he would have been with us in the very same team hotel. Our thoughts and prayers were with him and his lovely family. I still think of him a lot.

The match against France was Jason Leonard's hundredth England cap, so he led the side out, and it was a shame he had to go off with an ankle injury before half time. We began OK. Jason Robinson made a great run from a self-taken lineout. Dan Luger broke clear through the French defence but ran out of support. Our backs were looking dangerous, but the first score was Jonny Wilkinson's long-range penalty when the ball bounced up and down on the bar like a trampoline.

With Charlie Hodgson as virtually an alternative stand-off, their back row had a double target which threw them off their game – they didn't know who to go for. We used a similar tactic of playing Catt in the World Cup semi-final. Having Hodgson playing at No. 12, and acting as first receiver a lot of the time, we certainly succeeded in putting off the French back row – Betsen was taken off before the end.

Hodgson fluffed a clearance kick quite early on, letting Olivier Magne, their flanker, charge it down and score. But we were soon in front again with two more penalties from Wilkinson. Our backs, especially Robinson, were giving the opposition a lot of problems, and when Hodgson broke through it was a certain try if he hadn't somehow failed to notice Will Greenwood on his shoulder. Then Jonny put over another penalty to make it 12—7 at the break.

In the second half we started OK and had most of the possession. Ben Cohen made a lot of ground up the right flank, and got the ball to Will Greenwood who floated a well-timed long pass out to Robinson and in Jason went, right under the posts. I thought when he went over like that early in the second half that we would blast them apart, like we did two years ago, but we then produced what I said at the time was the worst 25 minutes since I had taken over. With a 15-point lead, which a Wilkinson drop goal soon turned into 18 points, we looked to be coasting. But when Thomas Castaignède came on in the 64th minute as a replacement for Aurelien Rougerie, some slick work put their full back Clément Poitrenaud over for a score. Merceron's conversion was miles off, so that still left them 13 points adrift at 25—12. A late try from their centre Damien Traille made it quite a bit closer, but we held out and the result was the win we needed, and on the whole deserved. All the same, it was disappointing to have conceded three tries, though I think we would still have won, even if the game had gone on longer, as we were fitter and better than them. Jonny Wilkinson registered his 600th point in international rugby with his fifth penalty, and was happy to do most of the scoring

So we didn't play all that well against France, but that was the first hurdle of the Grand Slam, and we were over it.

Wales

A week later we went to Cardiff to take on Wales, a game I always expected would be tough. In the end we won 26—9, but they gave us a real run for our money, especially in the first half when they were in my opinion the better side. Wales were definitely a good team, and they showed a lot of passion.

I thought they would come out of the blocks fast, taking the game to us from the start, and that's what they did. A lot of pressure over the first fifteen minutes earned them a penalty, but Jonny Wilkinson struck back with one of his own and then a brilliant drop goal. We began to come back at them, with good work by the forwards which earned another penalty, but then shortly before the break their centre Mark Taylor got clear through and a try looked a certainty. There were two men outside him but somehow he didn't get the pass away and our defence held. We had two objectives that day – to win the game and not to concede a try – and we achieved our objectives. Before the half-time whistle Phil Christophers was sin-binned for taking out Gareth Thomas without the ball, and we were down to fourteen men but Ceri Sweeney missed the penalty, so we still led 9—6 at half time.

The problems were identified and sorted out in the changing room, and after the break we started to play a more structured and controlled game. Will Greenwood went through two tackles to score under the posts – his sixth try against Wales. They must hate the sight of him! Then, after the conversion, we put the Welsh on the back foot with some powerful forward play and good combinations among the backs. Joe Worsley got a try from close range, Wilkinson converting, which made it 23—6. And that was about it. Credit to Wales, they never stopped battling. We kept our line clean, although Jonny took a worry-ing knock near the end. I thought Will Greenwood in particular had a fine game. In fact he was brilliant, world-class, and Lawrence Dallaglio also had a tremendous game. We lacked a bit of discipline, which kept us on the back foot, but as I said at the time, 'Hopefully, we'll get a bit better every game and keep nudging forward.'

Italy

In the Italy match at Twickenham there was a fantastic first twenty minutes, just amazing. In that time England racked up a total of 33 points with two tries from full back Josh Lewsey, and one each from Steve Thompson, James Simpson-Daniel and Mike Tindall.

First to score after only two minutes was Lewsey after the ball had gone down the line at speed through Wilkinson and Simpson-Daniel. Seven minutes later a second try came from Thompson after a smart pick-and-go by Dawson. The clock was still only on thirteen minutes when Simpson-Daniel got the next after a brilliant two-on-one from Lewsey. Wilkinson nailed the easy conversion, but almost straight away was lining up another, this time after Lewsey's second try, a superb individual effort. On the half-hour centre Tindall was put in for England's fifth try after some fine work from Dawson and Lewsey again. Tindall went over on the scissor from a Dawson pick-and-go – and that seemed to signal the start of the Italian resistance, because after that somehow we seemed to take our foot off the pedal and couldn't get the ball off the Italians. In fact, although we ran out winners 40—5 we spent most of the match defending. The really bad news was that Wilkinson had to go off with his shoulder injured again, and to make matters worse his replacement Charlie Hodgson had to go off almost at once as well. Hodgson's injury was going to keep him out of the game for a year.

After the game my thoughts were that we would have to up our performance a couple of gears if we were going to achieve our aims. But you have to look at the positives. We had a lot of new faces, and we had defended well. But it was a very quiet dressing room.

Scotland

The Scotland match two weeks later at Twickenham was a hard-fought affair, although we quickly ran up a lead with two penalties from Wilkinson. Then things looked even worse for the Scots when two of their players were sin-binned within minutes of each other. First Andrew Mower went off for a high tackle on Lewsey. Then their No. 8 Simon Taylor followed him for a tackle on Mike Tindall that was so late it was practically the next day. But, credit to the Scots, they kept their heads up and when they were still down to thirteen men Chris Paterson slotted a penalty after a fine run by Bryan Redpath.

Then Jason Robinson was the third person to join the sin-bin brigade for a high tackle on Kenny Logan. While he was off, Paterson levelled the scores with a fine kick which kept Scotland very much in the game. But then we put together the best move of the match so far to send Lewsey over in the corner – his third try in two games.

That made it 13—6 to us, but the Scots forwards were still slugging it out up front and Paterson used their advantage to slot over another penalty, answered by Wilkinson just before the break.

The guys got into gear in the second half and, when Redpath was smartly caught by Dawson at the base of the scrum near their line, Ben Cohen went over for an easy try, converted by Wilkinson. I had the idea of trying Jason Robinson at centre, and the experiment seemed to be paying off because he quickly got in on the act with a fine try through the midfield. Grayson had come on for Wilkinson, and he slotted the conversion with ease. The Scots didn't give up though, they began to press again, but the steam went out of their effort near the end when Matt Dawson did a neat show-and-go, releasing Jason for his second try.

I was pleased with our effort, all things considered. Certainly I was a lot more satisfied than after the Italy game. Scotland did well enough. They got stuck in and proved it was a true Six Nations championship. On our side there were a lot of good individual performances, with Josh Lewsey in particular doing plenty of good things, but I was worried at how easily we gave away possession – we turned a lot of ball over in that game.

Ireland

Then it was showdown time at Lansdowne Road, with both sides going for the Slam. Ireland were playing with the wind, and there was some frantic play at the start. A glitch on Steve Thompson's radar sent his lineout throw to their flanker Keith Gleeson, and the ball was taken on by Marcus Horan. We kept them out but gave away a penalty, which their fly half Humphreys didn't need as he put over a smart drop goal.

We had the perfect answer to that, which was a converted try within the next five minutes. A wheeled Ireland scrum allowed Richard Hill to pressurise Peter Stringer. Matt Dawson pounced on the loose ball and his break released Dallaglio to go over under the posts.

Around ten minutes before half time Ireland were very dangerous, persistently attacking our line with good breaks from Brian O'Driscoll and Geordan Murphy from full back. But our defence was rock solid, and we made certain that no points were scored. Wilkinson stretched the lead to 10—6 with a right-footed drop goal, and then another just before the half-hour – again on his wrong foot – from thirty-five metres out.

After the break Tindall scored the try that put the writing on the wall for Ireland. Our forwards had made good ground before a way opened for Mike, who barged through the cover on an angled run once the gap had been made by Grayson and Greenwood.

There were about twenty minutes left on the clock when we really put our foot on the gas, and our forwards started to swarm all over the Irish. Dallaglio made a great run and was held up just short of the line, but it didn't matter because Greenwood grabbed the third try when he was pushed over after a five-metre scrum. Wilkinson added the extras and, with Tindall going off, I tried Jason Robinson at centre again, like I did against Scotland. Ten minutes from time Greenwood intercepted a tired pass from Murphy and strolled over for his second try in injury time. Finally, well into injury time, replacement Dan Luger added a fifth try after the ball was spun out to Lewsey and he put the wing over. Jonny converted. The final score was England 42—Ireland 6.

Grand Slam champions

After the game I said how delighted I was by how the guys had reacted to the stress of the occasion. 'We have put a lot of pressure on ourselves all week,' I told them. 'I can't say how good these guys are. They are the toughest guys I have ever worked with, physically and mentally. I was confident we were going to win if we held on to the ball. Ireland were a good team but I am delighted with the outcome.'

At the end of the 2003 Six Nations England had put together a run of twenty-one consecutive home victories, won thirty-one of their past thirty-five games, and finally laid to rest the ghost of Grand Slam failures against all three Celtic nations.

It was the perfect start to the World Cup year, in such stark contrast to 1999.

26

RECORD SUMMER
TOUR

Unlike New Zealand when they came to Twickenham nine months earlier, we went on the June 2003 southern hemisphere tour to New Zealand and Australia with a full-strength team. We took some flak in certain quarters for that decision, but I knew it was the right one, and that winning would give us huge momentum for the World Cup. Test match rugby to me should always be about putting out your strongest side, regardless of the World Cup coming up or whatever. When New Zealand came to Twickenham, leaving a few major players at home, I just didn't think that was the way to do it. The way to the World Cup was to go game by game, so when you arrived at the World Cup tournament you knew exactly what position you were in. So even if we'd lost down there it would have been the right decision to take the strongest team. We had to know exactly where we were.

First we played the Maoris at New Plymouth, which is in the middle of nowhere, and we stayed in a hotel that was totally different from what we were used to. It was good fun, a real country town, and we enjoyed it. The Maoris had hardly lost a game against international teams, but we beat them comfortably, and that was our second team. The weather that night was terrible, pouring with rain, and we played against the wind at the start. The New Zealand media in their papers were incredibly negative, trotting out yet again that 'boring England' tag, but the conditions were almost unplayable so I don't know what we were supposed to do. I was amazed that in New Zealand, which is such a great rugby country, there should have been such a lack of knowledge in some parts of the media. Maybe it was just because we were English, but some of the stuff they were putting in the papers was laughable. What rankled with them I think was that it wasn't our Test match team, it was our second team, and I think they were just surprised by the power of that side. It was a great night, a great win.

In the run-up to the Test some of their media were brilliant. *The Lord of the Rings* movie had recently been shot in New Zealand by Peter Jackson, who was of course a New Zealander, and a lot of people out there were bowled over by that movie. It didn't take their media long to decide the English team were 'white orcs' and, because of the way we played, they decided we weren't just white orcs but white orcs on steroids – that's what they called us. But we didn't mind. In fact we built on it. For the World Cup we added a special section to our Black Book with a picture of every player in the squad next to a picture of a character from the movie. We also reproduced the article itself: '. . . *The rest of the pack were simply giant gargoyles, raw-boned, cauli-flower-ear monoliths that intimidated and unsettled. When they ran onto the field, it was like watching a tribe of white orcs on steroids. Forget their hardness – has there ever been an uglier forward pack . . .*' It was great!

In the test we played with thirteen men for ten minutes, when Back and Dallaglio were sin-binned, and that included about five minutes right on our own line – those scrums on our line will go down in history, the way we kept them out. The most amazing thing was that while for ten minutes we had thirteen of our men against fifteen All Blacks, we still managed to win that ten-minute period 3—0 – they didn't score a point. It was an epic game, we don't win down there too often, and it was brilliant to do that before the World Cup. One of the headlines the next day summed up the New Zealand point of view. 'The World Cup,' it said, 'has just got considerably harder.'

We didn't play all that well for a lot of that match. But we won, we still beat New Zealand. The last time we beat them on their own turf had been thirty years earlier. Martin Johnson put in a massive performance, so did Steve Thompson, while Dallaglio and wing Ben Cohen were also among the standouts. But for me and most of those who watched that game, it was Jonny Wilkinson who did the business. His work with the boot was just extraordinary. His tally was a drop goal and four penalties, all of them difficult in those terrible conditions. But there was one on the touchline which had everyone in the stand applauding, whichever side they were backing. He just hit this ball from the touchline into a gale force wind and it went like an arrow, it was the most incredible kick. Carlos Spencer by contrast, who was kicking for the All Blacks, missed a couple that would have been called easy in normal conditions, but here it was wet, windy and very difficult. But Wilkinson's kicking that night was unbelievable. People watching that game were just in awe of what he was doing. For the first time the New Zealanders were saying, 'Hang on, this is serious!'

New Zealand dominated the first half territorially, with England launching a couple of good counter-attacks, but it was Jonny's kicking that gave us the edge when we went into the break six points apiece. Then, early in the second half, he sent over another penalty to give England the lead. Not so long after that Back and Dallaglio were sin-binned within seconds of each other, we were down to thirteen men, and the All Blacks threw everything they had at us. They camped on our line, they tried everything, but we kept them out. And then Jonny put us clear with that incredible penalty.

In the final quarter Carlos Spencer put Howlett away for the only try of the match, which he converted. That made it 15—13. But for the last twenty minutes we kept them out, just like we had been doing all day. Spencer missed another penalty, and then so too for once did Wilkinson, from the halfway line. And then the final whistle blew for a historic win.

It was a very tough game. There was an ugly incident when Josh Lewsey had his head stamped on by their second row, Ali Williams. That left a really bad flavour, and we assumed Williams would get banned for six months. But he got off, and it was from that moment onwards that I said, 'Right, that's it, from now on the England team is going to travel with a QC.' Legal systems vary from country to country, so I decided that from then on we should always have someone to represent our players travelling with us.

In the changing room afterwards everyone was smiling as if to say, 'How did we do that? Winning a test match against the All Blacks is difficult, but to win when you're playing badly and with thirteen men?' Of course, the conditions were appalling. We didn't care about how prettily we played – we just had to win. And it was very valuable to our preparation. I had a chance to see how the New Zealand game had changed, how they were playing wide. But I never really thought we would be playing New Zealand at the World Cup anyway. I suspected right from the start, given the way the draw was structured, that we would be meeting Australia in the final. Actually to win gave the team huge confidence, to know we could go to New Zealand and even play badly, even play with thirteen men, and still come away with a win! It was just a great trip, one of those great, great trips.

The Wallabies: foreshadowing the World Cup final

As mentioned, I already had a feeling we would be playing Australia in the World Cup final, so this was the moment to show them what we could do. Both the New Zealand games had been played in appalling conditions, but Melbourne's Telstra Dome had a roof. I went there in advance to check things, and the first thing they said was, 'You'll obviously want the roof open because you're English, and the English like to play in the rain.' And I said, 'Yes, I am English, but I want the roof shut.' In the southern hemisphere, it doesn't matter how good you are, the image of English rugby is always the same: big, slow, boring and kicking goals. And in fact we hadn't been that way at least since I'd been in charge. I kept telling them that this team with people like Martin Johnson had some fantastic ball-players, and it was in perfect conditions that we would play our best.

So we played with the roof closed, in perfect conditions, when it was pouring with rain outside. But because we were playing in the dry under that shut roof, the team played really well. We outscored the Wallabies by three tries to one in a victory by 25—15 that could have been even more. There were tries for centres Will Greenwood and Mike Tindall, as well as a brilliant second half effort from wing Ben Cohen. The game had hardly started when Dallaglio stole an early Wallaby lineout, and terrific recycling of the ball at pace sucked in the defenders before it finally went wide and Greenwood burst through a tackle to dot down the ball near the posts for an easy conversion.

We kept up the pressure throughout that half, and always looked like scoring, although the Wallabies slotted a penalty for a silly mistake.

But not long afterwards Tindall was over in the left corner after the ball had been taken up from our 22 with quick hands from Wilkinson, Thompson and Greenwood. Jonny hit the post with the conversion, and we went into the break 12—3 up.

The second half saw the Wallabies creep up with a couple of penalties against just one for us, and then Jonny Wilkinson broke through, giving a show of the ball to the Wallaby defence, and then popping it up to Cohen, who straightened his running line brilliantly before leaving full back Chris Latham for dead with a side-step and an accelerating run.

The Wallabies never looked like coming back after that, though their wing, Sailor, cut through for a fine try in the right corner. Martin Johnson and Steve Thompson were everywhere. We played some fantastic fifteen-man rugby. But we also put on this spectacular sixty-metre rolling maul. It should have been a penalty try – how can you go sixty yards and then they suddenly stop it on their line if not by collapsing it? Then critics in the media said we were cheating. John Eales, for instance, said a few things which seemed strange. When he looked at the game later he may have been a bit embarrassed by some of the things he said about the maul being illegal.

In fact we didn't score from it, but it certainly rattled the Australians. So the next day their media decided we had peaked too early. You can certainly peak fitness-wise, but not in terms of the way you play. We just had a great game that night. Australia had a few players missing, true, but it was a very good Australian team, playing at home. England had never won in Australia, which is an incredible statistic – that was the first we had ever won, and we did it with room to spare. It was a great win, one of our best performances from the whole team. That was perhaps the first time we really demonstrated our plan from A to Z, as opposed to just plan A or plan B. I don't think people can now describe the way we play because there are too many varieties, and that's one of the strengths of the team.

Those two test victories were really three victories if you include the Maoris game – most of the players who played in that Maori team were in the World Cup squad – and for us comfortably to beat the Maoris with their terrific record was huge. That trio of wins set us up for the World Cup. It amazed me that so many experts at home were saying we shouldn't be doing this, we shouldn't be exposing ourselves just before the World Cup. What if we lost? Well, if we had lost it would still have been the right decision because in my opinion you want to know where you are. As it was, we knew we were better than both those teams. It gave us huge confidence. We were thinking about the World Cup even when we played in Melbourne, because while in Australia we stopped off at Perth for three days to check the hotels and the training grounds. Perth was going to be the place where we would be based for the first two or three weeks of the World Cup and I wanted our World Cup squad to get the feel of it.

The press conference – laying down the gauntlet

My philosophy of meeting pressure with pressure sometimes comes out in strange ways, and that's how it came out in the press conference in Melbourne after the match against the Wallabies. For the entire week leading up to the match, the Aussie press had been after me to get me to rise to the comments that had been coming from the Australian camp.

'The team's too old . . .'

'Dad's Army . . .'

'They don't score tries . . .'

'Boring . . .'

Those were some of the quips. I'd lived in Australia, so I knew this was just the sort of thing that the Aussies like to do. When we returned for the World Cup the headlines would read, 'Is that all you've got?' referring to Wilkinson's stunning display against South Africa in Perth.

It's just banter in a sharp, competitive way.

Normally I wouldn't respond in kind. We were fastidious about coaching our players to resist the temptation of being goaded into an exchange of words. However in this particular situation, sitting in a press conference in Melbourne just after the game, I suppose I was feeling a bit aggressive with respect to some of the press. I usually try to be the same in a winning situation or a losing one. I am usually conscious of setting the tone for the team to follow. This time I decided on a different approach. When the first question came from the Australian media, I went on the front foot. Knowing how the draw was structured,

I had a strange feeling that we would meet Australia in the World Cup final, so I started playing the Aussies at their own game. If I'd known how much of a stir it would cause, I would have done it sooner.

The first question came: 'How high did you rate England's performance tonight?'

I answered it in brief and then added my own additional thoughts.

'I must be missing something here. I thought sport was all about winning? Everything seems to have changed here in Australia, certainly seems to have with respect to rugby union since I lived here. I thought you Aussies were all about winning and not about marks out of ten for performance. Eddie Jones and the Wallabies have been trying to wind us up all week about what an old, tired, slow and boring team we are. Well, all that's bullshit!'

The look of complete shock on all of their faces in that moment was priceless.

'We've beaten the Wallabies five times in a row now.

'For the match at the Telstra Dome, you guys all asked us both whether we wanted to play with the roof open or closed. I wanted the roof shut so that the game could be played in perfect conditions, giving the best chance of a great running game. Eddie Jones wanted it open and to introduce the uncertainty of weather conditions. And you call us boring?'

I suppose it wasn't very gracious or sporting in the traditional sort of way. Once they had recovered their composure the journalists scribbled furiously. For the first time I was doing what I thought the Aussies did in their own media; I was putting the questions back to them. It was cold and calculating. I'm not sure they had ever had an opposing coach serve it up to them.

How different to my first press conference all those years ago, I thought to myself.

The headlines in the following day's papers read, 'Woodward, the new Douglas Jardine'.

Douglas Jardine had of course been captain of the touring England cricket team in the notorious 'bodyline' series of test matches in 1932–33 when, in accordance with Jardine's plan, Harold Larwood and the other England fast bowlers fired barrages of short-pitched, high-rearing balls at the Australian batsmen with the aim of intimidating them. The great Don Bradman had been putting England to the sword at that time with a series of record innings, and desperate measures were needed. Jardine had been tasked by his cricketing superiors to 'win at all costs'. And that's exactly what he did. He had observed Bradman's reaction to the fast, short-pitched ball and identified a weakness there which he sought to exploit. The Aussies were very unhappy about it. There were even calls for seccession from the Commonwealth.

'I don't get it,' said one of the players at the airport the next day. 'I thought Douglas Jardine was a hero for winning that series?'

I had thought so too. So I bought a DVD documentary of the events of those days that had so strained relations between our two countries. It was an Australian version of course, but included interviews with Jardine's family on the impact which it had had on his life. Apparently Douglas Jardine was never allowed to play cricket for England again. Despite the fact that he had carried out their instructions, the cricket authorities abandoned their successful captain and chose to denigrate him.

The new Douglas Jardine? I thought as I ejected the DVD from my laptop on the plane. *Perfect!*

The reaction was exactly what I and the players wanted.

Later that year, we had the privilege of holding the press Christmas party at Lord's in the famous Long Room. There on the north wall is a portrait of Douglas Jardine in a huge frame, immortalised forever. I stood under that picture and tried to imagine what that man must have endured in battling an incredibly entrenched participative sporting culture when he returned to England.

A summer of ideal preparation

England had just beaten the All Blacks for only the second time in history in New Zealand. We had defeated the Wallabies for the very first time in history on their home ground. We were the number one team in the world.

We returned from Australia confident that we could hold our own against any team in the world as long as we had the right preparation.

Thankfully, we came home to three straight months of uninterrupted training with the World Cup squad on a brand new pitch at Pennyhill Park. It was an exciting summer indeed. After the summer tour, the players had four weeks from the end of June until the end of July for individual rest and training, pre-habilitation and rehabilitation work. On 21 July and in the ensuing seven weeks to 8 September, when the World Cup squad was announced, forty-two players trained as a team but competed individually for the thirty places available in the World Cup squad. And after a short week off, those thirty players went on to train for an additional three weeks before it was time to board the plane for Perth for the seven weeks of the World Cup. In all, the squad had ten straight weeks of fully England-controlled time. During this period the elite squad of forty-two were completely in our hands. Even though the first games in the 2003–04 season began in the last week of August, our forty-two players were relieved of their club duties for two weeks, and the World Cup squad of thirty were away from their-clubs for an additional twelve weeks.

So from the end of May, and the final of the 2003 Zurich Premiership, right up to 23 November when we returned home, the top players in the country were completely in our control. It was any coach's dream. Finally we could do exactly what we wanted and prepare the players our way. But instead of pushing the players hard as we had in '99 in an effort to build fitness, now all we had to do was maintain our fitness and build on our skills. It was just what we'd been aiming for, and it represented a huge partnership between the RFU and the Zurich Premiership clubs. It amounted to another twenty training days on top of the usual training days we had in the autumn, and that's outside the three Test weeks we had in that time. It was fantastic, and the preparation really showed in the players' performances.

Digging up the pitch

The pitch at Pennyhill Park had been completely dug up and re-laid between the Ireland game of the Six Nations and the end of the summer tour. It was now on a par with the best pitches in the world where before it had been simply adequate.

The project had started just before the Six Nations. The problem was that, while the pitch at Pennyhill was very convenient, it was also very unpredictable in its state, usually being either bone dry and rock hard or waterlogged and boggy. There seemed to be no in-between. Most injuries in rugby occur in training on unsuitable surfaces. If we wanted to be a world-class team we had to have world-class facilities. Only this was no small project, and we didn't own the land. If we wanted to build a pitch, the RFU would have to partner with Pennyhill Park.

My relationship with the RFU had changed over the years since Francis Baron had been appointed CEO. Francis and I had developed a very successful system for managing the expenditure and improvements in the England team. We had worked out a very clear set of guidelines for managing the elite squad, and I was free to operate anywhere within those guidelines with complete control over how I accomplished my aims. Francis got out of my way and let me do my job in the best way I knew how. When something came up that was outside those guidelines, such as my idea with the pitch at Pennyhill Park, we had a simple solution. I would put the idea to Francis, and, if he felt it had merit, he in turn would put the idea to the management board. If they felt they could do it, my initiative would be approved. Otherwise, it was up to me to work out a way to make it happen. In the case of a new pitch at Pennyhill Park, I was sure the idea had merit, but the investment required was probably going to be in excess of £150,000. It's at times like these that I'm so grateful for the fantastic relationships we've been building with our core business partners over the years. My first step was to talk with Danny Pecorelli, who owns and runs the hotel.

'Danny, I've got an idea . . .'

Danny was used to my ideas, but this one really appealed to him. As always, he was pleased to help us.

My next step had been to speak with Keith Kent, the groundsman at Twickenham. I first met Keith when we played New Zealand at the Manchester United ground in the autumn of 1997. Since then I was delighted that he had won the position of head groundkeeper at Twickenham two years previously. His whole approach and professionalism can be summed up in his very first words to me after he was appointed.

'Right, Clive, how do you want the pitch?'

Keith could create a pitch that would suit the game England wanted to play. With Keith, the coach came first and the grass second. We have always got along well. The team of groundsmen at Twickenham are really part of our One Team.

The RFU put up some money, so did Pennyhill Park (after all, we couldn't exactly take the pitch with us if we left), and Keith Kent managed the work from start to finish. The pitch at Pennyhill Park was completely reconstructed and expanded, and now Keith keeps both surfaces in top condition. It was the best preparation for the World Cup we could possibly have hoped for. Did it win us the World Cup? I don't know, but I wouldn't like to have prepared without it.

House of Pain

But it didn't stop there. I also wanted full gym facilities for the players – on the pitch! So Danny agreed to put in a concrete slab near the new pitch, and I did a deal with a company, GL Events Owen Brown, who provided temporary buildings, pavilions and marquees for functions. In exchange for allowing them to bring their key customers to lunch with the players, and watch some closed training sessions over the summer, they agreed to let us 'borrow' a pavilion for a few months. It was a huge gift worth many tens of thousands of pounds. Dave Reddin then arranged that all the proper gym equipment from Twickenham was put in trucks and brought to Pennyhill Park. The players could walk right from the pitch into the gym. The pavilion became synonymous with hard sessions with Dave, so the players dubbed it the House of Pain. It was excellent to have the facility so close and convenient. Too bad it was only temporary.

Right through the long hot summer we were up at 6.30 a.m. to meet the players at 7.30 a.m. every morning. We'd start with either the weights condition programme or skills exercises before breakfast, and we'd finish each day with some light-hearted games or competitions amongst the mini-teams into which we'd divided the squad. Each week on average we had three fitness or health tests, six weights sessions, five skills sessions, seven recovery periods with specific programmes for each player, three rest periods (enforced stays in bed, actually) during the day to enhance physical gains – all between Monday evening and Friday afternoon. We could see the players growing physically and mentally stronger day by day, and believed that the intense training in the heat would prepare us for the Australian climate.

Wales, France friendlies – end of a winning streak

In the run-up to the 1999 World Cup, the warm-up games had produced some entertaining games but also a lot of mismatches – for example, we had played the United States at Twickenham in a game that saw us win by 106—8. So for the 2003 World Cup I was determined that we should play real opposition. What I was looking for was full preparation for the World Cup, so the side which we put out for the first warm-up, against Wales at the Millennium Stadium in Cardiff on 23 August, only contained a handful of front-liners. We were still working on the composition of the final England squad, and this was a powerful but basically second-string team. A lot of those players had shown their paces in that gritty win over the New Zealand Maoris back in June.

That Wales warm-up game was played in absolutely perfect conditions, just like we had played in Melbourne against Australia. We were really hoping for perfect conditions in Australia for the World Cup, and yet the media across the world went on repeating that England would come unstuck in Australia because of the hard grounds. I couldn't believe what they were saying! In reality we wanted perfect conditions and hard grounds, which would suit us more than any other team in the World Cup, because we were fast and skilful and strong.

We hammered the Welsh 43—9 that sunny August day, putting over five tries. Alex King was at fly half and contributed 16 points – two conversions, a drop goal and three penalties – but even so didn't have an especially good day with the boot. Our forwards were brilliant – people like Simon Shaw, Julian White and the rest – these guys absolutely demolished Wales. Shaw is a wonderful player, and he's had his share of bad luck; but now with Johnson retiring in 2004 he has got his chance. At Cardiff that day he put in a man-of-the-match performance. Not bad when you consider that he became a father for the first time that week, an event that reminded me of the huge support that the players' wives and girlfriends have given them to succeed.

We kept up the pressure through the first half but didn't turn it into enough points. At the break we were seven ahead thanks to a try by Lewis Moody, but it should have been more. Then in the second half we were all over them. Luger scored after good work from the pack. Then it was Joe Worsley's turn with a pick-up from the base of the scrum. Stuart Abbott at centre was next to score, hitting the line at pace with a good angle after the pack, especially Grewcock, had put in some more good work. Finally, Dorian West went over from short range. That five-try win gave the opposition something to think about and some idea of England's strength in depth.

Next came the first of two matches against France. This was at the Stade Vélodrome in Marseilles, which is a venue where France have yet to lose – New Zealand, Australia, and South Africa have all gone down to them there. But we so nearly did it, losing 17—16 by a single point. Up to that moment we had had fourteen straight victories, and if we had won that game, if you include the World cup matches, it would have been a record twenty-five wins in a row before eventually losing to Ireland at Twickenham in 2004. I know this didn't happen on the scoreboard by one point, but it's a good indication of the excellence of this team.

However, our minds were not on the stats, we were entirely concentrating on preparing for the World Cup. France were in effect fielding their first team against our second, which didn't have Martin Johnson, Jonny Wilkinson or Jason Robinson, and they won by a whisker, Grayson missing a drop goal by inches in injury time that would have given us the match. But even without a victory that game gave us a great psychological advantage.

That Marseilles game also saw the new-look England shirts for the first time. There were teething troubles – at first the numbers kept coming off the backs – but there's no doubt the skin-tight kit did make the players harder to get hold of, and was therefore a part of our all-angles-covered preparation. They've framed that e-mail I sent Nike about the baggy shirt.

Mike Tindall did well in that Marseilles match, scoring a fine try when he powered through two tackles to get to the line from the French 22. Austin Healey also had a great game at scrum half, while Martin Corry and Lewis Moody kept the French, particularly fly half Frédéric Michalak, very much on the back foot. For France, their lock Fabien Pelous had a pretty good game, and full back Nicolas Brusque scored a good try in the first half. So they just shaded it.

It was another story two weeks later at Twickenham, when we put five tries past France in a thorough demolition job – victory to England 45—15. This time we had most of our frontline players on the field, while the French had left some of theirs behind. But the extent of our domination sent out signals to all the opposition, particularly a blistering spell before the break which saw us go over their line three times. The match at Twickenham was the only warm-up that Martin Johnson and Jonny Wilkinson got, and they oozed class for as long as they were on the field – I took both off shortly after the break. That was the day Geordan Murphy broke his leg playing for Ireland in another World Cup warm-up, so I don't think I can be accused of being unduly protective.

A couple of tries from Ben Cohen and one from Jason Robinson at full back underlined our dominance in that pre-break spell. Cohen's first came after a neat grubber by Wilkinson, and his second arrived only three minutes later. Again it was Wilkinson, with a break and a pop-up pass, who set it in motion. Jason Robinson went over next with one of his thrilling fifty-metre runs, and at half time the score was 33—3. Then Balshaw scored immediately after the break, collecting a switched kick-off from the French and motoring past Xavier Garbajosa on the left wing before a lot of people had even got back to their seats. Balshaw had a terrific match, and one that rightly got him into the World Cup squad. After that the French kept us out, more or less, and even got a couple of tries themselves, though Balshaw twice came within a whisker of scoring. The guys were really enjoying themselves in their skin-tight gear, with Steve Thompson giving a searing performance.

After the match we were officially placed top of the IRB's inaugural world rankings, as well as being the Zurich world number one side, so I had achieved my 1999 aim of England going into the 2003 World Cup as favourites to win. That was a hugely hot summer and, as I said, we trained the whole time at Pennyhill Park with an eye on the hot, dry, perfect conditions we were expecting – and looking forward to – in Australia. When we got to Australia it rained, and rained a lot. Quite funny really. So after all that we played in the rain.

Logistics sorted

It's no coincidence that England started winning around the time that first Nathan Martin, then Louise Ramsay, came on board. Louise had organised the logistics of moving the team around and inducting new players into the culture with military precision. She had broken down each day of the seven-week World Cup tournament into hourly time segments, with a comprehensive 'to do' list for each major event, and with clear delegation and lines of responsibility where she needed assistance or help from others. Over the summer she had been on a scouting tour of all the hotels we might possibly stay in, and she had made diagrams and a logistical breakdown of every route we would travel, with contingency plans clearly mapped out if anything went wrong. There were literally hundreds of pages in her notebook, all fully categorised and tabbed for easy access. Anyone who needed to could access the right information in just a few moments and reference the exact requirements of any event spanning the tournament. It was the most amazing example of organisation I'd ever seen, and yet another reason why I was supremely confident that we were preparing as well off the pitch as on it.

No talk of retiring

I had been watching the French play Scotland in April in the Six Nations. The Scottish winger Kenny Logan announced in an emotional interview after the game that it was his last game at Murrayfield, that he was retiring after the World Cup and would never play there again. I couldn't believe it. I immediately wrote an e-mail to all the players basically stating that I would not consider any player for selection for the World Cup who wanted to talk about retirement before it was all over. We introduced a new Teamship Rule to cover it. I felt strongly that if we were going to be focused on the job in hand this was no time for our team to be concerned with anyone's retirement.

An important aspect of our World Cup preparation was that we didn't discuss matters outside what we were actually doing. We didn't even talk about the World Cup in our team meetings in the War Room until a month before our departure, just after the France match when the final squad was announced. The players all knew what they were training for, so rather than focus intently on the World Cup, as we had for the '99 tournament, we instead chose to say very little, if not absolutely nothing, about it. By the time we did start talking about the tournament with just four weeks to go, the entire squad was very fresh. We didn't go overboard about the magnitude of the event – we simply prepared in the most professional way we could.

We're ready

By the end of September we were ready. Our quiet, determined preparation over three months had been invaluable. We didn't rush, we didn't push too hard. We didn't have to motivate the players in any way, shape or form. For the first time I could ever remember our preparation was flawless. If anything, that in itself was a distraction. We weren't used to everything going so right. I think it eventually showed in our matches, too, in that we had so much more potential in the team than we showed during the tournament.

In less than four years, since our bitter defeat in the quarter-final against South Africa in Paris during the '99 World Cup, we had achieved all the goals I laid out in my World Cup report.

We would arrive as the number one team in the Zurich world rankings.

We would arrive, I believed, as the best-prepared team in the tournament.

According to the bookmakers, we would arrive at the World Cup as favourites to win.

And quite aside from any goal I had set, we were going into the 2003 World Cup with ten straight wins over southern hemisphere sides, a feat never before accomplished by any English team over our antipodean counterparts.

In our Leadership, Teamship and Partnership we were as One Team. We were operating in the Winning Zone, and we had done everything possible to give our players every chance.

I must at this point mention Andy Robinson again. It is not easy being second-in-command when you clearly have the ability to be number one. He deserves the Rugby World Cup success more than anyone I can name, not only for his brilliance in coaching but also for his knowledge of how to support me under sometimes extreme pressure. He has the ability to take over from me and I just hope, if that happens, that he finds someone as good as I had to be his number two.

27
THE 2003 IRB RUGBY WORLD CUP

From the moment England landed in Perth on Thursday 2 October, the pressure was on. My little banter with the press a few months earlier certainly hadn't been forgotten. 'Jardine' was back on Australian soil.

Even though we had arrived as favourites, and were ranked number one and very well prepared, the Australian press would give us little credit until after the final. It was all fun, really, and I was happy to look at it that way. Living in Australia for almost five years had given me a valuable insight into Australian culture.

For the first time ever when going into a major tournament or series of internationals, I felt confident. England's preparation had been spot on. I knew we'd give this group of players every chance of winning. What we had to do now during the tournament was to get the selection right, call the right substitutions and, most importantly, ensure nothing happened off the pitch that could derail us.

The support team: pressure

Of course there were still the old jokes about England being too old, too slow, too boring – a bunch of guys who peaked between tournaments and choked in the big matches, just like all Pommy sporting teams. But now they had added a new twist.

'The RFU has more money. It's not fair,' ran the storylines day after day. Of course, it wasn't true, but I wasn't looking to correct anyone. If they wanted to think we had a huge war chest and were therefore unstoppable, far be it from me to change their minds!

Right from the start it was pretty obvious that my idea of preparation and support for the team was different from everyone else's. Take the matter of accommodation. The IRB officially held the World Cup, and so they arranged and paid for all accommodation and transport, as is the custom with touring test sides. The IRB budgets for each team covered thirty players staying in twin-share rooms, as well as twelve members of the support and coaching teams staying in single rooms. I wanted to change that. Our players were adults, professional sports people, and making them stay in twin-share accommodation was something we had stopped years before. The RFU would have to pick up the extra expense. If they didn't, the players would have done it themselves. The management board at the RFU agreed, and signed off on the expense. They too had been on a journey of sorts, and they were up to speed on how the team needed to operate.

But leaving nothing to chance, we needed more. The IRB allowed for twelve members of the support team, and that was not enough for me. After careful consideration I felt that eighteen people were essential for England's success. On this, however, the management board didn't agree; they felt that four people on our World Cup support team were unnecessary. These were:

Referee Steve Lander: In the last World Cup, the IRB had changed a ruling about lineouts just before a crucial pool match, and I wasn't taking any risks with this one. Steve Lander, I felt, was important to the team because, the day before each game, we always met the match referee, and Steve could speak their language and understand their leanings and preferences. We also had him working in training sessions, refereeing every contact situation. Any player stupidly giving away a penalty would get it from everyone: 'You've just cost us the World Cup. How does it feel?' He was just like another coach. As it turned out, his guidance and expertise would prove vital.

Chef Dave Campbell: Dave was one of the senior chefs at Pennyhill Park, and Dave Reddin had been working with him for years to perfect our players' nutrition programme. Dave Campbell knew exactly what we wanted, and would make certain that no bad or spoiled food products would make it to our tables. Of course we didn't suspect any foul play when Jonny had got sick in South

Africa back in 2000, but I was not going to take any chances with the team this time. So I couldn't see how we could go without him. You just can't teach every hotel's chef a new way of doing things. As it was, the hotels where we stayed were incredibly co-operative with Dave, and very interested in his vast knowledge of sports nutrition.

Visual Awareness Coach Sherylle Calder: It was almost unthinkable for me to travel to Australia without Sherylle Calder. Her training programmes were a huge hit with the players and she was needed every day to supervise and give feedback to selected individuals. Her work was enjoyable, and the friendly competition between players that it created was also very healthy. Her CTC had added strength to our defence and had helped to improve our attacking game. It was thanks to her training that we were rarely out of position.

QC Richard Smith: I just had a hunch that we would need to have a good legal advisor at hand. Without pointing to any single specific reason why we should need him, I could think of hundreds of scenarios where we might. Who could possibly foresee the trouble we might get into, given some unusual combination of circumstances? Taking Richard Smith along certainly attracted a lot of adverse attention, but I argued that having a professional, balanced legal mind available might well be needed if a major situation arose.

A resourceful solution

The members of the management board felt they had already pushed the boat out far enough to help me with the extra expenses for the players, but with these extra support people I was getting into an area where they couldn't help me. So, as long as it didn't warrant any extra costs, I was left to my own devices. Either I found a way to make it happen, or they stayed at home.

Two companies sorted it out by offering sponsorship. Uncle Ben's Rice, a division of Master Foods, offered to sponsor our chef David Campbell if the media were allowed to cover the England squad's diet during the World Cup. I spoke with some friends at the *Sun* newspaper and offered them exclusive rights to report on what chef David was feeding the team. They loved the idea, and so pictures of David and stories of our menu went out to the nation in the *Sun*'s home segment. EBS, the electronic broking service for foreign exchange, agreed to sponsor David's hat. We put their logo on his chef's hat and that went into every picture during the tournament too.

As an added bonus, we invited both companies to bring a few of their special clients along to Pennyhill Park to meet the players, to watch, and even to take part in training – something that was unique. We were happy to do it when these partners were helping us out so much. Between the two, we raised enough money in sponsorship to fund our four extra people, plus we put a bit back into the RFU. Both Francis and the management board were happy with the outcome. I would like to thank both companies for their invaluable support; these individuals certainly made a massive difference to our success.

Of course, the reports in the Australian media were very critical of the fact that we had a chef, a referee, a QC, and a host of medical and therapeutic specialists. As for the resources side, yes, the RFU did have the largest player base, to the best of my knowledge, but no, we didn't have huge budgets for the elite squad. As I understood it, we actually had smaller budgets than our main rivals. But we'd always been in a situation where we had to learn to do more with less, and we had become very resourceful over the years. Our extra people were not paid a salary to come to the World Cup; they were happy simply to come along for the experience. In fact they probably would have paid their own expenses, but I just felt it wouldn't be right. I was grateful that each one of them was with us, and they proved invaluable team-members.

No one else in the squad but Francis Baron knew what I was doing to make everything work. All that the players knew was that everything was perfectly in place. There were absolutely no excuses for not winning. We had taken care of every contingency imaginable. It was the opportunity of a lifetime which all of them had dreamed about for years.

So I just listened to criticism over our budgets and got on with it. My attitude must have seemed strange to everyone else.

Settling in

From the time we arrived we had ten days in Perth to get settled into the climate and time zone of Australia. Because of our excellent preparation, we were ready, so our time leading up to the first pool match, against Georgia, was simply about having lots of rest, recovering from jetlag, and getting used to the warm dry weather customary in Australia. Apart from a few light runs on the pitch, we didn't do a lot of training. We had a very relaxed week and a half.

It really helped that we were in familiar surroundings. A part of our strategy in coming down to Australia for the summer tour had been to spend extra time visiting the hotels and playing facilities we would see in the World Cup. As I said before, after we left Melbourne in late June I had deliberately stopped with the team for three days in Perth. This was in line with our attitude to logistics and the benefit of familiarity at Pennyhill Park.

None of the players had really wanted to do this. They had just finished a tough season and an even tougher summer tour, and were longing to get home to their families and their beds. They could have done just that by hopping on the first plane, and it was a real testament to the Teamship of the senior players that they went along with the idea. So for three days we had stayed at the Sheraton hotel, practised at the nearby school which would be our training ground, and ran light sessions at the Subiaco Oval. England had never played in Perth before. South Africa however had only recently played the Wallabies there. I didn't want that to be an advantage in their favour.

Incidentally, while we were in Perth during the summer we had also done a one-on-one debrief with each player. You might think that this would be a regular part of coaching at an elite level – feeding back extensive information to players on their strengths and weaknesses – but we rarely have time to do it in the course of our training. The players normally travel home the day after a Test match, and we didn't have sufficient training days or Test week days to speak to everyone in this kind of detail about their individual games. The players didn't necessarily like these debriefing sessions because they were long and exacting, as with employee reviews, but they fully co-operated, and I believe it made a massive difference to our summer training.

So those three days of mental preparation in the summer had been designed to reduce the risk of any disruptions due to an unfamiliar environment. We had been to Melbourne to play Australia, so that base was covered, but we hadn't yet been to Brisbane or Sydney. That would of course have displayed the presumption that we were definitely going to make it to the quarter-finals, but I regret not doing it. It was an oversight that would cost us dearly and indeed nearly ended our World Cup tournament.

But that was later. First we had Georgia and South Africa to think about. I always believed that the South Africa game would be our most important match. Like the All Blacks pool match in 1999, I believed that if we won that game we would make it to the final. Thankfully, by the beginning of the tournament, we were quite at home in Perth and ready for anything.

Warming up in Perth

For our first match in the World Cup, against Georgia on 12 October at the Subiaco Oval, Perth, there was a lot of debate about whether we should send out our strongest team against comparative minnows. The second match we were to play, against South Africa, was the big game of the tournament for us, a must-win game, and I felt we needed to start the whole thing with our strongest team, and take the risk of injury. As it turned out we lost both Richard Hill and Matt Dawson in that Georgia game – two of our best players – but we compensated well, and that's where our strength-in-depth policy paid off, because Kyran Bracken played fantastically well against South Africa, and it was Hill's replacement, Lewis Moody, who charged down the South African fly half Louis Koen's clearance kick. That charge-down set up a try for Will Greenwood, which was probably the crucial point in the match, shifting domination decisively in England's direction.

While on the subject of Moody's charge-down skills, I should point out he did another near charge-down on Mat Rogers in the last minutes of the World Cup final a month later, causing Rogers to slice his kick. It was from the resulting lineout, of course, that England built up a situation which allowed Jonny Wilkinson to score the drop goal that made England world champions.

The Georgia match was a good beginning, a win for us by 84—6. They were quite a tough team, not a bad side at all, but after a slow start we got into our stride and began to play some good rugby. Jonny Wilkinson got the show on the road with a penalty, although it had taken time to break down the Georgians, and they also slotted a penalty in the eighth minute. Then Mike Tindall went over after a good forward drive, Wilkinson breaking the first line of defence before off-loading. Steve Thompson got the third with a pick-up from the back of a ruck. Then Neil Back secured our bonus point with the fourth. Georgia never gave up, but in all we ran in twelve tries for an 84—6 win that was pretty satisfactory except for those two injuries. Greenwood got a brace of tries, so did Ben Cohen, while there was one each for Robinson, Tindall, Dawson, Thompson, Dallaglio, Back, and replacements Luger and Regan. Jonny Wilkinson was his usual dead-eye with the boot, landing seven kicks from seven.

Preparing for South Africa

Feeling confident we were playing well as a team, we had just six days to prepare for what was in my mind our key match in the tournament. Like New Zealand in our pool match in '99, if any team was going to disrupt England's road to the World Cup, it would be South Africa in Perth. For those six days leading up to the match, we had to stay focused. Two rather strange occurrences served to bolster my confidence.

I discovered quite by accident that the South African team were training with tackle bags marked with England players' numbers, No. 10 for example for Jonny Wilkinson. That was OK, but I also heard how they were being highly aggressive with these tackle bags and targeting certain ones. To my mind it wasn't a great way to prepare a team for a test match. I had also got wind of some very unusual training that the Springbok side had been involved with before the World Cup. More of this was to surface later, but none of it was conducive to a regular Test match encounter. All it did was to give me even greater confidence in our team.

Above: In a key game of the World Cup campaign, against South Africa, Will Greenwood scores after a great Lewis Moody charge down. We were on the way.

Right: Jason Robinson carves through the Welsh defence in the quarter-final in Brisbane. After a very nervous first half, we won our way through to the semis.

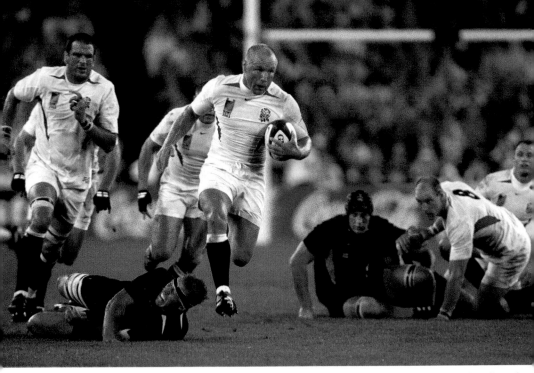

Against France in the semi-final, Neil Back was world class and, along with Richard Hill and Lawrence Dallaglio, nullified the French back row into insignificance.

In the final, Martin Johnson, as always, led by example. No one in the history of English rugby deserved to lift the Cup more than he did.

To play great rugby union is one thing, to play in two codes is quite another. I cannot speak highly enough of Jason Robinson and it is fitting that he scored England's only try.

Look at the players' faces. Jonny Wilkinson, the world's greatest player, encapsulated six years of work with his drop goal in that one magic moment.

Just after the final whistle, words failed us.

One Team with the World Cup.

Was it all worth it? Yes.

Back in England, Freddie joined us at Pennyhill Park, more thrilled to see Jonny and the World Cup than to see me.

The Queen honoured the team with an invitation to Buckingham Palace. She seemed to enjoy the occasion almost as much as we did.

The news of a knighthood was announced while I was with the family in Verbier. This was one skiing holiday I didn't miss.

Jayne and I playing the 11th at Augusta – Amen Corner was more spectacular than I could ever have imagined.

What a great year – 2003. With rugby's most prized trophies (*left to right*): the Six Nations Trophy (Grand Slam), World Cup, Calcutta Cup and Cook Cup.

There are some events in World Cup rugby that you simply cannot prevent or prepare for. One of those happened to the England team the very next day. We were in our final training session on Friday before the game when all of a sudden the press swooped down on our private session at the school. Cars and vans flooded the car park, people came running with their cameras and microphones, and no less than three helicopters were hovering fifty metres over the pitch. We had security guards maintaining our privacy, and were trained to deal with pressure, but this was something different altogether – it's a bit hard to talk over the sound of a hovering helicopter, let alone concentrate.

Apparently what attracted the media was a rumour that Prince Harry, then on a gap year working at a country property in a remote part of Queensland, was here to watch our last training session. Everyone, of course, wanted his picture.

'Look, I know we've had a few injuries,' I told them, 'but we're not at the stage where we have to call Prince Harry into the squad. I assure you he's not here.' The press still refused to believe me. Of course, Prince Harry wouldn't have dreamed of interrupting our training sessions. He just wanted to be there for the game. He and his brother have been great supporters of the team for many years and we've enjoyed their enthusiasm.

If it had happened earlier in the week, it would have been less of an issue, but in the day before a match your sessions have to be absolutely private and confidential. We set our whole series of calls and our player line-up around the analysis we have on the other team. If that was leaked on the Friday before the game, we wouldn't have any time to change our strategy by the next day.

All I could do was to call the team in and tell them not to panic. We would just get on with it, like always. We changed our final training slightly in terms of the last team run, and then committed to rehearsing our play just a little bit more than usual in our walk-through at Subiaco Oval the next day.

I suppose I could have made a massive scene about the situation, but that would simply have attracted yet more unwanted critical attention. Under the laws of the land, there was nothing we could do to stop it, and that was exactly what the ARU advised when we made a few quiet enquiries in the following days. I felt it was against the spirit of the competition and tournament and even in violation of the RFU's participation agreement, but how on earth can you stop something like that?

South Africa

By the time of the World Cup I had been doing the coaching job for England for six years, and I can say that the pool match against South Africa was the most pressurised game I'd ever been involved in. The pressure on the team to win that match was huge, because we all felt that if we won it we would go on to win the World Cup. Also there was a lot of history to the game because of what had happened at Twickenham in autumn 2002. So it was a colossal occasion. You can look at it from the stands and say we didn't really do that well, but under that amount of pressure I think the team played really, really well to win 25—6.

There was a lot from some South Africans before that game about Martin Johnson being a dirty player and so on, and I still don't understand why some teams, be they the Australians, the South Africans, the French, whoever, continued to try and wind our guys up. Our players just sat quietly in our camp – everyone just took it on board without a word. I would have gone nuts if any of our guys had made statements like that about other players, but they just didn't seem to learn. The best way is to say nothing, because all those comments just helped us.

People also said that we missed Richard Hill. Richard is a world-class player, but so is Lewis Moody. In this instance, I don't think Richard would have made that much difference. We beat South Africa fair and square in a World Cup game, and people were still asking questions – but that was a game we had to win. And win it we did, by a good margin. What's more, Moody's charge-down was critical. Incidentally, that charge-down was no fluke. We had been working on the technique, and Moody knew how to do it, it's a technical thing.

We took the lead early on with Jonny Wilkinson kicking a penalty. Both Robinson and Cohen were looking threatening, especially when Cohen nearly created a try for Mike Tindall in the eleventh minute, but we still hadn't broken through to their line. Koen landed a penalty to get South Africa off the mark, and then he notched up another just before the break. But in the second half our backs were looking increasingly dangerous as the game went on, and Wilkinson racked up a couple of penalties, even though we still hadn't yet gone over for a try. The killer blow for the Springboks came at the end of the third quarter with Will Greenwood's score from Moody's charge-down. Jonny slotted two more drop goals to ease England clear, so in the second half we scored 19 points without letting the Springboks through at any stage. That meant it was just about certain that we would go through to the knockout stages with quarter- and semi-final matches against Wales and France. It was also England's fifth successive win against the Springboks.

We'd won. In my view our biggest potential stumbling block was now out of the way. Assuming we won against Samoa and Uruguay, we would meet Wales in the quarter-final in Brisbane instead of playing the All Blacks for our semi-final berth. Just over two weeks into the tournament we were feeling good.

28

IN STRIFE IN MELBOURNE

We flew to Melbourne on Sunday for our next pool match against Samoa in seven days' time, and checked back into the Sheraton Towers where we had stayed when we beat Australia just a few months before. Everything was very familiar, and that of course made a major difference psychologically.

The selection options for this match were excellent, and we felt we were able to rest quite a few key players, unlike in the '99 World Cup. In those days I wasn't confident of the experience of our second team, but in this World Cup there was a very small margin between the starting XV and the rest of the squad, and it was highly confidence-boosting to know we had a depth of players that hadn't been there before. However, that's not to take anything away from the Samoans. They are a team you always have to watch, and they have the ability to beat anyone on their day.

So in selecting for the Samoa match we changed a few of the players, brought in some new faces, and moved the squad around a bit. And sure enough, the Samoans gave us a scare in the opening stages – the way they played that day would have caused problems for every single team in the championship. I knew we had the team to win it, but Samoa were a very, very good side, and they scored one cracking try. All the same, at the end of the day we won the game comfortably, and that's what you've got to look at. Too many people were getting carried away after the match with how the team was playing, rather than that we were the team who actually won the game. The World Cup was about winning, and moving on to the next game.

The Samoans got in front with a penalty in the fourth minute, but the excitement really started two minutes later when they attacked from deep, moving the ball very fast from the breakdown and spreading it wide. Lome Fa'atau made a clear break down the wing and a superb passage of continuity play ended with their captain Semo Sititi charging over for the try. That was the first try we had conceded in the World Cup. Earl Va'a's conversion made that 10—0 within ten minutes of play.

Our forwards took the game to them up front after that, and the pack's dominance led to a pushover try for Neil Back. Two penalties from Jonny – who had earlier missed a sitter, to everyone's jaw-dropping disbelief – against two of theirs saw us trailing by 16—13 at the break.

In the third quarter we made some changes, with Thompson, Moody and Vickery coming on for Regan, Worsley and White, and the forwards' constant pressure on the Samoan line earned us a penalty try in the fifty-second minute, which put us ahead for the first time, until Va'a lined up another penalty to make it 22—20.

Wilkinson cancelled that with a drop goal, and then put up a brilliant kick behind the Samoan defence for Iain Balshaw, who dived over for the try, a signature move of Dave Aldred. Phil Vickery added another after the England backs ran some explosive plays, and with the conversions we were ahead 35—22. That was about it, although the Samoans kept coming right to the finish. The crowd rose to them at the end for their part in the best match of the tournament so far. It was a great World Cup game, and they had some fantastic players. Someone at the IRB has got to make a serious decision and some serious investment in those Pacific Island countries. If they do that, then I think a Samoan team capable of winning the World Cup is a definite possibility. Otherwise, their great players are always going to go and qualify for other countries. Certainly New Zealand has taken huge advantage of that. But for the World Cup to grow we have to keep adding teams, not reducing them.

Sixteen men on the pitch – QC

Although Samoa had tested us the whole way, England's fitness and Second-Half Thinking told in the end. But with only a few minutes on the clock, the England team were confronted with as grave a situation as we could have imagined: an unfortunate accident which turned into something that came close to derailing England's tournament hopes.

It all happened innocently enough. When a player goes off the pitch for injury or blood replacement, for that moment there are only fourteen men on the pitch playing rugby. If that happens at a critical time, it can be a disadvantage which may just cost the game. So we'd been practising the steps we would take in such an eventuality, and in particular the importance of everyone on the bench keeping an eye on the game so that we never missed the opportunity to get a replacement player on without any delay. The entire squad had been training all week on this system of ours for bringing substitutes onto the pitch. We stepped our players through how to handle the situation: if you're told to get off or you have an injury, always walk to the substitute, and always work it so that there is a minimum time with fewer players. Quite simply, we had a policy of not playing unless we had fifteen men on the pitch.

In those dying few minutes against Samoa, Mike Tindall had received an injury and limped off the other side of the pitch to have it sorted out. Meanwhile, I was up in the coaches' box liaising via Andy Robinson, who was on the microphone communicating with the coaches at the touchline. I hated being in the box because you never got to see what was really going on. In this instance, I saw that Tindall had gone off, leaving fourteen men on the pitch, and I also knew we had Dan Luger ready to go on in his place. Now I couldn't believe what I was seeing. We had practised this all week and here was the exact scenario we were trying to prevent. I shouted into the microphone to get Luger on, now!

Dave Reddin had been managing the touchline for England brilliantly. But all through the game he had been having a challenging time with the fifth official, Steve Walsh, something I was not aware of. For every match there is a referee on the pitch, two touch judges, and then a fourth and a fifth official whose jobs are to keep an eye on each of the two teams and see that the substitutions are made correctly. Steve Walsh was the fifth official in charge of the Samoan side and should have had nothing to do with own side. Dave is a solid character and good under pressure, but he's not one to take a step back in the heat of the game. Tindall was off the pitch on the other side of the field. When I shouted into the microphone to get Luger on, Dave did just that, practically shoving him in the back to send him past the touch judge. Steve Walsh was unhappy about this, and to make things worse Mike Tindall must have realised he hadn't followed our system because he then promptly stepped back onto the pitch.

For thirty-two seconds, England had sixteen men on the pitch in the final minutes of a game that, though hard fought, was clearly ours. The mistake was soon rectified and there was no advantage either way as a result, so in terms of the outcome of the game it really wasn't a major issue.

It's actually not all that uncommon an occurrence, either. In the heat of the game, when the pressure is on, mistakes like this are prone to happen. That was exactly why we had been practising the substitution routine. England might not have been in much trouble over it, but for one small event which compounded the problem.

The altercation between Dave Reddin and Steve Walsh had worsened after the match, sending Dave Reddin to the match commissioner to report the incident. This was really a non-event, but it added heat to the situation and gave everyone cause to call a full and formal enquiry. England were now at risk of facing disciplinary action, not just for the incidents on the touchline but for the extra man on the pitch, too. There are no hard and fast rules for what happens in the scenario like ours of having an extra man on the pitch. That meant the rules and therefore the punishment would be fully open to interpretation, and you could bet that anyone who might have wanted England to be fined, docked points on the competition table, or even disqualified from the tournament, would be pulling out all the stops to make it happen.

Called to court

On Monday the team flew into the Gold Coast, a beach-side city about an hour's drive south of Brisbane. We had planned an easy week leading up to the Uruguay match in Brisbane, but now I, Dave Reddin and a few of the players had been called to an official hearing in Sydney by the IRB. No sooner had we arrived at the Gold Coast than we had to board another plane to Sydney. I could tell from the tone of the summons that it was going to get difficult. I was just thankful we had Richard Smith, our QC and legal advisor, on the team. I could never have anticipated this particular series of events, but it just goes to show the level of preparation required to operate successfully at this elite level.

In court Richard Smith was simply brilliant. The matter was held before a disciplinary committee in a court room in Sydney, and a solicitor representing the IRB lined up against our QC over the allegations. The gentleman chairing the committee was Irish and had an extensive legal background. The difference in experience between Richard and the solicitor acting on behalf of the IRB was clear. The IRB may have thought they were going to give us a hard time, but Richard dismantled their arguments with quiet and incisive ease. I was following the events as best I could but wasn't too certain of all the nuances. But when we went into a meeting room during a short recess I found the normally quiet Richard was more than cross.

I'd missed it, but apparently everyone had agreed there would be certain issues that would not be brought into the argument. The other solicitor was floundering and so had reverted to the issues which had been ruled out. Richard was furious, and after the break went on the front foot. Even to my non-legal brain it was obvious he was simply destroying their argument.

In the end, England was given a fine of £10,000 and Dave Reddin was banned from the touchline for two weeks. Dave of course did not deserve this but took it on the chin and got on with the business of winning the next game. Flying back to the Gold Coast, I finally breathed a sigh of relief. We had made a mistake but had got away with it, avoiding loss of competition points or, the worst case scenario, disqualification from the tournament. I'm just glad I stuck to my guns and brought Richard along when many were questioning the validity.

As for Richard, well, he was worth his weight in gold. This disciplinary hearing showed him at his best and he never thought about charging the RFU for his services. He was just delighted to have seven weeks as part of the England rugby team. It's awesome the way great partnerships work. I intend to travel with Richard Smith again!

TESTED IN BRISBANE 29

For everyone else who didn't have the pleasure of flying to Sydney to watch Richard Smith QC in action, Zurich had organised a golf tournament for the players. It's funny that the only person who was really interested in golf was at a disciplinary hearing on the one day we had golf on the agenda. Dave Reddin likes a game of golf too, but he didn't get one either. I'd still wager I'm the only coach ever to bring his golf clubs with him to the World Cup. Apart from the golf day, I'm not sure when I thought I'd get to use them, but you never know. So far everything had gone well in our preparation and on the pitch. We had escaped in Sydney for our transgression against Samoa. From there it should have been a relatively easy couple of weeks to the semi-final. But then, just when I thought everything was going right, the wheels started to fall off in the England camp.

England rugby is all about 'head space'. When we have focused preparation, and get our head space right without distractions, we're unstoppable. When distractions cloud our mind, our preparation suffers. In Queensland, our distractions came in the form of a lack of privacy – the media and press journalists were booked to stay in the same hotel as the team. Usually we will do everything we can to avoid this happening because we like to be aware of the times when we are on or off duty. It's not that the media meant to be a distraction. Indeed, I'm sure they would have been horrified if they had known. We normally get along really well and work as partners. It was just that, during our supposed rest week on the Gold Coast, the players couldn't go anywhere to relax in the hotel. It was absolutely the wrong situation. The team were meant to be having a break, a chance to get away from everything. The stories of the courtroom drama from the previous week were still hanging around, and the journalists were being driven by their editors to fill more newspaper inches with copy.

Meanwhile, there was the Uruguay match, where England played well against an obviously weaker side. They weren't one of the better sides and we beat them 111—13 to go into the knockout stages with a record of played four, won four. I picked Dallaglio for that game, which meant he went through the whole tournament playing every single second of every single game. At the time people were saying we should rest him, but we thought he would benefit from the extra game, so he needed to play. That Uruguay game really got him back to his best, and by the time of the semi-final I think there's no doubt he was definitely one of the standout players.

Wales quarter-final

If the distractions were bad before the Uruguay match, they were even worse in the lead up to our quarter-final match against Wales. We had moved to the Hilton in Brisbane and unfortunately the journalists had moved too – again into the same hotel. It has an atrium which goes from the hotel lobby right to the ceiling. Clear-glass lifts face into the atrium, and from them you can look down into the coffee lounge and restaurant as well as the whole lobby which is all open-plan. Just trying to get out for a quiet coffee or a sandwich was a problem. It was disconcerting for everyone.

Another problem was that in that week of the quarter-final the players had their wives and families joining them. We've always believed that for a long tour like this it was good for everyone to spend time with loved ones. However, the media were unaccustomed to seeing us operate as a group at such close quarters, particularly with our families during what should have been private times. The close proximity and constant observation of the journalists only prompted more questions, criticism and intrusions. So the two weeks of preparation in Queensland was not our best period, to say the least. It all caught up with us, and it showed on the pitch against Wales.

That first forty minutes in the World Cup quarter-final at the Suncorp Stadium, Brisbane was probably the worst England had played for four years. In fact, we'd saved our worst forty minutes since the '99 World Cup for the Welsh in the 2003 World Cup.

We fielded a full-strength squad against a team we had beaten 26—9 only six months before in the Grand Slam, but Wales played a great game, and we were falling apart. For the first time, I think everyone was focused on the next match, not the one at hand. Wilkinson missed his first penalty but slotted the second. Then a terrible cross-field kick went down the throat of Shane Williams, who ripped our defence to shreds for Stephen Jones to score. Not long after that, Colin Charvis turned down an easy pot at goal to go for the lineout, and helped himself to a try. At half time we were down 10—3. There was a real chance we would blow the whole tournament right here in this match.

Walking down to the changing room, visions of John Hart's post-1999 demise in New Zealand crowded my mind. There was no question, if we lost in the quarter-final to an admittedly in-form Wales side, there would be no going home to my job or perhaps even to England at all! We were going to get on a plane the next day, and at this stage of the tournament it was either going to be a flight to Sydney or a flight to London. I've since told Jayne that if we'd lost, we would probably have moved to Cuba!

Tensions were high at half time. We are usually quite calm and businesslike in creating the right conditions for starting the second half of a game. Not today. Johnno was at his best and – in the way that only Johnno can – simply reminded everyone that he had no intention of going home after this match. This gave Robbo and me a few precious minutes to make some changes to the team. We were under huge pressure, and we had to get it right. Greenwood was playing well, so too was Tindall, but under pressure Jonny was having to get stuck into the rucks, which he has no problem doing, but we didn't have another naturally good kicker there in support. So we moved Tindall to the wing and brought on Mike Catt to share the mid-field duties with Wilko.

The second half was different. It was the whole team, not just Mike – though he did make a big difference in taking the pressure off Wilkinson's kicking game. Jason Robinson took a lineout to himself on the edge of his own 22, double-side-stepped through an invisible gap in the Wales midfield, stepped on the gas a little, and disappeared down the middle with a change of pace that left the Welsh on their backsides. He sprinted sixty metres before unloading to Will Greenwood who went over in the corner. Wilkinson converted, and after that Jonny began to put over kicks from everywhere. Jonny Wilkinson was fantastic that day – my man of the match. The Welsh did manage to close the gap to eight points when Iestyn Harris's cross-field kick put Martyn Williams over in the corner, but we held on to win by 28—17.

I was extremely relieved. Under the most pressure we made the correct calls – this is what experience brings to a major competition. Thinking correctly under pressure at half time saved us. The Welsh were a very good team – I knew to my own cost that they would always be very competitive – but I also knew that if we played like that against the French, we'd have no chance, so we were going to have to up the ante.

Losing it with the press

In the press conference immediately following the game I'd had enough.

On top of the distractions of the previous week from the media, now even our own stalwart English journalists seemed to be turning against us. Even though we'd won against Wales, we hadn't won that well, and the journalists all seemed to believe that they'd been watching the true England side. In short, and I know it's a generalization so I apologise to any journalist who still had faith in England, they seemed to have collectively put their belief in France to win the semi-final the following week. They all wanted to know why England had played so poorly. I wasn't giving anything away, and that made them simply more aggressive in their questioning.

There was one French journalist from *L'Equipe* newspaper in particular who really went to town on it. He kept asking questions that underlined what he saw as England's inability to perform when it mattered. It wasn't so much the questions as much as his tone. He picked on Jonny Wilkinson several times as highly underperforming. It just wasn't true.

'All this money on preparation and you're lucky to win in a quarter-final match against Wales.' As if we were already beaten by France and should hold our heads in disgrace.

I went on the front foot. Every now and again you just have to let loose.

Jonny didn't warrant any more pressure, and this was heading in the wrong direction. I decided to give them something better to talk about. I will meet pressure with pressure if that's what it takes, and I'm not a politician trying to get elected, I'm a rugby coach.

'Mate, we are where we are. We'll be right for next week. You think we've had a poor game and you've written us off. Well I'm confident. The French couldn't beat us last time and they won't this time.'

Everyone thought I'd completely lost the plot. It was clear to them now that England had no hope against France. From that moment everyone began predicting a France vs New Zealand final. There were two people who thought it would be England vs Australia, me and Eddie Jones – one of the few times we have agreed.

The media had been around the hotel so much over the past two weeks, they'd seen the players at rest trying to relax with their jetlagged families, returning from a strenuous training session, and even just out of bed eating breakfast. It was all very normal, but they read too much into it – do you know anyone who looks their best at breakfast!

Looking back now even I see the irony. Here I am almost paranoid about preparation, and the only hotels and venues we didn't visit with the team in planning our tournament were the Gold Coast and Brisbane. So as not to send the wrong message of misplaced assurance to our competitors or the world's rugby media, we hadn't visited Brisbane. We had researched the hotels and found they were adequate (Louise had visited them and we were happy with them), but I hadn't expected to be sharing them with quite so many journalists. It's no mistake then that these two locations turned into the only places where all the players were uncomfortable and a bit out of sorts. It amazes me how many times I have to learn this lesson about preparation and mindset.

The ramifications of losing the quarter-final to Wales that day would have been huge, but that is sport. It made me realise that, although I might at times seem unreasonable in my demands for thorough prep-aration and the need for the correct environment for the team, it was warranted. My belief has only been strengthened. You have to look for the unexpected and try to cover every base. It may seem as if we have developed a maniacal approach to this area, but that week was a prime example of Dislocated Expectation nearly getting the better of us. As we boarded the plane to fly to Sydney, we had scraped through our greatest individual and personal challenge of the tournament. We were all now acutely aware of what it meant to lose our concentration and underperform. There was a lot of thinking on that flight south.

Semi-final in Sydney

In the coach from the airport I began thinking about where we were staying for the next week. Unlike the journalists who doubted England's form, I was supremely confident about the coming week's game.

Some months before, when Louise had been organising hotel details for the eventuality that we would make the quarter-final, semi-final and final, she had checked six different hotels where we might stay, depending on how our pool matches went and which quarter-final we found ourselves in. Subsequently, when she rattled off the names of the four possible hotels in Sydney, one in particular stood out.

The Manly Pacific. I knew it well. England had stayed there in 1999 when we played the centenary game in our pre-World Cup summer tour at what was then Stadium Australia. It was also the hotel where Jayne and I had first stayed when we arrived in Sydney all those years ago.

On the coach, going through the familiar streets of Manly, I couldn't help but think back over the incredible journey I'd been on since my first days here in Sydney. The frustration I had felt for England rugby at the end of my international career was now completely transformed into a passion for winning and building an elite England set-up to make it happen. When I first set foot on Manly beach, I never thought it would. Now here I was driving along the esplanade towards the hotel. It was for me a little surreal. This place had been a very large part of my life. I'd lived here, played here, married Jayne here, and we'd had two great children in the Manly Cottage Hospital up the road. Now here I was back, coach of the England team and fighting to win a World Cup. Funny how things work out sometimes, isn't it?

Jayne arrived from Brisbane later in the day. The room we had was just above the very same room where we'd stayed in 1985. I felt good. We were in Sydney. The team were ready. The management were fantastic. Everyone was doing just what they had to do. Energy levels were high.

France in the semi-final

Our semi-final game against France on 16 November was the fourth match of the year against them, and we won it convincingly 24—7. The French afterwards said that the weather had been against them, but the last time we'd played them, at Twickenham, we had put 40 points past them in a game that was played in perfect conditions. The truth is we were hoping for the same, and were disappointed to see the rain bucketing down. I believe England would have had the advantage if the conditions had been perfect. But we played very well in the wet – in fact England were just fantastic. We did really, really well; that was our best game in the World Cup by a mile.

But I can't help thinking France had lost the game before they'd even walked onto the pitch. I think mentally they made a big error by announcing that Fabien Galthié would be retiring after the World Cup. None of our guys did that, world cups are not retirement parties. To me, the French seemed too concerned about Galthié and his last game for France, and I thought the retirement announcement should have been left until January. Besides getting mixed up about that, the French also seemed to lose all confidence when the rain started to pour down, even when then they were still in the bus going to the ground, or so I heard. They seemed to have decided they couldn't win the game because it was raining. Frankly I was staggered, I just couldn't understand their attitude. As I said at the press conference after the game, I had been on holiday in France and I knew it rained there too. It's a nonsense to think those rainy conditions particularly suited England. What I was trying to say was that firm conditions were the best for us. We were a very skilful team; the front row of Woodman, Thompson, Vickery – these guys could all run, handle ball, do the works, so we wanted perfect conditions. But the wet didn't faze us in the least because our mindset was that we were determined to win whether it was blowing a hurricane or it was 100 degrees. We played the conditions and we played extremely well. The World Cup was about winning, and I kept saying to everyone that it was about winning. Well, we won again, and now we were in the World Cup final, and I told the people at the press conference that this team could beat anyone, anywhere at any time, in any conditions.

Our whole team was playing really well. I think Dallaglio and Back especially were outstanding that night. They sorted out the French danger men, Betsen and Michalak for instance; they just didn't give them any space or time at all. The pressure had its effect, because the French looked a beaten team to me fairly early on. It's amazing how strong the mind is. I honestly think they'd decided it wasn't going to be their night. Which was great for us.

After ten minutes Jonny was in a decent position for a drop goal which he put over. But very soon afterwards Betsen grabbed a loose ball from the back of a lineout and crashed over the England line. Michalak put over a wonderful conversion from the touchline in pouring rain, but that was the only one he slotted in the whole match, and that solitary converted try was France's only score.

The French discipline wasn't great after that. Their wing Christophe Dominici had to trip Jason Robinson when he was steaming past him, and that got him a yellow card, plus he injured himself in the process of fouling Jason and was out of the game permanently. Our forwards were exerting terrific pressure, and Jonny had one easy penalty, then a neat drop goal, and finally a tremendous long-distance shot that put us 12—7 ahead at the break.

More French frustration in the second half saw Betsen sin-binned for a late tackle on Wilkinson, which Jonny punished by slotting a penalty that put clear water between the sides. Then he put over a superb drop from the back of the ruck, and their coach Bernard Laporte called off Michalak and brought on Merceron. That didn't make much difference and, although it would have been nice to score, we spent the last quarter of the game camped in their 22. It was good to be able to bring on Jason Leonard not long before time – that was his 112th cap, a world record.

The French really seemed to fall apart in the second half, which surprised us. We certainly put huge pressure on their fly half Michalak, and when they took him off it seemed like it was game over. And even more significant was when they took off their prop, Jean-Jacques Crenca, a world-class player in that French pack whom we really respected. They took him off when there was still twenty minutes to go, and I thought, *Hullo, they've given up*.

It's worth noting too that when the final whistle went, our guys just shook hands and walked off the pitch – no celebrations with the crowd – despite the fact that we were in the final and England supporters were all round us cheering their heads off. In the other semi-final, where Australia beat New Zealand, the Australians did a huge lap of honour. Perhaps it was because they were playing at home, or maybe it was a spontaneous celebration of a great win against the All Blacks. Either way I remember watching that and thinking, *Interesting, that says a lot about their mindset*. What a contrast between the actions of our team and theirs: we saw the France match as another game we had to win so we could get to the final and win that too. No doubt Australia beat the All Blacks in a massive game. And it was not so different from the France–England match in that it was between two great rivals. But when I saw the Wallabies celebrating to that extent, it told me that perhaps they were relieved to get into the final and that maybe that game had been their World Cup final.

30
THE WORLD CUP FINAL

I had always thought it would be an England–Australia final. Like us, they hadn't played very well, whereas the All Blacks had played really well. But the All Blacks hadn't played any of the real heavies – they hadn't come up against any of them except South Africa. And I always believed Australia would beat the All Blacks. I said that if the final was between England and Australia, as I believed it would be, that to me would be the dream final. And so it proved. The occasion was so big, Australia, the host nation, against us. It was massive.

I realised from the end of the semi-final that this coming week was going to take some managing. I was determined to enjoy it and was even more determined that everyone in the squad was going to enjoy it too. In a meeting early on in the week I reminded everyone of the need to stay focused on what we were there to do – this was no time to get distracted by invitations or corporate hospitality. We would continue to work with our sponsors in all the normal ways that we do, but the possibility of the team being derailed by the huge interest in them was very considerable.

My week was just great. Professionally speaking I felt as though everything had come together for this one week. Everyone within the management team was awesome. I didn't see much of Phil Pask, Richard Wegrzyk or Barney Kenny, our physios, which meant they were doing exactly what they did best, looking after the players. These guys work incredibly hard and are so well respected by the players for it. They have a very special relationship with them.

The week flew by, the press conferences were rather upbeat affairs, I even managed to be fairly light-hearted myself. The journalists who'd written us off against the French were quick to get back behind the team, and I must say I enjoyed this week with the media more than any other. Not bad since that was before we'd won the World Cup.

Jess arrived in Sydney on the Wednesday and Joe arrived on Thursday. Together with Jayne we spent a good few hours of relaxation time visiting favourite places in Manly and sharing a few nice meals together.

The England fans were wonderful. Manly was full of them each day, and it gave us a great boost to have their backing.

So the scene was set. I found myself in the final team meeting, ready to board the coach to go to the stadium. I reminded everyone of the need to think correctly under pressure, we were not to get caught up in the emotion of the occasion. We should see it as another game and not leave anything on the training pitch. So, I asked them to all do their jobs, win and then we could go home.

My abiding memory of this week is of the eight players not selected to play or bench for the World Cup final. They were Julian White, Mark Regan, Simon Shaw, Joe Worsley, Andy Gomarsall, Paul Grayson, Dan Luger and Stuart Abbott. Danny Grewcock was in this list too although he had retired injured. They were magnificent in everything they did, the way they supported the team, trained with the team and handled their huge disappointment. That proved to me that the One Team concept worked under the most intense pressure imaginable. These players are the real heroes of the World Cup final week.

It was raining when Martin led the guys out that night in the Telstra Stadium in Sydney, but that didn't stop the Wallabies from moving the ball wide from the beginning, and coming at us, which suited us fine. But in the sixth minute they got a scrum in our 22, and their fly half Stephen Larkham, who had a great game, put up a brilliantly accurate bomb in the corner for his wing Lote Tuqiri to gather for a try. Flatley missed the conversion, and for the rest of the half we were on top.

Some good driving play gave a penalty for Wilkinson after 12 minutes. Then five minutes later Larkham had to go to the blood bin after trying to tackle Ben Cohen – and that was one of their key men off. What made it worse for Larkham was that while he was tackling Cohen the ball was miles away, so he gave away a penalty as well, which Jonny duly slotted. Not much later, Richard Hill pounced on an Australian error and took the ball through with his feet. From the ruck it went down the line for a certain try, but suddenly that went out of the window when Ben Kay spilled it with the line in front of him. Aargh! But then at least Wilkinson put us 9—5 ahead with another penalty.

We were still pressing, Mike Tindall raising hell down the left side, and then Jason Robinson took the ball to them, creating a ruck again on the left. Lawrence Dallaglio burst onto the ball at pace as Dawson fired it out, and he crashed through the Australian defence. Jonny was on his right and took it on further before spinning the ball out left to Jason Robinson. Jason was away, he just slid under the clutching arms and was over the line before they knew it. Try! It was one of the tournament's great moments.

Jonny missed the conversion, and at the break we went in 14—5 up, which if anything understated our dominance. Normally a very safe pair of hands, Ben Kay had dropped the ball on the line, and there'd been quite a few errors, so I think if we'd gone in about 25 ahead at half time that would have been a fair reflection.

Then in the second half, we had a mass of possession. Anyone watching the video will scratch his head and wonder how England could have had so much possession and still have lost that half 9—0. The answer is, you can't play rugby when you give away penalties every time you scrum. And we just gave away penalty after penalty. I thought we were a better team than Australia, going into that game, by quite a few points. But as it turned out, through all the circumstances, we ended up just shading it in the final minute of extra time. It was very strange. Scrums led to penalties, time after time.

As far as we were concerned we were just scrummaging. With Vickery and Woodman we had gone out there to destroy the Australian scrum, which is what we did. But in doing so we kept getting penalised because the referee saw it that way. The key change of the game was when we brought on Jason Leonard, who came on at full time for Phil Vickery. That was tough on Phil, because obviously he was having a fantastic game. But we were getting penalised for just scrummaging. So I said to Jason, 'With all your experience now, you sort it out.' And what Jason did to sort it out, and he's on record saying it, is: 'I went on, and I didn't scrummage.' It's anathema for a prop to go on and just lean and hold the scrum. But we were only going to lose that game if we went on giving away penalties. So he didn't do what Vickery or Woodman had done – it would mean getting penalised.

We were all over them at the start of the second half, but then we started getting penalised in the scrum, and making mistakes we didn't need to. Flatley put over a penalty in the forty-eighth minute, the first time they were in our territory, and again in the sixty-first. The Australian defence was good, and they didn't give away much. Jonny had a couple of misses with his drops, and every scrum was a major hassle for the ref. But we still had most of the possession and played most of the rugby. In the final quarter Will Greenwood was clear through, but Mat Rogers got his toe to the ball at the last minute and put it in touch – Will couldn't believe it! Then there was another bad scrum and another penalty – Flatley stepped forward and suddenly the score was 14—14. Our forwards had controlled the ball brilliantly throughout the second half, and here we were, coming out into an extra time of ten minutes each way after losing the half 9—0.

Extra time

In extra time Wilkinson put over a penalty from almost halfway, then he and Flatley exchanged penalties, making it 17—14 at the extra time break. We were still dominating, but English hands in the ruck gave Flatley a chance to make it 17—17, and it was a chance he took.

We were approaching the end of extra time. It was now or never.

Wilkinson took the restart and kicked long and hard down the middle, finding Wallaby flanker George Smith who ran into a white wall around his 22. Gregan got the ruck ball to Mat Rogers, who attempted to kick for a long touch, but sliced it. Now, Phil Larder had tirelessly drilled the players on charge-downs as the start of our counter-attack policy. As a replacement Lewis Moody had the freshest legs. He got right down the pitch and put the pressure on Rogers. It worked. Rogers's sliced kick meant it was England's throw in a lineout between the halfway line and the Australian 22.

England had just one minute and ten seconds on the clock to win the match. Luckily we had also been working on our performance under pressure in the last minutes of games. Everyone knew that it only took twenty seconds to score, and that if we could just make five phases we would have an 85 per cent chance of scoring either a try, or a penalty or a drop goal. Any one would do.

I was on my feet down at the touchline. I'd come down from the box at the halfway mark of extra time. This was no time to be away from the pitch. The whole team knew this was our chance.

The final minute of extra time

We all knew what had to happen. The Zigzag pattern would give us the best chance at drop goal. The touch judge put the ball in Steve Thompson's hands. Here we go.

Steve Thompson throws long and finds replacement flanker Lewis Moody at the tail.

We could all see the lineout call Ben Kay had made. It was a bold move, exactly what we would have wanted them to do. It's my guess that the whole of Australia, and most of England too, thought the ball was going to Martin Johnson at the front of the lineout. He was the safe bet. Clearly all the Wallabies in defence thought so, too. The close pass is always less risky than the long pass. More things can go wrong throwing it to the tail of the lineout, but that's exactly where Steve Thompson had gone with it. Ben Kay had made the correct decision under pressure. In that one moment, Simon Hardy's and Andy Robinson's countless hours since the North American tour in 2001 perfecting our lineouts paid off. Sherylle Calder's dedication to Steve's vision skills was also evident as the ball was perfectly thrown to Lewis Moody. Under pressure, at the end of the match, exhausted, our training prevailed.

Moody makes a clean take and the ball goes down the line to Mike Catt, who takes it on the burst, setting up a ruck.

Mike knew the Zigzag pattern like he'd written it. The first contact was essential. The hours and hours of contact drills with Andy Robinson all came together in that moment. Everyone executed the ruck perfectly.

Dawson delays the pass out, apparently waiting for Wilkinson to position himself for the drop everyone's expecting.

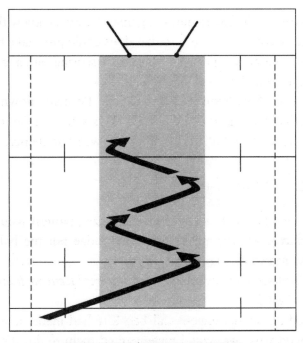

ENGLAND'S 'ZIGZAG' ROUTINE

Dawson had control of the game. He knew that Zigzag called for positioning Jonny Wilkinson right in front of the uprights. There were only fifty seconds on the clock now, but still he was in no rush. He could see we were too far out for a drop goal. That was thinking correctly under pressure. He knew he had to get a better position for Jonny.

But instead of passing, Dawson dummies and darts through, making ten to fifteen clear yards up the middle.

After countless hours analysing games with ProZone, Matt was clearly seeing the pitch as if from above. He saw the empty space on the pitch. And his fitness at this critical time after that gruelling hundred minutes of the match ensured he was still up for it. The incredible work by Dave Reddin and the medical support team to keep these men fit and fresh all came together. Even though we had a fresh scrum half on the bench, we were convinced Dawson's fitness and thinking were up to it. We were right.

Neil Back is at the base of the ruck that forms round Dawson, and he puts the ball out to Martin Johnson.

A half dozen people on the pitch could have filled the role left vacant by Dawson at the bottom of the ruck. Every movement of the ball was vital in those few seconds. Our thousands of drills for passing skills meant that we didn't have just one person who could handle that role. The Zigzag pattern was working perfectly. We were moving up field to within range.

Johnno crashes on another few yards, sucking in the Australian defenders, one of whom at least seems to come in illegally from the side.

The Wallabies all looked miles off-side, but there was no signal from the referee André Watson, not even an indication he would acknowledge the infringement. T-CUP again. The players knew where we were, they knew we were within range. Dawson came into the scrum half position at the back of the ruck. Standing on the touch line, Andy Gomarsall grabbed my arm.

'Clive, they're going to do it . . .'

Dawson waits, looks, and then fires the ball back to Wilkinson on the Wallaby 22.

After running the pattern some thousands of times, Zigzag is executed perfectly. It's all up to Jonny now. Dave Alred has been working with Jonny since he was thirteen years old, hours and hours every week, year after year. This is the moment he had been training so fanatically for. Christ, it's going to happen. It's going to be a drop goal for England . . .

Wilkinson takes the ball cleanly and drop kicks it towards the uprights with his right foot.

The ball is in the air. 82,957 people at Telstra Stadium collectively hold their breaths. Millions more around the world join them.

The ball is headed right toward the goal posts . . .

Destiny

At most, Jonny's drop kick would have been in the air for four seconds, possibly less. Yet in that moment standing on the touchline, with Andy Gomarsall firmly gripping my left forearm, time slowed to a crawl. The intense roar of the huge crowd melted away into a distant hum. As

Jonny struck the ball with his right foot – and he's left-footed – I was willing the ball to go through the uprights. It seemed that destiny was bringing World Cup sporting glory back to England for the first time since 1966.

There were some strange coincidences between our Rugby World Cup and that of our distant national football heroes of the 1966 Football World Cup.

In both matches, England's opponents scored first.

On both occasions, England hit back just six minutes later – in '66 with a header by Geoff Hurst and in '03 with a penalty kick by Jonny Wilkinson.

In both matches, England led the game until the last minute of normal time. On both occasions England had seemed in control, had heard their fans celebrating in the stands, only for a never-say-die opposition to equalise with the last kick of the game in regulation time.

There was a member of the Cohen family in both teams, George Cohen in '66 and his nephew Ben Cohen in '03, some thirty-seven years later.

There were also many comparisons to be made between the captains, Martin Johnson and Bobby Moore, between myself and the coach of the '66 World Cup team, Sir Alf Ramsey, and between Jonny Wilkinson and the hero of the '66 team, Geoff Hurst – both wore the number 10 and both were twenty-four years old at the time their brilliance won the matches.

England secured victory in both matches in the dying seconds of extra time. In '66 Hurst completed his hat trick in a 4—2 win at Wembley, while Wilkinson kicked his first drop goal of the night with just thirty-five seconds left on the clock in extra time.

More than just the series of coincidences on the pitch, I also had to wonder at the strange series of events that, against all odds, led me to be in the position of head coach of the England side with all the business tools I needed to transform the squad into a team of highly prepared elite athletes.

As a boy I was inspired by the '66 World Cup heroes, then fell into playing rugby, and eventually came to love the game and play at the top international level. But being so disappointed by lost opportunity as a player, I searched hard for that sensation of winning in its highest ideal. I went to Australia, and discovered that the apparent invincibility of the southern hemisphere was really just a myth. I was then drawn to starting a coaching career at Henley – anyone who knew me as a player could hardly believe the incongruity of it – where I was gripped with the competitive spirit and decided to coach rugby seriously, becoming coach of England just six years later.

Returning to Sydney for the semi-final had been like completing the circle, Manly coming back into my life again after all those years.

It had been thirty-seven years since England won the Football World Cup in 1966, thirty-seven years between England's two World Cup glories. And the final score of 20—17 adds up to 37!

As the ball sailed through the air reaching the peak in its lobbing arc towards the middle of the uprights, the trials and tribulations of the past six years, the incredible highs and the crushing lows, the massive effort from wonderfully talented coaches to build this team of players, the huge effort, dedication and sacrifice from all of the players, the transformation of the entire England set-up, the elation of seeing the team execute this last pattern flawlessly, all concentrated into one sheer moment of intense living energy, the purest sensation of which any sportsperson can dream. This was what it's all about. This was Winning!

The rain was still pouring. The scores were level. The clock showed a hundred minutes. After what seemed an eternity, Jonny Wilkinson's drop kick sailed cleanly between the posts.

WORLD CUP GLORY 31

*Martin Johnson has it. He drives. There's thirty-five seconds to go.
This is the one ... It's coming back for Jonny Wilkinson ... He
drops for World Cup glory ... It's up ... It's over! He's done it!
Jonny Wilkinson is England's hero yet again. And there's no time for
Australia to come back. England have just won the World Cup ...*
                              – Ian Robertson, BBC Radio Five Live

On the touch line, everyone was going nuts. In the stands and all around
me, there was wild screaming and shouting. You could almost hear
the estimated twenty million England supporters around the world
screaming their support from their homes or in the thousands of pubs
where they were watching the game on TV.

But I wasn't shouting. I was watching the referee. After a moment's
hesitation, André Watson raised his right hand to indicate the score.
England were 20—17 up on the Wallabies with thirty-five seconds on
the clock.

Now it was my turn to scream.

At the players.

The game wasn't over when the kick went through. Luckily the
Wallabies were as shell-shocked as we were. I was screaming for the
players to get back into position for the restart, but of course no-one
could hear me because the entire stadium had erupted.

By the time Larkham kicked for the restart, there were only seconds
remaining. But the Wallabies still had a chance to score. If we lost
possession the game wouldn't stop until the ball was grounded. That
restart was a complete disaster from our point of view. We were all so
out of position. The ball was caught by Trevor Woodman, a prop

forward, where one of the backs would normally be in a position to catch it. Luckily the Aussies weren't thinking too clearly either. If they'd taken a little more time in the restart we would have been in serious trouble. Woodman set up the ruck and the ball went to Mike Catt first pass.

In vain I was screaming out again at the top of my lungs.

'KICK IT OUT, MIKE! KICK IT OUT!'

Of course he couldn't hear me, but he knew what to do. Mike Catt immediately hoofed the ball into the stands. It went right over my head. I never watched where the ball landed. I was again staring at the match referee. He casually looked down at his watch, then calmly blew his whistle to indicate full time, his expression suggesting he felt he had refereed an epic final, which he had.

Martin Johnson raised both arms and looked to the heavens. Neil Back raced to the stands to pluck his four-year-old daughter Olivia from the crowd. She would remain with him all of the long night ahead. Jonny Wilkinson and Will Greenwood were jumping around shouting, 'World Cup! World Cup!'

Everyone was hugging and dancing and celebrating, exhausted and elated.

I walked straight to the Australian coach, Eddie Jones, further down the touchline to my left. I shook his hand and gave him a hug. I was speechless. 'There's nothing I can say,' I shouted in his ear so that he could hear me over the roar of the crowd.

'No, well done. Go and join your team.' There was nothing else to do or say. It had been a momentous night but as he wasn't on the winning side I dread to think how he was feeling.

Wild celebrations

The players were all going wild. So too the coaches. Even the seven members of our support team who weren't allowed onto the pitch or in the changing rooms during the game managed to find their way down to us. We were all rejoicing and applauding the extended team effort that brought us to this climactic point.

Jayne, Jess and Joe had watched the game from high up in the stadium. Now they had made their way down to the edge of the pitch.

I would have missed them but Phil Vickery pointed them out to me. After our semi-final win, Jayne had spent all the next day on the phone getting flights for the children. It was too huge a trip for Freddie who was nine, but Jayne somehow managed flights for Jess and Joe to come all the way to Australia for just four days. As they approached the fence around the pitch the supporters realised they belonged to me and they hoisted first Jayne, then Jess and finally Joe over their heads and onto the pitch. What a moment.

The Wallabies had stayed on the pitch as well. Their players' and coaches' sportsmanship was beyond anything we could have expected. Too bad their prime minister John Howard didn't get the same message before he began handing out medals in the awards ceremony. When Martin Johnson accepted the Webb Ellis Trophy on behalf of the England team, he raised it in the air above his head in a triumphant gesture. The England team, and the crowd erupted in glorious approval.

On and on the celebrations went. It was easily an hour, maybe an hour and a half before we were all back in the changing rooms again. It didn't stop there. No one wanted it to end. All sorts of dignitaries and VIPs came in to visit. Tessa Jowell, Secretary of State, came to offer her best wishes. Prince Harry was ecstatic, of course. And even John Howard finally had a smile on his face.

Everyone was madly checking their mobile phones for text messages from friends and loved ones. But there were no calls and no messages. Apparently the whole system had crashed with the intense traffic over-load. I never received a single text from anyone. We were all hoping they would come through the next day but they never did. Fittingly, our World Cup celebrations that hour were largely alone, as one team. It took a long, long time for everyone to get showered and changed. All the players, all the management, all the RFU officials, we were all transfixed by what we had achieved. No one wanted it to end.

Two hours after the match we finally made it to a press conference in the stadium. Three people walked into the room after me: Jonny Wilkinson, Lawrence Dallaglio and Martin Johnson carrying the Webb Ellis Cup. There was a slight ripple of applause as the cameras clicked furiously. I don't think anyone could really believe that England was there with the cup in their hands as victors and world champions. We handled the press well, answering questions efficiently and quickly. The players were humble and gracious. I was just glad I didn't get into any arguments. When asked how I felt about the game my stock answer was, 'I don't really care. We won. That's all that matters.'

We didn't leave the stadium until at least 2 a.m.

After the press conference, the four of us hopped into a mini van to join the rest of the team who had gone by coach into the city to celebrate at a restaurant on Sydney Harbour. With the water in the background and a beer in my hand we toasted our great victory and the celebrations continued. It was marvellous to be there with all the members of the England team and all our friends, spouses and families. After an hour I was completely knackered. When the coach driver announced he was taking the bus back to the hotel, only a few of us took up the offer of an early night.

I was on that bus along with one or two of the other management and their wives. Jonny and his girlfriend came, too. Jayne was there but it took us quite a while to persuade Jess and Joe to come back. It was about 3.30 a.m. by then. What a great ride that was back to the Manly Pacific. It was still raining, it was the middle of the night, but I will always remember sitting on that bus with some very special people with whom I had come through a lot. We had done it.

We arrived back at the Manly Pacific somewhere between 4 a.m. and 5 a.m. Even at that hour there were thousands of England supporters milling around outside, obviously waiting for their triumphant England team to return.

A word here for our amazing supporters. All through the tournament, and especially once we'd arrived in Sydney, there wasn't a training session we left for without a wonderful crowd. They were simply magnificent, and it made me very proud to have that kind of support. A huge thank you to every single person who backed us both in Sydney and at home. It made a difference, a big difference.

When Jonny walked off the bus, the crowd went wild. We struggled to make it through the chaos of that ecstatic cheering crowd. It was the perfect way to cap an incredible night, an amazing victory, and an unbelievable six-year journey.

We all crashed into our beds and into a deep sleep.

SYDNEY MORNING HERALD

=== 1385 days to go (to the next World Cup) ===

Rugby World Cup
PUBLIC NOTICE
To England and its sports fans

Regarding your magnificent football team's 20–17 triumph in the Rugby World Cup final on November 22, on behalf of all Australians, we would like to admit the following:

You were not too old (although we hoped you would be when the game went into extra-time).

You were not too slow.

You scored as many tries as we did.

You kicked no more penalty goals than we did.

You ran the ball as much as we did.

You did it with one of your own as coach (even though he did spend some formative years playing at Manly).

You are better singers than we are (and just quietly, Swing Low, Sweet Chariot is growing on us, as is Jonny without an 'h').

You played with class, toughness and grace.

You were bloody superior ... and

You are, for the first time in 37 years, winners of a football World Cup.

AS A RESULT:

We believe Twickenham is a most fitting home for Bill (our pet name for the Webb Ellis Trophy), though we humbly remind you that, unlike the Ashes, you have to hand it over if you don't win next time.

We concede the time has come to forgive you for using Australia as a dumping ground for your poor, weak and defenceless — even if the practice continues unabated every fourth summer.

We'll stop including the Socceroos' victory on our boastful list of triumphs over you and concede, upon reflection, it was only a friendly and you substituted your entire team at half-time.

We will no longer characterise your fans as beer-swilling, pot-bellied louts or knife-wielding hooligans and try to remember the sporting and enthusiastic supporters who did so much to make the final memorable.

We will stop calling for the International Rugby Board to change the scoring system. In fact, if you can guarantee us a final as good as that one again, we'll ask them to actually increase the value of penalty and drop goals.

WE OFFICIALLY REMOVE THE 215-YEAR-OLD CHIP(S) FROM OUR WEARY SHOULDERS AND ENCOURAGE ALL AUSTRALIANS TO BE NICE TO ANY PERSON OF ENGLISH PERSUASION THEY COME INTO CONTACT WITH FOR THE REST OF THE WEEK ... well, at least until the close of business today.

P.S. GO THE WALLABIES, who through their magnificent efforts did us all proud on the field and even more so off it, with the magnanimous manner in which they and our fans accepted defeat at the hands of you Pommy bastards (sorry, that one slipped through the editing process).

Newspaper Article November 24, 2003

The best day of my life

I was still beaming when I woke up a few hours later. It's a rare opportunity to be a part of something truly extraordinary like winning the World Cup. For a fleeting moment, as I first opened my eyes to see the same room, in the same hotel, with the same sound of the waves that I had heard some eighteen years ago on my first night in Australia with Jayne, it all felt like one long action-packed dream. But the feeling of elation didn't fade as consciousness returned. It was real. We had won the World Cup.

That Sunday with the family was special. We all spoke to Freddie and arranged for him to meet us as soon as we landed. We saw some close friends, all of whom had dropped everything and jumped on flights via outer Mongolia or whatever it took to get to Sydney for Saturday. We walked a few hundred yards down the beach to the Blue Café for a late breakfast. The cheers and congratulations from supporters and wellwishers continued. Everywhere we looked we saw white-shirted fans with huge smiles pasted across their faces. It was intensely gratifying.

Waiting for my bacon and eggs I leafed through the *Sydney Morning Herald* to see what the world would say. There, in a full-page spread in the *Sydney Morning Herald*, was an article with a public apology on behalf of the Australian people (see p. 399). It did make me smile.

I do love Australia and the Australian people, although I'm not sure they feel the same way about me.

From the café the surf looked heavenly, so finally, with time to ourselves, the kids and I hired body boards and wetsuits and spent the rest of the day on the beach. The banter from the other people on the waves was great. I must have heard 'Go the Wallabies' a hundred times as kids with beaming smiles cut through the swell to splash water my way. For lunch we had cold beer from a local pub and fresh fish and chips right on the beach. It was perfect. It was well into the afternoon before, tired but extremely happy, we went back to the hotel to prepare for the International Rugby Board's Awards Dinner scheduled for that night.

It was comical really. Unfortunately, we weren't the most popular guests of honour. It was decidedly quiet when we arrived. I think the black tie crowd had been hoping the Wallabies would come walking victorious through the door to thunderous applause. Instead they got the England team, and with most of us having had a few drinks through the day, it was a ticklish affair to say the least. In the Rules of Engagement it stated that the winning team had to attend the annual IRB dinner, so we did. We were honoured. Jonny was awarded player of the season, England were team of the year and I was coach of the year. The really funny bit was that all the way through dinner we watched, on huge screens around the room, the 1999 final of the Wallabies beating France. Not once but over and over again. I wonder if in 2007 they will show the final from 2003? I doubt it somehow.

Back in Manly we all changed into our casual clothes and met at a bar once again to celebrate late into the night with a host of England supporters. It was a great way to end a fabulous day of celebrations with the team, family and friends.

Leaving for home

The next day we had one final team meeting around midday before departing for the airport. It was an official thanks and congratulations to everyone involved. The Webb Ellis Trophy was sitting right at the front of the room. We couldn't take our eyes off it.

British Airways had renamed a special Boeing 747 'Sweet Chariot' for our return. Most of the other passengers were England fans returning home, too, many of whom had actually been at the game; we were all going home together. For the entire twelve-hour leg of our journey to Singapore none of the players kept in their seats. All were up and moving around the entire plane. They chatted with their supporters, who were thrilled to relive the momentous victory with their guys. The trophy even made it to the back of the plane so that everyone could have a first-hand look. It was all like one big flying party.

On the second leg from Singapore to London, however, everyone was completely exhausted and crashed into their seats, consumed by sleep. The lights were down, the plane was quiet and the Webb Ellis Trophy was tucked safely under a player's arm. As my eyes finally closed and fatigue overwhelmed me, I couldn't help but think what a great end it was to an amazing journey. I went to sleep thinking it was good to be going home.

The World Cup final is the only game in seventy-five matches over six years that I never watched again, never analysed with ProZone and never debriefed with the players. It is indeed the only match where it just didn't seem to matter how we had played. We had won. England were 2003 World Cup Champions. Nothing could take that away.

32

CAUSE FOR CELEBRATION

It was just after 4 a.m. Tuesday morning when 'Sweet Chariot' landed at Heathrow some twenty-four hours after taking off from Sydney. The sleep had revitalised everyone and the excitement had returned. We were coming home victorious, with trophy in hand. The plane pulled up short of the concourse as stairs were wheeled into place for our official arrival. The team left the plane as one to be greeted on the tarmac by VIPs, media and camera crews. One of the people waiting was the president of the RFU Robert Horner. Robert had only just got back from Sydney himself. It was great to see him there at 4.30 a.m. to meet the team. Since he became president of the RFU in July of 2003 Robert has overseen 19 England matches in this one season. He has said he's enjoyed every minute of his time as president, and on our side we've enjoyed having Robert's quiet, supportive and dignified presence with us throughout. There are many wonderful and talented men on the RFU council and he's one of them.

The others on the plane had to wait as the official welcome home got under way. At least they had a good view. It had been a very special journey home on that flight.

After a short while the welcome was ended and we went into the terminal and through to the immigration hall. We were glad it was brief because we were all ready to go home for much needed rest. We'd celebrated. Now it was time to regroup with our families, many of whom had seen so little of us over the last year. We had arranged for other family members that hadn't travelled to Australia to meet us all for breakfast at Pennyhill Park. A full team reunion. When we were all ready, we moved to the exit of the arrivals hall.

Just as the front few of the group reached the exit, we seemed to hit a snag. Everyone had stopped in front of me, so I walked to the front of the line. There were several policemen and women waiting for us, and a very senior police officer, called 'Ma'am' by everyone, wanted a word. I must say, she handled the situation very well. Apparently, unknown to us, thousands of people had got up in the middle of the night and driven down to Terminal Four at Heathrow to meet us! That was the first moment when I began to realise the extent of the excitement back home over winning the World Cup. I think Heathrow and the police had been surprised, too, but they were controlling the situation well. There were all kinds of people there, both very young and old. The last thing we wanted was for any one to be hurt if the crowd surged forward.

We agreed with the senior police officer to go into the arrivals hall in groups, and thus lessen the fear of one huge reaction to the players. When it came to our turn to walk through to the wellwishers, I grabbed Jayne by the hand. We rounded the corner and were greeted by shouts, cheers, whistles and thunderous applause. In front of me there were thousands of people, all cheering their England team home. It was astonishing. We were all overwhelmed by the wonderful spontaneity and warmth of the greeting.

The arrivals hall was filled with people. All I could see was a sea of faces craning for a glimpse of their heroes. Right the way out onto the curb and into the car-park the crowd went.

It took an hour for the team just to make their way to the waiting coach. This was our normal England team coach and everyone said Hi to our regular driver, Chris, very happy to see a familiar face as they clambered on board. On the drive out of Heathrow, people were lining the streets everywhere, hanging out of car windows, waving St George's flags and cheering their hearts out. It was incredible. It was five in the morning! What sane person is up at that crazy hour? I was later informed that in fact nearly 10,000 ecstatic people had swarmed to the airport. The car parks at Heathrow were full. After that people just parked up on kerbs, and even just abandoned their cars on roundabouts. Cars had apparently been parked more than a mile away, while people trudged through the dawn half-light of late November just to greet the team. It was a truly awesome scene, one that none of us will ever forget.

We drove along the familiar route back to Pennyhill Park. Supporters were still following, beeping their horns and waving out of windows at the team. The coach was a bit uncomfortable. We'd all crammed in together due to the numbers of people at the airport. Players were sitting on top of one another but, even though they were tired and looking forward to getting home, they were so happy. We were met by familiar faces at the hotel. Everyone came out to see us. The best moment in getting to Pennyhill Park was seeing Freddie holding the World Cup and chatting with Jonny. He was more pleased to see Jonny and the World Cup than to see me. After a hot breakfast for all families and friends, we held our last press conference at the hotel and then said our goodbyes.

At home later that day, the residents in our village of Cookham had hung a banner of congratulations across our village high street, and our own neighbours had decorated the house in welcome. Words fail me when I try to explain what it was like finally to walk through our front door. I had Jayne and all the kids together and I was home. And we'd done it!

London celebrates

Two weeks after our tremendous welcome at the airport, the team were invited by the Government and the Greater London Council to be the guests of honour in a parade through central London. It was a great accolade. Early on the morning of 8 December we assembled at the Intercontinental Hotel, Park Lane. It was the first time we'd been together as a team since saying goodbye at Pennyhill Park. We were all rested by then, so it was great to see the genuine affection this group had for each other after such a challenging tournament. O_2 were sponsoring the event and had acquired two open-topped double-decker London buses which had been completely repainted and redesigned with huge images of the team. It was December, so the weather wasn't too good. The rain had been pouring down most of the night so hard that we would have been surprised to see even a few thousand people, pretty much just friends and family really, waiting at our final destination of Trafalgar Square. As we boarded the buses I was delighted to see that it had stopped raining. It wasn't sunny, but it wasn't throwing it down either. We were all fairly wrapped up against the cold but underneath we were wearing our World Cup suits; I asked the team to leave their overcoats behind so that we would look like a team. One or two had had enough common sense to wear vests under their clothes, and I wish I had been one of them. I think I was one of the coldest on the bus that day.

That ride through the streets of London will stay with me for the rest of my life. I asked the team of players to get on the first bus and rode just behind with all the management. The supporters were brilliant. The authorities estimate that nearly a million people turned out to celebrate with us. They were everywhere and the St George's flag was in abundance. We even had tickertape in Trafalgar Square as we were all made honorary Freemen of the City of London. (It still doesn't mean I can park anywhere I like though.) We were a bit worried about one or two people hanging right up lamp posts and on the ledges of buildings, and I still don't know how those people who followed the time-honoured tradition of jumping into the fountain at Trafalgar Square managed to avoid hypothermia.

After the parade we had lunch together with our wives and girlfriends at the Intercontinental, and then once again we boarded our England coach, this time to attend a very special invitation to afternoon tea. I had the great honour of introducing the whole touring party to Her Majesty the Queen at Buckingham Palace – it's times like this you just hope to remember everyone's name. I came unstuck when I got to Tony Spreadbury, a great referee known to all of us as 'Spreaders'. My mind went blank and 'Spreaders' it was! The Queen and all the senior Royals were excellent in every way, and to see the guys supping tea and eating tiny sandwiches with her corgis was just great.

We rounded off our exceptional day by attending an evening champagne reception at No. 10 Downing Street with the Prime Minister, the Right Honourable Tony Blair, and a cross-party guest list of senior politicians.

It was an unforgettable day, the crowning moment in a massive effort by a dedicated group of individuals intent on winning. The sheer volume of celebrations in Trafalgar Square highlighted what a momentous spirit had been awoken in the English public by our sporting achievements. It consumed everyone involved in the team for more than six months. The effect of winning the World Cup for England was beginning to sink in, and I felt enormously proud.

Knight of the realm

December passed in a whirl. There was a lot of catching up on the time I'd been away on tour, and a lot of work to be done – as usual, the Six Nations tournament was looming. But I did find the time to send a Christmas card (my first, I'm afraid I'm not too good with cards) that I'd dreamt of sending for six months, whenever I'd thought about life after the World Cup. It was a great pleasure to write personally to the people who had played an important role in encouraging England's efforts over the years (see below). I also had a lot of fun designing the card. It was also a busy month for special occasions as we had sponsors and other partners to see and thank for all of their wonderful support.

However, out of all these occasions one day in December stands out as the most memorable. I'd just arrived home for a family dinner when Jayne handed me an envelope. I had been awarded an OBE a couple of years earlier so I recognised the markings on the outside. I joked with Jayne, amazed she'd not opened it before I got home, and then took out the letter. A knighthood! I couldn't believe it. There had been speculation in the media, but this was the sort of thing that happened to other people. I never expected it to happen to me. I accepted the honour with deep gratitude and felt that it reflected the team's massive achievement over years of hard work. I was also delighted to learn that the whole playing team and senior coaching staff were to be recognised in the Queen's New Year's Honours List, too. There are only one or two people still to be rewarded, but I know this is in hand.

Letting go

The one difficulty that I experienced as a leader on returning home was readjusting. I don't just mean from the nomadic hotel existence. This is always hard, and at home I'm regularly shouted at because I act as though towels hang themselves up, clothes put themselves away, and beds make themselves! No, this was different.

I had been answerable for the whole touring party and the England team for quite some time – from May really – but once we were back in England the whole scenario changed. I tried to be on hand to cover all the bases and organise everything as we usually do, as one team, but it was beyond my control – so many people were so incredibly excited about the team's achievements. I was concerned that people would be left out or overlooked, and I was worried about some events and activities that the team were involved in, but our World Cup victory had taken on a life of its own and we were all caught up in the whirlwind. I couldn't cover everything. It would prove to have a knock-on effect on the team, but in the end I just had to let go. Even so, the overwhelming events of that December will make the entire experience of winning so much more memorable for all of us.

I will end the chapter with part of the Epilogue from Raymond Skyrme's *The Rugby World Cup 2003: A verse chronicle*, kindly sent to me by the author:

> All of England was glued to the screen.
> Such a sight young fans had never seen.
> Since nineteen sixty-six
> Albion's Trophies are nix:
> Such a triumph impresses the Queen!
> Long she's known for what honour they strive;
> Despite slips, how they've kept hopes alive.
> England, IRB votes,
> Had Best Team, Player, and Coach:
> How can she not dub Woodward 'Sir Clive'?
>
> When the triumphal return has been made
> Will the team get a ticker parade?
> A banquet at Guildhall
> Or that drive up the Mall
> To the final Royal Accolade?
>
> All of Rugbydom wishes them well.
> May no naysayers England's joy quell.
> But (to come back to earth)
> England must prove her worth
> In 07! Time only will tell!
>
> On that prophetic note we depart,
> Each his own champion's chance to chart.
> When the tourney begins
> (Whether North or South wins)
> Let strength, speed, and skill all play their part!

33

A NEW YEAR, A NEW ERA

It is my job on behalf of the players to move on and do what is required to be successful in our preparation, giving England the best chance of winning. So we will continue to do more with less, and to think of creative ways to make our resources go further. That we were victorious against the odds makes winning even sweeter. In that respect, we have parlayed the tremendous buoyant spirit generated by our success into some interesting new initiatives.

Changing rooms, changing again

We feel it's important at this time to re-examine every area of the elite environment, so in early January of this year, when some ideas for improvements came up in a management team meeting, we were keen to move on them. Not since our first real transformation in early 1998 had we made any dramatic improvements to the England changing rooms over the years, but like any room at home, there are times when you just need a new approach or a spring cleaning. Once again Rob Chappelhow and his team contributed some brilliant design and production work, kindly sponsored by O_2, and it totally transformed the room for the players. If you're passing Twickenham, drop by – you can always visit and have a look around the ground.

Between the ears

We believe the team that wins the next World Cup will be the team with the most 'between the ears'. In that regard we have continued our quest to help our players achieve maximum performance. Dave Alred is working harder than ever in this particular area, and Sherylle Calder has come on board full-time with the England team, although that took a little persuasion among those who remain on the more conservative side of the game. England have also employed a company called Matchpower whose job it is to create specialised programmes for the players to test intelligence and to improve decision-making under pressure. Interestingly, some of the Matchpower team are from Israel. There must be quite a lot of thinking going on over there.

New facility: Pennyhill Park

Following on from our tremendously positive experience with laying out the new pitch in the summer before the World Cup, we are now pulling our partners and sponsors together to erect a permanent building next to the pitch at Pennyhill Park. My aim is to build the best training facility for rugby in the world. It would have a permanent gym, but I would also want to be able not only to video our training sessions (which Tony Biscombe has been doing for years), but also take the team straight back from the pitch into the War Room to review our performance – instant feedback and correction – and then go out and do it again after our debrief. This is a major project, and in my view it's just the right thing for all of the coaches and technicians to aim for. The building in its current design will contain a full gym for Dave Reddin, a Pressure Room for Dave Alred, a Contact Room for Phil Larder, a Coaching/Team War Room for Andy Robinson and Joe Lydon, and a scaled-down Medical Room for treatment while training.

Of course all that would be in addition to the amazing improvements which Pennyhill Park have already made of their own accord to their terrific hotel facilities. They have just invested millions of pounds in building the most wonderful spa facilities, which I've been told are the best in Europe. The players are not there to enjoy spa treatments of course, but we use many of the facilities in our recovery processes after games, and for individual treatment of players' injuries. The new building signifies the management team's approach to moving on. We don't want to settle for the norm, but would much rather stretch the boundaries and explore where we could really take our elite performance strategies.

Summary of the elite business processes

There is absolutely no doubt in my mind that England won the World Cup because we applied business principles to the management of a professional sport. And I firmly believe the principles found in the England story can be applied to any sport or business situation. Indeed, I have been privileged to work with England rugby's corporate sponsors and partners doing just that. It's one of my ways of giving our sponsors more than they normally could expect from their investment in our sport. I enjoy meeting their teams, and hopefully the England rugby story has inspired many to strive for Winning! While working with our partners I learn heaps of great business ideas to refine, adapt and bring back into the rugby arena. It allows me to put in practice what I've always firmly believed – that sport actually has a huge amount to learn from business.

To summarise, there are seven steps that we've followed in the process of Winning!

1. **Set the vision, inspire the team:** In our case, our vision was Winning! in elite rugby, in the broader sense of the word, defined in the Seven Elements of Winning! (Scoreboard, Performance, Team, Enjoyable Experience, Competition, Supporters, Consistency. See p. 272.)
2. **Design the experience that supports your goal:** The England rugby experience needed shaking up, and the players needed a new challenge in the modern professional arena. We designed an elite rugby experience or atmosphere for the players which would inspire them to work harder than they ever thought possible, and which would remove all distractions, thus creating a 'no excuses' environment. But we also designed an experience or atmosphere for our management team that would be just as important to them as the players. This we then shared with our partners and sponsors.
3. **Build an infrastructure of effective systems in the core parts of your business:** We focused on our core parts of rugby (Leadership, Coaching, Fitness/Nutrition, Psychology, Medical/Recovery,

Analysis/IT and Management) and developed world-class performance standards in each area to measure and manage our performance.

4. **Laying the foundation for a strong elite team culture:** Starting with our *This Is England* Teamship Rules, and evolving into One Team, we created a strong culture within the elite squad, a 'this is how we do it here' philosophy that pervades everything we do, without us having continually to reinvent the wheel. It is a living, breathing, dynamic part of our organisation. And with that framework in place, we followed these steps in a process of continual improvement.

5. **Think: Mindset:** We observed the emerging culture of our team and influenced the mindset of the organisation with a clear level of thinking that strengthened the process as it gained momentum.

6. **Plan: Organisation:** We prepared very carefully to implement new ideas within the organisation. If a new initiative was not supporting our aims, we dropped it quickly. In the early days of England rugby, for every ten ideas we tried, nine fell by the wayside over the years.

7. **Do: Coaching/Playing:** We identified three key times within the cycle of the year when we could implement new ideas and develop the coaching strategy needed to win. For this it is imperative to build in the all-important time for preparation.

I realise that we will never really 'finish' our work in any one of the above seven areas. Even now, we are back in the process of building. The nearest we came to our desired level of achievement in each step of this process was in the lead-up to the World Cup itself.

Winning! mindset

We also now have a clear set of principles and thinking tools that help guide us in developing our culture. Our Winning! mindset consists of seven concepts that we have instilled into the very way in which we do things in the England camp (see diagram on p. 417). They are:

1. **Enjoyment:** First and foremost, for each member group of our team, including leaders, team-mates, partners and supporters.
2. **ChangeThinking!:** A combination of thinking differently, and laterally, about old problems or situations usually taken for granted; and 6-F Thinking, thinking vertically in many different ways so as to provide the depth and detail required to do things that one per cent better than anyone else.
3. **Critical non-essentials:** All the factors in our elite rugby environment that help us to make our player experience hassle-free, thus creating the best environment in which to prepare mentally for games.
4. **Build on success:** When we experienced setbacks – and every team will do so, because winning doesn't happen in a straight line – we learned not to panic but to look for just one or two major lessons from our performance, at all times remembering to see the bigger picture and make sure everyone has a perspective of the given situation. But when we had success, that was when we strove to fully debrief so as to learn why we excelled and how to repeat that part of our performance.
5. **Second-Half Thinking:** This is when we put our heads back into the right frame of mind at half time and learnt to play each forty minutes as if it were a game in itself. This separation allowed us to build on strong first halves and more easily regroup from poor ones, as in the Wales quarter-final.
6. **One Team:** This is a powerful model for organisational culture, which is something that's hard to define and therefore difficult for managers and team-members to work on. One Team helped us all to recognise what it meant to be part of an elite rugby culture where everyone's noses were pointing in the same direction.

I have, in the pages of this book, tried to share with you some of the structures and ideas that the England rugby team have adapted and operated over a fairly long period of time. I believe these guiding principles are transferable from one sport to another or from one business to another. You will have noticed that I have not felt inclined to share the innermost workings of the team – we still intend to beat our opposition whenever we can. And to do so we need to continue to be a fast-moving organisation, adapting and changing to what is in front of us. Improvement and growth are a never-ending process for us. I believe these concepts will be the key to our future development and evolution. More than just in our philosophies and framework for thinking about England rugby, we are beginning once again to look at everything we do with a view to simplifying the rather complex task of getting our team of players to the pitch ready to win. The challenge is to win in these areas before we even get to the pitch.

7 ELEMENTS OF WINNING!

You know you're Winning! when you've achieved . . .
1. More points on the scoreboard.
2. A performance of World Class standards in the core areas of your game.
3. A team that really clicks in the heat of the match.
4. An experience off the pitch that is enjoyable and inspires the whole organisation.
5. Real competition against a team you know can beat you.
6. 75,000 people on their feet going nuts – a performance your supporters wildly applaud.
7. Knowing you can do it on a consistent basis.

About winning in the future

In the long term, World Cup tournaments will come and go. So will the players and coaches, including me. I would hate to think that the current success of England rugby is only a small blip in history. Instead I would love for us all to look back in thirty years' time and appreciate that this year was just the start of a massive period of success.

Since the World Cup we certainly haven't been sitting still – although at times it has felt like it in the wake of the huge celebrations that consumed the country. In the light of our success, I would have thought

Tribute to England's heroes
Picture courtesy of Nike, from window of the Rugby Store, Twickenham

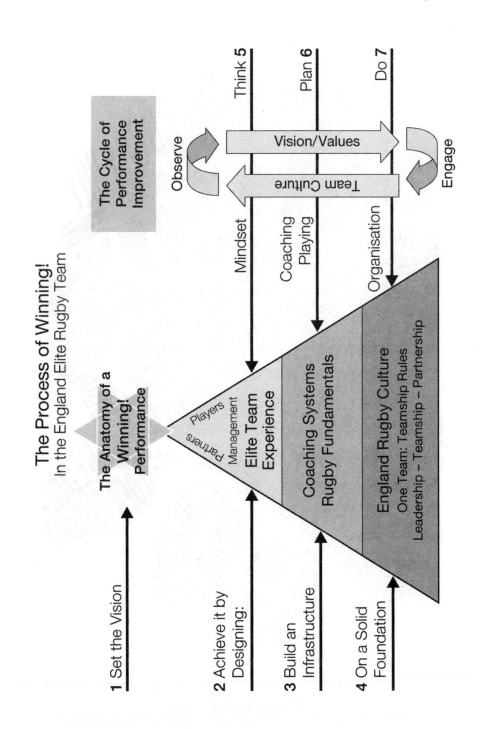

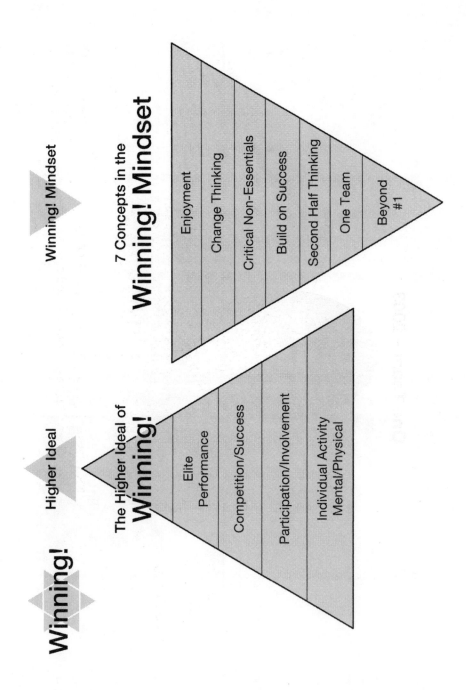

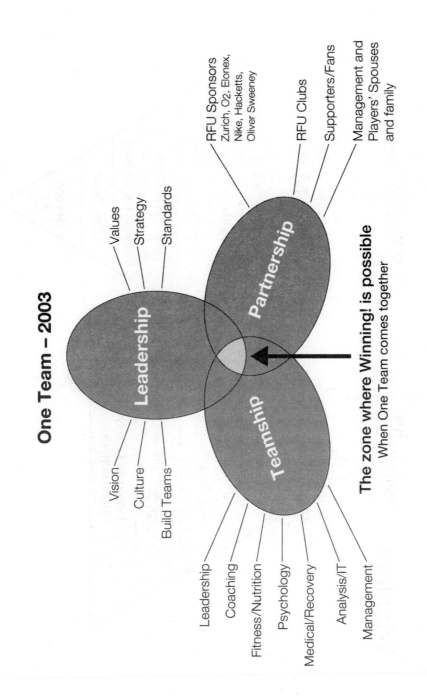

One Team – 2003

Values
Strategy
Standards

Leadership

Vision
Culture
Build Teams

Partnership

RFU Sponsors
Zurich, O₂, Elonex,
Nike, Hacketts,
Oliver Sweeney

RFU Clubs

Supporters/Fans

Management and
Players' Spouses
and family

Teamship

Leadership
Coaching
Fitness/Nutrition
Psychology
Medical/Recovery
Analysis/IT
Management

The zone where Winning! is possible
When One Team comes together

it obvious to the RFU and the Premiership clubs what England can do as a national side when we have time with our players. Yet since our victory on 22 November we have found ourselves in the same old situation I encountered in my early days. Since winning the World Cup our access to the players has been as restricted as in any year before. We've had no training days with the team at all outside of Test weeks – not the World Cup winning team, but a new team, a team that needs to rebuild, renew and progress. Just as England was finally getting the same level of access to its players as our southern-hemisphere counterparts – and indeed the same level of access as Ireland, whose provincial set-up now mirrors that of Australia or New Zealand – we have again reverted to the situation where we have only limited access to the players.

Some would argue that it is only fair that clubs can call on their star players, the new superstars and heroes of England rugby, to compensate for giving us so much access for the first half of the season. To those I would like to offer this simple truism of sport: you are only as good as your last victory. In the months after the World Cup, more than half the squad who travelled to Australia had retired or were not available due to injury. With such a raft of inexperienced players, this was the time we needed our preparation days more than any other, yet we had less. There are times when perhaps I have to be philosophical about a situation, but my job as coach of the England team is to do everything possible to give our players and England the best chance of winning, not sitting on a fence or being a diplomat.

We had been spoiled having such great preparation with the players across the summer and early autumn in the lead-up to the World Cup. But being realistic, since experience must count for something, I knew the trend would *not* continue following the World Cup. Remember, success doesn't happen in a straight line. Sometimes you have to experience frustration before you break through to the next successful stage in winning. That's just the process in action.

So will we always win? As for the short term of the England elite squad, the simple answer is no. We might not always be victorious. But one thing is for certain. We in the England set-up are charged with developing and coaching elite athletes striving for a sensation as deeply meaningful and satisfying as any in the world, the peak state of which all true sports people dream.

The compulsion is strong.

We will always strive for Winning!

That is why we are here.

Clive Woodward
Head Coach
England Rugby
2004

ENGLAND TEAM MANAGEMENT

WORKSHOP 1 1997

ROGER UTTLEY – ENGLAND ...

Roger Miles Uttley was born in ...
... 8 and lock during a career ...
He toured with the British Lions in ...
forwards coach to the 1997 ...
Manager from September 1997 ...

JOHN MITCHELL – ENGLAND ASSISTA...

John Eric Paul Mitchell was ...
player-coach in 1996 and ...
He toured Britain with ...
Hamilton, Waikato, ...
Assistant Coach in September ...
2000. He was the coach of ...

PHIL LARDER – ASSISTANT COACH

Phil Larder played rugby league ...
thirteen years later he was ...
the 1997 rugby league World Cup ...
first round. He first became ...
remained in the coaching staff ...
British Lions in 2001.

DAVE ALRED – ASSISTANT COACH

Dave Alred is responsible for ...
players. His experience is based on ...
rugby league and American football ...

ENGLAND TEAM MANAGEMENT

ROGER UTTLEY – ENGLAND TEAM MANAGER

Roger Miles Uttley was born in Blackpool and won 23 England caps at flanker, No. 8 and lock during a career in which he played for Gosforth and Wasps. He toured with the British Lions in 1974, playing in all four tests, and was forwards coach to the 1989 Lions in Australia. Roger was England Team Manager from September 1997 until January 1999.

JOHN MITCHELL – ENGLAND ASSISTANT COACH

John Eric Paul Mitchell was born in Hawera, New Zealand, and became Sale's player-coach in 1996 and helped them reach the Pilkington Cup in May 1997. He toured Britain with the All Blacks in 1993 and played for Fraser-Tech, Hamilton, Waikato, Lyon Olympique and Garryowen. John became England Assistant Coach in September 1997 and left to return to New Zealand in April 2000. He was the coach of the All Blacks for the 2003 World Cup.

PHIL LARDER – ASSISTANT COACH

Phil Larder played rugby league for Oldham and started coaching in 1982. Thirteen years later he was in charge of the Great Britain team that reached the 1995 rugby league World Cup final and beat favourites Australia in the first round. He first became involved with the England squad in 1997 and has remained in the coaching staff ever since. He coached and toured with the British Lions in 2001.

DAVE ALRED – ASSISTANT COACH

Dave Alred is responsible for improving the kicking skills of the England players. His experience is based on a broad playing spectrum in rugby union, rugby league and American football. He has enjoyed great success with England squad members including Rob Andrew, Paul Grayson and Jonny Wilkinson. Dave worked with the England squad for the 1995 World Cup and has been part of Clive Woodward's coaching team from September 1997 in a part-time capacity until moving over full time in 2000 to the present day.

TERRY CRYSTAL – ENGLAND TEAM DOCTOR

Terry Crystal was born in Leeds and went to Argentina in 1990 and Australia and Fiji the following year as tour doctor before being appointed to the team doctor role in January 1994. As well as his duties as a general practitioner, while working with England he was also involved with a sports clinic at a BUPA hospital in Leeds. Terry was succeeded as team doctor by Dr Simon Kemp in 2001.

KEVIN MURPHY – TEAM PHYSIOTHERAPIST

Kevin Murphy was born in Chester and began his England duties in 1986 having fulfilled a similar role with the British Lions in New Zealand three years earlier. He was honorary physiotherapist with the Great Britain team at two Olympic and Commonwealth games and ran a private practice in Sale. Kevin worked with the England squad until 2001.

PAT FOX – TEAM FITNESS ADVISOR

Pat Fox was born in Christchurch New Zealand and worked with the All Blacks, Otago, Auckland, North Harbour, the Americas Cup Yachting squad and various New Zealand Sports Groups including cricket, soccer, netball and tennis. He joined Wasps in 1990. He was succeeded in the team fitness role by Dave Reddin.

PHIL KEITH-ROACH – SCRUMMAGING ADVISOR

Phil Keith-Roach, a former hooker, played for Gloucester, Rosslyn Park and won three Blues at Cambridge from 1969 to 1971. He has assisted various England representative sides in addition to the senior England squad including England 'A', England Under-21 and the schools 18-Group. Phil has also worked with Wasps and remains a member of the England coaching team.

RICHARD WEGRZYK – TEAM MASSEUR

Richard Wegrzyk was born in Taplow, Buckinghamshire and has been the team masseur with England for well over 100 test matches. He has also toured with the British Lions in 1997 and 2001 and has lectured at St Mary's University College.

TONY BISCOMBE – VIDEO ANALYST

Tony joined the Rugby Football Union in 1989 and since 1998 has been the National Technical Support Manager for the RFU. Tony is responsible, with his department, for managing the video analysis carried out for the elite England squad and all the other England representative sides.

TOM SEARS – PRESS OFFICER

Tom joined the RFU in 1997 as press officer and worked with the England squad throughout the 1997 autumn test series and the 1998 Five Nations Championship. He joined Northampton Rugby Club as Press Officer in 1999 and then went on to perform the same role at Worcestershire Cricket Club.

DAN ARNOLD – BAGGAGE MASTER

Dan toured Australia with the England squad in 1997 and the southern hemisphere tour of 1998. He continued to work at the RFU in an administrative capacity in the coaching department of the RFU before leaving the RFU.

ANDY ROBINSON – COACH

Andy Robinson joined England's coaching staff just before the 2000 South Africa tour and in doing so restored the partnership with Clive Woodward, which they had enjoyed with the England Under-21 team and at Bath. Andy played in seven Bath Cup-winning teams and gained eight caps for his country as well as touring with the British team in 1989. He coached at Bath for a three-year period, which included a Heineken Cup final success and was assistant coach on the Lions tour to Australia in 2001.

BRIAN ASHTON – ASSISTANT COACH

Brian Ashton took his first coaching role with England in 1985. His reappointment in 2000 followed a spell as Ireland coach and a successful period working at Bath. Brian stayed with the senior England team until 2002 when he accepted the post of National Academy Manager with the RFU Performance Department.

DAVE REDDIN – ASSISTANT COACH

Dave Reddin began working with the senior England squad in 1997 after two seasons with Leicester Tigers. His time with England also included work with the national Under-21 development team at the SANZA tournament in 1998.

He is responsible for the physical preparation of the players and implementing their detailed training and dietary programmes.

SIMON HARDY – ASSISTANT COACH

Simon Hardy played for Saracens, Wasps and England Under-23s before starting his coaching career. He became part-time throwing coach to England in 1999 and full-time lineout coach in 2000. Simon had been throwing coach to Bath, Gloucester, Leicester Tigers, Northampton Saints and NEC Harlequins before joining England full time. Simon has coached England international hookers including Steve Thompson, Dorian West and Mark Regan. Simon also coaches Zurich Premiership clubs around the country as part of his full-time role with England. Simon was part of the coaching team that won the RWC in 2003.

DR SIMON KEMP – TEAM DOCTOR

Simon Kemp joined the RFU in 2001, succeeding Terry Crystal, and was part of the England touring party to North America in the same year. Simon joined the RFU after a successful spell at Fulham Football Club and he has also worked in New Zealand.

STEVE LANDER – REFEREE ADVISOR

Steve started refereeing with the Oxon society in 1983 and joined the international panel in 1995. His first test in charge was the Five Nations Championship match between Scotland and Wales. Steve has been the Referee Advisor to the England squad during a successful spell, which has included the 2003 Grand Slam and RWC.

NATHAN MARTIN – HEAD OF PERFORMANCE SERVICES

A former Royal Marine, Nathan Martin joined the RFU in 2000 and was heavily involved in organising the administration and logistics of the North American tour in 2001 and England matches until the appointment of Louise Ramsay as England Team Manager in the autumn of the same year. Nathan is currently the Head of Performance Services for the RFU Performance Department.

LOUISE RAMSAY – ENGLAND TEAM MANAGER

Louise joined the England squad in 2001 after a very successful career working with a number of summer and winter British Olympic teams for which she was awarded the MBE. Louise was an integral member of the England RWC

2003 management team and toured with England to Argentina in 2002 and New Zealand and Australia in 2003.

KAREN BURNETT – PA TO CLIVE WOODWARD

Karen joined the RFU in August 2001 after working with Gavin Hastings' hospitality and sponsorship group. She was responsible for Clive Woodward's diary and administration until leaving in February 2003 to return to Gavin Hastings' company.

ADRIAN FIRTH – MEDIA RELATIONS MANAGER

Adrian Firth joined the RFU in 2000 after spending time working with a number of PR agencies in the sports field. He toured South Africa in 2000 and Argentina in 2002 and left the RFU in the same year. He has gone on to work in other PR-related posts including the Professional Rugby Players' Association.

ENGLAND UNDER CLIVE WOODWARD 1997–2003 RWC Final

MATCH 1   15 November 1997, Twickenham

ENGLAND 15 (5PG) AUSTRALIA 15 (1G 1PG 1T)

England: M B Perry; D L Rees, W J H Greenwood, P R de Glanville, A A Adebayo; M J Catt, K P P Bracken; J Leonard, A E Long, W R Green, M O Johnson, G S Archer, L B N Dallaglio *(captain)*, A J Diprose, R A Hill

Substitutions P J Grayson for de Glanville (7–23 mins); R Cockerill for Long (15–16 mins; 40 mins), A S Healey for Adebayo (65 mins)

Scorer *Penalty Goals:* Catt (5)

Australia: S J Larkham; B N Tune, T J Horan, P W Howard, J W Roff; E J Flatley, G M Gregan; R L L Harry, M A Foley, A T Blades, J F Langford, J A Eales *(captain)*, O D A Finegan, V Ofahengaue, B J Robinson

Substitutions D J Wilson for Robinson (40 mins); A D Heath for Blades (65 mins)

Scorers *Tries:* Gregan, Tune   *Conversion:* Roff   *Penalty Goal:* Roff

Referee A J Watson (South Africa)

MATCH 2   22 November 1997, Old Trafford, Manchester

ENGLAND 8 (1PG 1T) NEW ZEALAND 25 (2G 2PG 1T)

England: M B Perry; D L Rees, W J H Greenwood, P R de Glanville, A A Adebayo; M J Catt, K P P Bracken; J Leonard, R Cockerill, D J Garforth, M O Johnson, G S Archer, L B N Dallaglio *(captain)*, A J Diprose, R A Hill

Substitutions N A Back for Diprose (40 mins); A S Healey for Adebayo (55 mins)

Scorers *Try:* de Glanville   *Penalty Goal:* Catt

New Zealand: C M Cullen; J W Wilson, F E Bunce, A Ieremia, J T Lomu; A P Mehrtens, J W Marshall *(captain)*; C W Dowd, N J Hewitt, O M Brown, I D Jones, R M Brooke, T C Randell, Z V Brooke, J A Kronfeld

Substitutions A F Blowers for Z Brooke (52 mins); S J McLeod for Ieremia (59 mins); J P Preston for Wilson (79 mins)

Scorers *Tries:* Jones, Wilson, Randell   *Conversions:* Mehrtens (2)   *Penalty Goals:* Mehrtens (2)

Referee P L Marshall (Australia)

MATCH 3   29 November 1997, Twickenham

ENGLAND 11 (2PG 1T) SOUTH AFRICA 29 (3G 1PG 1T)

England: M B Perry; J Bentley, W J H Greenwood, N J J Greenstock, D L Rees; M J Catt, M J S Dawson; J Leonard, R Cockerill, D J Garforth, D J Grewcock, G S Archer, L B N Dallaglio (*captain*), R A Hill, N A Back

Substitutions P J Grayson for Catt (40 mins); C M A Sheasby for Hill (57 mins); A S Healey for Bentley (64 mins); S D Shaw for Grewcock (68 mins)

Scorers *Try:* Greenstock   *Penalty Goals:* Catt (2)

South Africa: P C Montgomery; J T Small, A H Snyman, D J Muir, P W G Rossouw; H W Honiball, W Swanepoel; J P du Randt, J Dalton, A C Garvey, K Otto, M G Andrews, A D Aitken, G H Teichmann (*captain*), A G Venter

Substitution R B Skinstad for Venter (31–38 mins)

Scorers *Tries:* Garvey, Snyman, Andrews, Swanepoel   *Conversions:* Honiball (2), Montgomery   *Penalty Goal:* Honiball

Referee C J Hawke (New Zealand)

MATCH 4   6 December 1997, Twickenham

ENGLAND 26 (1G 3PG 2T) NEW ZEALAND 26 (2G 4PG)

England: M B Perry; D L Rees, W J H Greenwood, P R de Glanville, A S Healey; P J Grayson, K P P Bracken; J Leonard, R Cockerill, D J Garforth, M O Johnson, G S Archer, L B N Dallaglio (*captain*), R A Hill, N A Back

Substitutions T R G Stimpson for Rees (6–17 mins) and de Glanville (59 mins); C M A Sheasby for Back (19–28 mins); M J S Dawson for Bracken (59 mins); M P Regan for Cockerill (63 mins)

Scorers *Tries:* Rees, Hill, Dallaglio   *Conversion:* Grayson   *Penalty Goals:* Grayson (3)

New Zealand: C M Cullen; J W Wilson, F E Bunce, W K Little, J T Lomu; A P Mehrtens, J W Marshall (*captain*); M R Allen, N J Hewitt, O M Brown, I D Jones, R M Brooke, T C Randell, Z V Brooke, J A Kronfeld

Substitutions C C Riechelmann for Kronfeld (31–34 mins); C J Spencer for Little (65 mins); S J McLeod for Bunce (75 mins)

Scorers *Tries:* Mehrtens, Little   *Conversions:* Mehrtens (2)   *Penalty Goals:* Mehrtens (4)

Referee J M Fleming (Scotland)

MATCH 5   7 February 1998, Stade de France, Paris

FRANCE 24 (1G 2PG 2DG 1T) ENGLAND 17 (4PG 1T)

France: J-L Sadourny; P Bernat-Salles, C Lamaison, S Glas, C Dominici; T Castaignède, P Carbonneau; C Califano, R Ibañez (*captain*), F Tournaire, O Brouzet, F Pelous, P Benetton, T Lièvremont, O Magne

Substitutions M Lièvremont for Benetton (15 mins); T Cléda for T Lièvremont (54 mins)

Scorers *Tries:* Bernat-Salles, Dominici   *Conversion:* Lamaison   *Penalty Goals:* Lamaison (2)   *Dropped Goals:* Castaignède, Sadourny

England: M J Catt; D L Rees, W J H Greenwood, J C Guscott, A S Healey; P J Grayson, K P P Bracken; J Leonard, M P Regan, D J Garforth, M O Johnson, G S Archer, L B N Dallaglio (*captain*), R A Hill, N A Back

Substitution D E West for Regan (70 mins)

Scorers *Try:* Back   *Penalty Goals:* Grayson (4)

Referee D T M McHugh (Ireland)

MATCH 6   21 February 1998, Twickenham

ENGLAND 60 (7G 2PG 1T) WALES 26 (3G 1T)

England: M B Perry; D L Rees, W J H Greenwood, J C Guscott, A S Healey; P J Grayson, K P P Bracken; J Leonard, R Cockerill, P J Vickery, M O Johnson, G S Archer, L B N Dallaglio (*captain*), R A Hill, N A Back

Substitutions D J Grewcock for Johnson (56 mins); D J Garforth for Vickery (56 mins); A J Diprose for Hill (56 mins); M J Catt for Grayson (70 mins); P R de Glanville for Greenwood (70 mins); M J S Dawson for Bracken (70 mins)

Scorers *Tries:* Rees (2), Back, Bracken, Dallaglio, Healey, Greenwood, Dawson *Conversions:* Grayson (7)   *Penalty Goals:* Grayson (2)

Wales: N R Jenkins; G Thomas, A G Bateman, I S Gibbs, N K Walker; A C Thomas, R Howley (*captain*); A L P Lewis, B H Williams, D Young, G O Llewellyn, M J Voyle, C L Charvis, L S Quinnell, M E Williams

Substitutions W T Proctor for Walker (3 mins); R C Appleyard for Quinnell (48 mins); L B Davies for Bateman (65 mins); J M Humphreys for B Williams (65 mins); C Stephens for Voyle (73 mins); L Mustoe for Lewis (77 mins)

Scorers *Tries:* Bateman (2), G Thomas, Gibbs   *Conversions:* Jenkins (3)

Referee C J Hawke (New Zealand)

MATCH 7   22 March 1998, Murrayfield

SCOTLAND 20 (2G 2PG) ENGLAND 34 (4G 1PG 1DG)

Scotland: D J Lee; A G Stanger, G P J Townsend, A V Tait, S L Longstaff; C M Chalmers, G Armstrong (*captain*); D I W Hilton, G C Bulloch, A P Burnell, D F Cronin, G W Weir, R I Wainwright, E W Peters, A J Roxburgh

Substitutions S B Grimes for Cronin (53 mins); C A Murray for Chalmers (72 mins)

Scorers *Tries:* Stanger, Longstaff   *Conversions:* Lee (2)   *Penalty Goals:* Chalmers (2)

England: M B Perry; A S Healey, W J H Greenwood, J C Guscott, A A Adebayo; P J Grayson, M J S Dawson; J Leonard, R Cockerill, D J Garforth, M O Johnson, G S Archer, L B N Dallaglio (*captain*), D Ryan, N A Back

Substitutions A J Diprose for Ryan (68 mins); P R de Glanville for Healey (71 mins); D J Grewcock for Johnson (74 mins); D E West for Cockerill (83 mins)

Scorers *Tries:* pen try, Dawson, Healey, Grayson   *Conversions:* Grayson (4)   *Penalty Goal:* Grayson   *Dropped Goal:* Grayson

Referee C Thomas (Wales)

MATCH 8   4 April 1998, Twickenham

ENGLAND 35 (3G 3PG 1T) IRELAND 17 (2G 1PG)

England: M B Perry; M J Catt, W J H Greenwood, J C Guscott, A S Healey; P J Grayson, M J S Dawson; J Leonard, R Cockerill, D J Garforth, M O Johnson, G S Archer, L B N Dallaglio (*captain*), A J Diprose, N A Back

Substitutions D J Grewcock for Archer (52 mins); P R de Glanville for Greenwood (52 mins); J P Wilkinson for Catt (78 mins)

Scorers *Tries:* Perry, Catt, Cockerill, de Glanville   *Conversions:* Grayson (3)   *Penalty Goals:* Grayson (3)

Ireland: C P Clarke; R M Wallace, K M Maggs, M C McCall, D A Hickie; E P Elwood, C D McGuinness; R Corrigan, K G M Wood (*captain*), P S Wallace, P S Johns, M E O'Kelly, D S Corkery, V C P Costello, A J Ward

Substitutions K P Keane for McCall (45 mins); D G Humphreys for Clarke (69 mins)
Scorers *Tries:* Hickie (2) *Conversions:* Elwood (2) *Penalty Goal:* Elwood
Referee W D Bevan (Wales)

MATCH 9   6 June 1998, Suncorp Stadium, Brisbane

AUSTRALIA 76 (6G 5T 3PG) ENGLAND 0
Australia: M C Burke; B N Tune, D J Herbert, T J Horan, J W Roff; S J Larkham,
  G M Gregan; R L L Harry, P N Kearns, A T Blades, T M Bowman, J A Eales
  (*captain*), M J Cockbain, R S T Kefu, D J Wilson
Substitutions O D A Finegan for Cockbain (45 mins); V Ofahengaue for Kefu (50 mins);
  D J Crowley for Harry (61 mins); J S Little for Burke (66 mins)
Scorers *Tries:* Larkham (3), Tune (3), Horan (2), Burke, Gregan, Kefu *Conversions:*
  Burke (4), Larkham (2) *Penalty Goals:* Burke (3)
England: T R G Stimpson; S P Brown, M B Perry, S C W Ravenscroft, A S Healey; J P
  Wilkinson, S Benton; G C Rowntree, R Cockerill, P J Vickery, G S Archer, D J
  Grewcock, B Sturnham, A J Diprose (*captain*), R J Pool-Jones
Substitutions B B Clarke for Pool-Jones (temp 26–40 mins); S Potter for Ravenscroft
  (temp 26–34 mins); D E Chapman for Stimpson (66 mins)
Referee A J Watson (South Africa)

MATCH 10   20 June 1998, Carisbrook, Dunedin

NEW ZEALAND 64 (5G 3PG 4T) ENGLAND 22 (2G 1PG 1T)
New Zealand: C M Cullen; J W Wilson, M A Mayerhofler, W K Little, J T Lomu; A P
  Mehrtens, O F J Tonu'u; C W Dowd, A D Oliver, O M Brown, I D Jones, R M
  Brooke, M N Jones, T C Randell (*captain*), J A Kronfeld
Substitutions T J Blackadder for M Jones (20 mins); M D Robinson for Tonu'u
  (62 mins)
Scorers *Tries:* Cullen (2), Randell (2), Wilson (2), Lomu, Kronfeld, Mayerhofler *Conver-
  sions:* Mehrtens (5) *Penalty Goals:* Mehrtens (3)
England: M B Perry; T R G Stimpson, N D Beal, O J Lewsey, A S Healey; J P Wilkinson,
  M J S Dawson (*captain*); G C Rowntree, R Cockerill, P J Vickery, G S Archer, D J
  Grewcock, B B Clarke, S O Ojomoh, P H Sanderson
Substitutions T D Beim for Wilkinson (43 mins); W R Green for Rowntree (temp
  10–18 mins) and for Vickery (55 mins); B Sturnham for Ojomoh (temp 35–
  55 mins); P B T Greening for Cockerill (55 mins); D Sims for Archer (76 mins)
Scorers *Tries:* Cockerill, Dawson, Beim *Conversions:* Stimpson (2) *Penalty Goal:*
  Stimpson
Referee W J Erickson (Australia)

MATCH 11   27 June 1998, Eden Park, Auckland

NEW ZEALAND 40 (5G 1T) ENGLAND 10 (1G 1PG)
New Zealand: C M Cullen; J W Wilson, C S Ralph, M A Mayerhofler, J T Lomu; A P
  Mehrtens, O F J Tonu'u; C W Dowd, A D Oliver, O M Brown, I D Jones, R M
  Brooke, T J Blackadder, T C Randell (*captain*), J A Kronfeld
Substitutions C J Spencer for Mayerhofler (40 mins); N J Hewitt for Oliver (temp
  40–50 mins and temp 71–76 mins); I Maka for Blackadder (50 mins); J Vidiri for
  Lomu (62 mins); M P Carter for I Jones (65 mins); C H Hoeft for Dowd (temp
  7–9 mins and 75 mins); C W Dowd for Hewitt (76 mins)

Scorers *Tries:* Wilson (2), Mayerhofler, Vidiri, Maka, Randell *Conversions:* Spencer (3), Mehrtens (2)

England: M B Perry; T D Beim, N D Beal, J J N Baxendell, A S Healey; O J Lewsey, M J S Dawson (*captain*); G C Rowntree, R Cockerill, P J Vickery, R J Fidler, D Sims, B B Clarke, A J Diprose, P H Sanderson

Substitutions B Sturnham for Sanderson (temp 19–21 mins); T R G Stimpson for Beim (36 mins); S C W Ravenscroft for Healey (70 mins); P B T Greening for Cockerill (76 mins)

Scorer *Try:* Dawson *Conversion:* Dawson *Penalty Goal:* Dawson

Referee P L Marshall (Australia)

MATCH 12 4 July 1998, Newlands, Cape Town

SOUTH AFRICA 18 (1G 2PG 1T) ENGLAND 0

South Africa: P C Montgomery; C S Terblanche, A H Snyman, P G Muller, P W G Rossouw; H W Honiball, J H van der Westhuizen; R B Kempson, J Dalton, A C Garvey, K Otto, M G Andrews, J C Erasmus, G H Teichmann (*captain*), A G Venter

Substitutions R B Skinstad for Otto (temp 10–19 mins); A-H Le Roux for Kempson (75 mins)

Scorers *Tries:* van der Westhuizen, Terblanche *Conversion:* Montgomery *Penalty Goals:* Montgomery (2)

England: M B Perry; S P Brown, N D Beal, J J N Baxendell, P C Sampson; O J Lewsey, M J S Dawson (*captain*); G C Rowntree, R Cockerill, P J Vickery, D Sims, R J Fidler, B B Clarke, A J Diprose, P H Sanderson

Substitution T R G Stimpson for Sampson (55 mins)

Referee C J Hawke (New Zealand)

MATCH 13 14 November 1998, The Alfred McAlpine Stadium, Huddersfield

ENGLAND 110 (15G 1T) THE NETHERLANDS 0

England: M B Perry; D D Luger, W J H Greenwood, J C Guscott, A S Healey; P J Grayson, M J S Dawson; J Leonard, R Cockerill, D J Garforth, G S Archer, M O Johnson (*captain*), B B Clarke, M E Corry, N A Back

Substitutions T A K Rodber for Archer (50 mins); G C Rowntree for Garforth (50 mins); R A Hill for Clarke (50 mins); N D Beal for Perry (50 mins)

Scorers *Tries:* Back (4), Guscott (4), penalty try, Greenwood, Cockerill, Corry, Dawson, Luger, Healey, Beal *Conversions:* Grayson (15)

The Netherlands: A Webber; O Winkels, R van der Walle, G Everts, G Viguurs; B Vervoort, M Marcker (*captain*); J J van der Esch, A Seybel, R Philippo, P Faas, R Donkers, R van der Ven, C Elisara, N Holten

Substitutions H Brat for van der Esch (45 mins); S Ramaker for Vervoort (65 mins); R Lips for Marcker (76 mins)

Referee R Duhau (France)

MATCH 14 22 November 1998, The Alfred McAlpine Stadium, Huddersfield

ENGLAND 23 (2G 3PG) ITALY 15 (4PG 1DG)

England: M B Perry; A S Healey, W J H Greenwood, J C Guscott, D D Luger; P J Grayson, M J S Dawson; J Leonard, R Cockerill, D J Garforth, M O Johnson (*captain*), G S Archer, B B Clarke, M E Corry, N A Back

Substitutions G C Rowntree for Garforth (50 mins); R A Hill for Clarke (50 mins); T A K Rodber for Archer (50 mins);

Scorers *Tries:* Luger, Greenwood *Conversions:* Grayson (2), *Penalty Goals:* Grayson (3)

Italy: M J Pini; F Roselli, C Stoica, M Dallan, L Martin; D Dominguez, A Troncon; M Cuttitta, A Moscardi, G P De Carli, C Checchinato, W Cristofoletto, M Giovanelli (*captain*), C Caione, M Bergamasco

Substitutions O Arancio for Bergamasco (60 mins); G Lanzi for Cristofoletto (84 mins); A Castellani for Cuttitta (84 mins)

Scorer *Penalty Goals:* Dominguez (4) *Dropped Goal:* Dominguez

Referee D Mené (France)

MATCH 15 28 November 1998, Twickenham

ENGLAND 11 (2PG 1T) AUSTRALIA 12 (4PG)

England: M B Perry; T Underwood, P R de Glanville, J C Guscott, A S Healey; P J Grayson, M J S Dawson; J Leonard, R Cockerill, D J Garforth, M O Johnson, T A K Rodber, L B N Dallaglio (*captain*), R A Hill, N A Back

Substitution M J Catt for Grayson (33 mins)

Scorers *Try:* Guscott *Penalty Goals:* Catt (2)

Australia: C E Latham; J S Little, D J Herbert, N P Grey, J W Roff; S J Larkham, G M Gregan; E P Noriega, P N Kearns, A T Blades, T M Bowman, J A Eales (*captain*), M J Cockbain, R S T Kefu, D J Wilson

Substitutions M A Foley for Kearns (46 mins); O D A Finegan for Cockbain (50 mins)

Scorer *Penalty Goals:* Eales (4)

Referee P G Honiss (New Zealand)

MATCH 16 5 December 1998, Twickenham

ENGLAND 13 (1G 2PG) SOUTH AFRICA 7 (1G)

England: N D Beal; T Underwood, P R de Glanville, J C Guscott, D D Luger; M J Catt, M J S Dawson; J Leonard, R Cockerill, D J Garforth, M O Johnson, T A K Rodber, L B N Dallaglio (*captain*), R A Hill, N A Back

Substitutions D L Rees for Underwood (8 mins); A S Healey for Rees (22 mins); M E Corry for de Glanville (temp 59–62 mins); A D King for Catt (temp 59–62 mins) and for de Glanville (62 mins); D J Grewcock for Rodber (67 mins)

Scorers *Try:* Guscott *Conversion:* Dawson *Penalty Goals:* Dawson (2)

South Africa: P C Montgomery; C S Terblanche, A H Snyman, J C Stewart, P W G Rossouw; H W Honiball, J H van der Westhuizen; R B Kempson, J Dalton, A C Garvey, K Otto, M G Andrews, J C Erasmus, G H Teichmann (*captain*), R B Skinstad

Substitutions A-H le Roux for Kempson (temp 26–40 mins) and for Garvey (59 mins); A G Venter for Andrews (48 mins); W Swanepoel for van der Westhuizen (60 mins)

Scorers *Try:* Rossouw *Conversion:* Montgomery

Referee P D O'Brien (New Zealand)

MATCH 17   20 February 1999, Twickenham

ENGLAND 24 (3G 1PG) SCOTLAND 21 (3G)

England: N D Beal; D L Rees, J P Wilkinson, J C Guscott, D D Luger; M J Catt, M J S Dawson; J Leonard, R Cockerill, D J Garforth, M O Johnson, T A K Rodber, L B N Dallaglio (*captain*), R A Hill, N A Back

Substitutions D J Grewcock for Johnson (67 mins); K P P Bracken for Dawson (69 mins)

Scores *Tries:* Rodber, Luger, Beal *Conversions:* Wilkinson (3) *Penalty Goal:* Wilkinson

Scotland: G H Metcalfe; C A Murray, A V Tait, J A Leslie, K M Logan; G P J Townsend, G Armstrong (*captain*); T J Smith, G C Bulloch, A P Burnell, S Murray, S B Grimes, P Walton, E W Peters, M D Leslie

Substitutions A C Pountney for Walton (53 mins); D I W Hilton for Burnell (68 mins)

Scorers *Tries:* Tait 2, Townsend *Conversions:* Logan (3)

Referee D T M McHugh (Ireland)

MATCH 18   6 March 1999, Lansdowne Road, Dublin

IRELAND 15 (5PG) ENGLAND 27 (1G 4PG 1DG 1T)

Ireland: C M P O'Shea; J P Bishop, K M Maggs, R A J Henderson, G T Dempsey; D G Humphreys, C D McGuinness; P M Clohessy, K G M Wood, P S Wallace, P S Johns (*captain*), J W Davidson, D O'Cuinneagain, V C P Costello, A J Ward

Substitutions E R P Miller for Costello (64 mins); J M Fitzpatrick for Clohessy (65 mins)

Scorer *Penalty Goals:* Humphreys (5)

England: M B Perry; D L Rees, J P Wilkinson, J C Guscott, D D Luger; P J Grayson, K P P Bracken; J Leonard, R Cockerill, D J Garforth, M O Johnson, T A K Rodber, R A Hill, L B N Dallaglio (*captain*), N A Back

Substitution N McCarthy for Cockerill (temp 66–67 mins)

Scorers *Tries:* Rodber, Perry *Conversion:* Wilkinson *Penalty Goals:* Wilkinson (4) *Dropped Goal:* Grayson

Referee P D O'Brien (New Zealand)

MATCH 19   20 March 1999, Twickenham

ENGLAND 21 (7PG) FRANCE 10 (1G 1PG)

England: M B Perry; D L Rees, J P Wilkinson, J C Guscott, D D Luger; M J Catt, K P P Bracken; J Leonard, R Cockerill, D J Garforth, M O Johnson, T A K Rodber, R A Hill, L B N Dallaglio (*captain*), N A Back

Substitutions M J S Dawson for Bracken (34 mins); M E Corry for Hill (49 mins); N D Beal for Rees (66 mins); V E Ubogu for Garforth (79 mins)

Scorer *Penalty Goals:* Wilkinson (7)

France: E Ntamack; X Garbajosa, P Giordani, F Comba, C Dominici; T Castaignède, P Carbonneau; S Marconnet, R Ibañez (*captain*), F Tournaire, O Brouzet, F Pelous, T Lièvremont, C Juillet, R Castel

Substitutions C Califano for Marconnet (47 mins); D Auradou for Pelous (65 mins); M Raynaud for Lièvremont (65 mins)

Scorers *Try:* Comba *Conversion:* Castaignède *Penalty Goal:* Castaignède

Referee C J Hawke (New Zealand) replaced by J M Fleming (Scotland) (39 mins)

MATCH 20   11 April 1999, Wembley

WALES 32 (2G 6PG) ENGLAND 31 (2G 4PG 1T)

Wales: S P Howarth; G Thomas, M Taylor, I S Gibbs, D R James; N R Jenkins, R Howley (*captain*); P J D Rogers, G R Jenkins, B R Evans, J C Quinnell, C P Wyatt, C L Charvis, L S Quinnell, B D Sinkinson

Substitutions N J Walne for Thomas (63 mins); A L P Lewis for Rogers (68 mins); D Young for Evans (68 mins)

Scorers *Tries:* Howarth, Gibbs   *Conversions:* N Jenkins (2)   *Penalty Goals:* N Jenkins (6)

England: M B Perry; D D Luger, J P Wilkinson, B-J Mather, S M Hanley; M J Catt, M J S Dawson; J Leonard, R Cockerill, D J Garforth, M O Johnson, T A K Rodber, R A Hill, L B N Dallaglio (*captain*), N A Back

Substitution V E Ubogu for Garforth (68 mins)

Scorers *Tries:* Luger, Hanley, Hill   *Conversions:* Wilkinson (2)   *Penalty Goals:* Wilkinson (4)

Referee A J Watson (South Africa)

MATCH 21   26 June 1999, Stadium Australia, Sydney

AUSTRALIA 22 (1G 3T) ENGLAND 15 (1G 1PG 1T)

Australia: C E Latham; B N Tune, D J Herbert, N P Grey, J W Roff; T J Horan, G M Gregan; G M Panoho, J A Paul, E P Noriega, J P Welborn, D T Giffin, M J Cockbain, R S T Kefu, D J Wilson (*captain*)

Substitutions D J Crowley for Panoho (30 mins); C P Strauss for Kefu (46 mins); R W Williams for Cockbain (80 mins); M C Burke for Tune (81 mins)

Scorers *Tries:* Tune (2), Roff, Wilson   *Conversion:* Roff

England: M B Perry; D L Rees, M J Catt, J C Guscott, D D Luger; J P Wilkinson, K P P Bracken; J Leonard, R Cockerill, D J Garforth, M O Johnson (*captain*), T A K Rodber, R A Hill, M E Corry, N A Back

Substitutions M J S Dawson for Bracken (51 mins); P B T Greening for Cockerill (53 mins); D J Grewcock for Rodber (64 mins); V E Ubogu for Garforth (73 mins); B B Clarke for Corry (73 mins); P R de Glanville for Catt (79 mins); N D Beal for Perry (temp 54–61 mins)

Scorers *Tries:* Perry (2)   *Conversion:* Wilkinson   *Penalty Goal:* Wilkinson

Referee C J Hawke (New Zealand)

MATCH 22   21 August 1999, Twickenham

ENGLAND 106 (13G 3T) UNITED STATES 8 (1PG 1T)

England: M B Perry; A S Healey, P R de Glanville, J C Guscott, D D Luger; J P Wilkinson, M J S Dawson; G C Rowntree, P B T Greening, P J Vickery, M O Johnson (*captain*), D J Grewcock, R A Hill, L B N Dallaglio, N A Back

Substitutions T J Woodman for Rowntree (55 mins); W R Green for Vickery (55 mins); T R G Stimpson for Perry (59 mins); T A K Rodber for Grewcock (62 mins); N McCarthy for Greening (67 mins)

Scorers *Tries:* Guscott (4), Perry (2), Luger (2), Back (2), Hill, Johnson, Dawson, Greening, penalty try, De Glanville   *Conversions:* Wilkinson (13)

United States: K Shuman; V A Anitoni, J Grobler, T Takau, A Saulala; D Niu, K Dalzell; G Sucher, T W Billups, R Lehner, L Gross, A Parker, D Hodges, D Lyle (*captain*), F Mounga

Substitutions C Morrow for Anitoni (11 mins); R A Lumkong for Mounga (40 mins); M A Williams for Niu (61 mins); K Khasigian for Billups (61 mins); S Paga for Hodges (66 mins); M L'Huillier for Lehner (73 mins)
Scorers *Try:* Sucher *Penalty Goal:* Dalzell
Referee P G Honiss (New Zealand)

MATCH 23   28 August 1999, Twickenham

ENGLAND 36 (4G 1PG 1T) CANADA 11 (2PG 1T)

England: M B Perry; A S Healey, W J H Greenwood, J C Guscott, D D Luger; J P Wilkinson, M J S Dawson; G C Rowntree, P B T Greening, P J Vickery, M O Johnson (*captain*), D J Grewcock, R A Hill, L B N Dallaglio, N A Back
Substitutions M E Corry for Johnson (temp 7–14 mins); J Leonard for Rowntree (50 mins); R Cockerill for Greening (50 mins); D J Garforth for Vickery (50 mins); N D Beal for Healey (50 mins); T R G Stimpson for Perry (59 mins); M J Catt for Guscott (73 mins)
Scorers *Tries:* Greenwood (2), Perry, Luger, Dawson *Conversions:* Wilkinson (4) *Penalty Goal:* Wilkinson
Canada: D S Stewart; W U Stanley, D C Lougheed, S Bryan, C Smith; G L Rees (*captain*), M Williams; R Snow, P Dunkley, J Thiel, J Tait, M James, R Banks, A J Charron, D Baugh
Substitutions J Hutchinson for Baugh (46 mins); M Schmid for Banks (56 mins); D Major for Snow (64 mins); R Ross for Rees (71 mins); D W Penney for Thiel (76 mins); M E Cardinal for Dunkley (79 mins)
Scorers *Try:* Stanley *Penalty Goals:* Rees (2)
Referee J Dumé (France)

MATCH 24   2 October 1999, Twickenham

ENGLAND 67 (6G 5PG 2T) ITALY 7 (1G)

England: M B Perry; A S Healey, W J H Greenwood, P R de Glanville, D D Luger; J P Wilkinson, M J S Dawson; J Leonard, R Cockerill, P J Vickery, M O Johnson (*captain*), D J Grewcock, R A Hill, L B N Dallaglio, N A Back
Substitutions J C Guscott for Greenwood (35 mins); P B T Greening for Cockerill (56 mins); G C Rowntree for Leonard (65 mins); D J Garforth for Vickery (65 mins); M E Corry for Grewcock (78 mins); N D Beal for Perry (78 mins)
Scorers *Tries:* Perry, de Glanville, Luger, Wilkinson, Dawson, Hill, Back, Corry *Conversions:* Wilkinson (6) *Penalty Goals:* Wilkinson (5)
Italy: M J Pini; P Vaccari, A C Stoica, L Martin, N Zisti; D Dominguez, A Troncon; P Pucciariello, A Moscardi, F Properzi-Curti, W Cristofoletto, M Giacheri, M Giovanelli (*captain*), O Arancio, M Bergamasco
Substitutions A de Rossi for Bergamasco (18 mins); N Mazzucato for Pini (20 mins); C Checchinato for Cristofoletto (54 mins); F Mazzariol for Dominguez (76 mins)
Scorer *Try:* Dominguez *Conversion:* Dominguez
Referee A J Watson (South Africa)

MATCH 25 9 October 1999, Twickenham

ENGLAND 16 (1G 3PG) NEW ZEALAND 30 (3G 3PG)

England: M B Perry; A S Healey, P R de Glanville, J C Guscott, D D Luger; J P Wilkinson, M J S Dawson; J Leonard, R Cockerill, P J Vickery, M O Johnson (*captain*), D J Grewcock, R A Hill, L B N Dallaglio, N A Back

Substitutions D J Garforth for Vickery (53 mins); T A K Rodber for Grewcock (60 mins); P B T Greening for Cockerill (71 mins); P J Grayson for Wilkinson (71 mins); M E Corry for Hill (temp 12–18 mins) and for Back (81 mins)

Scorers *Try:* de Glanville *Conversion:* Wilkinson *Penalty Goals:* Wilkinson (3)

New Zealand: J W Wilson; T J F Umaga, C M Cullen, A Ieremia, J T Lomu; A P Mehrtens, J W Marshall; C H Hoeft, A D Oliver, C W Dowd, N M Maxwell, R M Brooke, R D Thorne, T C Randell (*captain*), J A Kronfeld

Substitutions B T Kelleher for Marshall (64 mins); R K Willis for Brooke (65 mins); D P E Gibson for Ieremia (68 mins); T E Brown for Mehrtens (81 mins); G E Feek for Dowd (temp 29–31 mins and 39–40 mins)

Scorers *Tries:* Wilson, Lomu, Kelleher *Conversions:* Mehrtens (3) *Penalty Goals:* Mehrtens (3)

Referee P L Marshall (Australia)

MATCH 26 15 October 1999, Twickenham

ENGLAND 101 (12G 4PG 1T) TONGA 10 (1G 1PG)

England: M B Perry; A S Healey, W J H Greenwood, J C Guscott, D D Luger; P J Grayson, M J S Dawson; G C Rowntree, P B T Greening, P J Vickery, M O Johnson (*captain*), G S Archer, J P R Worsley, L B N Dallaglio, R A Hill

Substitutions N D Beal for Dawson (31 mins); D J Grewcock for Johnson (50 mins); M J Catt for Greenwood (50 mins); R Cockerill for Dallaglio (59 mins)

Scorers *Tries:* Greening (2), Luger (2), Greenwood (2), Healey (2), Guscott (2), Hill, Dawson, Perry *Conversions:* Grayson (12) *Penalty Goals:* Grayson (4)

Tonga: S Tu'ipulotu; T Tiueti, F Tatafu, S Finau, S Taupeaafe; E Vunipola (*captain*), S Martens; N Ta'ufo'ou, F Vunipola, T Taumoepeau, I Fatani, B H Kivalu, D Edwards, K Tu'ipulotu, S Koloi

Substitutions T Faiga'anuku for Edwards (38 mins); F Mafi for K Tu'ipulotu (40 mins); I Tapueluela for F Vunipola (temp 31–43 mins) and for S Tu'ipulotu (53 mins); E Taione for Taupeaafe (58 mins); S M Tu'ipulotu for Martens (58 mins); V Toloke for Kivalu (60 mins); L Maka for F Vunipola (69 mins)

Scorers *Try:* Tiueti *Conversion:* S Tu'ipulotu *Penalty Goal:* S Tu'ipulotu

Referee W J Erickson (Australia)

MATCH 27 20 October 1999, Twickenham

ENGLAND 45 (2G 7PG 2T) FIJI 24 (3G 1PG)

England: M B Perry; N D Beal, W J H Greenwood, M J Catt, D D Luger; J P Wilkinson, A S Healey; J Leonard, P B T Greening, D J Garforth, M O Johnson (*captain*), G S Archer, J P R Worsley, L B N Dallaglio, N A Back

Substitutions G C Rowntree for Leonard (27 mins); P R de Glanville for Luger (39 mins); M J S Dawson for Healey (40 mins); T A K Rodber for Archer (44 mins); P J Grayson for Wilkinson (70 mins); R Cockerill for Greening (70 mins); R A Hill for Worsley (temp 40–78 mins) and for Perry (78 mins)

Scorers *Tries:* Greening, Luger, Back, Beal *Conversions:* Wilkinson, Dawson *Penalty Goals:* Wilkinson (7)

Fiji: A Uluinayau; M Vunibaka, V Satala, M Nakauta, I Tikomaimakogai; W Serevi, M Rauluni; D Rouse, G Smith (*captain*), J Veitayaki, S Raiwalui, E Katalau, K Sewabu, I Tawake, S N Tawake

Substitutions N Little for Serevi (48 mins); I Male for I Tawake (48 mins); W Sotutu for Vunibaka (56 mins); I Rasila for Smith (73 mins); E Naituivau for Rouse (73 mins); J Rauluni for Tikomaimakogai (76 mins)

Scorers *Try:* Satala, Nakauta, Tikomaimakogai *Conversions:* Little (3) *Penalty Goal:* Serevi

Referee C Thomas (Wales)

MATCH 28   24 October 1999, Stade de France, Paris

SOUTH AFRICA 44 (2G 5PG 5DG) ENGLAND 21 (7PG)

South Africa: P C Montgomery; D J Kayser, R F Fleck, P G Muller, P W G Rossouw; J H de Beer, J H van der Westhuizen (*captain*); J P du Randt, A E Drotské, I J Visagie, K Otto, M G Andrews, J C Erasmus, R B Skinstad, A G Venter

Substitutions A-H le Roux for du Randt (62 mins); P A van den Berg for Andrews (67 mins); A N Vos for Skinstad (76 mins); C S Terblanche for Kayser (temp 63–66 mins)

Scorers *Tries:* Rossouw, van der Westhuizen *Conversions:* de Beer (2) *Penalty Goals:* de Beer (5) *Dropped Goals:* de Beer (5)

England: M B Perry; N D Beal, W J H Greenwood, P R de Glanville, D D Luger; P J Grayson, M J S Dawson; J Leonard, P B T Greening, P J Vickery, M O Johnson (*captain*), D J Grewcock, R A Hill, L B N Dallaglio, N A Back

Substitutions A S Healey for Beal (55 mins); J P Wilkinson for Grayson (55 mins); M J Catt for de Glanville (71 mins); M E Corry for Dawson (72 mins)

Scorers *Penalty Goals:* Grayson (6), Wilkinson

Referee J M Fleming (Scotland)

MATCH 29   5 February 2000, Twickenham

ENGLAND 50 (4G 4PG 2T) IRELAND 18 (1G 2PG 1T)

England: M B Perry; A S Healey, M J Tindall, M J Catt, B C Cohen; J P Wilkinson, M J S Dawson (*captain*); J Leonard, P B T Greening, P J Vickery, G S Archer, S D Shaw, R A Hill, L B N Dallaglio, N A Back

Substitutions I R Balshaw for Perry (70 mins); T J Woodman for Leonard (70 mins); M E Corry for Shaw (76 mins)

Scorers *Tries:* Healey (2), Cohen (2), Back, Tindall *Conversions:* Wilkinson (4) *Penalty Goals:* Wilkinson (4)

Ireland: C M P O'Shea; J P Bishop, B G O'Driscoll, M J Mullins, K M Maggs; D G Humphreys, T A Tierney; P M Clohessy, K G M Wood (*captain*), P S Wallace, R E Casey, M E O'Kelly, D O'Cuinneagain, A G Foley, K Dawson

Substitutions M J Galwey for Casey (40 mins); T Brennan for O'Cuinneagain (47 mins); G T Dempsey for O'Shea (47 mins)

Scorers *Tries:* Maggs, Galwey *Conversion:* Humphreys *Penalty Goals:* Humphreys (2)

Referee S R Walsh (New Zealand)

MATCH 30   19 February 2000, Stade de France, Paris

FRANCE 9 (3PG) ENGLAND 15 (5PG)

France: R Dourthe; E Ntamack, D Venditti, T Lombard, C Dominici; T Castaignède, F Galthié; C Califano, M Dal Maso, F Tournaire, L Matiu, O Brouzet, A Benazzi, F Pelous (*captain*), O Magne

Substitutions T Lièvremont for Matiu (40 mins); S Betsen for Benazzi (62 mins); R Ibañez for Dal Maso (72 mins); P de Villiers for Tournaire (72 mins)

Scorer *Penalty Goals:* Dourthe (3)

England: M B Perry; A S Healey, M J Tindall, M J Catt, B C Cohen; J P Wilkinson, M J S Dawson (*captain*); J Leonard, P B T Greening, P J Vickery, G S Archer, S D Shaw, R A Hill, L B N Dallaglio, N A Back

Substitutions I R Balshaw for Perry (62 mins); M E Corry for Hill (75 mins)

Scorer *Penalty Goals:* Wilkinson (5)

Referee S J Dickinson (Australia)

MATCH 31   4 March 2000, Twickenham

ENGLAND 46 (3G 5PG 2T) WALES 12 (3PG 1DG)

England: M B Perry; A S Healey, M J Tindall, M J Catt, B C Cohen; J P Wilkinson, M J S Dawson (*captain*); J Leonard, P B T Greening, P J Vickery, G S Archer, S D Shaw, R A Hill, L B N Dallaglio, N A Back

Substitution M E Corry for Shaw (71 mins)

Scorers *Tries:* Greening, Back, Cohen, Hill, Dallaglio   *Conversions:* Wilkinson (3) *Penalty Goals:* Wilkinson (5)

Wales: S P Howarth; G Thomas, A G Bateman, M Taylor, S M Williams; N R Jenkins, R Howley; P J D Rogers, G R Jenkins, D Young (*captain*), J C Quinnell, C P Wyatt, C L Charvis, L S Quinnell, B D Sinkinson

Substitutions S C John for Young (23 mins); I M Gough for J C Quinnell (63 mins); B Williams for Charvis (temp 50–60 mins) and for G R Jenkins (71 mins); M E Williams for L S Quinnell (80 mins)

Scorer *Penalty Goals:* N R Jenkins (3)   *Dropped Goal:* N R Jenkins

Referee J M Fleming (Scotland)

MATCH 32   18 March 2000, Stadio Flaminio, Rome

ITALY 12 (1G 1T) ENGLAND 59 (5G 2PG 1DG 3T)

Italy: C Pilat; A C Stoica, L Martin, N Zisti, D Dallan; D Dominguez, A Troncon (*captain*); A Lo Cicero, A Moscardi, C Paoletti, C Checchinato, A Gritti, W Cristofoletto, A De Rossi, M Bergamasco

Substitutions G Preo for Dallan (58 mins); M Cuttitta for Paoletti (58 mins); A Persico for Bergamasco (77 mins)

Scorers *Tries:* Martin, Stoica   *Conversion:* Dominguez

England: M B Perry; A S Healey, M J Tindall, M J Catt, B C Cohen; J P Wilkinson, M J S Dawson (*captain*); J Leonard, P B T Greening, D J Garforth, G S Archer, S D Shaw, R A Hill, L B N Dallaglio, N A Back

Substitutions I R Balshaw for Tindall (62 mins); T J Woodman for Leonard (71 mins); J P R Worsley for Hill (71 mins); A D King for Wilkinson (73 mins); A C T Gomarsall for Dawson (78 mins); N McCarthy for Greening (78 mins); M E Corry for Archer (78 mins)

Scorers *Tries:* Healey (3), Penalty try, Cohen (2), Dawson (2)   *Conversions:* Wilkinson (4), King   *Penalty Goals:* Wilkinson (2)   *Dropped Goal:* Back
Referee A Lewis (Ireland)

MATCH 33   2 April 2000, Murrayfield

SCOTLAND 19 (1G 4PG) ENGLAND 13 (1G 2PG)

Scotland: C D Paterson; C C Moir, G P J Townsend, J G McLaren, G H Metcalfe; D W Hodge, A D Nicol (*captain*); T J Smith, S J Brotherstone, M J Stewart, S Murray, R Metcalfe, J P R White, M D Leslie, A C Pountney
Substitutions G R McIlwham for Stewart (69 mins); S J Reid for Leslie (temp 39–40 mins)
Scorer *Try:* Hodge   *Conversion:* Hodge   *Penalty Goals:* Hodge (4)
England: M B Perry; A S Healey, M J Tindall, M J Catt, B C Cohen; J P Wilkinson, M J S Dawson (*captain*); J Leonard, P B T Greening, P J Vickery, G S Archer, S D Shaw, R A Hill, L B N Dallaglio, N A Back
Substitutions I R Balshaw for Cohen (58 mins); M E Corry for Archer (64 mins); J P R Worsley for Hill (82 mins)
Scorers *Try:* Dallaglio   *Conversion:* Wilkinson   *Penalty Goals:* Wilkinson (2)
Referee C Thomas (Wales)

MATCH 34   17 June 2000, Loftus Versfeld, Pretoria

SOUTH AFRICA 18 (6PG) ENGLAND 13 (1G 2PG)

South Africa: P C Montgomery; B J Paulse, R F Fleck, D W Barry, P W G Rossouw; A J J van Straaten, J H van der Westhuizen; R B Kempson, C F Marais, W Meyer, C S Boome, K Otto, J C Erasmus, A N Vos (*captain*), A G Venter
Substitutions C P J Krige for Erasmus (20 mins); G M Delport for Fleck (temp 20–40 mins and 74 mins); A-H le Roux for Krige (temp 44–47 mins) and for Kempson (74 mins); P A van den Berg for Vos (temp 35–39 mins) and for Boome (73 mins); C M Williams for Barry (temp 32–40 mins)
Scorer *Penalty Goals:* Van Straaten (6)
England: M B Perry; T R G Stimpson, M J Tindall, M J Catt, D D Luger; A S Healey, K P P Bracken; J Leonard, P B T Greening, J M White, M O Johnson (*captain*), D J Grewcock, R A Hill, L B N Dallaglio, N A Back
Substitutions S D Shaw for Johnson (72 mins); L D Lloyd for Catt (74 mins); J P R Worsley for Grewcock (81 mins); M P Regan for Hill (temp 41–49 mins); D L Flatman for White (temp 59–67 mins)
Scorers *Try:* Luger   *Conversion:* Stimpson   *Penalty Goals:* Stimpson (2)
Referee C J Hawke (New Zealand)

MATCH 35   24 June 2000, Free State Stadium, Bloemfontein

SOUTH AFRICA 22 (1G 5PG) ENGLAND 27 (8PG 1DG)

South Africa: P C Montgomery; B J Paulse, R F Fleck, D W Barry, P W G Rossouw; A J J van Straaten, J H van der Westhuizen; R B Kempson, C F Marais, I J Visagie, C S Boome, K Otto, C P J Krige, A N Vos (*captain*), A G Venter
Substitutions C M Williams for Van Straaten (40 mins); A-H le Roux for Visagie (61 mins)
Scorers *Try:* Van der Westhuizen   *Conversion:* Montgomery   *Penalty Goals:* Van Straaten (4), Montgomery

England: M B Perry; A S Healey, M J Tindall, M J Catt, B C Cohen; J P Wilkinson, K P P Bracken; J Leonard, P B T Greening, J M White, M O Johnson (*captain*), D J Grewcock, R A Hill, L B N Dallaglio, N A Back

Substitutions S D Shaw for Grewcock (54 mins); J P R Worsley for Hill (61 mins); L D Lloyd for Tindall (71 mins); D L Flatman for Hill (temp 22–27 mins) and for White (81 mins)

Scorer *Penalty Goals:* Wilkinson (8)   *Dropped Goal:* Wilkinson

Referee S J Dickinson (Australia)

MATCH 36   18 November 2000, Twickenham

ENGLAND 22 (1G 4PG 1DG) AUSTRALIA 19 (1G 4PG)

England: M B Perry; A S Healey, M J Tindall, M J Catt, D D Luger; J P Wilkinson, K P P Bracken; J Leonard, P B T Greening, P J Vickery, M O Johnson (*captain*), D J Grewcock, R A Hill, L B N Dallaglio, N A Back

Substitutions D L Flatman for Vickery (temp 22–24 mins); I R Balshaw for Healey (55 mins); M J S Dawson for Bracken (61 mins); M P Regan for Greening (85 mins)

Scorers *Try:* Luger   *Conversion:* Wilkinson   *Penalty Goals:* Wilkinson (4)   *Dropped Goal:* Wilkinson

Australia: C E Latham; M C Burke, D J Herbert, S A Mortlock, J W C Roff; R B Kafer, S J Cordingley; W K Young, M A Foley, F J Dyson, D T Giffin, J A Eales (*captain*), R W Williams, R S T Kefu, G B Smith

Substitutions G M Panoho for Dyson (30 mins); N P Grey for Kafer (39 mins); J A Paul for Foley (40 mins); M R Connors for Williams (45 mins); R W Williams for Kefu (58 mins); P R Waugh for Smith (76 mins); M J Cockbain for Giffin (77 mins); F J Dyson for Panoho (82 mins)

Scorer *Try:* Burke   *Conversion:* Burke   *Penalty Goals:* Burke (4)

Referee A J Watson (South Africa)

MATCH 37   25 November 2000, Twickenham

ENGLAND 19 (1G 3PG 1DG) ARGENTINA 0

England: I R Balshaw; B C Cohen, M J Tindall, M J Catt, D D Luger; J P Wilkinson, M J S Dawson; J Leonard, M P Regan, J M White, M O Johnson (*captain*), D J Grewcock, R A Hill, L B N Dallaglio, N A Back

Substitutions P J Vickery for White (40 mins); D L Flatman for Vickery (temp 50–57 mins); W J H Greenwood for Tindall (57 mins); Flatman for Leonard (69 mins); M E Corry for Hill (74 mins); D E West for Regan (77 mins)

Scorers *Try:* Cohen   *Conversion:* Wilkinson   *Penalty Goals:* Wilkinson (3)   *Dropped Goals:* Wilkinson

Argentina: F Contepomi; O Bartolucci, J Orengo, L Arbizu (*captain*), I Corleto; G Quesada, A Pichot; R Grau, F Mendez, O Hasan, C I Fernandez Lobbe, A Allub, S Phelan, G Longo, R Martin

Substitution G Ugartemendia for Allub (64 mins)

Referee A Lewis (Ireland)

MATCH 38   2 December 2000, Twickenham

ENGLAND 25 (1G 6PG) SOUTH AFRICA 17 (4PG 1T)

England: M B Perry; B C Cohen, M J Tindall, W J H Greenwood, D D Luger; J P Wilkinson, M J S Dawson; J Leonard, P B T Greening, J M White, M O Johnson (*captain*), D J Grewcock, R A Hill, L B N Dallaglio, N A Back

Substitutions M P Regan for Hill (temp 21–33 mins) and for Greening (temp 40–60 mins); M E Corry for Back (temp 17–33 mins); I R Balshaw for Luger (40 mins); P J Vickery for White (40 mins); A S Healey for Greenwood (80 mins)

Scorers *Try:* Greenwood   *Conversion:* Wilkinson   *Penalty Goals:* Wilkinson (6)

South Africa: P C Montgomery; B J Paulse, R F Fleck, J C Mulder, C S Terblanche; A J J van Straaten, J H van der Westhuizen; R B Kempson, J W Smit, W Meyer, P A van den Berg, M G Andrews, C P J Krige, A N Vos (*captain*), A G Venter

Substitutions G Esterhuizen for Mulder (temp 26–40 mins); A J Venter for Van den Berg (59 mins); A-H le Roux for Meyer (61 mins); D J van Zyl for van der Westhuizen (73 mins); W Brosnihan for A J Venter (80 mins)

Scorer *Try:* Van Straaten   *Penalty Goals:* Van Straaten (4)

Referee D T M McHugh (Ireland)

MATCH 39   3 February 2001, Millennium Stadium, Cardiff

WALES 15 (1G 1PG 1T) ENGLAND 44 (4G 2PG 2T)

Wales: S M Jones; G Thomas, M Taylor, I S Gibbs, D R James; N R Jenkins, R Howley; D R Morris, R C McBryde, D Young (*captain*), I M Gough, C P Wyatt, C L Charvis, L S Quinnell, M E Williams

Substitutions A P Moore for Wyatt (45 mins); M A Jones for Thomas (54 mins); A G Bateman for Taylor (64 mins); S C John for Morris (64 mins); R H StJ B Moon for Howley (80 mins)

Scorers *Tries:* Howley, Quinnell   *Conversion:* Jenkins   *Penalty Goal:* Jenkins

England: I R Balshaw; B C Cohen, W J H Greenwood, M J Catt, D D Luger; J P Wilkinson, M J S Dawson; J Leonard, D E West, P J Vickery, M O Johnson (*captain*), D J Grewcock, R A Hill, L B N Dallaglio, N A Back

Substitutions A S Healey for Luger (7 mins); T J Woodman for Leonard (59 mins); M B Perry for Balshaw (59 mins); M E Corry for Dallaglio (69 mins); M J Tindall for Catt (69 mins)

Scorers *Tries:* Greenwood (3), Dawson (2), Cohen   *Conversions:* Wilkinson (4)   *Penalty Goals:* Wilkinson (2)

Referee J Dumé (France)

MATCH 40   17 February 2001, Twickenham

ENGLAND 80 (9G 4PG 1T) ITALY 23 (2G 3PG)

England: I R Balshaw; A S Healey, W J H Greenwood, M J Catt, B C Cohen; J P Wilkinson, M J S Dawson; J Leonard, D E West, P J Vickery, M O Johnson (*captain*), D J Grewcock, R A Hill, L B N Dallaglio, N A Back

Substitutions M P Regan for West (50 mins); J P R Worsley for Back (50 mins); J Robinson for Cohen (50 mins); K P P Bracken for Dawson (57 mins); T J Woodman for Leonard (68 mins); M E Corry for Grewcock (73 mins)

Scorers *Tries:* Healey (2), Balshaw (2), Cohen, Regan, Worsley, Greenwood, Wilkinson, Dallaglio   *Conversions:* Wilkinson (9)   *Penalty Goals:* Wilkinson (4)

Italy: A Scanavacca; L Martin, C Stoica, W Pozzebon, D Dallan; G Raineri, J-M Queirolo; A Lo Cicero, A Moscardi (*captain*), A Muraro, A Gritti, W Visser, C Caione, C Checchinato, M Bergamasco

Substitutions G P de Carli for Muraro (49 mins); M Rivaro for Pozzebon (66 mins); D Dal Maso for Caione (68 mins)

Scorers *Tries:* Dallan, Checchinato   *Conversions:* Scanavacca (2)   *Penalty Goals:* Scanavacca (3)

Referee S J Dickinson (Australia)

MATCH 41   3 March 2001, Twickenham

ENGLAND 43 (5G 1PG 1T) SCOTLAND 3 (1PG)

England: I R Balshaw; A S Healey, W J H Greenwood, M J Catt, B C Cohen; J P Wilkinson, M J S Dawson; J Leonard, D E West, P J Vickery, M O Johnson (*captain*), D J Grewcock, R A Hill, L B N Dallaglio, N A Back

Substitutions M P Regan for West (40 mins); J Robinson for Catt (62 mins); J P R Worsley for Back (68 mins); K P P Bracken for Dawson (73 mins)

Scorers *Tries:* Dallaglio (2), Balshaw (2), Hill, Greenwood   *Conversions:* Wilkinson (5)   *Penalty Goal:* Wilkinson

Scotland: C D Paterson; C A Murray, A J Bulloch, J A Leslie, K M Logan; D W Hodge, A D Nicol (*captain*); T J Smith, G C Bulloch, M J Stewart, S Murray, R Metcalfe, M D Leslie, S M Taylor, A C Pountney

Substitutions G R McIlwham for Stewart (45 mins); S B Grimes for Metcalfe (46 mins); B W Redpath for Nicol (60 mins); J M Craig for C Murray (70 mins); J G McLaren for A Bulloch (75 mins)

Scorer *Penalty Goal:* Hodge

Referee R Davies (Wales)

MATCH 42   7 April 2001, Twickenham

ENGLAND 48 (6G 2PG) FRANCE 19 (1G 3PG 1DG)

England: I R Balshaw; A S Healey, W J H Greenwood, M J Catt, B C Cohen; J P Wilkinson, M J S Dawson; J Leonard, P B T Greening, J M White, M O Johnson (*captain*), S W Borthwick, R A Hill, L B N Dallaglio, N A Back

Substitutions D E West for Greening (temp 19–28 mins); M E Corry for Borthwick (temp 30–78 mins); D L Flatman for Leonard (temp 38–40 mins); J Robinson for Cohen (62 mins); J P R Worsley for Hill (77 mins); M B Perry for Balshaw (77 mins); K P P Bracken for Dawson (80 mins)

Scorers *Tries:* Balshaw, Hill, Greenwood, Greening, Catt, Perry   *Conversions:* Wilkinson (6)   *Penalty Goals:* Wilkinson (2)

France: J-L Sadourny; P Bernat-Salles, S Glas, X Garbajosa, C Dominici; G Merceron, F Galthié; S Marconnet, R Ibañez, P de Villiers, L Nallet, A Benazzi, C Milhères, F Pelous (*captain*), O Magne

Substitutions D Auradou for Benazzi (45 mins); T Lièvremont for Nallet (45 mins); F Landreau for Ibanez (56 mins); A Galasso for de Villiers (81 mins)

Scorers *Try:* Bernat-Salles   *Conversion:* Merceron   *Penalty Goals:* Merceron (3)   *Drop Goal:* Merceron

Referee W T S Henning (South Africa) replaced by D T M McHugh (Ireland) (45 mins)

MATCH 43   2 June 2001, Fletcher's Field, Markham, Toronto

CANADA 10 (1G 1PG) ENGLAND 22 (1G 3T)

Canada: W U Stanley; N Witkowski, J Cannon, R P Ross, S Fauth; D S Stewart, M Williams; R G A Snow, P Dunkley, J D Thiel, E R P Knaggs, J N Tait, G A Dixon, A J Charron (*captain*), D Baugh

Substitutions D Burleigh for Dunkley (18 mins); M R Schmid for Knaggs (69 mins); D Major for Baugh (69 mins)

Scorers Try: Fauth   *Conversion:* Ross   *Penalty Goal:* Ross

England: O J Lewsey; P C Sampson, L D Lloyd, J Noon, M Stephenson; D J H Walder, K P P Bracken (*captain*); G C Rowntree, D E West, J M White, S W Borthwick, B J Kay, M E Corry, J P R Worsley, L W Moody

Substitutions T R G Stimpson for Stephenson (temp 5–40 mins), S D Shaw for Borthwick (64 mins); P H Sanderson for Worsley (64 mins)

Scorers Tries: Lewsey (2), West, Bracken   *Conversion:* Walder

Referee N Whitehouse (Wales)

MATCH 44   9 June 2001, Swangard Stadium, Burnaby, Vancouver

CANADA 20 (2G 2PG) ENGLAND 59 (5G 3PG 3T)

Canada: W U Stanley; N Witkowski, J Cannon, R P Ross, S Fauth; D S Stewart, M Williams; R G A Snow, D Burleigh, J D Thiel, A J Charron (*captain*), J N Tait, G A Dixon, R Banks, D Baugh

Substitutions K Nichols for Witkowski (temp 6–16 mins) and for Stanley (70 mins); D Major for Thiel (65 mins); M R Schmid for Baugh (65 mins); E R P Knaggs for Tait (68 mins); K Wirachowski for Banks (73 mins)

Scorers Tries: Baugh, Fauth   *Conversions:* Ross (2)   *Penalty Goals:* Ross (2)

England: O J Lewsey; P C Sampson, L D Lloyd, J Noon, M Stephenson; D J H Walder, K P P Bracken (*captain*); G C Rowntree, D E West, J M White, S D Shaw, B J Kay, S White-Cooper, J P R Worsley, L W Moody

Substitutions M B Wood for Bracken (36 mins); T R G Stimpson for Sampson (39 mins); S W Borthwick for Kay (42 mins), D L Flatman for White-Cooper (temp 37 to 40 mins) and for Rowntree (61 mins), P H Sanderson for Worsley (62 mins); A D King for Noon (70 mins); M P Regan for West (62 mins)

Scorers Tries: Shaw (2), Walder (2), penalty try, Worsley, Wood, Noon   *Conversions:* Walder (5)   *Penalty Goals:* Walder (3)

Referee J Jutge (France)

MATCH 45   16 June 2001, Balboa Park, San Francisco

UNITED STATES 19 (2G 1T) ENGLAND 48 (4G 4T)

United States: K Shuman; J Naivalu, P Eloff, J Grobler, J Naqica; G Wells, K Dalzell; M MacDonald, K Khasigian, P Still, L Gross, E Reed, D Hodges (*captain*), D Lyle, K Schubert

Substitutions O Fifita for Schubert (40 mins); A Magelby for Reed (68 mins)

Scorers Tries: Naqica (2), Grobler   *Conversions:* Wells (2)

England: O J Lewsey; L D Lloyd, F H H Waters, J Noon, M Stephenson; D J H Walder, K P P Bracken (*captain*); G C Rowntree, D E West, J M White, S D Shaw, S W Borthwick, S White-Cooper, J P R Worsley, L W Moody

Substitutions P H Sanderson for Moody (temp 9–12 mins) and for Worsley (62 mins), O Barkley for Noon (48 mins); A E Long for West (68 mins); D L Flatman for

White-Cooper (temp 29 to 38 mins) and for Rowntree (68 mins); T Palmer for Borthwick (73 mins); T Voyce for Walder (73 mins); M B Wood for Bracken (79 mins); Noon for Waters (79 mins)

Scorers *Tries:* Lewsey (2), Lloyd (2), West, Sanderson, Worsley, Moody   *Conversions:* Walder (4)

Referee A D Turner (South Africa)

MATCH 46   20 October 2001, Lansdowne Road, Dublin

IRELAND 20 (5PG 1T) ENGLAND 14 (3PG 1T)

Ireland: G T Dempsey; S P Horgan, B G O'Driscoll, K M Maggs, D A Hickie; D G Humphreys, P A Stringer; P M Clohessy, K G M Wood (*captain*), J J Hayes, M J Galwey, M E O'Kelly, E R P Miller, A G Foley, D P Wallace

Substitutions R J R O'Gara for Humphreys (59 mins); T Brennan for Galwey (66 mins); E Byrne for Clohessy (66 mins); K Dawson for Foley (77 mins); M J Mullins for O'Driscoll (77 mins)

Scorers *Try:* Wood   *Penalty Goals:* Humphreys (3), O'Gara (2)

England: I R Balshaw; D D Luger, W J H Greenwood, M J Catt, J Robinson; J P Wilkinson, M J S Dawson (*captain*); J Leonard, P B T Greening, J M White, S D Shaw, D J Grewcock, M E Corry, R A Hill, N A Back

Substitutions K P P Bracken for Dawson (37 mins); D E West for Greening (40 mins); A S Healey for Luger (60 mins); L W Moody for Corry (75 mins); G C Rowntree for White (75 mins)

Scorers *Try:* Healey   *Penalty Goals:* Wilkinson (3)

Referee P G Honiss (New Zealand)

MATCH 47   10 November 2001, Twickenham

ENGLAND 21 (5PG 2DG) AUSTRALIA 15 (1G 1PG 1T)

England: J Robinson; A S Healey, W J H Greenwood, M J Catt, D D Luger; J P Wilkinson, K P P Bracken; G C Rowntree, D E West, P J Vickery, B J Kay, D J Grewcock, R A Hill, J P R Worsley, N A Back (*captain*)

Scorers *Penalty Goals:* Wilkinson (5)   *Dropped Goals:* Wilkinson (2)

Australia: M C Burke; C E Latham, D J Herbert, N P Grey, J W Roff; S J Larkham, G M Gregan (*captain*); N B Stiles, M A Foley, B J Darwin, J B Harrison, D T Giffin, O D A Finegan, R S T Kefu, G B Smith

Substitutions M J Cockbain for Harrison (50 mins); G S G Bond for Herbert (68 mins); P R Waugh for Smith (68 mins); R C Moore for Darwin (80 mins)

Scorers *Tries:* Burke, Waugh   *Conversion:* Burke   *Penalty Goal:* Burke

Referee P D O'Brien (New Zealand)

MATCH 48   17 November 2001, Twickenham

ENGLAND 134 (14G 2PG 6T) ROMANIA 0

England: J Robinson; B C Cohen, W J H Greenwood, M J Tindall, D D Luger; C Hodgson, A S Healey; G C Rowntree, M P Regan, J Leonard, B J Kay, S W Borthwick, L W Moody, J P R Worsley, N A Back (*captain*)

Substitutions K P P Bracken, J M White and A Sanderson for Healey, Rowntree and Back (40 mins); D J Grewcock for Kay (62 mins); M J Catt for Greenwood (63 mins)

Scorers *Tries:* Robinson (4), Cohen (3), Luger (3), Hodgson (2), Moody (2), Tindall (2),

Healey, Sanderson, Regan, Worsley   *Conversions:* Hodgson (14)   *Penalty Goals:* Hodgson (2)

Romania: G Brezoianu; I Teodorescu, F Dobre, N Oprea, V Ghioc; I Tofan, L Sirbu; D Dima, P Balan, M Sociacu, C Petre, V Nedelcu, F Corodeanu, A Petrache (*captain*), R Samuil

Substitutions M Dragomir for Petre (39 mins); M Ciolacu for Oprea (40 mins); G Pasache and S Florea for Samuil & Sociacu (57 mins); P Toderasc for Dima (65 mins); M Codea for Sirbu (76 mins)

Referee P C Deluca (Argentina)

MATCH 49   24 November 2001, Twickenham

ENGLAND 29 (7PG 1DG 1T) SOUTH AFRICA 9 (3PG)

England: J Robinson; A S Healey, W J H Greenwood, M J Catt, D D Luger; J P Wilkinson, K P P Bracken; G C Rowntree, D E West, P J Vickery, M O Johnson (*captain*), D J Grewcock, R A Hill, J P R Worsley, N A Back

Substitutions L W Moody for Hill (57 mins); B J Kay for Back (temp 76–78 mins) and for Johnson (79 mins); M J Tindall for Catt (78 mins)

Scorers *Try:* Luger   *Penalty Goals:* Wilkinson (7)   *Dropped Goal:* Catt

South Africa: C A Jantjes; B J Paulse, T M Halstead, A J J van Straaten, D B Hall; L J Koen, J H van der Westhuizen; A-H le Roux, W J Smit, W Meyer, V Matfield, M G Andrews, A N Vos, R B Skinstad (*captain*), A J Venter

Substitutions I J Visagie for Meyer (temp 24–31 mins and 40 mins); A G Venter for Andrews (temp 44–49 mins and 66 mins); L van Biljon and C P J Krige for Smit and Vos (66 mins)

Scorer *Penalty Goals:* Van Straaten (3)

Referee S J Dickinson (Australia) replaced by D T M McHugh (Ireland) (12 mins)

MATCH 50   2 February 2002, Murrayfield

SCOTLAND 3 (1PG) ENGLAND 29 (3G 1PG 1T)

Scotland: G H Metcalfe; B J Laney, J G McLaren, G P J Townsend, C D Paterson; D W Hodge, B W Redpath; T J Smith, G C Bulloch, M J Stewart, S Murray, S B Grimes, J P R White, S M Taylor, A C Pountney (*captain*)

Substitution: G Graham for Smith (63 mins)

Scorer *Penalty Goal:* Hodge

England: J Robinson; A S Healey, W J H Greenwood, M J Tindall, B C Cohen; J P Wilkinson, K P P Bracken; G C Rowntree, S Thompson, J M White, M O Johnson (*captain*), B J Kay, R A Hill, J P R Worsley, N A Back

Substitutions: N Duncombe for Bracken (40 mins); D J Grewcock for Kay (69 mins); I R Balshaw for Tindall (72 mins); J Leonard for White (75 mins); C Hodgson for Wilkinson (82 mins)

Scorers *Tries:* Robinson (2), Tindall, Cohen   *Conversions:* Wilkinson (2), Hodgson   *Penalty Goal:* Wilkinson

Referee S R Walsh (New Zealand)

MATCH 51 16 February 2002, Twickenham

ENGLAND 45 (6G 1PG) IRELAND 11 (2PG 1T)

England: J Robinson; A S Healey, W J H Greenwood, M J Tindall, B C Cohen; J P Wilkinson, K P P Bracken; G C Rowntree, S Thompson, P J Vickery, M O Johnson (*captain*), B J Kay, R A Hill, J P R Worsley, N A Back

Substitutions J Leonard for Rowntree (16 mins); D J Grewcock for Johnson (60 mins); L W Moody for Hill (60 mins); I R Balshaw for Healey (60 mins); N Duncombe for Bracken (77 mins); C Hodgson for Wilkinson (77 mins)

Scorers *Tries:* Greenwood (2), Wilkinson, Cohen, Worsley, Kay *Conversions:* Wilkinson (6) *Penalty Goal:* Wilkinson

Ireland: G T Dempsey; G E A Murphy, B G O'Driscoll, K M Maggs, D A Hickie; D G Humphreys, P A Stringer; P M Clohessy, F J Sheahan, J J Hayes, M J Galwey (*captain*), M E O'Kelly, E R P Miller, A G Foley, D P Wallace

Substitutions R A J Henderson for Murphy (8 mins); R J R O'Gara for Henderson (40 mins); J S Byrne for Sheahan (52 mins); S H Easterby for Miller (57 mins); G W Longwell for Galwey (57 mins); P S Wallace for Clohessy (78 mins)

Scorers Try: O'Gara *Penalty Goals:* Humphreys (2)

Referee P L Marshall (Australia)

MATCH 52 2 March 2002, Stade de France, Paris

FRANCE 20 (2G 2PG) ENGLAND 15 (1G 1PG 1T)

France: N Brusque; A Rougerie, T Marsh, D Traille, D Bory; G Merceron, F Galthié (*captain*); J-J Crenca, R Ibañez, P de Villiers, D Auradou, O Brouzet, S Betsen, I Harinordoquy, O Magne

Substitutions F Pelous for Auradou (60 mins); O Milloud for Crenca (60 mins); P Mignoni for Galthié (67 mins); O Azam for Ibañez (74 mins); R Martin for Betsen (57 to 63 mins) and for Harinordoquy (78 mins)

Scorers *Tries:* Merceron, Harinordoquy *Conversions:* Merceron (2) *Penalty Goals:* Merceron (2)

England: J Robinson; A S Healey, W J H Greenwood, M J Tindall, B C Cohen; J P Wilkinson, K P P Bracken; G C Rowntree, S Thompson, P J Vickery, M O Johnson (*captain*), B J Kay, R A Hill, J P R Worsley, N A Back

Substitutions H Paul for Tindall (39 mins); M E Corry for Back (temp 47 to 54 mins) and for Worsley (60 mins); J Leonard for Rowntree (74 mins); D D Luger for Wilkinson (74 mins); D E West for Thompson (74 mins); D J Grewcock for Kay (74 mins)

Scorers *Tries:* Robinson, Cohen *Conversion:* Wilkinson *Penalty Goal:* Wilkinson

Referee A J Watson (South Africa)

MATCH 53 23 March 2002, Twickenham

ENGLAND 50 (5G 4PG 1DG) WALES 10 (1G 1PG)

England: A S Healey; D D Luger, W J H Greenwood, M J Tindall, B C Cohen; J P Wilkinson, K P P Bracken; G C Rowntree, S Thompson, J M White, D J Grewcock, B J Kay, L W Moody, R A Hill, N A Back (*captain*)

Substitutions M E Corry for Kay (temp 19 to 27 mins); M J S Dawson for Bracken (59 mins); T R G Stimpson for Tindall (63 mins); D E West for Thompson (69 mins); J P R Worsley for Moody (temp 42–53 mins) and for Hill (80 mins)

Scorers *Tries:* Luger (2), Greenwood, Wilkinson, Stimpson *Conversions:* Wilkinson (5) *Penalty Goals:* Wilkinson (4) *Drop Goal:* Wilkinson

Wales: K A Morgan; D R James, G Thomas, A W N Marinos, C S Morgan; I R Harris, R Howley; I D Thomas, R C McBryde, C T Anthony, A P Moore, C P Wyatt, N J Budgett, L S Quinnell (*captain*), M E Williams

Substitutions G R Williams for G Thomas (48 mins); C L Charvis for M Williams (50 mins); G O Llewellyn for Wyatt (54 mins); D Peel for Howley (59 mins); B Williams for McBryde (69 mins)

Scorers *Try:* Harris *Conversion:* Harris *Penalty Goal:* Harris

Referee A J Cole (Australia)

MATCH 54   7 April 2002, Stadio Flaminio, Rome

ITALY 9 (3PG) ENGLAND 45 (6G 1PG)

Italy: G Peens; N Mazzucato, C Stoica, G Raineri, D Dallan; D Dominguez, A Troncon; G de Carli, A Moscardi (*captain*), F Pucciariello, M Bortolami, M Giacheri, A Persico, M Phillips, Mauro Bergamasco

Substitutions C Zanoletti for Raineri (48 mins); A de Rossi for Phillips (48 mins); C Nieto for Pucciariello (59 mins); S Dellape for Giacheri (59 mins); R Pez for Peens (73 mins); A Moretti for Moscardi (76 mins); F Pucciariello for De Carli (80 mins); M Mazzantini for Stoica (82 mins)

Scorer *Penalty Goals:* Dominguez (3)

England: J Robinson; D D Luger, W J H Greenwood, M J Tindall, B C Cohen; J P Wilkinson, K P P Bracken; G C Rowntree, S Thompson, J M White, D J Grewcock, B J Kay, L W Moody, R A Hill, N A Back (*captain*)

Substitutions M O Johnson for Grewcock (temp 19–23 mins and 55 mins); M J S Dawson for Bracken (55 mins); J Leonard for Rowntree (55 mins); L B N Dallaglio for Back (55 mins); A S Healey for Cohen (69 mins); D E West for Thompson 72 mins); C Hodgson for Tindall (76 mins)

Scorers *Tries:* Greenwood (2), Cohen, Robinson, Dallaglio, Healey *Conversions:* Wilkinson (5), Dawson *Penalty Goal:* Wilkinson

Referee S M Lawrence (South Africa)

MATCH 55   22 June 2002, Vélez Sarsfield Stadium, Buenos Aires

ARGENTINA 18 (6PG) ENGLAND 26 (2G 4PG)

Argentina: I Corleto; G F Camardon, J Orengo, F Contepomi, D L Albanese; G Quesada, A Pichot (*captain*); M Reggiardo, F E Mendez, O J Hasan, C I Fernandez Lobbe, R Alvarez, S Phelan, G Longo, R A Martin

Substitutions L Ostiglia for Alvarez (temp 43–57 mins) and for Phelan (68 mins); D Giannantonio for Quesada (temp 60–67 mins); R D Grau for Reggiardo (66 mins); M E Ledesma for Mendez (72 mins)

Scorer *Penalty Goals:* Quesada (6)

England: M J Horak; T R G Stimpson, G Appleford, B Johnston, P Christophers; C Hodgson, A C T Gomarsall; D L Flatman, S Thompson, P J Vickery (*captain*), A Codling, B J Kay, A Sanderson, J P R Worsley, L W Moody

Scorers *Tries:* Kay, Christophers *Conversions:* Hodgson (2) *Penalty Goals:* Hodgson (3), Stimpson

Referee A C Rolland (Ireland)

MATCH 56   9 November 2002, Twickenham

ENGLAND 31 (2G 3PG 1DG 1T) NEW ZEALAND 28 (4G)

England: J Robinson; J Simpson-Daniel, W J H Greenwood, M J Tindall, B C Cohen; J P Wilkinson, M J S Dawson; T J Woodman, S Thompson, P J Vickery, M O Johnson (*captain*), D J Grewcock, L W Moody, L B N Dallaglio, R A Hill

Substitutions B Johnston for Greenwood (40 mins); N A Back for Hill (temp 49–62 mins) and for Dallaglio (70 mins); B J Kay for Grewcock (61 mins); A S Healey for Simpson-Daniel (77 mins)

Scorers *Tries:* Moody, Wilkinson, Cohen   *Conversions:* Wilkinson (2)   *Penalty Goals:* Wilkinson (3)   *Dropped Goal:* Wilkinson

New Zealand: B A Blair; D C Howlett, J F Umaga, K R Lowen, J T Lomu; C J Spencer, S J Devine; J M McDonnell, A K Hore, K J Meeuws, A J Williams, K J Robinson, T C Randell (*captain*), S R Broomhall, M R Holah

Substitutions D D Lee for Devine (30 mins); A P Mehrtens for Spencer (40 mins); M P Robinson for Umaga (temp 37–40 mins) and for Lowen (47 mins); B M Mika for K Robinson (62 mins)

Scorers *Tries:* Lomu (2), Howlett, Lee   *Conversions:* Blair (2), Mehrtens (2)

Referee J I Kaplan (South Africa)

MATCH 57   16 November 2002, Twickenham

ENGLAND 32 (2G 6PG) AUSTRALIA 31 (2G 4PG 1T)

England: J Robinson; J Simpson-Daniel, W J H Greenwood, M J Tindall, B C Cohen; J P Wilkinson, M J S Dawson; J Leonard, S Thompson, P J Vickery, M O Johnson (*captain*), B J Kay, L W Moody, R A Hill, N A Back

Substitutions: L B N Dallaglio for Hill (temp 41–51 mins); A S Healey for Tindall (80 mins)

Scorers *Tries:* Cohen (2)   *Conversions:* Wilkinson (2)   *Penalty Goals:* Wilkinson (6)

Australia: S J Larkham; W J Sailor, M C Burke, D J Herbert, S A Mortlock; E J Flatley, G M Gregan (*captain*); W K Young, J A Paul, E P Noriega, D J Vickerman, J B Harrison, M J Cockbain, R S T Kefu, G B Smith

Substitutions D T Giffin for Vickerman (55 mins); A L Freier for Paul (69 mins); D N Croft for Harrison (temp 70 to 80 mins) and for Smith (80 mins); M J Giteau for Herbert (73 mins); B J Darwin for Noriega (77 mins)

Scorers *Tries:* Flatley (2), Sailor   *Conversions:* Burke (2)   *Penalty Goals:* Burke (4)

Referee P G Honiss (New Zealand)

MATCH 58   23 November 2002, Twickenham

ENGLAND 53 (6G 2PG 1T) SOUTH AFRICA 3 (1PG)

England: J Robinson; B C Cohen, W J H Greenwood, M J Tindall, P D Christophers; J P Wilkinson, M J S Dawson; J Leonard, S Thompson, P J Vickery, M O Johnson (*captain*), B J Kay, L W Moody, R A Hill, N A Back

Substitutions L B N Dallaglio for Moody (15 mins); A S Healey for Wilkinson (44 mins); A C T Gomarsall for Dawson (57 mins); D J Grewcock for Kay (71 mins); T R G Stimpson for Greenwood (72 mins)

Scorers *Tries:* Greenwood (2), Cohen, Back, Hill, Dallaglio, penalty try   *Conversions:* Gomarsall (2), Stimpson (2), Wilkinson, Dawson   *Penalty Goals:* Wilkinson (2)

South Africa: W W Greeff; B J Paulse, R F Fleck, A D James, F Lombard; A S Pretorius,

J H Conradie; W G Roux, J Dalton, P D Carstens, J J Labuschagne, A J Venter, C P J Krigé (*captain*), J C van Niekerk, P J Wannenburg

Substitutions N Jordaan for Conradie (11 mins); R B Russell for Paulse (47 mins); A A Jacobs & L van Biljon for Pretorius and Dalton (55 mins); C J van der Linde for Carstens (62 mins)

Scorer *Penalty Goal:* Pretorius

Referee P D O'Brien (New Zealand)

MATCH 59   15 February 2003, Twickenham

ENGLAND 25 (1G 5PG 1DG) FRANCE 17 (1G 2T)

England: J Robinson; D D Luger, W J H Greenwood, C Hodgson, B C Cohen; J P Wilkinson, A C T Gomarsall; J Leonard, S Thompson, J M White, M O Johnson (*captain*), B J Kay, L W Moody, R A Hill, N A Back

Substitutions G C Rowntree for Leonard (33 mins); L B N Dallaglio for Moody (44 mins); D J Grewcock for Kay (84 mins); M P Regan for Rowntree (temp 47 mins to 56 mins)

Scorers *Try:* Robinson *Conversion:* Wilkinson *Penalty Goals:* Wilkinson (5) *Dropped Goal:* Wilkinson

France: C Poitrenaud; A Rougerie, X Garbajosa, D Traille, V Clerc; G Merceron, F Galthié (*captain*); J-J Crenca, R Ibañez, C Califano, F Pelous, O Brouzet, S Betsen, I Harinordoquy, O Magne

Substitutions S Marconnet for Califano (62 mins); S Chabal for Betsen (62 mins); T Castaignède for Rougerie (64 mins); J-B Rué for Ibañez (74 mins)

Scorers *Tries:* Magne, Poitrenaud, Traille *Conversion:* Merceron

Referee P G Honiss (New Zealand)

MATCH 60   22 February 2003, Millennium Stadium, Cardiff

WALES 9 (3PG) ENGLAND 26 (2G 2PG 2DG)

Wales: K A Morgan; Gareth Thomas, M Taylor, T Shanklin, G R Williams; C Sweeney, G J Cooper; I D Thomas, J M Humphreys (*captain*), B R Evans, R Sidoli, S M Williams, D R Jones, Gavin Thomas, M E Williams

Substitutions G J Williams for Humphreys (57 mins); C L Charvis for Gavin Thomas (57 mins); G Jenkins for Evans (57 mins); M J Watkins for Shanklin (65 mins); I R Harris for G R Williams (66 mins); G O Llewellyn for S Williams (73 mins)

Scorer *Penalty Goals:* Sweeney (3)

England: J Robinson; D D Luger, W J H Greenwood, C Hodgson, B C Cohen; J P Wilkinson, K P P Bracken; G C Rowntree, S Thompson, R Morris, M O Johnson (*captain*), B J Kay, R A Hill, L B N Dallaglio, N A Back

Substitutions P D Christophers for Robinson (39 mins); J P R Worsley for Back (56 mins); D J Grewcock for Kay (63 mins); J Simpson-Daniel for Hill (temp 40 mins to 50 mins) and for Wilkinson (77 mins); A C T Gomarsall for Luger (77 mins)

Scorers *Tries:* Greenwood, Worsley *Conversions:* Wilkinson (2) *Penalty Goals:* Wilkinson (2) *Dropped Goals:* Wilkinson (2)

Referee S R Walsh (New Zealand)

MATCH 61   9 March 2003, Twickenham

ENGLAND 40 (5G 1T) ITALY 5 (1T)

England: O J Lewsey; J Simpson-Daniel, W J H Greenwood, M J Tindall, D D Luger; J P Wilkinson (*captain*), M J S Dawson; G C Rowntree, S Thompson, R Morris, D J Grewcock, B J Kay, J P R Worsley, L B N Dallaglio, R A Hill

Substitutions C Hodgson for Wilkinson (47 mins); O J Smith for Hodgson (53 mins); S D Shaw for Kay (57 mins); M A Worsley for Morris (59 mins); M P Regan for Thompson (65 mins); A Sanderson for Dallaglio (temp 19–26 mins) and for Hill (65 mins); K P P Bracken for Lewsey (71 mins)

Scorers *Tries:* Lewsey (2), Thompson, Simpson-Daniel, Tindall, Luger   *Conversion:* Wilkinson (4), Dawson

Italy: Mirco Bergamasco; N Mazzucato, P Vaccari, G Raineri, D Dallan; R Pez, A Troncon (*captain*); G P De Carli, C Festuccia, R Martinez-Frugoni, C Bezzi, M Giacheri, A De Rossi, M Phillips, A R Persico

Substitutions A Masi for Dallan (16 mins); M Bortolami for Giacheri (temp 6– 11 mins and 47 mins); L Castrogiovanni for De Carli (49 mins); G Peens for Vaccari (65 mins); M Mazzantini for Troncon (68 mins); S Palmer for Phillips (71 mins); F Ongaro for Festuccia (74 mins)

Scorers *Try:* Mirco Bergamasco

Referee A C Rolland (Ireland)

MATCH 62   22 March 2003, Twickenham

ENGLAND 40 (4G 4PG) SCOTLAND 9 (3PG)

England: O J Lewsey; J Robinson, W J H Greenwood, M J Tindall, B C Cohen; J P Wilkinson, M J S Dawson; G C Rowntree, S Thompson, J Leonard, M O Johnson (*captain*), B J Kay, R A Hill, L B N Dallaglio, N A Back

Substitutions D D Luger for Tindall (56 mins); D J Grewcock for Kay (62 mins); P J Grayson for Wilkinson (66 mins); T J Woodman for Rowntree (66 mins); J P R Worsley for Dallaglio (74 mins)

Scorers *Tries:* Robinson (2), Lewsey, Cohen   *Conversions:* Wilkinson (3), Grayson   *Penalty Goals:* Wilkinson (4)

Scotland: G H Metcalfe; C D Paterson, J G McLaren, A Craig, K M Logan; G P J Townsend, B W Redpath (*captain*); T J Smith, G C Bulloch, B A F Douglas, S Murray, N J Hines, J P R White, S M Taylor, A L Mower

Substitutions S B Grimes for Murray (51 mins); K N Utterson for McLaren (56 mins); R S Beattie for Mower (67 mins); G Kerr for Douglas (72 mins)

Scorer *Penalty Goals:* Paterson (3)

Referee A Lewis (Ireland)

MATCH 63   30 March 2003, Lansdowne Road, Dublin

IRELAND 6 (1PG 1DG) ENGLAND 42 (4G 1PG 2DG 1T)

Ireland: G E A Murphy; J P Bishop, B G O'Driscoll (*captain*), K M Maggs, D A Hickie; D G Humphreys, P A Stringer; M J Horan, J S Byrne, J J Hayes, G W Longwell, M E O'Kelly, V C P Costello, A G Foley, K D Gleeson

Substitutions P J O'Connell for Longwell (57 mins); R J R O'Gara for Humphreys (63 mins); A Quinlan for Costello (68 mins); J M Fitzpatrick for Horan (75 mins); G T Dempsey for O'Driscoll (81 mins)

Scorer *Penalty Goal:* Humphreys   *Dropped Goal:* Humphreys

England: O J Lewsey; J Robinson, W J H Greenwood, M J Tindall, B C Cohen; J P Wilkinson, M J S Dawson; G C Rowntree, S Thompson, J Leonard, M O Johnson (*captain*), B J Kay, R A Hill, L B N Dallaglio, N A Back

Substitutions J P R Worsley for Hill (temp 22–29 mins); K P P Bracken for Dawson (temp 25–34 mins and 68–71 mins); T J Woodman for Rowntree (temp 37–40 mins and 45 mins); D J Grewcock for Kay (temp 45–51 mins); P J Grayson for Wilkinson (temp 54–60 mins); D D Luger for Tindall (68 mins)

Scorers *Tries:* Greenwood (2), Dallaglio, Tindall, Luger *Conversions:* Wilkinson (3), Grayson *Penalty Goal:* Wilkinson *Dropped Goals:* Wilkinson (2)

Referee J I Kaplan (South Africa)

MATCH 64   14 June 2003, WestpacTrust Stadium, Wellington

NEW ZEALAND 13 (1G 2PG) ENGLAND 15 (4PG 1DG)

New Zealand: D C Howlett; J T Rokocoko, M Nonu, J F Umaga, C S Ralph; C J Spencer, J W Marshall; D N Hewett, A D Oliver, G M Somerville, C R Jack, A J Williams, R D Thorne (*captain*), R So'oialo, R H McCaw

Substitutions S J Devine for Marshall (48 mins); K F Mealamu for Oliver (56 mins); M Muliaina for Rokokoko (72 mins); J Collins for So'oialo (73 mins)

Scorers *Try:* Howlett *Conversion:* Spencer *Penalty Goals:* Spencer (2)

England: O J Lewsey; J Robinson, W J H Greenwood, M J Tindall, B C Cohen; J P Wilkinson, K P P Bracken; G C Rowntree, S Thompson, J Leonard, M O Johnson (*captain*), B J Kay, R A Hill, L B N Dallaglio, N A Back

Substitutions P J Vickery for Leonard (40 mins); J P R Worsley for Hill (72 mins); D D Luger for Lewsey (77 mins)

Scorer *Penalty Goals:* Wilkinson (4) *Dropped Goal:* Wilkinson

Referee S J Dickinson (Australia)

MATCH 65   21 June 2003, Telstra Dome, Melbourne

AUSTRALIA 14 (3PG 1T) ENGLAND 25 (2G 2PG 1T)

Australia: C E Latham; W J Sailor, M Turinui, S Kefu, J W Roff; N P Grey, G M Gregan (*captain*); W K Young, J A Paul, E P Noriega, D T Giffin, N C Sharpe, D J Lyons, R S T Kefu, P R Waugh

Substitutions D J Vickerman for Sharpe (44 mins); B J Cannon for Paul (53 mins); M S Rogers for Turinui (58 mins); B J Darwin for Noriega (65 mins); L Tuqiri for Grey (65 mins)

Scorers *Try:* Sailor *Penalty Goals:* Roff (3)

England: J Robinson; O J Lewsey, W J H Greenwood, M J Tindall, B C Cohen; J P Wilkinson, K P P Bracken; T J Woodman, S Thompson, P J Vickery, M O Johnson (*captain*), B J Kay, R A Hill, L B N Dallaglio, N A Back

Substitutions J P R Worsley and M J S Dawson for Hill and Bracken (53 mins); S W Borthwick for Kay (temp 62–67 mins)

Scorers *Tries:* Greenwood, Tindall, Cohen *Conversions:* Wilkinson (2) *Penalty Goals:* Wilkinson (2)

Referee D T M McHugh (Ireland)

MATCH 66   23 August 2003, Millennium Stadium, Cardiff

WALES 9 (3PG) ENGLAND 43 (3G 3PG 1DG 2T)

Wales: G R Williams; G Thomas, M Taylor, S Parker, M A Jones; S M Jones (*captain*), G J Cooper; I D Thomas, R C McBryde, G Jenkins, R Sidoli, C P Wyatt, C L Charvis, D R Jones, M E Williams

Substitutions G J Williams for McBryde (61 mins); J Thomas for Wyatt (62 mins); A Jones for Jenkins (72 mins); Gavin Thomas for D R Jones (72 mins)

Scorer *Penalty Goals:* S Jones (3)

England: D Scarbrough; D D Luger, J Noon, S Abbott, J Simpson-Daniel; A D King, A C T Gomarsall; J Leonard (*captain*), M P Regan, J White, D J Grewcock, S D Shaw, M E Corry, J P R Worsley, L W Moody

Substitutions D E West for Regan (37 mins); O J Smith for Luger (57 mins); A Sanderson for Moody (62 mins); D J H Walder for King (71 mins); W R Green for White (72 mins); S W Borthwick for Shaw (temp 11–16 mins)

Scorers *Tries:* Moody, Luger, Worsley, Abbott, West *Conversions:* King (2), Walder *Penalty Goals:* King (3) *Dropped Goal:* King

Referee P C Deluca (Argentina)

MATCH 67   30 August 2003, Stade Vélodrome, Marseilles

FRANCE 17 (3PG 1DG 1T) ENGLAND 16 (1G 3PG)

France: N Brusque; A Rougerie, Y Jauzion, D Traille, C Dominici; F Michalak, F Galthié (*captain*); J-J Crenca, Y Bru, S Marconnet, F Pelous, J Thion, S Betsen, I Harinordoquy, O Magne

Substitutions B Liebenberg for Traille (54 mins); R Ibañez for Bru (54 mins); D Auradou for Thion (65 mins); P Tabacco for Betsen (65 mins); O Milloud for Crenca (temp 5–9 mins, 38–41 mins and 66 mins); S Chabal for Magne (75 mins)

Scorers *Try:* Brusque *Penalty Goals:* Michalak (3) *Dropped Goal:* Michalak

England: I R Balshaw; O J Lewsey, O J Smith, M J Tindall, B C Cohen; P J Grayson, A S Healey; G C Rowntree, D E West (*captain*), J M White, S W Borthwick, D J Grewcock, M E Corry, A Sanderson, L W Moody

Substitutions S Thompson for West (50 mins); J Noon for Cohen (temp 10 to 16 mins) and for Balshaw (54 mins); J Leonard for White (temp 6–8 mins) and for Rowntree (61 mins); S D Shaw for Borthwick (61 mins); A C T Gomarsall for Tindall (76 mins)

Scorers *Try:* Tindall *Conversion:* Grayson *Penalty Goals:* Grayson (3)

Referee S M Lawrence (South Africa)

MATCH 68   6 September 2003, Twickenham

ENGLAND 45 (4G 4PG 1T) FRANCE 14 (2PG 1DG 1T)

England: J Robinson; I R Balshaw, W J H Greenwood, S Abbott, B C Cohen; J P Wilkinson, K P P Bracken; T J Woodman, S Thompson, J M White, M O Johnson (*captain*), B J Kay, R A Hill, M E Corry, N A Back

Substitutions M J S Dawson for Bracken (34 mins); P J Grayson for Wilkinson (43 mins); S D Shaw for Johnson (43 mins); L W Moody for Corry (57 mins); O J Lewsey for Cohen (temp 47–53 mins) and for Abbott (60 mins); J Leonard for White (63 mins); D E West for Moody (temp 68–72 mins) and for Thompson (73 mins)

Scorers *Tries:* Cohen (2), Robinson, Balshaw, Lewsey *Conversions:* Wilkinson (3), Grayson *Penalty Goals:* Wilkinson (4)

France: C Poitrenaud; X Garbajosa, Y Jauzion, B Liebenberg, C Dominici; G Merceron, D Yachvili; O Milloud, R Ibañez (*captain*), J-B Poux, D Auradou, O Brouzet, P Tabacco, C Labit, S Chabal

Substitutions A Rougerie for Dominici (40 mins); O Magne for Chabal (50 mins); F Pelous for Brouzet (58 mins); Y Bru for Ibañez (70 mins); I Harinordoquy for Tabacco (73 mins); S Marconnet for Milloud (temp 62 to 73 mins) and for Poux (73 mins)

Scorers *Try:* Rougerie   *Penalty Goals:* Merceron (2)   *Dropped Goal:* Jauzion
Referee N Williams (Wales)

MATCH 69   12 October 2003, Subiaco Oval, Perth

ENGLAND 84 (9G 2PG 3T) GEORGIA 6 (2PG)

England: J Robinson; O J Lewsey, W J H Greenwood, M J Tindall, B C Cohen; J P Wilkinson, M J S Dawson; T J Woodman, S Thompson, P J Vickery, M O Johnson (*captain*), B J Kay, R A Hill, L B N Dallaglio, N A Back

Substitutions D D Luger for Tindall (35 mins); A C T Gomarsall for Dawson (35 mins); M P Regan for Thompson (40 mins); P J Grayson for Wilkinson (46 mins); L W Moody for Hill (51 mins); J Leonard for Woodman (temp 28 to 29 mins) and for Vickery (51 mins)

Scorers *Tries:* Greenwood (2), Cohen (2), Robinson, Tindall, Dawson, Thompson, Dallaglio, Back, Luger, Regan   *Conversions:* Wilkinson (5), Grayson (4)   *Penalty Goals:* Wilkinson (2)

Georgia: B Khamashuridze; M Urjukashvili, T Zibzibadze, I Guiorgadze, V Katsadze (*captain*); P Jimsheladze, I Abusseridze; G Shvelidze, A Guiorgadze, A Margvelash-vili, Z Mtchedlishvili, V Didebulidze, G Labadze, G Chkhaidze, G Yachvili

Substitutions S Nikolaenko for Margvelashvili (40 mins); V Nadiradze for Didebulidze (43 mins); D Bolghashvili for Yachvili (66 mins); D Dadunashvili for A Guiorgadze (72 mins); B Khekhelashvili for Khamashuridze (75 mins); M Kvirikashvili for Jimsh-eladze (75 mins); I Machkhaneli for Chkhaidze (80 mins)

Referee P C Deluca (Argentina)

MATCH 70   18 October 2003, Subiaco Oval, Perth

ENGLAND 25 (1G 4PG 2DG) SOUTH AFRICA 6 (2PG)

England: J Robinson; O J Lewsey, W J H Greenwood, M J Tindall, B C Cohen; J P Wilkinson, K P P Bracken; T J Woodman, S Thompson, P J Vickery, M O Johnson (*captain*), B J Kay, L W Moody, L B N Dallaglio, N A Back

Substitutions D D Luger for Tindall (70 mins); J Leonard for Woodman (73 mins); J P R Worsley for Back (temp 46–51 mins)

Scorers *Try:* Greenwood   *Conversion:* Wilkinson   *Penalty Goals:* Wilkinson (4)   *Dropped Goals:* Wilkinson (2)

South Africa: J N B van der Westhuyzen; A K Willemse, G P Müller, D W Barry, G M Delport; L J Koen, J H van der Westhuizen; C J Bezuidenhout, D Coetzee, R E Bands, J P Botha, V Matfield, C P J Krigé (*captain*), J H Smith, J C van Niekerk

Substitutions J W Smit for Coetzee (temp 44–51 mins and 57 mins); L D Sephaka for Bands (6–13 mins and 68 mins); D J Hougaard for Koen (68 mins)

Scorer *Penalty Goals:* Koen (2)
Referee P L Marshall (Australia)

MATCH 71   26 October 2003, Telstra Dome, Melbourne

ENGLAND 35 (3G 2PG 1DG 1T) SAMOA 22 (1G 5PG)

England: J Robinson; I R Balshaw, S Abbott, M J Tindall, B C Cohen; J P Wilkinson, M J S Dawson; J Leonard, M P Regan, J M White, M O Johnson (*captain*), B J Kay, J P R Worsley, L B N Dallaglio, N A Back

Substitutions S Thompson for Regan (48 mins); P J Vickery for White (48 mins); L W Moody for Worsley (48 mins); M J Catt for Abbott (71 mins)

Scorers *Tries:* Back, penalty try, Balshaw, Vickery   *Conversions:* Wilkinson (3) *Penalty Goals:* Wilkinson (2)   *Dropped Goal:* Wilkinson

Samoa: T Vili; L Fa'atau, T Fanolua, B P Lima, S Tagicakibau; E Va'a, S So'oialo; K Lealamanua, J Meredith, J Tomuli, O Palepoi, L Lafaiali'i, P Poulos, S Sititi (*captain*), M Fa'asavalu

Substitutions D Rasmussen for Fanolua (45 mins); S Lemalu for Tomuli (52 mins); K Viliamu for Poulos (62 mins); D Tuiavi'i for Lafaiali'i (65 mins); D Feaunati for Tagicakibau (72 mins); D Tyrell for So'oialo (75 mins); M Schwlager for Meredith (75 mins)

Scorers *Try:* Sititi   *Conversion:* Va'a   *Penalty Goals:* Va'a (5)

Referee J I Kaplan (South Africa)

MATCH 72   2 November 2003, Suncorp Stadium, Brisbane

ENGLAND 111 (13G 4T) URUGUAY 13 (1G 2PG)

England: O J Lewsey; I R Balshaw, S Abbott, M J Catt, D D Luger; P J Grayson, A C T Gomarsall; J Leonard, D E West, P J Vickery (*captain*), M E Corry, D J Grewcock, J P R Worsley, L B N Dallaglio, L W Moody

Substitutions M O Johnson for Corry (43 mins); J Robinson for Balshaw (43 mins); J M White for Vickery (52 mins); K P P Bracken for Gomarsall (61 mins); W J H Greenwood for Grayson (61 mins)

Scorers *Tries:* Lewsey (5), Balshaw (2), Robinson (2), Gomarsall (2), Catt (2), Moody, Luger, Abbott, Greenwood   *Conversions:* Grayson (11), Catt (2)

Uruguay: J-R Menchaca; J Pastore, D Aguirre (*captain*), J de Freitas, J Viana; S Aguirre, J Campomar; E Berruti, D Lamelas, P Lemoine, J-C Bado, J-M Alvarez, N Brignoni, R Capo, N Grille

Substitutions M Gutierrez for Grille (43 mins); R Sanchez for Berruti (43 mins); J Alzueta for Alvarez (52 mins); D Reyes for De Freitas (temp 5–10 mins) and for Viana (52 mins); J-A Perez for Lamelas (56 mins); G Storace for Lemoine (69 mins); E Caffera for Menchaca (71 mins)

Scorers *Try:* Lemoine   *Conversion:* Menchaca   *Penalty Goals:* Menchaca (2)

Referee N Williams (Wales)

MATCH 73   9 November 2003, Suncorp Stadium, Brisbane

ENGLAND 28 (1G 6PG 1DG) WALES 17 (1G 2T)

England: J Robinson; D D Luger, W J H Greenwood, M J Tindall, B C Cohen; J P Wilkinson, M J S Dawson; J Leonard, S Thompson, P J Vickery, M O Johnson (*captain*), B J Kay, L W Moody, L B N Dallaglio, N A Back

Substitutions M J Catt for Luger (40 mins); T J Woodman for Leonard (44 mins); S Abbott for Greenwood (52 mins); K P P Bracken for Dawson (67 mins)

Scorers *Try:* Greenwood   *Conversion:* Wilkinson   *Penalty Goals:* Wilkinson (6) *Dropped Goal:* Wilkinson

Wales: G. Thomas; M A Jones, M Taylor, I R Harris, S M Williams; S M Jones, G J Cooper; I D Thomas, R C McBryde, A Jones, B Cockbain, R Sidoli, D R Jones, J Thomas C L Charvis (*captain*)

Substitutions G Jenkins for A Jones (28 mins); G O Llewellyn for Cockbain (48 mins); M E Williams for J Thomas (57 mins); D Peel for Cooper (64 mins); Davies for McBryde (64 mins); C Sweeney for S Jones (temp 58–72 mins)

Scorers *Tries:* S Jones, Charvis, M E Williams   *Conversion:* Harris

Referee A C Rolland (Ireland)

MATCH 74   16 November 2003, Telstra Stadium, Sydney

ENGLAND 24 (5PG 3DG) FRANCE 7 (1G)

England: O J Lewsey; J Robinson, W J H Greenwood, M J Catt, B C Cohen; J P Wilkinson, M J S Dawson; T J Woodman, S Thompson, P J Vickery, M O Johnson (*captain*), B J Kay, R A Hill, L B N Dallaglio, N A Back

Substitutions M J Tindall for Catt (68 mins); K P P Bracken for Dawson (temp 39–40 mins and 69 mins); L W Moody for Hill (73 mins); J Leonard for Vickery (temp 4–5 mins) and for Woodman (78 mins); D E West for Thompson (78 mins)

Scorer *Penalty Goals:* Wilkinson (5)   *Dropped Goals:* Wilkinson (3)

France: N Brusque; A Rougerie, T Marsh, Y Jauzion, C Dominici; F Michalak, F Galthié (*captain*); J-J Crenca, R Ibañez, S Marconnet, F Pelous, J Thion, S Betsen, I Harinordoquy, O Magne

Substitutions C Poitrenaud for Dominici (33 mins); O Milloud for Crenca (61 mins); G Merceron for Michalak (63 mins); C Labit for Betsen (63 mins)

Scorers *Try:* Betsen   *Conversion:* Michalak

Referee P D O'Brien (New Zealand)

MATCH 75   22 November 2003, Telstra Stadium, Sydney

ENGLAND 20 (4PG 1DG 1T) AUSTRALIA 17 (4PG 1T) (including extra time)

England: J Robinson; O J Lewsey, W J H Greenwood, M J Tindall, B C Cohen; J P Wilkinson, M J S Dawson; T J Woodman, S Thompson, P J Vickery, M O Johnson (*captain*), B J Kay, R A Hill, L B N Dallaglio, N A Back

Substitutions M J Catt for Tindall (78 mins); J Leonard for Vickery (80 mins); I R Balshaw for Lewsey (85 mins); L W Moody for Hill (93 mins)

Scorers *Try:* Robinson   *Penalty Goals:* Wilkinson (4)   *Dropped Goal:* Wilkinson

Australia: M S Rogers; W J Sailor, S A Mortlock, E J Flatley, L Tuqiri; S J Larkham, G M Gregan (*captain*); W K Young, B J Cannon, A K E Baxter, J B Harrison, N C Sharpe, G B Smith, D J Lyons, P R Waugh

Substitutions D T Giffin for Sharpe (48 mins); J A Paul for Cannon (56 mins); M J Cockbain for Lyons (56 mins); J W Roff for Sailor (70 mins); M J Dunning for Young (92 mins); M J Giteau for Larkham (temp 18–30 mins; 55–63 mins; 85–93 mins)

Scorers *Try:* Tuqiri   *Penalty Goals:* Flatley (4)

Referee A J Watson (South Africa)

Index